WRITING TRAVEL
IN CENTRAL ASIAN HISTORY

WRITING TRAVEL IN CENTRAL ASIAN HISTORY

Edited by Nile Green

Indiana University Press

Bloomington and Indianapolis

This book is a publication of

Indiana University Press
Office of Scholarly Publishing
Herman B Wells Library 350
1320 East 10th Street
Bloomington, Indiana 47405 USA

iupress.indiana.edu

Telephone   800-842-6796
Fax   812-855-7931

∞ The paper used in this publication meets the minimum require-
ments of the American National Standard for Information Sciences—Permanence of Paper for Printed Library Materials, ANSI
Z39.48-1992.

Manufactured in the United States of America

Library of Congress Cataloging-in-Publication Data

Writing travel in Central Asian history / edited by Nile Green.
    pages cm
    This volume had its origins in the conference "The Roads to
Oxiana: The Writing of Travel at the Crossroads of Asia," hosted by
the UCLA Program on Central Asia in November 2010.
    Includes bibliographical references and index.
    ISBN 978-0-253-01134-3 (cloth : alk. paper) -- ISBN 978-0-253-
01135-0 (pbk. : alk. paper) -- ISBN 978-0-253-01148-0 (ebook)
    1. Asia, Central—Description and travel—Congresses. 2. Travel
writing—History—Congresses. 3. Travel writing—History and
criticism—Congresses. 4. Visitors, Foreign—Asia, Central—
History—Congresses. I. Green, Nile.
DS327.7.W75 2013
915.804—dc23
                                                    2013034752

1 2 3 4 5 19 18 17 16 15 14

To the memory of Owen Lattimore

Contents

Preface and Acknowledgments

THIS VOLUME HAD its origins in the conference "The Roads to Oxiana: The Writing of Travel at the Crossroads of Asia," hosted by the Program on Central Asia at the University of California, Los Angeles (UCLA), in November 2010. The conference was in turn linked to a series of Program on Central Asia seminars and conferences addressing the intersection of mobility and literature. For both funding of and organizational assistance with the original conference, I am grateful to the UCLA International Institute and the UCLA Asia Institute. I would like to extend especial gratitude to my colleagues C. Cindy Fan and R. Bin Wong for generous support of Central Asian studies and to Nick Menzies and Elizabeth Leicester for superb organizational acumen. I would also like to thank Sebouh Aslanian, Ra'anan Boustan, Robert Buswell, Randal Johnson, Nancy Levine, Hannah Reiss, Rahim Shayegan, Monica L. Smith, Sanjay Subrahmanyam, and Ronald Vroon for their close involvement in various Program on Central Asia activities and to Ali Behdad for acting as panel chair at the "Roads to Oxiana" conference. I am also grateful to the several other scholars who wrote or presented papers in relation to the conference and book project: Roshan Abraham, Dhara Anjaria, David Chioni Moore, and Daniel J. Sheffield.

In tracking down the travel texts and secondary literature consulted for the introduction, I am especially thankful for the opportunity to use the rare book holdings of the Forschungsstelle zur historischen Reisekultur (Research Hall on Historical Travel Culture) in Eutin, Germany. I have also relied greatly on the British Library and the Young Research Library at UCLA; my special thanks to Dr. David Hirsch, Librarian for Middle Eastern, Islamic, South Asian, Central Asian, and Jewish Studies at UCLA. I would also like to thank the American Institute for Afghanistan Studies for the award of the John F. Richards Fellowship (2011), which funded research in Kabul and Germany. For suggestions and advice on a variety of Central Asian matters, I offer thanks to Ingeborg Baldauf, Thomas Barfield, Jason BeDuhn, Alanna Cooper, William Dalrymple, Touraj Daryaee, Johan Elverskog, Frantz Grenet, Zsuzsanna Gulasci, Andrew Hale, Cheri Hunter, Ali F. Igmen, Nikki Keddie, Arash Khazeni, Karen Leonard, Claude Markovits, John Mock, Christine Noelle-Karimi, Elena Sadovskaya, Richard Salomon, John Schoeberlein, Martin Schwartz, Nicholas Sims-Williams, Ursula Sims-Williams, Jon Thompson, and Joel Walker. Final thanks to Rebecca Tolen at Indiana University Press for believing in the value of this project.

The publishers gratefully acknowledge the following organizations for permission to print illustrations: Fidra Books for figure 5.2, and the Anahita Gallery, Santa Fe, New Mexico, for figure 8.1.

WRITING TRAVEL
IN CENTRAL ASIAN HISTORY

Introduction

Writing, Travel, and the Global History of Central Asia

Nile Green

From a Silk Road to a Road of Texts

From the medieval *Divisament dou monde* of Marco Polo to the modernist prose of Robert Byron's *The Road to Oxiana*, Central Asia has been made known to the wider world through the medium of travel writing.[1] At a time when Central Asia is increasingly drawn into global political affairs, such travel writings allow us to map the cultural dimensions of an earlier geopolitics that ranges from Qing Chinese empire builders to Russian missionaries and Japanese archaeologists. By reading the polyglottal prose written at the crossroads of Asia, the following chapters trace distinct stages of global connectivity by joining the early modern age of camel caravans and horsemen with the modern age of railroads and motorcars. Focusing on little-known travel writings of literary and ethnographic no less than historical interest, the chapters explore the different meanings given to Central Asia in the far corners of the world during the region's most intensive periods of globalization between the sixteenth and twentieth centuries. By framing Central Asia as a cultural contact zone between different peoples and polities as much as a transit zone for material commodities such as silk, cotton, and oil, this book aims to connect Central Asia to the larger field of global history. The aim here is to add new layers to our understanding of both Central Asia and globalization, giving due recognition to the shifting politics and fluctuating trade patterns of the region but asking how these "hard" developments were inseparable from the cultural productions of the travelers who were globalization in human terms—and vice versa, for as we will see in the following chapters, neither the commerce nor politics of

Central Asia can be fully understood in isolation from the travel accounts that so often formed the basis of mercantile and military action.

In laying out a general model, we can suggest a distinct "informational" profile for the travel writings on the region, a profile that is quite different from that of other historically inaccessible regions such as the islands of the South Pacific or the interior of Africa, conceived as they were in terms of the romantic imagination and the civilizing mission respectively. If this profile was not unique to Central Asian travel writings, then it was certainly emphatic in them. Except in certain expressions of Russian (or perhaps Japanese) Orientalism, Central Asia rarely appeared a place of imagination and enchantment (excepting, on its edges, Tibet), seldom as a perilously pestilent vector zone from which few returned alive, and never as an unspoiled Eden or "New World" populated by noble savages.[2] It is for this reason that the terminology used here is of travel "writing" rather than travel "literature," with its suggestion of primarily aesthetic intentions, for self-consciously literary works form only a small proportion of the more robustly informational writings on the region. Given the range of languages and literatures brought together here, the term "travel writing" is used to define a broad category of texts—including visual texts—that emerged from acts of travel and often (but not always) described them. We are therefore speaking about a much wider body of writings than the singular genre of the travelogue and its equivalents in Asian literatures. And so the writings examined in this volume include merchant manuals and histories, ethnographies and autobiographies, archaeological reports and poetic notebooks as well as straightforward travelogues. In keeping with the informational profile that so many of these works have in common, it is worth drawing on Mary Campbell's adage that "the travel book is a kind of witness: it is generically aimed at the truth."[3] For the purposes of this volume, we might qualify this statement by saying that travel writings aimed to communicate "the truth" about Central Asia as it related to the experiences of the people who traveled there and the needs of the societies (and economies and polities) for whom they wrote. To write travel was to make use of a key cultural technology that helped enable more concrete forms of global connection between Central Asia and the wider world. Whether enabling commerce, conquest, or conversion, travel writings laid the informational basis for subsequent interactions. In keeping with this logic of interaction between different peoples, knowledge orders, and state systems, the term "Central Asia" is defined broadly in this volume to refer to the vast stretch of the Eurasian landmass lying between the shifting and ill-defined borders of the early modern Russian, Chinese, Iranian, and Mughal Indian states. Despite its long history of state formation in its own right, the region can be conceived in conceptual if not literal terms as a vast "borderland" entered at different times by the diverse peoples of Eurasia and, in more recent times, beyond.[4]

Reflecting recent attempts to draw mobility and circulation into our understanding of the formation of apparently stationary nations or regions, this volume also aims to use travel writings to factor mobility and interaction into the making of Central

Asia itself as the region opened to an incrementally global cast of actors.[5] In terms
of its human geography, Central Asia was not a geographical constant, and its accessibility to the persons who ventured there changed considerably over the long period
surveyed in this introduction, most especially in the modern period when biological
transport was suddenly and repeatedly replaced by train, automobile, and airplane
travel. Between the early modern and modern periods in particular, this resulted in
the opening of the region to a far wider diversity of travelers, whether in terms of class,
profession, gender, or nationality. What we are facing, then, is a historical-geographi-
cal process, and the accounts discussed in the following chapters come from travelers
who not only witnessed but were party to it. As we will see, this process of the opening
of Central Asia led in turn to more varied literary representations of the region, which
was transformed in the distant areas where those texts were received from primarily
a commercial zone into an ethnological or archaeological goldfield, a musical soundscape, or a socialist utopia. Travel writing, then, both participated in and documented
the larger transformations of historical geography, so connecting this volume's cul-
turalist approach to the more familiar framing of the region through commerce and
geopolitics.

In this way, the chapters in this volume provide fine-grained studies of the concrete and discursive connections made between Central Asia and far distant regions
of the world, connections that help us "globalize" the study of a region that is often
relegated to the margins of world history.[6] Just as Jonathan Bloom has reimagined the
Silk Road as a "Paper Road," and Philippe Forêt and Andreas Kaplony have traced the
evolution of visual and cartographic representations of Central Asia, this volume goes
a step further by documenting a process in cultural history by which Central Asia was
transformed into a textual space that was understood through the various discursive
models carried by travelers from across the world.[7] Made up of variant languages and
genres, shared assumptions and private idiosyncrasies, the travel writings under scru-
tiny here were the cultural traffic of what became a road of texts that eventually connected Central Asia with peoples as far away as Japan and the United States.

Historicizing Travel Writing in Central Asia: Three Periods

In order to locate the specific travelers and texts that are studied in the following chapters in the cultural dimensions of a longer process of globalization, the remainder of
this introduction presents a structured survey of the development and diversification
of travel writing about Central Asia. While the chapters focus on the lesser-studied
later eras of travel in the region, this introductory essay presents a *longue durée* survey that places the chapters' case studies into a lengthier and incremental process of
global exchange. In order to chart the many byways of this road of texts, the following
pages present a clear periodization: from antiquity to around 1500, from around 1500
to 1850, and from 1850 to 1940. Obviously, such a stark model is intended to suggest
general patterns rather than absolute rules. Even so, each of these periods can be seen

as having its particular features characterized by particular types of traveler and text. This is emphatically not to say that examples of one period's defining travelers and genres cannot be found in other periods, but it is to propose that traveling writers of different periods emerged out of different social and intellectual backgrounds no less than their travel writings manifested changing concerns and epistemologies.

If this speaks to the shifts in travelers and their representations of Central Asia, then the usefulness of periodization is also in recognizing that, in terms of human geography, the space of Central Asia was itself repeatedly transformed over time. This reflects not only the shifting fortunes of commercial transit routes and indigenous production centers. It also reflects the changing accessibility of the region as the encroaching frontiers of expansive neighbors brought Central Asia "closer" to the populations of the Chinese, Russian, and British empires while developments in technology outside the region and of infrastructure within it afforded easier access through the railroads, roads, and airlines that replaced the preindustrial transport system of mules and camels. No longer only a silk road, the road of texts that we pursue here was sequentially fueled by straw, coal, and gasoline. These were the raw materials of travel writing that help us connect culture to commerce, the soft and hard factors of globalization.

It is important to bear in mind that while in large part overlapping with other models of periodization, what is proposed here are textual as much as historical periods, even if the history of these texts is shown to be linked to the wider pattern of Central Asia's interactions with the world. Since the range of visitors in the long first period was far more limited than in the two shorter subsequent periods, the first period cannot properly be considered an age of "globalization." For this reason, the book's chapters deal with the second and third periods of travel writing for which it makes sense to speak of global rather than merely regional or, at best, Eurasian interactions. However, since these later periods cannot be understood in isolation, it is important to contextualize them in relation to what (and who) came before. The remainder of this introduction serves as a larger schematic survey of incrementally global interactions with Central Asia that were witnessed—and enabled—by the union of travel and writing. It is one of the contentions of this volume that in Central Asia as in other regions of the world, writing—and the variable efficiency of the distribution networks by which different texts were disseminated—served as one of the crucial technologies of globalization.

The first and longest period of Central Asian travel dates from antiquity to around 1500. This was the age of the region's greatest inaccessibility, a product not only of its inherent physical geography but also of its enclosure by powerful buffer empires that themselves presented considerable social and political obstacles to travelers from beyond them. While a sequence of travelers from distant literate societies did reach the region in this period, the comparatively lower general literacy of the ancient and medieval periods meant that fewer travelers were writers, while the sheer passage of time has inevitably also contributed to the relative paucity of surviving writings. In this first period, travel was also more likely to be regional, exhibiting a general correlation: the earlier the date of the text, the more proximate to Central Asia its provenance. This correlation intersects with another general characteristic of the period: the farther away from Central Asia the writer's origin, the less direct and reliable the information he recorded, as it was often passed on by several transmitters before being committed to writing. In other words, the pre-1500 period saw fewer travel writings that were the firsthand products of actual travelers. This is as true of the early Arabic and Persian accounts of Central Asia as of Greco-Roman geographies and arguably even the famous Marco Polo.

Long-distance travel was tremendously expensive and dangerous in this period, such that travelers required both the support of wealthy organizations and high levels of commitment. It is certainly true that there were distinct periods of greater connectivity, the thirteenth- and fourteenth-century Pax Mongolica being the great example. But distant states were not often able to act as effective protectors, patrons, or organizers of travel in this first period, especially on their frontiers, while the fundamental logistics of land travel did not dramatically change between antiquity and the early modern period. Even taking into account the achievements of Central Asia's medieval and late medieval states, the tribal zones outside of the cities remained dangerously outside state control until the late nineteenth century.

As a result of these dangers, two of the most characteristic forms of travel writing to emerge from this first period are mercantile and religious texts based on expeditions that drew on the material resources, prestige, and customs of safe passage provided to representatives of collective merchant investment or religious organizations. Even when not concerned with the practical or proselytizing dimensions of trade and religion, travel writings from the period frame the region in religious terms through attempting to relate it to the geographies of the Scriptures or the biographies of the holy.[8] Out of these religious and mercantile concerns (and in turn conceptions) of the region appeared the third major type of travel writing from the period, that which emerged from diplomatic negotiations, for such exchanges were often entrusted to the religious figures or merchants seen as having the requisite prestige, inviolability, and connections.

Dating between around 1500 and 1850, Central Asia's second period of travel writing did not see substantial easing in the logistics of travel by way of any lessening of the physical inaccessibility or costs of reaching the region. But it did see, firstly, the appearance of more varied and complex organizations that supported travel and, secondly, the emergence of more effective and reliable forms of collecting and disseminating knowledge. These were in part the result of the new states that appeared in and around the region, by way of the Safavid, Mughal, and Shaybanid polities whose rise roughly coincides with the opening of the period; the Ming and Qing empires that between them endured throughout this period; and the Russian and

British Indian states that drew closer to Central Asia through the eighteenth and the first half of the nineteenth century. The typical characteristics of "early modernity" allow us to separate this period from the much longer first period of Central Asian travel in order to point to interactions that we can more credibly recognize as global in scale and scope. Even so, this was not yet the full-blown era of globalization that was heralded by imperial conquest and mechanized travel in the third period discussed below. Nonetheless, there was much that was new. An early modern infrastructure of travel emerged through the support of both mercantile and state sponsors by way of such merchant companies as the British Muscovy Company (chartered in 1555) and new learned societies such as the Saint Petersburg (and later Imperial) Academy of Sciences (founded in 1724). This second period also saw Asian merchant networks—particularly those based in India—become more efficient and organized sponsors of regularized travel, though we still know relatively little about their written forms of information gathering.[9]

Many other travel sponsors also emerged in this second period, with early modern states playing a gradually increasing role. For whether in Beijing or Saint Petersburg, bureaucratic cadres and learned societies were appendages of increasingly efficient imperial states that were keen to promote utilizable knowledge of physical and human geography. The result was that new types of traveler and of travel writing made their appearance, what Jaś Elsner and Joan-Pau Rubiés have called "the empirical traveler" with his "new authoritative discourse on human geography."[10] If merchants did not disappear between 1500 and 1850, then the regularizing of the maritime routes to China certainly cut away Central Asia's old role as a transit route between China and Europe, even as this prompted British and especially Russian merchants to report on the commercial produce of the region itself. But it was the new "scientific" traveler and the more deliberately observational and quantifiable methods of knowledge collection that introduced the period's most important innovation to travel writing, albeit seen in different discursive expressions in Chinese and Persian no less than Russian and German writings from the time. The Chinese conquest of Xinjiang (New Territory) in 1759 under the Qing and the Russian foundation of Orenburg in 1734 and the series of frontier fortresses that encroached on the Kazakh steppes brought Central Asia closer to the expanding populations and intellectuals of these formerly distant states. As we have already noted, the new types of traveler and text were often connected to both the expansion of new empires and the retraction of older ones in the areas surrounding Central Asia, lending a distinctly imperial cast to many writings of the period that was quite dissimilar from the sponsorship of nonstate mercantile and religious entities in the previous centuries. Even so, the "steppe road" of this period remained a rough and dangerous sequence of routes along which the danger of being kidnapped into slavery loomed large well into the nineteenth century.

The third period of travel stretched between around 1850 and 1940, its curtailment with the closing of the Chinese and Soviet borders showing that globalization is never an automatic or unstoppable process. The dating parameters here are marked by two interdependent transformations that greatly affected travel in and out of Central Asia: the Russian colonization of western Central Asia and the region's subsequent connection to the European rail network. From the 1860s, with the reassertion of Chinese rule in the eastern regions of Central Asia, the political and, with it, the social and urban geography of the remainder of Central Asia was also transformed. In both cases, independent Muslim rule came to an end. The contingent nature of these expansions brought with it a flurry of new types of political traveler, the spies and surveyors whose writings form the textual contributions of the Great Game, whose writings were as likely to be in Persian and Urdu as in Russian and English. Yet this era of imperial annexation of Central Asia brought with it not only expressly political travel writings but also the new genres of exploratory, ethnographic, and archaeological travel writings, which, if inseparable from empire, were at least distinct from the political reports of the Great Game. In many cases, the new scholarly travelers writing such texts were not themselves imperial citizens, but taking advantage of the easier access and (for Europeans at least) stability of the area to travel in pursuit of genuinely scientific and artistic concerns. In addition to the political and archaeo-exploratory texts, the final new body of writings to emerge in this last period is that of the journalistic and even touristic traveler, for the expansion of the Trans-Caspian Railway, and from the 1920s the appearance of motorable roads and then airports in Central Asia, led to the most rapid of all openings of the region to new social and professional types of traveler, from the journalist to the rally driver.

Then, in the 1930s and 1940s, what had been for centuries porous frontiers were rapidly subjected to unprecedented levels of control by the Soviet and then Chinese Communist authorities.[11] The incremental expansion of global exchanges that had greatly expanded since the coming of the railroad half a century earlier entered a rapid reversal as the more closely defined borders that had been mapped by 1900 were transformed into concrete and militarized boundaries. The chapters in this volume observe this date of around 1940, which signals not only the substantial closing of Central Asia to global traffic but also the entry of the totalitarian state as the primary agent of mobility. The mass deportations of Tatars, Koreans, and many others that marked this new period, and whatever writings survive from them, must await their own volume. With this end point in mind, we can now turn toward the three periods in more detail, to examine some representative examples of the forms of travel and writing that connected Central Asia to the wider world.

Monkish Diplomats and Unreliable Geographers (Antiquity to c. 1500)

The earliest surviving European accounts of Central Asia were those written by often semi-legendary Greek writers such as Aristeas of Proconnesus (fl. 7th century BCE), whose now lost travel poem *Arimaspea*, was quoted by many later writers in antiquity.[12] Despite his own extensive travels in Egypt, the historian Herodotus (d. c. 425

BCE) relied for his knowledge of Central Asia on other travelers, and it was mainly through the histories written in the wake of Alexander's conquests that Central Asia entered the Graeco-Roman imagination, particularly through book 4 of Arrian's *Anabasis Alexandrou*.[13] Despite brief mentions of Turkic peoples by the Byzantine historian Theophylact Simocatta, by the late antique period the contacts forged in the Hellenic era had been lost and knowledge of Central Asia appeared in the form of the hagiographical travel accounts of Philostratus's *Vita Apollonii*.[14] It was, however, during late antiquity that one of the most enduring institutional supports and motivations of Central Asian travel writing were to emerge through the missionary activities of the Christian church. Given the sheer range of culture areas through which Christianity expanded in late antiquity, accounts of church founding and missionary journeys appeared in a variety of languages, including such Asian languages as Syriac.[15]

However, it was in Chinese that the most extensive and accurate early medieval travel account of Central Asia was written as a result of the travels of the Buddhist monk Xuanzang (Hsüan-tsang, c. 602–664), who, in his motivating search for manuscripts, echoed the religious profile of many other writing travelers in this first period.[16] Setting off in 629, Xuanzang spent the next fifteen years traveling west through Central Asia and then south across the Hindu Kush into India, reaching as far south as the Pallava capital at Kanchipuram in south India. Along the way, he stayed at the numerous Buddhist monasteries that lined the roads through Central Asia, most notably at Turfan, Kucha, and Bamiyan, so pointing to the importance of religious institutions in providing the practical wherewithal for travel in this period. This pattern would be repeated after the region's Islamization in the ways in which Sufi shrines and *khanaqah* monasteries provided the staging posts for later medieval travelers. Even so, Xuanzang's lifetime coincided with the Central Asian conquests and embassies of the Tang dynasty (618–907), developments that led to a fascination with Central Asian exotica among the Tang elite.[17] As a result, the *Da Tang Xiyu Ji* (Great Tang Dynasty Record of the Western Regions), Xuanzang's extraordinarily detailed account of what he had seen on his travels, was only one of a series of Chinese travel accounts to be written in this period.[18] Others were written by fellow monks, such as Huichao's *Wang Wu Tianzhuguo Zhuan* (Record on the Five Indian Kingdoms,) of around 740, some of whom served as imperial agents, such as the monk and ambassador to Samarqand, Wukong (fl. 750–89), a pattern we will see again with regard to Christian monastic emissaries. Combined with the eleventh-century Song dynasty reports on the Liao/Khitan empire, such encounters created in Chinese what was by far the most detailed and accurate medieval body of writing on Central Asia.[19]

In the thirteenth century, the Mongol conquests and subsequent Pax Mongolica enabled a rapid expansion of contact between Europe, China, and the Middle East, with Central Asia in between. Among medieval European accounts of Central Asia from this period, it is the travels of merchants such as the Polo family that are the best known.[20] As seen in the long debates on whether the sources of Marco Polo's information drew on direct observation or oral mercantile lore, the information circuits of medieval traders were more often spoken than written. But the thirteenth century also saw the rise of what G. F. Hudson termed a "religious *Weltpolitik*," and, based as it was on literate and mobile monks, it was the religious profile of *Weltpolitik* that brought the largest expansion of European travel writings on Central Asia.[21] The most important Latinate emissaries were the Italian Franciscan monk Giovanni do Plan di Carpini (John of Plano Carpini, 1182/85–1252), who undertook a journey through Central Asia to the Mongol court between 1245 and 1247, and the Flemish Franciscan Willem van Ruysbroeck (William of Rubruck, c. 1220–c. 1293), who made a similar journey between 1253 and 1255.[22] Plan di Carpini's *Ystoria Mongalorum* (History of the Mongols) and van Ruysbroeck's *Itinerarium* (Itinerary) were both "histories" in the medieval Latin sense, attempting to provide reliable data on both the past and the present of the peoples and regions the authors had encountered on their journeys. If the *Itinerarium* did contain more first-person narrative than the *Ystoria Mongalorum*, then this was incidental to the writers' common aim of using travel and writing to supply reliable strategic information to their royal and ecclesiastical sponsors. Yet even as both books were written in Latin, their writers drew on a sequence of interpreters who afforded them access to the multilingual spaces of Central Asia, and while these polyglot voices were largely subsumed in the final texts, the genealogy of both the *Itinerarium* and the *Ystoria Mongalorum* positions them as multivocal products of the Central Asian "road of texts."[23]

The same might be said in a different way of such histories of the Mongols as *La Flor des estoires d'orient* (Flowers of the Stories of the East) by the itinerant Armenian noble Hethum (Hayton of Corycus, d. c. 1320), which was translated into medieval French, Latin, English, and Castilian.[24] While the larger number were written in either Latin or its Romance vernaculars, other accounts of Central Asia appeared in Syriac, such as the autobiographical history of the Nestorian monk and diplomat Bar Sawma (c. 1220–1294), who was himself probably of Turkic Uighur origin and acted as a mediator between the Mongols and Franks in an attempt to forge an alliance against the Mamluks.[25] In the same period, Kirakos Kaidzekatski (c. 1202–1271) wrote an Armenian travel account of the embassy of the Armenian King Hethum I of Cilicia (r. 1226–70) to the Mongols.[26] Approaching the Mongol court from the other direction were Chinese emissaries, such as the Taoist monk Qiu Chuji (1148–1227), whose *Qiu Changchun Xiyou Ji* (Travels to the West of Qiu Changchun) was published in block print, so marking the transition of Central Asian travel writings into print.[27] In 1259, another Chinese scholar, Chang De, was dispatched on behalf of the Mongol ruler Möngke (r. 1251–59) and recorded his journey in another of the several Chinese travelogues of the period.[28] There was then a whole series of monkish diplomats involved in what before the discovery of the Americas was indeed a *Weltpolitik*. But this was more than a question of politics. It was also a question of knowledge or what Samuel Adshead conceptualized as the expansion of the "basic information circuit" under the Pax

Mongolica. According to Adshead, this expansion brought about "an integration of information, so that . . . a unified picture of a single world was assembled."[29] Through the informational profile of the writings that came out of Central Asian travel in the Mongol era, there emerged "a unified conceptualization of the world, with the geographies, histories and cultures of the parts coordinated with each other."[30] But like all globalizations, this Mongol version was fragile and reversible. While it did hand down a legacy of information to subsequent periods, the exchanges—particularly with Europe—would have to be made over in later centuries.

A number of similarities with the European works appear in the Arabic and Persian travel writings of this long first period. As in the Christian West, the region was at times conceived in terms of scriptural geographies, not least of lands bordered by the wall of Gog and Magog (*sadd Yajuj wa Majuj*).[31] There was also the recognition of the importance of the region's slave trade, which by at least the twelfth century was responsible for relocating large numbers of Central Asian peoples into the Muslim-ruled polities of northern India.[32] However, in the Middle East as in Europe, scriptural and moralistic conceptions of Central Asia lived alongside more empirical sources of information, and the earliest Arabic and Persian texts expressly devoted to the region comprised geographical and historical works that drew on information passed on by actual travelers.[33] Among the earliest proper travel accounts was that of Tamim ibn Bahr, who in 821 was sent as ambassador to the Uighur Turks and brought back information on the travel routes, horse armies, and tent dwellers of the steppe.[34] Once again, the purposes of many of these early Muslim works were expressly practical, whether with regard to knowledge of trade routes, as in the Arabic *Kitab al-Masalik wa'l Mamalik* (Book of Roads and Kingdoms) of Abu'l Qasim 'Ubaydullah ibn Khordadbeh (c. 820–912), or more general geopolitical information, as in the Persian *Hudud al-'Alam* (Limits of the World).[35]

The most important early Arabic travelogue as such on the region was that of Ahmad ibn Fadlan, who in 921 was sent from Baghdad as the 'Abbasid ambassador to the Volga Bulgars.[36] Although related to the western Central Asian regions that would later be absorbed by Muscovy, Ibn Fadlan's account brought back a wealth of information on the unknown Turkic and Rus peoples whom the 'Abbasids were then seeking to bring under their own suzerainty. Richly informative as his travel report was on the customs and practices of these unknown peoples, for Ibn Fadlan the western steppes formed a zone of radical alterity that lay beyond the known spheres of either Islamdom or Christendom.

Ibn Fadlan's focus on the peoples rather than the physical spaces of Central Asia was common to most early Arabic accounts of the region, with writers such as Jahiz (781–868) in his *Risala fi Manaqib al-Turk* (Treatise on the Qualities of the Turks) focusing on what they saw as the displeasing habits of the Turkic peoples.[37] This was a quite different conception of the region than that found in the accounts of later Arabic and Persian writers, to whom the gradually converted peoples of Central Asia presented the common legal and ritual idioms of Islam, with urban pockets of Judaism. If little is known of the biography of Ibn Fadlan, we know more about the writer of the most important medieval Arabic travel account of Central Asia, the illustrious Ibn Battuta (1304–1368/69), who included a long section on the region in his *Tuhfat al-Nuzzar fi Ghara'ib al-Amsar wa 'Aja'ib al-Asfar* (Gift to the Contemplators on the Strangeness of Cities and the Marvels of Travel).[38] Like his Christian contemporaries, Ibn Battuta straddled the realms of religious professional and diplomat, using his credentials as a scholar of Islamic law to pick up a sequence of diplomatic positions such as accompanying the Byzantine royal wife of Uzbeg Khan, the khan of the Golden Horde, back to Constantinople as a means of safely leaving the steppe. Even so, in its composition, Ibn Battuta's travelogue has more in common with Marco Polo's *Divisament dou monde* in that it was composed only on his return to Morocco at the end of his decades of travel and not written by himself but "dictated" to the local scholar Ibn Juzayy al-Kalbi (1321–1357). Writings were rarely made "in the field" during these centuries, presumably in part as a consequence of the expense and rarity of paper, as well as its sheer weight for those who could not afford pack animals. As with regard to the Greek and Christian traditions, other travel accounts were preserved in Persian hagiographical works that describe various Sufis treading the migration routes between Central Asia and India, not least those between the towns of north India and the early Sufi center of Ush.[39] For Muslims dwelling in the Mediterranean west or the Indian south, through a long sequence of Arabic and Persian writings, the towns of Central Asia had become known to Muslims as places of piety and pilgrimage as well as commerce.

The expansion between around 900 and 1500 of these Arabic and Persian writings on Central Asia shows the increasing familiarity and even domestication of the region's peoples. By the sixteenth century, in the Persian (and, in translation, Ottoman Turkish) *Khataynama* (Book of Cathay) that 'Ali Akbar completed in 1516, even the Ming emperor was being presented as a believer in Islam.[40] More reliably, the *Khataynama* also described the roads into China from Khotan, Kashmir, and Moghulistan, as well as the Qalmaq tribespeople and their obeisance to the Ming.[41] Such familiarization was one of the many tasks that the technology of writing could accomplish, but it was also weakened by a lack of reliable information. Such surer knowledge would only emerge in the next period, when increasing information was used to assess and articulate difference as much as to make claims of commonality.

Commerce, Ethnography, and Science (c. 1500–1850)

The second period saw the composition of a much larger body of travel writings on Central Asia. This was due in part to the appearance of new types of travelers who traversed the steppe under the sponsorship of the expanding Asian empires and European trading companies of the period, travelers who were now both more likely to be literate and more likely to be tasked with writing informational reports rather than accomplishing spiritual, mercantile, or diplomatic tasks. Writing, then, became an objective in its own right as travelers were as likely to be state-employed information gatherers as monks who happened to leave written records. In line with other early modern forms of representation, we see in such texts what Jaś Elsner and Joan-Pau Rubiés have termed a new "naturalistic and ethnographic paradigm."[42] State-sponsored data gathering about Central Asia was not entirely new to the period, as witnessed in such first-period texts as the Arabic *Kitab al-Masalik wa'l Mamalik* and, in its distribution if not composition, the Chinese *Da Tang Xiyu Ji*. But both the quantity of such writings and the variety of their sponsors are new to the second period, a literary expansion that is also reflected in their linguistic range, which points to a broader new sequence of interactions.

What is interesting here is that this literary expansion occurred in the same period that saw the final collapse of Chinese-European overland trade through the consolidation of the maritime routes to China, positioning the older Silk Road as the least productive agent of travel writings from outside the region. Yet the decreasing importance of the China trade did not mean an end to commerce, and the expanding and centralizing states that emerged all around Central Asia brought an increased demand for the region's own exports, especially warhorses. Three of the classic hallmarks of early modernity—centralizing states, intensifying trade, and increasing literacy—thus had their impact on putting the peoples and spaces of Central Asia into ink. If this increase in trade and writing suggests a mere intensification of patterns already discernible in the previous period, then what distinguishes the centuries between around 1500 and 1850 is the appearance of new forms of humanistic and ethnographic inquiry as well and, from the early 1800s, the appearance of writings related to the new physical sciences. Again, we see the pattern of travel writing serving as a technology for the transfer of information.

Throughout this second period—and especially between the sixteenth and eighteenth centuries—one of the most important linguistic media for such information was Persian, which in written form continued to serve as a cultural technology for interactions between Central Asia, India, and Iran. Indeed, the importance of the language as a written as well as spoken medium of information was seen even far into China.[43] Many if not most of its writers in both Central Asia and India learned Persian as a second language. In such cases, it was not a "natural" or mother tongue but rather a cultural tool that its writers deliberately learned to use. As a result, Persian was tremendously important for the mobility of peoples as well as books, ideas as well as identities, enabling educated, literate travelers to find work as state functionaries or court savants in the Persianate arena that stretched between Central Asia, India, and Iran, a milieu that is memorably evoked in Sanjay Subrahmanyam's chapter on the Persian writings of Central Asian travelers into India. It is therefore no coincidence that so many accounts of travel in and out of Central Asia survive in Persian, because mastery of the written language was itself a tool that enabled and encouraged educated men to travel and find service in the chanceries of distant states. A number of travel writings from this period were written by Central Asians leaving the region as well as travelers entering it from Iran or India. Showing how travel to Central Asia was in some cases inseparable from travel out of Central Asia, this points us to the process of circulation—whether of people or products, texts or ideas—which presents a more complex model of interaction than the one-way travel of outsiders into Central Asia. By taking up this important theme in the opening chapter, Subrahmanyam's study of such circulatory travel between Central Asia and India reminds us from the outset that the infrastructure of Persian-based knowledge and state employment that enabled Central Asians to travel to Mughal India also enabled them to come back. Ron Sela's chapter, which discusses early modern diplomatic exchanges between Russia and the Central Asian khanates, provokes the question of circulation in another direction. But in comparison to exchanges that were mediated through the symbolic language of Islam and the spoken language of Persian, these northwesterly exchanges suffered from a considerable deficit in the social capital of trust. If the roads to India and Russia presented travelers with comparable problems in terms of physical geography, then the challenges of human and cultural geography were far larger for the Russians and other early modern travelers from Europe. Not least among the challenges they faced as Christian "infidels" was the risk of being sold into slavery, that most influential but least documented motor of mobility across Central Asia that continued into the late nineteenth century.[44]

Even if many of the Russians who entered Central Asia were not to return, then many of the Central Asians who headed into India never returned either, albeit in many cases as a result of better conditions in Hindustan. The most famous of these "Turanis" in India is the deposed minor prince of Fergana, Zahir al-Din Babur (1483–1531), whose *Baburnama* describes the wanderings that ultimately saw him conquer Kabul and northern India, so laying the foundations of the Mughal (or Timurid) Empire. Apparently written en route, the *Baburnama* is a classic product of the road of texts because of its multilingualism. Originally written in Chaghatai Turkish, in 1590 it was translated into the better-understood Persian of its Indian reception zone; the text thus underwent a double *translatio* or "transfer" in language as well as space.[45] Another important Persian travel account from the period was written by Mahmud ibn Amir Wali Balkhi (b. 1596). Like Babur, he traveled out of Central Asia into India, though he returned home, pointing to the two-way nature of much of the travel enabled by Central Asia's connections with other regions.[46] The main text of Mahmud ibn Amir's *Bahr al-Asrar fi Ma'rifat al-Akhyar* (The Sea of Secrets concerning the Knowledge of the Noble) constitutes a world history rather than a travelogue, with the latter appearing only as an appendage and recounting a journey through India between 1625 and 1631. But if, like many travel writings, the *Bahr al-Asrar* is not a travelogue in generic terms, it does point to the region's widening connections in a period when improved communications in the settled imperial polities to the south and west allowed not only risk-calculating merchants but also bookish librarians like Mahmud ibn Amir to travel safely both from and to Central Asia. As a result, unlike several major texts of the previous period (including those of Marco Polo and Ibn Battuta), the *Bahr al-Asrar* was written by the traveler himself, perhaps signaling the literate traveler as a more typically early modern type. Moreover, in its detailed and apparently accurate accounts of the cultural practices of the various peoples it describes, the *Bahr al-Asrar* points to another important early modern development by way of its more precise standards of ethnographic description. Mobile persons and texts allowed different peoples clearer senses of commonality and difference. As Subrahmanyam discusses in his chapter, such descriptions also allow us to trace emerging notions of regional identity and even patriotism.

As late as the eighteenth century, Central Asian Muslims were still being drawn southward by the opportunities of the Mughal Empire, and a picaresque account of the travels of the Central Asian dervish Shah Palangposh (d. 1699) from Bukhara to Aurangabad appears in the Persian *Malfuzat-i Naqshbandiyya*.[47] By the time the Indian official 'Abd al-Karim Shahristani wrote his account of a journey in the opposite direction from India through western Central Asia and Iran to Iraq around 1740, the comparativism and empiricism of the *Bahr al-Asrar* was much more fully developed and had become a topic of discussion for the author in its own right, a theme taken up in Subrahmanyam's chapter.[48] Like other travelers in the next generations, 'Abd al-Karim Shahristani's travels were likewise in imperial service, albeit in that of the last Central Asian empire builder, Nadir Shah Afshar (r. 1736–47).[49] With the rapid rise of British control over his north Indian homeland in the decades after his return there, Shahristani's Persian travelogue, like so many products of the road of texts, was translated into English to aid the new imperial power.[50]

Even as Islam and Persian continued to form idioms of trust and communication during this second period of travel writing, Christianity and Latin also maintained their role in the motivating and recording of travel. During the sixteenth and seventeenth centuries, Christian monks continued to serve as emissaries, as they did earlier during the Mongol Empire, albeit in the most celebrated cases with Jesuits rather than Franciscans. As with the multilingual genealogies of medieval Latin texts, the inviolate persons of the actual travelers themselves similarly reflected the complex interactions of Central Asian travel. This is best seen in the case of the Portuguese former soldier and Jesuit Bento de Góis (1562–1607), whose diplomatic sponsor on his momentous journey from India across the Pamirs through Yarkand and into China was the Mughal emperor Akbar (r. 1556–1605).[51] As recounted in both de Góis's own epistolary reports from the road and the narrative written by his Beijing-based fellow Jesuit Matteo Ricci (1552–1610), the writing of de Góis's journey was, like its medieval predecessors, directed toward the provision of information on the unconverted peoples of Central Asia and the routes that led to their cities. If these were no longer searches for Prester John in Asia, they were still underwritten by a "religious *Weltpolitik*" that the Reformation and the rise of the Ottomans had done nothing to diminish.

Christianity—albeit in its Russian Orthodox form—was also important in the early Russian expansion into Central Asia. Building on the policies of conquer and convert that had seen Kazan and Astrakhan successfully brought under the control of Muscovy, Orthodox missionaries moved farther into Central Asia in the seventeenth century. But between the 1620s and 1660s, it was former soldiers and merchants such as the Pazukhin brothers who brought to Russia the first reliable information about Central Asia, even if their travel writings were sometimes in the statist genre of the *rospros'*, or interrogation report. As Ron Sela describes in his chapter, these early diplomatic missions, with their emphasis on establishing trade and freeing Russian captives, set the trend for subsequent Russian exploration of and eventual conquest of the region.[52] As responses to the Central Asian slave trade, the Russian missions also echoed the Iranian diplomatic expeditions discussed in the chapter by Abbas Amanat and Arash Khazeni, pointing again to the interplay between enforced and voluntary mobility in the region.

Like slaves, merchants also represent continuity between the first and second periods, though by the second period, there are significant differences in the number of merchants, the regions from which they came, and the detail in which they wrote. An early example is what is probably the earliest English account of Central Asia, the 1580 *Discoverie of the Countries of Tartaria, Scithia, & Cataya, by the North-East, with the Manners, Fashions, and Orders which are Used in these Countries*, by the Bristol merchant John Frampton. Both the subtitle and summary in the official Stationers' Register describe Frampton's *Discoverie* as depicting "the mervulous wonders that haue ben seene in those Cuntreyes."[53] In fact, the book contains no original information and is largely based on the book of Marco Polo, an English translation of which Frampton had published a year earlier.[54] Even so, this second period would see the European trading companies and the expanding European book trade combining to form important sponsors of more reliable travel writing. In some cases, travel accounts were put into printed circulation, as with the account of the 1558 journey to Bukhara (Boghar) of the Muscovy Company agent Anthony Jenkinson (1529–1611), published in 1589 through the efforts of one of the early modern traveler's greatest informational impresarios, Richard Hakluyt.[55] Like other texts of its kind, Jenkinson's is concerned mainly with providing information of practical benefit to merchants.

From the eighteenth century onward, such merchant guides became increasingly reliable, as in the account of George Thompson and Reynold Hogg's 1739 journey to Bukhara and Khiva, which was published as part of the travelogue of the freelance merchant Jonas Hanway (1712–1786).[56] Collated in Hanway's book were not only written descriptions of Central Asia's marts and products but also accounts of Turkoman and other tribespeople, statistics on taxes, forms of measurement, and, moreover, maps. While some European merchants of the period were seeking an overland route to India, others such as James Spilman (who in 1739 failed to reach Bukhara) were attempting to open markets in Central Asia

itself.[57] However, the tiny number of Europeans who reached the area could neither compare nor compete with the influx of Chinese merchants into the regions
conquered by the Qing in the 1750s.[58]

Although Spilman's attempt to reach Bukhara from Saint Petersburg failed, the
Indian merchant Mir 'Izzatullah was more successful in the proxy overland journey
from Delhi he made between 1812 and 1813 on behalf of the East India Company vet-
erinarian William Moorcroft (1767–1825).[59] If we have already seen the pan-European
collusion of trade interests and the book market spurring the literary passage of travel
writings from translation in one European language to another, then in the Persian
Ma'asir-i Bukhara, which Mir 'Izzatullah wrote for Moorcroft—itself translated into
English in 1825 and 1872—we see the literary interweaving of European and Indian
interests in Central Asia. If 'Izzatullah's and Moorcroft's aims were to gather information on the Bukharan horse trade in order to better supply the colonial Indian Army,
then they were by no means the only seekers of Central Asia's animal resources in this
period, and accounts of the region's wild horses and equestrian marketplaces became
a notable feature of the Russian periodical press.[60] As a widening range of actors
appeared in Central Asia, its multilingual road of texts became both more globalized
and interwoven at the same time.[61] Like their Russian and British Indian counterparts,
employees of the Iranian Qajar state wrote corresponding travel accounts in Persian of
their attempts to tap the same supplies of textiles and horses.[62] Yet as we see in Amanat
and Khazeni's chapter, as neighboring states sought to exercise influence on Central
Asia's governance and trade, emissaries sent from Iran were no less at risk than their
European counterparts. This was all the more true in view of the slave trade in Central
Asia that contributed so greatly to the wealth of the region's tribes in the early modern
period and continued even after the consolidation of Russian power in the 1860s and
1870s.[63] In discussing the captive diary of the Iranian official Mahmud Taqi Ashtiyani,
who in the 1860s spent nine years as a prisoner of Turkmen tribesmen, Amanat and
Khazeni bring to life the region's centuries-old slave trade, of which the unfortunate
Ashtiyani was one of the last victims. The diary, written on the cusp of two ages—just
before the Russian conquest of the region and the ending of the tribes' slave trade—
stands at a point of transition between the second and third periods of travel writing on Central Asia. Ashtiyani's captive narrative reminds us of how dangerous the
"steppe road" still was at this time and how fragile the protection that membership in
the Islamicate or Persianate ecumene offered to travelers, especially to Shi'ites.

Trade, though, is perhaps the greatest manager of risks, and despite these dangers,
the second period saw an increase in traffic other than in slaves, including the overland
trade with Europe via Muscovy. Such trade—or in some cases rumors of it—brought
with it an increase in curiosity about uncharted regions that in turn fed a growing
book trade in travel accounts of Central Asia. One example is the Dutch travelogue
of the sailor Jan Struys (c. 1629–c. 1694), which like others of its kind purports to
recount travels in Muscovy and Persia as well as "Tartary" or Central Asia proper.[64]

Struys's travelogue was originally printed in 1676 in the key port and print emporium of Amsterdam, and bootleg editions rapidly appeared in several European languages. Although only partly based on genuine travels and probably wholly ghostwritten, Struys's travelogue is at least more reliable than the almost entirely fictitious *Voyage into Tartary* of Heliogenes de l'Epy, which, published in London in 1689, traded on Struys's success.[65] While de Epy's travels were fictional, they were not without purpose, and like such better-known fictional travelogues of the eighteenth century as Johnson's *History of Rasselas* (1759) and Voltaire's *Candide* (1759), Epy's *Voyage into Tartary* drew Central Asia into serious debates on comparative politics.[66]

If trade-related writings were not new to the period, then the interdependent emergence of European military and intellectual interests in Central Asia were. While the "religious *Weltpolitik*" of the thirteenth century had framed Mongol Central Asia as a potential ally for Europe, with the expansion of Russian imperial interests in the eighteenth and early nineteenth centuries, the region was reconceived as a potential space of control or subjugation.[67] As with the better-informed merchant accounts appearing from the presses of western Europe by the later eighteenth century, Russian travel accounts similarly saw the gradual dispelling of geographical legends of vast gold supplies and easy routes into India.[68] Rather than merchant travels, from the eighteenth century, many of the major Russian accounts were written by army officers on either reconnaissance or diplomatic missions, as in the 1771 journey of Nikolaj Ryčkov to the Kazakh steppes and the 1819 mission to Khiva of Nikolaj Murav'ev (d. 1866), both of which were in turn translated into French and German.[69] The 1843 Russian travelogue on Bukhara and Samarqand by the czarist diplomat Nikolai Vladimirovich Khanykov (1819–1878) is likewise filled with exacting details on the two khanates' legal, educational, governmental, market, and health conditions.[70]

While the Russian language provided one linguistic outlet for the travel writings that accompanied these new interests, both Russians and non-Russians in imperial service turned to French and German, the other major literary languages employed by intellectuals across Europe, with German emerging as an especially important language for travel writings on Central Asia, a role it maintained into the early twentieth century. One of the most important early Russian-German accounts was written by Grigorij Fedorovič Gens (1787–1845) during his period as president of the Russian imperial Asian Boundary Commission.[71] Far more systematic in its nonjudgmental descriptions of the villages, inhabitants, foodstuffs, lifestyles, economies, natural resources, and languages of Khiva, Bukhara, and Khokand, Gens's *Nachrichten* (Reports) was very much part of the new ethnography that emerged from the nexus of empire and Enlightenment.[72] However, this imperially sponsored emphasis on more accurate data on the peoples and resources of Central Asia was not unique to Russian expansion, and the Chinese Qing imperial conquests of the seventeenth and eighteenth centuries saw both the writing and the publication of correspondingly detailed travel surveys.[73] As Laura Hostetler discusses in her chapter on eighteenth-century

Qing imperial ethnography, these texts also in some cases contain detailed pictorial representations of Central Asia's inhabitants. For both Asian and European travelers, such visual information became an increasingly important feature. But what was perhaps more specific to China in this period is the representation of Central Asia as an artistic as well as a political and ethnographic space, an aestheticization that would not feature significantly in European writings until at least the 1850s. In China, this development was seen most fully in the second period in the various Qing printed editions of the *Journey to the West* by Wu Cheng'en (1500–1582), the fictionalized account of the travels of the seventh-century monk Xuanzang, some of which contain dramatic illustrations of Xuanzang's adventures with the witches and monsters who dwelled in this mythologized Central Asia.[74]

If Chinese and Russian imperial ethnography formed one new mode of travel writing, then the rise of the natural sciences formed another. Compared to explorations of even the most distant regions of the Pacific, overland scientific expeditions to Central Asia were far more fraught. The redoubtable German botanist and explorer Samuel Gottlieb Gmelin (1744–1774) would get no farther into Central Asia than the eastern side of the Caspian before he was kidnapped by tribesmen and ultimately perished in captivity.[75] Other botanists were more successful, however; while collecting the samples that would make up his landmark *Flora Altaica* (1833) and *Flora Rossica* (1841–53), the German-Estonian botanist Carl Friedrich von Ledebour (1785–1851) wrote an account of his 1826 journey through the Altai mountains and Kirgiz steppe that was one of the earliest texts to conceptualize Central Asia as a natural environment.[76] The new scientific travelogues of Ledebour, a professor in the Russian-controlled Estonian university city of Tartu, and Gmelin, a professor of botany in the imperial capital of Saint Petersburg, contributed greatly to Russian understanding of the natural resources coming under their command. Geological travelers would not extensively travel in Central Asia until the 1860s, but when they did so, it was very much part of the new pattern of imperial resource-oriented knowledge. For Nikolaj Severcov (1827–1885) provided important geological maps of frontier zones while Ivan Mushketov (1850–1902) served as president of the Imperial Russian Geographical Society and as mining adviser to the governor-general of Turkestan. By reconceptualizing Central Asia as a space of plant and mineral riches, the travel writings of Russian imperial scientists served as a cultural technology that laid the groundwork for more tangible interactions by way of mining and cotton farming.[77] These were not long in coming. After the 1851 signing of the Sino-Russian Treaty of Kulja, which officially opened the Chinese-ruled region of Ili to Russian trade, in 1871 Russia seized control of Kulja and the agriculturally rich Ili Valley. Again, travel writing was the soft enabler of the hard traffic of globalization.

From Great Games to Railroad Savants (1850–1940)

Marked by the coming of Russian rule and the industrialization of travel, the third period saw new interactions with Central Asia enabled by the older cultural technology of travel writing. The first of these interactions was the new strategic value lent to the region as a result of the high-stakes travel of the late Great Game, which reached its peak in the mid-nineteenth century as British rule crept toward the mountain borders of Central Asia with the conquest of Punjab in 1849 and as the Russians vanquished the Central Asian khanates in the 1860s. The second of these new interactions was the rise of archaeological travel, which saw the region become exploitable beyond its mercantile, and natural wealth. The third was the rapid expansion of journalistic and artistic travel in the region as a result of the Trans-Caspian Railway and then automobile and airplane travel in the early twentieth century. All three of these new modes of travel and the writings they produced were linked inextricably to the expansion of Russian imperial control over Central Asia between 1865 and 1884 as the Russians captured the khanates of Tashkent, Bukhara, Samarqand, Khiva, Khoqand, and Merv. The colonization of the region radically changed the social and urban geography of Central Asia itself, not only by introducing settler communities and the urban enclaves constructed for them, but also by the rapid connection of Central Asia to western Europe by rail. The result was the most radical shifting of travel between Europe and Central Asia in history, massively reducing the time (and expense and danger) of European travel to the region that had previously been carried out at the biological speed of humans and animals rather than the industrial speed of trains. Whether with regard to military, journalistic, or archaeological travel, the construction of not only the Trans-Caspian (1879–98) but also the Trans-Siberian (1891–1916) railroads suddenly opened Central Asia to far larger numbers and more diversified travelers than ever in its history.[78] Although the Russian imperial authorities did regulate the entry of foreign visitors to the region, the aim was primarily to keep out spies and vagrants. As a result, the new middle-class railroad travelers were able to reach Central Asia with relatively little bureaucratic or transportational difficulty. Japan's transformation into a modernized imperial power also brought new Asian travelers to the region whose interests, modes of travel, and writing forms closely overlapped with those of European explorers. The cultural fruits of this imperially empowered industrialization of travel were the fresh conceptions of the region voiced in the writings of the savants, ideologues, and spies who carried their various concerns into—and back out of—Central Asia.[79]

Turning first to the Great Game travel writers, what was most distinctive about the strategic conception of the region they created was not so much the heightened detail and accuracy of its information gathering, for this link between imperialism and empiricism was a continuation of the scientific investigations introduced in the early modern period. Rather, what was new was the secrecy of their writings (the result of more reliable communication methods with Central Asia) and their upland focus on previously ignored mountain regions (the result of greater knowledge of and access to the surrounding lowlands). The secretive nature of Great Game travel writing was a direct contrast to the commercially published and widely distributed European texts of the previous period. Moreover, the space depicted in these writings was in many cases a very different Central Asia than that presented by earlier writers.

If it was to the Russians that the khanates would begin to fall from the 1860s, in Turkish and Persian no less than in German prose, the steppes were now being conceived as spaces of untapped usable resources and not merely the *dasht*, or wasteland, of former times. In Asian as well as European languages, the nineteenth century saw Central Asia represented in increasingly detailed and "resource-oriented" terms. The best early Russian example from this period is Petr Petrovitch Semenov (1827–1914), who traveled across Central Asia as far as the Tian Shan mountains on behalf of the Russian Geographical Society and the czar's government, writing reports as a geographer, statistician, and spy.[80] But the Russian Empire was by no means the only state to dispatch investigators to the region, even if it was to prove the most militarily effective one. From the midnineteenth century, the Ottoman and Qajar governments in Istanbul and Tehran also sent new kinds of explorers to collect information on the political structures and natural resources of the last surviving khanates and the surrounding steppes.[81] An Iranian counterpart to Semenov's travelogue is the Persian *Sifaratnama-yi Khwarazm* (Khiva Travelogue) by the Iranian diplomat Riza Quli Khan Hidayat (1800–1871), also written in the 1850s.[82] Like the European works that were its interlocutors—the *Sifaratnama-yi Khwarazm* was after all originally published in Paris—the Persian text paid great attention to the climate history, water sources, and livestock markets of the steppe. In a period that saw the Qajar Iranian state invest in the training of cartographers and printers as well as diplomats, the *Sifaratnama-yi Khwarazm* is only one of numerous Persian travel accounts that in printed word and lithographic illustration depict the ungoverned plains that earlier Muslim travelers had overlooked in favor of the towns.

If Central Asia was now a place of underused nature, this by no means lent a prosaic pen to its literary representation, and Persian texts such as the *Sifaratnama-yi Khwarazm* contain highly polished and evocative prose. This interplay between state-funded exploration of the natural environment and literary inspiration even reached as far as Britain, where the reports of Great Game explorers helped inform poets and other creative writers. As Kate Teltscher describes in her chapter, the romanticization of the river Oxus in Matthew Arnold's poem *Sohrab and Rustum* (1853) was only a small part of a flurry of writings devoted to Central Asia's last mysterious river.[83] The emergence of this more aesthetic vision of Central Asia in both British and Russian imperial writings reflects the widening awareness of Central Asia among artistic circles, and not only the mercantile, military, or bureaucratic circles of previous times. As we will see, it was a development that would reach its peak in the early 1900s, when the opening of the railroads and the writing of tourist guidebooks allowed poets, painters, and musicians to travel to the region in person. But before then, the armchair travels of poets such as Arnold also helped inspire genuine explorers, pointing to the symbiosis of the public poetry and the secretive prose of the Great Game era.

Poets and explorers also held something else in common, for theirs was an isolated and backwater Central Asia of scarcely populated mountains and secluded passes that stood in firm contrast to the bustling commercial towns and lowland trade routes that had been the focus of early modern writers. Far away from the Romantic likes of Jean-Jacques Rousseau in the Alps, this new focus on rivers and mountains had been less stressed, for whenever possible, travelers had always avoided the mountain areas of Central Asia. Mountain-climbing botanists such as von Ledebour were rare exceptions, and only a tiny number of accounts survive from more local travelers, such as the soldier Darvish Muhammad Khan, who penned a Persian account of the Kafir "infidels" of the Hindu Kush.[84] The originally secretive nature of these travels usually meant that the writings were published later, but in the wake of the Russian conquest in the 1880s, newspapers from Calcutta to Saint Petersburg and even New York heightened global interest in Central Asia, as evidenced by the excitable review of Lord Curzon's travel reports published in the *New York Times* in 1890 and numerous other American newspaper articles on the region's politics and cotton markets.[85] One of the newest elements of this strategic body of writing is its emphasis on mountain Central Asia, as seen in the 1868 account of the Karakorum Range given by the spy and tea planter Robert Barkley Shaw (1839–1879) as well as by George Nathaniel Curzon (1859–1925), who would shortly afterward be appointed as viceroy of India.[86]

The imperial nature of the Great Game's data collection meant that these travelers made up a varied caravan, with their reports written in a series of different languages, so adding a distinctly imperial profile to the literary productions of the road of texts. Many of the most important of these travel writers emerged from either the fringes or the actual colonies of the Russian and British empires, contributing further to the increasingly global connections of Central Asia. The most famous example is the Hungarian orientalist, spy, and explorer Ármin Vámbéry (1832–1913), whose celebrated account of his 1863 journey to Khiva, Bukhara, and Samarqand appeared first in his adopted English before quickly being translated into Russian, his native Hungarian, and even Turkish.[87] No mere self-publicist, Vámbéry also wrote in German on such major issues as the Anglo-Russian border question, which was arguably the key factor in the period's strategic reimagining of Central Asia.[88] Like other imperial adventurers and opportunists, Vámbéry instrumentalized his travel-won expertise in order to gain influence upon his return, though unlike the unswerving careerist Curzon, he vacillated between the roles of imperial informant and yarn-spinning showman.

If the writings of many Indian informants who risked their lives traveling to Central Asia were silenced in the secret archives of imperial intelligence, then there was at least one successful self-publicist, Munshi Mohana Lala (Mohan Lal Kashmiri, 1812–1877).[89] In addition to the travel diary that he eventually published in London, while he was in India, Mohana Lal wrote numerous articles on his Central Asian journeys in Bengali and English for such newspapers as the *Bengal Hurkaru* and the *Englishman*, winning fame that would culminate in a lecture tour of England and Germany.[90] However, most Indian Great Game travelers wrote only secret accounts of their journeys, as was the case of the Kashmiri Brahmin and civil servant Mehta Sher Singh, whose travelogue of 1866–67 provided the colonial government with detailed information on ways the Russian conquest of Tashkent in 1865 was affecting the Indian merchants who carried British goods into the region.[91] Still others, such as the unnamed Hindu pandits who, as part of the Great Trigonometric Survey, helped chart the Himalaya, found fame only vicariously through the anonymous publication of their travelogues in imperial journals.[92] Aimed as it was at delineating the boundaries of British India from Central Asia, this was again the creation in writing of a strategic geography.

The sponsorship of British imperial intelligence led to the creation of this increasingly linguistically diverse body of travel writing, and the employment of specialists from the Russian dependencies made further contributions to this diversification. The Swedish-language travel writings of the Swedish-Finnish military officer Gustaf Mannerheim (1867–1951) represent a case in point. As a Russian cavalry officer, Mannerheim played the leading role in an expedition to chart the Russian-Chinese border in the wake of the Russo-Japanese War, contributing again to the new strategic imaginary of Central Asia.[93] Another important Scandinavian traveler under Russian protection was the Danish military officer and explorer Ole Olufsen (1865–1929), whose travel writings not only helped chart the Pamirs but also provided arguably the richest ethnography of Bukharan life of the period, encyclopedic in its coverage of vegetation, animal husbandry, languages, building styles, foodstuffs, dress, narcotics, games, and government.[94] In addition to this Scandinavian entry to Central Asia, which would culminate in the exploratory travel writings of Sven Hedin (1865–1952), émigrés and officers from Central Europe seconded to Russian imperial service wrote a number of notable travelogues. There were also many German and Scandinavian (particularly Danish) visitors who had no affiliation with the Russian state. These traveling savants maintained the impetus of German-language publishing on Central Asia, and the period between around 1880 and 1920 saw a tremendous number of original and translated books on Central Asian travel appearing from such Leipzig-based presses as F. A. Brockhaus and S. Hirzel, with Berlin's publishers running a close second. One example is the account of an 1873 journey to Khiva as part of General von Kaufman's army of conquest written by the seconded Westphalian hussar lieutenant Hugo Stumm, who envisaged the region solely in terms of cavalry maneuvers and troop marches.[95] Another such account of the period was written by Heinrich Moser (1844–1923), the Saint Petersburg–based son of a Swiss watchmaker and pioneer of Russian industrialization, which gave particularly informative descriptions of the native craft industries of the newly conquered territories.[96] After expeditions in the 1870s to Chinese Central Asia in German state service, in 1877 the Prussian geologist Ferdinand von Richthofen (1833–1905) forged perhaps the most enduring concept to emerge from the scientific travels of the period, that of the *Seidenstrasse* or "Silk Road."[97] But perhaps the most unusual contribution of travel writing to imperial knowledge came through the work of Max H. Kuczynski (1890–1967), erstwhile professor of pathology at von Richthofen's University of Berlin. For through his travels to Central Asia during the 1920s, Kuczynski developed the notion of *ethnische Pathologie* (ethnic pathology), penning a psychoanalytical travelogue devoted to the folk medicines and masturbation practices of the Kirghiz.[98]

Nonetheless, even more than during the early modern period, the traffic enabled by the railroad network that connected imperial Russia to Europe was two-way and afforded circulation of people and ideas between these different world regions. The late nineteenth century thus saw Central Asian travelers reaching Europe and returning with ideas with which, through framing them in travel writings, they sought to transform their own societies. An example is the Tatar Muslim modernist Fatih Karimi (1870–1937), who in 1899 set off on the tour of Germany that he recorded in his *Yavrupa Siyahatnamese* (European Travelogue).[99] In counterpoint to the German accounts of Central Asian manners and customs, here was a study of European lifestyles that paid particular attention to the freedoms and education of women.[100] As a member of the modernist Jadid movement, Karimi attempted through his writings to promote such "modernization" on his return home, pointing to the intersection of travel and writing as a mechanism for social change. Echoing the large-scale movements of Slavic peoples in the Russian empire, migration became a prominent topic in the writings of Jadid intellectuals such as the Tatar Muhammad Zahir Bigiev (1870–1902), who in 1908 published his own travelogue, *Maverannahrda Siyahat* (Transoxanian Journey), in the Tatar intellectual capital of Kazan.[101] The railroad allowed far larger numbers of Central Asians to travel out of the region, especially on the hajj to Mecca but also through the migration of the thousands of Kalmyks who settled in Turkey, France and Southeastern Europe in the 1920s.[102] A number of these pilgrims and migrants wrote accounts of their journeys, though these travels out of Central Asia fall beyond our concerns here. In other cases, the new rail network allowed a new kind of Muslim intellectual tourist to enter even the most forbidding reaches of Central Asia via the Trans-Siberian Railway. Writing in Persian and Ottoman Turkish respectively, the travelogues of the Iranian Mahdi Quli Hidayat (1864–1955) and the Tatar 'Abd al-Rashid Ibrahim (1857–1944) record rich details of the rail journey and the globalized medley of characters met on the journey from Tehran and Istanbul to Vladivostok, from Polish commercial travelers to Korean railroad porters.[103] For such Muslim intellectuals, it was the railroad itself that served as a tool of ethnography as the new *rah-i ahan*, or "iron road," through the heart of Asia became the meeting place of the world.[104]

Moving from ethnographic to historical travels, by 1900, travel writings on Central Asia were also serving as a cultural technology for promoting change in other distant regions. The relationship between travel writing and nationalist ideology is seen in such works as Franz von Schwartz's account of Turkestan as the *Wiege*, or "cradle," of the Indo-Germanic peoples.[105] In such ways, the opening of Central Asia to traveling intellectuals led to the region becoming a space for discovering the racial cement of faraway nations. The intersection of imperial knowledge with historical and archaeological travel was also seen with regard to the sudden scramble for the antiquities of Central Asia between the 1890s and 1920s. As Imre Galambos shows in his study of Japanese archaeological travel writings, such works could also have nation-building agendas by trying to recover for imperial Japan a Buddhist heritage that other Japanese nationalists were suppressing in favor of a Shinto past. Like other travel writings, archaeological travelogues also had their material counterparts in the vast numbers of manuscripts, frescoes, and other antiquities that were carried out of the region.

In this way, such travel writings lent new kinds of value to the desert wastes of the Taklamakan and Gobi in particular, which in the civilizational rhetoric of the period could be seen as a cradle of ancient civilizations to rival Greece and Mesopotamia. Responding to British archaeological work in colonial India, Russian archaeologists set to work shortly after the conquests of Samarqand, Khiva, and Bukhara.[106] Farther east a few decades later, after the pioneering archaeological work of Vsevolod Ivanovich Roborovskiy (1856–1910) in the Turfan region between 1893 and 1895, archaeological travel expanded rapidly, emerging in Grand Tour Europe and being perfected in the biblical Levant. This form of travel was exported into Central Asia by such figures as the Russian Sergey Fedorovich Ol'denburg (1863–1934), the Anglo-Hungarian Sir Marc Aurel Stein (1862–1943), the French Paul Pelliot (1878–1945), and the German Albert von Le Coq (1860–1930). Collectively, they wrote many shelves' worth of popular and scholarly accounts of their travels that defined the region more in terms of its Buddhist past than its Muslim present.[107] In a period of Chinese recolonization of the "Western Regions" (Xiyu) and the Japanese colonization of parts of China, there were major political implications to this vision of primordial belongings, and many of the writings of the archaeological explorers were soon translated into both Chinese and Japanese.[108]

It was therefore not only Europeans who were attracted by the new archaeological discoveries, and with the period's widening variety of travelers, American and Japanese travelers entered the race for antiquities. The Americans included the former geologist Raphael Pumpelly (1837–1923), who carried out excavations in Russian Turkmenistan in the early 1900s after a career as a coal and oil prospector, during which he had surveyed the coal deposits of northern China.[109] Though derided at the time, Pumpelly made the earliest claims for an ancient civilization in the region; he is now recognized as the discoverer of the Central Asian Bronze Age. He was followed from the United States by the professional Harvard scholar, Langdon Warner (1881–1955), who in the 1920s pursued Stein and von le Coq further east by re-excavating the Mogao caves near Dunhuang.[110] These American cultural travelers were pioneers in their country's gradually awakening interest in a region that, even in a period of growing U.S. political engagement with the world, seemed to be as far from American naval and commercial interests as possible. Even so, from the late 1920s the American traveler and scholar Owen Lattimore (1900–1989) began to warn his compatriots that the region was in fact the geopolitical "pivot of Asia."[111]

From the opposite side of the Pacific—albeit often via the roundabout route of steamships to Europe and trains into Central Asia—came several Japanese parties, whose writings presented Central Asia as part of Japan's pan-Asian Buddhist heritage. As discussed in Imre Galambos's chapter, the earliest Japanese archaeological expeditions were led by Count Ōtani Kōzui (1876–1948). Between 1902 and 1914, Ōtani, a leader of the Jodo Shinshu (Pure Land) Buddhist sect, led or financed three journeys along with Tachibana Zuichō (1890–1968) and Nomura Eizaburō (1880–1936).[112] A range of Japanese written accounts of these expeditions survive, from Tachibana's *Chūa tanken* (Exploration of Central Asia) to the compilation *Shin Saiiki-ki* (New Record of the Western Regions), which was self-consciously modeled on Xuanzang's classical Chinese travelogue.[113] Based on these westerly discoveries of a lost Buddhist past, there also emerged a number of Japanese fictional works on Central Asian travel, such as the *Tonko* of the celebrated novelist Yasushi Inoue (1907–1991), which tells the story of a Chinese youth wandering westward and accidentally discovering the famous manuscript-laden cave at Dunhuang.[114] However, the Japanese expeditions can no more be separated from imperial politics than can those of such British explorers as Aurel Stein. Between the 1900s and 1930s, Japan's imperial expansion into mainland Asia evolved into an extensive Central Asian policy that paid special attention to Mongolia as a means of inserting Japanese influence between that of imperial Russia and the faltering Republic of China.[115]

As we have noted, the Japanese were not the only Asian participants in the reconceptualization of the desert wastes of Central Asia as the location of valuable cultural artifacts and nationalist pride. From the late 1920s, the Chinese archaeologist Huang Wenbi (1893–1966) led numerous expeditions, with the diaries of his first 1927–30 journey to Mongolia and Xinjiang forming the earliest direct archaeological vision of Central Asia in Chinese.[116] Yet even before Huang Wenbi's travels, in the early 1900s, the Chinese translation of Aurel Stein's archaeological reports and Édouard Chavannes's studies of Tang accounts of Central Asia fueled new Chinese conceptions of the region as being part of their own "national" past.[117] Even so, recent archival research shows that in the first decades of the twentieth century, Chinese scholars remained narrowly concerned with the discovery of Chinese-language manuscripts rather than with the multilingual codicological discoveries of Stein et al.[118] As a result, while Chinese officials before 1930 were complicit in allowing what was later referred to as the "plundering" of "foreign devils," Chinese scholars after 1930 used their newly-learned archaeological methods to uncover evidence for an ancient Han presence in Central Asia that would bolster China's political claims over the region. Through such new evaluations of Central Asian artifacts and ruins, travel and writing provided the ideological resources for the construction of national identities and political claims that linked Central Asia to both China and Japan.

With their vast camel trains and treacherous desert crossings, the great archaeo-logical expeditions of the 1920s were the last gasp of a mode of preindustrial travel that for thousands of years had sharply limited the number of visitors to Central Asia. But even if the archaeologists' crossings of the Taklamakan and Gobi were made by animal transport, their export of antiquities was an industrial enterprise, for their artifacts were carried on camel only as far as the nearest railheads of the Trans-SIberian and Trans-Caspian, whence they were swiftly borne northwest to Saint Petersburg, London, Berlin, and, in Count Ōtani's case, the Japanese port of Kobe. Ever since the opening of its first section in the 1886, the Trans-Caspian Railway had brought Central Asia into the new global era of industrialized travel. As early as the following year, in 1887, the train had entered travel writing through the works of such French travelers as Edgar Boulangier, whose *Voyage à Merv* contains one of the first accounts of Central Asian train travel and presents Central Asia as a seamless continuum with industrial Europe, where miners and machines were already hard at work.[119] If travel and exploration of intracontinen-tal regions had developed much more slowly than the interconnection of even the most dispersed coastal and island regions of the planet, then when the railroad reached as far as Andijan in the Fergana Valley in 1898, Central Asia became for the first time easily linked to both global markets and that late Victorian creation, the "world tourist."

By the late 1890s, the Trans-Caspian Railway was already becoming a tool of cul-ture by offering easier access to the region to artists, intellectuals, and journalists from western Europe. Even before the railroad reached Bukhara, the Russian conquests ini-tiated a kind of artistic conquest of the region through the orientalist paintings of Vas-ily Vereshchagin (1842–1904) and others. Patronized by no less a figure than Governor-General Kaufman, Vereshchagin produced some 250 drawings and paintings during his two tours of the region, in 1868 and 1870, which, when exhibited around Europe, triggered a new artistic interest in the region.[120] With the coming of the Trans-Caspian Railway, many other artists and dilettantes found themselves able to comfortably fol-low in Vereshchagin's wake. These new short-term visitors wrote new kinds of travel writing, such as that by the German scholar Max Albrecht, which, with its picturesque illustrations, accounts of harmlessly exotic peoples, and paean to the railroad, was composed for cultivated tourists such as himself.[121] The writings of Albrecht's aristo-cratic compatriot Hans-Hermann Duke of Schweinitz (d. 1918) gave reassuring advice about the different classes of ticket available and the comfort of sleeping wagons.[122] Other texts, such as *Transkaspien und seine Eisenbahn* (The Trans-Caspian and Its Railroad), a travel brochure written by the German surgeon Dr. O. Heyfelder, gave minute practical instructions, while General Tschernajew, the governor-general of Turkestan, published an article in the Russian newspaper *Nowoje Wremja* that pro-claimed "an academic railroad."[123]

Tschernajew was far from mistaken, and the railroad afforded access to new kinds of visitors pursuing cultural and at times idiosyncratic rather than well-funded impe-rial projects. As Ronald Vroon explores in his chapter in this volume on the eminent avant-garde poet Velimir Khlebnikov (1885–1922), the possibility of private travel through Russian Asia also fed the kind of distinctly anti-imperial imaginaries captured in the versified travel impressions recorded in the *Grossbuch* notebook that Khlebnikov filled on his journey. Moving from personal to community projects, the easier access to Russian-controlled Central Asia allowed the Anglo-Jewish bibliophile Elkan Nathan Adler (1861-1946) to reach Bukhara in 1897 and recover the codicological heritage of Judeo-Persian.[124] The railroad also opened the region to educated middle-class women, who were by this period graduating from the universities of western Europe and being admitted to its learned societies. A case in point is the female Fellow of the Royal Scottish Geographical Society Ella R. Christie (1861–1949), whose travelogue includes detailed assessments of the comforts and reliability of Central Asia's new train services.[125] Other new types of traveler to emerge from these developments were the anthropologists and musicologists whose writings presented Central Asia not as the barbaric lands of primitive nomads but as a sonic space created by long-term inhabitants whose folk melodies kept harmonious congruence with their geographical surroundings. Several pioneering female British, American, and Swiss musical travelers are studied in Tanya Merchant's chapter, which charts the zenith of global cultural exchange with Central Asia before the closing of the region's borders from both the Soviet and Chinese sides in the 1930s and early 1940s. Included among these music seekers is the pioneering Austrian musicologist Erich Moritz von Hornbostel (1877–1935), for whom the instruments and songs of the Kirghiz and Turkmen formed part of the globalizing comparative spectrum he would use to develop the Hornbostel-Sachs system of instrument classification with Curt Sachs.[126] But even if it was the artists and intellectuals who left the larger number of travel writings, they were only a small proportion of the travelers—and settlers—whom the railroads carried into the region, for by 1914, the Trans-Caspian Railway had brought a staggering 450,000 European settlers into Russian Central Asia.[127]

It was not only train travel that opened Central Asia to global immigration. By the 1920s and 1930s, it was the turn of motorized transport to carry in even more varied human traffic. While the novelty of driving was fresh, for those able to gain visas into Soviet or Chinese territory, Central Asia produced some of the most important early examples of the literature of automobilism. Sponsored as many of them were by rival European motorcar manufacturers, these journeys and the accounts written about them form the literary zenith of the process of incorporation of Central Asia into the global industrial marketplace, not least insofar as Central Asia formed only one leg of the global road trips that had by now become possible. The earliest great occasion for such writings was the 1907 Peking-to-Paris motor race, which spawned a series of travelogues including *La metá del mundo vista da un'automobile* by the Italian journalist (and later Fascist politician) Luigi Barzini (1874–1947), who won the race together with the duke Scipione Borghese.[128] Frivolous as such writings may seem, Barzini had earlier been a front-line correspondent during the Russo-Japanese War and had experienced hard travel aplenty. The other notable account of a Central Asian road trip was that of Clärenore Stinnes (1901–1990), the pioneering female motorcar racer who completed the first successful circumnavigation of the world by car between 1927 and 1929. Written in her native German, *Im Auto durch zwei Welten* (Through Two Worlds in an Automobile) was an instant success and was quickly re-published in Spanish.[129] In the vignettes of meeting German-speaking Mongolian officials and seeing telephone lines laid beside the road on the way into Ulan Bator, her book captured a moment of Central Asia's increasing connection to the world she was driving through.[130] These books, written in different European languages, presented their readers (and potential car customers) with a view of Central Asia as the ultimate road test.

Yet such feats were not only intended to advertise rival car companies, and motor travel also had important implications for the gendering of travel. For while a few hardy women such as Lady Catherina Macartney (1877–1949) and Ella Sykes (1863–1939) traveled through Central Asia by pack animal in the early 1900s, by the 1920s and 1930s, the motorcar rapidly opened the region to a series of European and American women. As Tanya Merchant's chapter shows, these women in turn took an interest in the women of Central Asia, who had for centuries been all but ignored in estimations of the region's material or cultural value.[131] Among these new motor travelers is the successful English travel writer Rosita Forbes (1890–1967), whose many adventures in the 1920s and 1930s included the drive from Kabul to Samarqand that she recounted in her *Forbidden Road*.[132] A few years later, in 1939, the avant-garde Swiss heroin addict Annemarie Schwarzenbach (1908–1942) and her journalist companion Ella Maillart (1903–1997) followed Forbes's trail by driving a Ford Model 18 Roadster from Geneva to Kabul while filing travel articles by telegraph for newspapers back home.[133] Such was the popularity of this new breed of roving journalist in the 1930s that it gave rise to a new kind of culture hero: the cartoon reporter Tintin. Created by the Belgian journalist Georges Remi, writing as Hergé, the first book of Tintin adventures was *Les Aventures de Tintin, reporter du "Petit Vingtième" au pays des Soviets*, published in 1929–30, which included a cartoon tour of Central Asia.[134] If by 1930, Tintin's was a Soviet Union of cars, trains, and airplanes, then his book of adventures was also a new kind of travel writing: it was anti-Communist propaganda commissioned by Hergé's right-wing Catholic employer, the Belgian newspaper editor Abbé Norbert Wallez (1882–1952).

Yet it was not only Belgian cartoon characters and the daughters of German industrialists who were able to embark on such car journeys. Asian travelers also made important contributions to the new genre of the automobile travelogue. Written four years after Stinnes's *Im Auto* were the Urdu and Persian accounts of the 1933 journey to Afghanistan of the Indian Muslim educationalist Sulayman Nadwi (1884–1953) and poet Muhammad Iqbal (1877–1938).[135] They reached Kabul in an imported American Buick, transcribing the vehicle's name into Urdu as a new addition to the Islamic vocabulary of travel. Such Indian writings were the textual response to the road-building projects of the 1920s and 1930s that brought the mountain valleys of

Afghanistan into easy driving distance of the British Indian city of Peshawar.[136] Even an aging poet like Muhammad Iqbal could now tour Afghan towns that a few years earlier could be seen only by hardy foot travelers. Trains, motorcars, and, from the late 1920s, airplanes brought not only more people but new kinds of people to Central Asia, more socially and professionally diverse visitors who included artists and musicians, journalists, and political idealists. A product of Weimar Berlin, the radical journalist Leo Matthias (1893–1970) could thus cast a critical gaze on Asia's industrialization in his 1933 travelogue *Griff in den Orient* (Gripping the East).[137]

Matthias's vision of Soviet Central Asia was quite different from that which attracted African American idealists such as the poet Langston Hughes (1902–1967), who spent five months touring Soviet Central Asia in 1932–33. The Missouri-born Hughes was one of almost a dozen African American idealists and leftists who traveled to the region as part of an officially organized visit that had originally been intended to be part of a propaganda film about the conditions of the African American factory worker.[138] Hughes left the official tour group and stayed on in Ashkabad in Turkmenistan, where he visited factories and spent time with local artists and writers before finally leaving via the Trans-Siberian Railway for Vladivostok. One of the many artistic and intellectual travelers enabled by the new infrastructure of travel, Hughes also wrote an account of his experiences, memorably titled *A Negro Looks at Soviet Central Asia*, which presents an explicit comparison between life in Soviet Central Asia and the American South.[139] The literary exchange was two-way, and with the publication of the Uzbek anthology *Langston Hyuz She'rlari* (Poems by Langston Hughes), he became the first American poet to be translated into a Central Asian language.[140] Along with the American female motor travelers, Langston Hughes and his companions formed part of a growing number of travelers between the Russian territories and the United States as Central Asia became a place where Americans (especially African Americans from the South) could taste a communist utopia for the worker that was all the more impressive in that cotton was farmed by worker collectives instead of slaves.[141] Travel writing, then, served as a political as well as a cultural technology for exporting sympathetic or even propagandistic accounts of the Soviet system to the surrounding world.

Other leftist fellow travelers came from Europe, such as the Budapest-born man of letters Arthur Koestler (1905–1983), who in the years before his turn away from Communism enthusiastically toured Turkmenistan in 1932. But as travel writing became a tool in the great ideological contests of the early twentieth century, it was the United States that saw the writing of the darkest depiction of Central Asia as a space of radical politics. The most vivid example is the 1922 book *Beasts, Men and Gods* by the Polish exile Ferdinand Ossendowski, who recounted his experiences as an officer serving the "Mad Baron" Roman Ungern von Sternberg in the horrendous millenarian battles for Mongolia.[142] During the same years, these global political contests were also found in writings from the other side of the ideological spectrum, such as the 1940

Das Neue Asien (The New Asia) by the Austrian journalistic globe-trotter Colin Ross (1885–1945). The leading German-language travel writer of the interwar period and subsequent Nazi foreign propaganda specialist, Ross laid out in his travel book the case for a "new Asia." In this Axis-inspired plan for a new global political geography, Central Asia and China would be united under Japan as the counterpart to a *Neues Europa* in which western Europe was joined with Africa and a defeated Soviet Union under German rule.[143]

Yet the writings of such ideological globe-trotters as Ross and Hughes represented the swan song of Central Asian travel writing. From the 1930s, the same totalitarian states that they championed were closing the region to all but the most controlled traffic. Borders between Chinese, Soviet, Afghan, and Mongolian territory that had been mapped by the geographical travelers of the late nineteenth century were increasingly sealed in response to the mass migration out of Central Asia in the 1920s. In 1920 alone, some 11,376 Turkmen households had fled Soviet rule by relocating to Afghanistan, while between 1920 and 1924, some 30,000 households escaped across the borders of Tajikistan.[144] Alarmed at the rapid escape of labor and capital, the Soviet authorities developed a new policy in which the border "was to be '*na zamok*,' or 'under lock and key,' in contrast to the loose flows of people, goods and money under the czar."[145] In response to similar mass migrations and the decline in diplomatic relations, the Soviet-Chinese border was also sealed and became one of the most militarized borders on the planet. By 1940, Central Asia's heady era of globalization had drawn to a commanding halt.

We have followed a series of cultural trails that from antiquity to the twentieth century chart Central Asia's increasing interaction with the surrounding world through a multilingual "road of texts." If much valuable scholarship has traced Central Asia's connections in antiquity with distant Rome and China, here we have sketched a broader picture by following the evidence of this literary trail. In outline at least, we have seen how the vague and sporadic early accounts of Central Asia written by a narrow range of religious and (less often) merchant travelers were gradually replaced by a more accurate and systematic series of accounts written by increasingly diverse groups of travelers. We have traced a slow widening of access to the region from antiquity to the early modern period, as religious and mercantile networks provided the chief premodern means of and motivations for travel. Then, we have followed the emergence in the early modern period of new imperial interests and their collusion with scientific investigations before the appearance of a less regulated "civil society" of rail travelers comprising the private scholars and journalists of the early twentieth century. If in putting forward the idea of a "road of texts," we have tried to enrich appreciation of Central Asia as a cultural as well as a mercantile and geopolitical zone, then this is not to divorce culture from its economic and political foundations. For through three stages of slowly increasing access to and representation of Central Asia, we have pointed to the role of the diversifying range of merchant, civil, and state institutions that funded travelers and their writings before movement was itself massively cheapened with the coming of rail, car, and air travel. In recognizing the political and other institutional allegiances of so many travelers from different regions, we have also seen that the nonaligned "liberal" traveler—the touristic amateur of European modernity—was a rare and late arrival in Central Asia.[146]

With so many currents of Asian, European, and even American modernity running through Central Asia, we have seen how the region became closely connected with the world at large. Travel writings served in this process as a cultural technology that aided the incorporation of the region into larger global developments, whether "hard" ones such as expanding states and markets or "soft" ones such as debates on politics and culture. The many different examples of travel writing surveyed in this introduction point to the different conceptions of Central Asia that were created through its interaction with a broadening global spectrum of travelers, conceptions that were inseparable from more concrete developments in trade and politics. These radically different ways of seeing the "same" space served as one of the cultural technologies of globalization as a once remote region and its peoples were incorporated into the knowledge and cultural systems of the wider world. In creating these various representations, travel writings served as discursive agents in helping shape and even provoke outside action and intervention in Central Asia. In such ways, the strikingly variant images of Central Asia created by the many different actors in its complex and connected history help us better explain the course of that history as Central Asia was successively transformed from the site of Prester John's court to an imperial horse market and a laboratory of socialism. The chapters that follow show in fine detail the role of travel writings in both recording and enabling Central Asia's incorporation into global history as the region was tied not only politically but also culturally into a wider world and its competing systems.

Notes

In researching this introduction, I am grateful for the resources of the Forschungsstelle zur historischen **Reisekultur** in Eutin (Germany). Thanks also to the American Institute for Afghanistan Studies, which granted me the John F. Richards Fellowship for research in Germany and Afghanistan. I am also grateful to Imre Galambos, Laura Hostetler, Arash Khazeni, Sanjay Subrahmanyam, and Kate Teltscher for comments and suggestions.

1. For general surveys and case studies, see Stewart Gordon, *When Asia Was the World: Traveling Merchants, Scholars, Warriors, and Monks Who Created the "Riches of the East"* (New York: Perseus Books, 2008); Svetlana Gorshenina, *Explorateurs en asie centrale: Voyageurs et aventuriers de Marco Polo à Ella Maillart* (Geneva: Éditions Olizane, 2003); and Komatsu Hisao, Obiya Chika, and John S. Schoeberlein, eds., *Migration in Central Asia: Its History and Current Problems* (Osaka: National Museum of Ethnology, 2000).

2. Cf. Johannes Fabian, *Out of Our Minds: Reason and Madness in the Exploration of Central Africa* (Berkeley: University of California Press, 2000); Matt K. Matsuda, *Empire of Love: Histories of France and the Pacific* (New York: Oxford University Press, 2005); and Anthony Pagden, *The Fall*

of Natural Man: The American Indian and the Origins of Comparative Anthropology (Cambridge: Cambridge University Press, 1982).

3. Mary B. Campbell, *The Witness and the Other World: Exotic European Travel Writing, 400–1600* (Ithaca: Cornell University Press, 1991), pp. 2–3, cited in Carl Thompson, *Travel Writing* (London: Routledge, 2011), p. 15.

4. Daniel R. Brower and Edward J. Lazzerini, "Introduction," in Brower and Lazzerini, eds., *Russia's Orient: Imperial Borderlands and Peoples, 1700–1917* (Bloomington: Indiana University Press, 1997), pp. xi–xx, and Witt Raczka, "Xinjiang and Its Central Asian Borderlands," *Central Asian Survey* 17, 3 (1998), pp. 373–407.

5. Claude Markovits, Jacques Pouchepadass, and Sanjay Subrahmanyam, eds., *Society and Circulation: Mobile People and Itinerant Cultures in South Asia, 1750–1950* (New Delhi: Permanent Black, 2003), and John Randolph and Eugene M. Avrutin, eds., *Russia in Motion: Cultures of Human Mobility since 1850* (Urbana: University of Illinois Press, 2012). For studies of more recent interactions, see Touraj Atabaki and Sanjyot Mehendale, eds., *Central Asia and the Caucasus: Transnationalism and Diaspora* (New York: Routledge, 2005).

6. Victor Lieberman, "Transcending East-West Dichotomies: State and Culture Formation in Six Ostensibly Disparate Areas," *Modern Asian Studies* 31, 3 (1997), pp. 463–546. For attempts to reverse this tendency, see S. A. M. Adshead, *Central Asia in World History* (New York: St Martin's Press, 1993); Peter B. Golden, *Central Asia in World History* (Oxford: Oxford University Press, 2011); and Timothy May, *The Mongol Conquests in World History* (London: Reaktion Books, 2011).

7. Jonathan Bloom, "Silk Road or Paper Road," *The Silk Road*, December 2005, pp. 21–26, and Philippe Forêt and Andreas Kaplony, eds., *The Journey of Maps and Images on the Silk Road* (Leiden: Brill, 2008).

8. Emeri van Donzel and Andrea Schmidt, *Gog and Magog in Early Eastern Christian and Islamic Sources: Sallam's Quest for Alexander's Wall* (Leiden: Brill, 2010).

9. Scott C. Levi, *The Indian Diaspora in Central Asia and Its Trade, 1550–1900* (Leiden: Brill, 2002), and Claude Markovits, *The Global World of Indian Merchants, 1750–1947: Traders of Sind from Bukhara to Panama* (Cambridge: Cambridge University Press, 2000).

10. Jaś Elsner and Joan-Pau Rubiés, "Introduction," in Elsner and Rubiés, eds., *Voyages and Visions: Towards a Cultural History of Travel* (London: Reaktion Books, 1999), p. 37.

11. Andrea M. Chandler, *Institutions of Isolation: Border Controls in the Soviet Union and Its Successor States, 1917–1993* (Montreal: McGill-Queen's University Press, 1998), ch. 5, and Charles Shaw, "Friendship under Lock and Key: The Soviet Central Asian Border, 1918–34," *Central Asian Survey* 30, 3–4 (2011), pp. 331–48.

12. James D. P. Bolton, *Aristeas of Proconnesus* (Oxford: Clarendon Press, 1962).

13. James Romm, ed., *The Landmark Arrian: The Campaigns of Alexander,* trans. Pamela Mensch (New York: Pantheon Books, 2010). More generally, see John R. Gardiner-Garden, *Greek Conceptions on Inner Asian Geography and Ethnography from Ephoros to Eratosthenes* (Bloomington: Indiana University, Research Institute for Inner Asian Studies, 1987), and Amélie Kuhrt and Susan Sherwin-White, eds., *Hellenism in the East: The Interaction of Greek and Non-Greek Civilizations from Syria to Central Asia after Alexander* (London: Duckworth, 1987).

14. Michael Whitby and Mary Whitby, trans., *The History of Theophylact Simocatta* (Oxford: Oxford University Press, 1986).

15. J. P. Asmussen, "The Sogdian and Uighur-Turkish Christian Literature in Central Asia before the Real Rise of Islam: A Survey," in L. A. Hercus et al., eds, *Indological and Buddhist Studies: Volume in Honour of Professor J. W. de Jong on His Sixtieth Birthday* (Canberra: Australian National University, 1982), pp. 11–29.

16. On Chinese travel accounts more generally, see Richard Strassberg, *Inscribed Landscapes: Travel Writing from Imperial China* (Berkeley: University of California Press, 1994).

17. Edward H. Schafer, *The Golden Peaches of Samarkand: A Study of T'ang Exotics* (Berkeley: University of California Press, 1963); on books, see ibid., ch. 19.

18. Rongxi Li, trans., *The Great Tang Dynasty Record of the Western Regions* (Berkeley: Numata Center for Buddhist Translation & Research, 1995).

19. Christian Lamouroux, "De l'étrangeté à la différence: Les récits des émissaires Song en pays Liao (XIe S.)," in Claudine Salmon, ed., *Récits de voyages asiatiques: Genres, mentalités, conception de l'espace* (Paris: École française d'Extrême-Orient, 1996), pp. 101–26.

20. Among the vast secondary literature, see most critically Frances Wood, *Did Marco Polo Go to China?* (London: Secker & Warburg, 1995).

21. Geoffrey F. Hudson, *Europe & China: A Survey of Their Relations from the Earliest Times to 1800* (London: E. Arnold & Co., 1931), p. 135.

22. Johannes Giessauf, *Die Mongolengeschichte des Johannes von Piano Carpine: Einführung, Text, Übersetzung, Kommentar* (Graz: Selbstverlag des Instituts für Geschichte der Karl-Franzens-Universität Graz, 1995), and William of Rubruck, *The Mission of Friar William of Rubruck: His Journey to the Court of the Great Khan Möngke, 1253–1255*, trans. Peter Jackson with introduction, notes, and appendices by Peter Jackson with David Morgan (London: Hakluyt Society, 1990). See also Christopher Dawson, ed., *The Mongol Mission: Narratives and Letters of the Franciscan Missionaries in Mongolia and China in the Thirteenth and Fourteenth Centuries* (New York: Sheed and Ward, 1955).

23. Claude *Kappler*, "Les Voyageurs et les langues orientales: Interprètes, traducteurs et connaisseurs," in Marion Debout, Denise Eekaute-Bardery, and Vincent Fourniau, eds., *Routes d'Asie: Marchands et voyageurs, XVe–XVIIIe siècle* (Istanbul: Isis Press, 1988).

24. For printed editions of the various versions, see Louis de Baecker, *L'Extrême Orient au moyen-âge: D'après les manuscrits d'un Flamand de Belgique, moine de Saint-Bertin à Saint-Omer et d'un prince d'Arménie, moine de Prémontré à Poitiers* (Paris: E. Leroux, 1877), pt. 2; Glenn Burger, *A Lytell Cronycle: Richard Pynson's Translation (c. 1520) of "La fleur des histoires de la terre d'Orient,"* (Toronto: University of Toronto Press, 1988); and Wesley R. Long, ed., *La Flor de las Ystorias de Orient, by Hayton, Prince of Gorigos; Edited from the Unique Ms, Escorial Z-I-2* (Chicago: University of Chicago Press, 1934).

25. E. A. Wallis, trans., *The Monk of Kublai Khan, Emperor of China; or The History of the Life and Travels of Rabban Sawma* (London: The Religious Track Society, 1928). See also Morris Rossabi, *Voyager from Xanadu: Rabban Sauma and the First Journey from China to the West* (Tokyo: Kodansha International, 1992).

26. John A. Boyle, "Kirakos of Ganjak on the Mongols," *Central Asiatic Journal* 7, 3 (1963), pp. 199–214.

27. Arthur Waley, trans., *The Travels of an Alchemist: The Journey of the Taoist, Ch'ang-Ch'un, from China to the Hindukush at the Summons of Chingiz Khan, Recorded by His Disciple, Li Chih-Ch'ang* (London: G. Routledge & Sons, 1931).

28. "Si Shi Ki: Record of an Embassy to the Regions in the West," in Emile Bretschneider, *Medieval Researches from Eastern Asiatic Sources* (repr., New York: Barnes & Noble, 1967), pp. 109–56.

29. Adshead (1993), p. 70.

30. Ibid., pp. 70–71.

31. Donzel and Schmidt (2010).

32. Peter Jackson, "Turkish Slaves on Islam's Indian Fronter," in Richard M. Eaton and Indrani Chatterjee, eds., *Slavery and South Asian History* (Bloomington: Indiana University Press, 2006).

33. Hansgerd Göckenjan and István Zimonyi, *Orientalische Berichte über die Völker Osteuropas und Zentralasiens im Mittelalter: Die Ğayhani-Tradition (Ibn Rusta, Gardīzī, Ḥudūd al-ʿĀlam, al-Bakrī und al-Marwazī)* (Wiesbaden: Harrassowitz in Kommission, 2001), and André Miquel, *La Géographie humaine du monde musulman jusqu'au milieu du 11e siècle* (Paris: Éditions de l'École des

hautes études en sciences sociales, 1973–88), vol. 2, *Géographie arabe et représentation du monde: La terre et l'étranger*, ch. 5.

34. Vladimir Minorsky, "Tamim ibn Bahr's Journey to the Uyghurs," *Bulletin of the School of Oriental and African Studies* 12, 2 (1948), pp. 275–305.

35. Manūchihr Sutūdah, ed., *Ḥudūd al-ʿĀlam min al-Mashriq ilā al-Maghrib* (Tehran: Kitābkhāna-i Tuhūrī, 1983), translated by V. Minorskij as *Ḥudūd al-ʿĀlam (The Regions of the World): A Persian Geography, 372 A.H./982 A.D.* (London: Luzac, 1937). The surviving abridgment of the *Kitāb al-Masālik* is printed in J. de Goeje, ed., *Bibliotheca Geographorum Arabicorum*, vol. 6 (Lugduni Batavorum [Leiden]: E. J. Brill, 1889).

36. Ibn Fadlān, *Risālat Ibn Faḍlān: Mabʿūth al-Khalīfa al-ʿAbbāsī al-Muqtadir ilá bilād al-Ṣaqālibah*, ed. Haydar Muhammad Ghaybah (Beirut: al-Sharikah al-ʿĀlamiyah lil-Kitāb, 1994), translated by Richard N. Frye as *Ibn Fadlan's Journey to Russia: A Tenth-Century Traveler from Baghdad to the Volga River* (Princeton: Markus Wiener, 2005).

37. Miquel (1975), pp. 204–5, 249–51.

38. Ibn Battuta, *The Travels of Ibn Battuta to Central Asia*, ed. Ibrahimov Nematulla Ibrahimovich (Princeton: Markus Wiener, 2010).

39. Thierry Zarcone, "Une route de sainteté islamique entre l'Asie centrale et l'Inde: La voie Ush-Kashghar-Srinagar," *Cahiers d'Asie Centrale* 1–2 (1996), pp. 227–54.

40. Kaveh Louis Hemmat, "Children of Cain in the Land of Error: A Central Asian Merchant's Treatise on Government and Society in Ming China," *Comparative Studies of South Asia, Africa and the Middle East* 30, 3 (2010), p. 440.

41. Īraj Afshār, ed., *Khatāynāma: Sharh-i Mushāhidāt-i Sayyid ʿAlī Akbar Khitāʾī, Muʿāsir-i Shāh Ismāʿīl Safavī dar Chīn* (Tehran: Markaz-i Asnād-i Farhangī-yi Āsiyā, 1357/1979), pp. 39–41 on roads and p. 157 on the Qalmaqs.

42. Elsner and Rubiés (1999), p. 29.

43. Liu Yingsheng, "A Lingua Franca along the Silk Road: Persian Language in China between the 14th and the 16th Centuries," in Ralph Kauz, ed., *Aspects of the Maritime Silk Road: From the Persian Gulf to the East China Sea* (Wiesbaden: Harrassowitz, 2010).

44. Benjamin D. Hopkins, "Race, Sex and Slavery: 'Forced Labour' in Central Asia and Afghanistan in the Early 19th Century," *Modern Asian Studies* 42, 4 (2008), pp. 629–71.

45. Zahiruddin Muhammad Babur Mirza, *Bâburnâma: Chaghatay Turkish Text with Abdul-Rahim Khankhanan's Persian Translation*, ed. and trans. W. M. Thackston, Jr. (Cambridge, MA: Department of Near Eastern Languages and Civilizations, Harvard University, 1993).

46. Mahmūd ibn Amīr Walī Balkhī, *Bahr al-Asrār fī Maʿrifat al-Akhyār*, ed. Hakīm Muhammad Saʿīd, Sayyid Muʿīn al-Haqq, and Ansār Zāhid Khān (Karachi: Pakistan Historical Society, 1984). For studies of the text, see Muzaffar Alam and Sanjay Subrahmanyam, *Indo-Persian Travels in the Age of Discoveries, 1400–1800* (Cambridge: Cambridge University Press, 2007), ch. 4, and Riazul Islam, "Travelogue of Mahmūd b. Amīr Walī," *Journal of the Pakistan Historical Society* 27, 2 (1979), pp. 88–120.

47. Shāh Mahmūd Awrangābādī, *Malfūzāt-i Naqshbandiyya: Hālāt-i Hazrat Bābā Shāh Musāfir Sāhib* (Hyderabad: Nizāmat-i ʿUmūr-i Mazhabī-yi Sarkār-i ʿĀlī, 1358/1939). For fuller discussion, see Nile Green, *Indian Sufism since the Seventeenth Century: Saints, Books and Empires in the Muslim Deccan* (London: Routledge, 2006), chs. 1 and 2.

48. ʿAbd al-Karīm ibn Khwāja ʿAqībat Mahmūd Kashmīrī, *Bayān-i Wāqiʿ: A Biography of Nādir Shāh Afshār and the Travels of the Author*, ed. K. B. Nasīm (Lahore: University of Punjab, 1970). For analysis, see Alam and Subrahmanyam (2007), ch. 6.

49. On continued contacts between South and Central Asia in this transitional period, see T. K. Beisembiev, "Farghana's Contacts with India in the 18th and 19th Centuries (According to the Khokand Chronicles)," *Journal of Asian History* 23 (1994), pp. 124–35.

50. Francis Gladwin, trans., *The Memoirs of Khojeh Abdulkurreem, A Cashmerian of Distinction* (London: J. S. Barr, 1793).

51. Hugues Didier, *Fantômes d'islam & de Chine: Le voyage de Bento de Góis S.J. (1603–1607)* (Paris: Fundação Calouste Gulbenkian, 2003), and, more generally, C. Wessels, *Early Jesuit Travellers in Central Asia, 1603–1721* (The Hague: Nijhoff, 1924).

52. On seventeenth-century Russian merchant accounts of the Central Asian khanates, Persia, and Mughal India, see also Matthew Romaniello, "Russia Encounters Islam: Merchant Narratives and the Early Modern Global Economy," *World History Connected* 10, 1 (2013), http://worldhistory-connected.press.illinois.edu/10.1/forum_romaniello.html (accessed July 3, 2013).

53. Cited in Edward G. Cox, *A Reference Guide to the Literature of Travel* (Seattle: University of Washington Publications, 1935), vol. 1, p. 246.

54. Donald Beecher, "The Legacy of John Frampton: Elizabethan Trader and Translator," *Renaissance Studies* 20, 3 (2006), pp. 320–39.

55. Richard Hakluyt, ed., *The Voyage of M. Anthony Ienkinson, Made from the Citie of Mosco in Russia, to the Citie of Boghar in Bactria* (London, 1589).

56. Jonas Hanway, *Historical Account of British Trade over the Caspian Sea, with a Journal of Travels, etc* (London: T. Osborne et al., 1753), vol. 1, pp. 237–70.

57. Anon. [James Spilman], *A Journey Through Russia Into Persia; by Two English Gentlemen, Who Went in the Year 1739, from Petersburg in Order to make a Discovery how the Trade from Great Britain might be carried on from Astracan over the Caspian* (London: R. Dodsley, 1742).

58. On the carefully controlled influx of Han merchants from the 1760s, see James A. Millward, *Beyond the Pass: Economy, Ethnicity, and Empire in Qing Central Asia, 1759-1864* (Stanford: Stanford University Press, 1998), chs. 4 and 5.

59. Maria Szuppe, "En quête de chevaux turkmènes: Le journal de voyage de Mīr 'Izzatullāh de Delhi à Boukhara en 1812–1813," *Cahiers d'Asie Centrale* 1–2 (1996), pp. 91–111. On Indian Muslim travelers in colonial service, see also John Bray, "Trader, Middleman or Spy? The Dilemmas of a Kashmiri Muslim in Early 19th-Century Tibet," in Anna Akasoy, Charles Burnett, and Ronit Yoeli-Tlalim, eds., *Islam and Tibet: Interactions along the Musk Routes* (Farnham: Ashgate, 2010).

60. Carole Ferret, "Des chevaux pour l'empire," *Cahiers d'Asie Centrale* 17–18 (2009), pp. 211–53.

61. Scott Levi, "India, Russia and the Eighteenth-Century Transformation of the Central Asian Caravan Trade," *Journal of the Economic and Social History of the Orient* 42, 4 (1999), pp. 519–48.

62. Arash Khazeni, "Across the Black Sands and the Red: Travel Writing, Nature, and the Reclamation of the Eurasian Steppe, circa 1850," *International Journal of Middle East Studies* 42, 4 (2010), pp. 591–614.

63. On reports of the continuation of slavery in Bukhara and elsewhere as late as the 1920s, see Hopkins (2008), pp. 666–69.

64. Jean Struys, *Drie aanmerkelijke en seer rampspoedige Reysen door Italien, Griekenlandt, Lij-flandt, Moscovien, Tartarijen, Meden, Persien, Oost-Indien, Japan, en verscheyden andere Gewesten* (Amsterdam, 1676). Also Kees Boterbloem, *The Fiction and Reality of Jan Struys: A Seventeenth-Century Dutch Globetrotter* (Basingstoke: Palgrave Macmillan, 2008).

65. Heliogenes de L'Epy, *A Voyage into Tartary: Containing a Curious Description of that Country, with Part of Greece and Turkey* (London, 1689).

66. E. F. Bleiler, "L'Epy's 'A Voyage into Tartary': An Enlightenment Ideal Society," *Extrapolation* 29, 2 (1988), pp. 95–111.

67. Catherine Poujol, "Les Voyageurs Russe en Asie Centrale au XVIIIe Siècle: Vers une science des itinéraires," in Debout et al. (1988), and Willard Sunderland, *Taming the Wild Field: Colonization and Empire on the Russian Steppe* (Ithaca: Cornell University Press, 2006).

68. Catherine Poujol, "Les voyageurs Russes et l'Asie Centrale: Naissance et declin de deux mythes, les réserves d'or et la voie vers l'Inde," *Central Asian Survey* 4, 3 (2007), pp. 59–73.

69. Nikolaj Petrovič Ryčkov, *Dnevnyja zapiski putešestvyja kapitana Nikolaja Ryčkova v Kir-gis-Kajsackoj stepe* (Saint Petersburg: Imp. Akad. Nauk, 1772), and Nikolaj Nikolaevič Murav'ev, *Putešestvie v Turkmeniju i Chivy v 1819 i 1820* (Moskow: Semen, 1822). On Russian accounts of neigh-boring Iran, see Elena Andreeva, *Russia and Iran in the Great Game: Travelogues and Orientalism* (New York: Routledge, 2007).

70. Humphrey Higgens, "Khanykov on Bukhara in 1841," *Central Asian Review* 15, 2 (1967), pp. 114–22.

71. Grigorij Fedorovič Gens, *Nachrichten über Chiwa, Buchara, Chokand und den nordwestli-chen Theil des chinesischen Staates* (Saint Petersburg: Akademie der Wissenschaften, 1839).

72. Katherine M. Faull, ed., *Anthropology and the German Enlightenment: Perspectives on Humanity* (Lewisburg: Bucknell University Press, 1995), and Larry Wolff and Marco Cipolloni, eds., *The Anthropology of the Enlightenment* (Palo Alto: Stanford University Press, 2007).

73. Laura Hostetler, *The Qing Colonial Enterprise: Ethnography and Cartography in Early Mod-ern China* (Chicago: University of Chicago Press, 2001), and Peter C. Perdue, *China Marches West: The Qing Conquest of Central Eurasia* (Cambridge: Belknap Press, 2005).

74. Cheng'en Wu, *Journey to the West*, 4 vols, trans. and ed. Anthony C. Yu (Chicago: University of Chicago Press, 1977–83).

75. Samuel Gottlieb Gmelin, *Reise durch Russland zur untersuchung der drey natur-reiche*, 4 vols (Saint Petersburg: Kayserliche Academie der Wissenschaften, 1770–84).

76. *Carl Friedrich von Ledebour, Reise durch das Altai-Gebirge und die soongorische Kirgisen-Steppe* (Berlin: G. Reimer, 1829).

77. V. Muschkbtow [Ivan Vasil'evich Mushketov], "Kurzer Bericht über eine geologische Reise in Turkestan, im Jahre 1875," *Verhandlungen der Russisch-Kaiserlichen Mineralogischen Gesell-schaft zu St. Petersburg*, 2nd series, vol. 12 (1877), pp. 117–236; Muschkbtow, *"Turkestan": Geo-logicheskoe i orograficheskoe opisanie po dannym," sobrannym" vo vremiâ puteshestviĭ s" 1874 g. po 1880 g* (Saint Peterburg: M. M. Stasiulevicha, 1886–1906); and Nikolaj Alekseevič Severcov, *Putešestvija po Turkestanskomu kraju i izsledovanie gornoj strany Tjan'-Šanja* (Saint Petersburg: s.n., 1873).

78. Nile Green, "The Rail Hajjis: The Trans-Siberian Railway and the Long Way to Mecca," in Venetia Porter, ed., *Hajj: Collected Essays* (London: British Museum, 2013).

79. François Lantz, "Mouvement et voies de communication en Asie centrale: L'avènement d'une colonie," *Cahiers d'Asie Centrale* 17–18 (2009), pp. 289–317, and Steven G. Marks, *Road to Power: The Trans-Siberian Railroad and the Colonization of Asian Russia, 1850–1917* (London: I. B. Tauris, 1991).

80. Petr Petrovitch Semenov, *Travels in the Tian'-Shan' 1856–1857*, trans. Liudmila Gilmour, Colin Thomas, and Marcus Wheeler, ed. and annot. by Colin Thomas (London: The Hakluyt Society, 1998).

81. Francois Georgeon, "Un voyageur ottoman à Khiva en 187," *Transmission du savoir dans le monde musulman périphérique, Lettre d'information* 10 (1990), pp. 89–94, and Christoph Herzog and Raoul Motika, "Orientalism 'Alla Turca': Late 19th/Early 20th Century Ottoman Voyages into the Muslim 'Outback'," *Die Welt des Islams* 40, 2 (2000), pp. 139–95.

82. Rizā Qulī Khān Hidāyat, *Sifāratnāma-yi Khwārazm: Relation de l'Ambassade au Kharezm (Khiva) de Riza Qouly Khan: Texte Persan*, ed. Charles Schefer (Paris: Ernest Leroux, 1876). For analy-sis, see Khazeni (2010) and Christine Noelle-Karimi, "'Different in all Respects': Bukhara and Khiva as Viewed by Kāğār Envoys," in Yavuz Köse with Tobias Völker, eds., *Şehrâyîn: Die Welt der Osmanen, Die Osmanen in der Welt: Wahrnehmungen, Begegnungen und Abgrenzungen / Illuminating the Otto-man World: Perceptions, Encounters and Boundaries* (Wiesbaden: Otto Harrassowitz, 2012).

83. C. W. J. Withers and I. M. Keighren, "Travels into Print: Authoring, Editing and Narratives of Travel and Exploration, c. 1815–c. 1857," *Transactions of the Institute of British Geographers* 36, 4 (2011), pp. 560–73.

84. Gianroberto Scarcia, ed. and trans., *Ṣifat-nāma-yi Darvīš Muḥammad Ḫān-i Ġāzī: Cronaca di una Crociata Musulmana contro i Kafiri di Laġmān nell'anno 1582* (Rome: Istituto Italiano per il Medio ed Estremo Oriente, 1965).

85. "New Publications: The New Central Asia; Russia in Central Asia in 1889 and the Anglo-Russian Question by the Hon. George N. Curzon, M.P.," *New York Times*, January 13, 1890.

86. George Nathaniel Curzon, *The Pamirs and the Source of the Oxus* (London: Royal Geographical Society, 1896), and Robert Shaw, *Visits to High Tartary, Yârkand, and Kâshgar (formerly Chinese Tartary), and Return Journey over the Karakoram Pass* (London: John Murray, 1871).

87. Ármin Vámbéry, *Travels in Central Asia: Being the Account of a Journey from Teheran across the Turkoman Desert on the Eastern Shore of the Caspian to Khiva, Bokhara, and Samarcand, Performed in the year 1863* (London: J. Murray, 1864); Vámbéry, *Puteshestvīe po Srednei Azīī: Opisanīe poīezdki iz Tegerana cherez Turkmenskuīu step' po vostochnomu beregu Kaspīĭskago morīa v Chivu, Bukharu i Samarkand, sovershennoĭ v 1863 godu* (Saint Petersburg: s.n., 1865); Vámbéry, *Vázlatok Közép-Ázsiából: Ujabb adalékok az oxusmelléki országok népismereti, társadalmi és politikai viszonyaihoz* (Budapest : Ráth Mór, 1868); and Vámbéry, *Bir Sahte Dervisin Asya-i Vustada Seyahatı* (Istanbul: Vakit Matbaası, 1295/1878).

88. Hermann Vámbéry, *Centralasien und die englisch-russische Grenzfrage: Gesammelte politische Schriften* (Leipzig: Brockhaus, 1873).

89. Munshi Mohan Lal, *Travel in the Punjab, Afganistan and Turkistan to Balk, Bokhara and Herat, and a Visit to Great Britain and Germany* (London: W. H. Allen & Co., 1846). More generally, see Hari Ram Gupta, *Life and Work of Mohan Lal Kashmiri, 1812–1877* (Lahore: Minerva, 1943).

90. On the newspaper articles, see Christopher A. Bayly, *Empire and Information: Intelligence Gathering and Social Communication in India, 1780–1870* (Cambridge: Cambridge University Press, 1997), p. 230.

91. Mehta Sher Singh, *Kashmir to Central Asia, 1866–1867: Routes & Events*, trans. Gulshan Majeed and Raja Bano (Srinagar: Jay Kay Book Shop, 2009).

92. T. G. Montgomerie, "Report on the Trans-Himalayan Explorations, in Connexion with the Great Trigonometrical Survey of India, during 1856–7: Route-Survey made by Pundit ———," *Proceedings of the Royal Geographical Society of London* 12, 3 (1867–68), pp. 146–75.

93. Carl Gustaf Emil Mannerheim, *Dagbok: Förd under min resa i Centralasien och Kina, 1906–07–08* (Helsingfors: Svenska Litteratursällskapet i Finland, 2010).

94. Ole Olufsen, "Zwei Vortrage über meine Reisen in Pamir, 1896–97 und 1898–99," *Zeitschrift der Gesellschaft für Erdk* (Berlin, 1897–1900), and Olufsen, *Bokhara, Khiva og Turkestan* (Copenhagen: Universitetsudvalget, 1906).

95. Hugo Stumm, *Aus Chiwa: Berichte* (Berlin: Mittler, 1873).

96. Heinrich Moser, *Durch Central-Asien: Reiseschilderungen* (Leipzig: Brockhaus, 1888).

97. Daniel C. Waugh, "Richthofen's 'Silk Roads': Towards the Archaeology of a Concept," *The Silk Road* 5, 1 (2007), pp. 1–10.

98. Max H. Kuczynski, *Steppe und Mensch: Kirkisische Reiseeindrücke und Betrachtungen über Leben, Kultur und Krankheit in ihren Zusammenhängen* (Leipzig: S. Hirzel, 1925).

99. Ingeborg Baldauf, "'Europa ist eine andere Welt und die Europäer sind andere Menschen': Kommentare eines reisenden tatarischen Aufklärers (1899/1902)," in Rudiger Hohls, Iris Schröder, and Hannes Siegrist, eds., *Europa und die Europäer: Quellen und Essays zur modernen europäischen Geschichte* (Stuttgart: Steiner, 2005), and Azade-Ayse Rorlich, "'The Temptation of the West': Two Tatar Travellers' Encounter with Europe at the End of the Nineteenth Century," *Central Asian Survey* 4, 3 (1985), pp. 39–58.

100. Baldauf (2005).

101. Komatsu Hisao, "Migration in Central Asia as Reflected in the Jadid Writings," in Komatsu et al. (2000), pp. 25–26.

102. Françoise Aubin, "Une Société d'émigrés: La colonie des Kalmouks en France," *L'Année sociologique* 17 (1966), pp. 133–212; Green (2013); Timur Kocaoglu, "Turkistan Abroad: The Political Migration—from the Soviet & Chinese Central Asia (1918–1997)," in Komatsu et al. (2000); and Sharifa Tosheva, "The Pilgrimage Books of Central Asia: Routes and Impressions (19th and Early 20th Centuries)," in Alexandre Papas, Thomas Welsford, and Thiery Zarcone, eds., *Central Asian Pilgrims: Hajj Routes and Pious Visits between Central Asia and the Hijaz* (Berlin: Klaus Schwarz Verlag, 2012). For statistical data on the emigration of Jews, Armenians, Indians, and Tatars out of Central Asia under czarist rule, see Rinat Shigabdinov and Georgii Nikitenko, "Migration Processes in the West of Central Asia in the Late Nineteenth and Twentieth Centuries," in Komatsu et al. (2000), pp. 88–92.

103. 'Abd al-Rashid Ibrahim, *'Alem-i Islam ve Japonya'da Intisari Islamiyet*, 2 vols. (Istanbul, 1910–13); Abdürrechid Ibrahim, trans. François Georgeon with Işık Tamdoğan-Abel, *Un Tatar au Japon: Voyage en Asie (1908–1910)* (Paris: Sindbad-Actes Sud, 2004); and Mihdī Qulī Hidāyat, *Safarnāma-yi Tasharruf bih Makka-yi Mu'azzama* (Tehran: Chāpkhāna-yi Majlis, n.d.). For a study of the Siberian sections of these texts, see Green (2013).

104. On such travel writings in Persian, see Nile Green, "From the Silk Road to the Railroad (and Back): The Means and Meaning of the Iranian Encounter with China," in *Iranian Studies* (forthcoming).

105. Franz von Schwartz, *Turkestan: Die Wiege der indogermanischen Völker* (Freiburg im Breisgau: Herder, 1900). Also Marlène Laruelle, "Le berceau aryen: Mythologie et idéologie au service de la colonisation du Turkestan," *Cahiers d'Asie Centrale* 17–18 (2009), pp. 107–31.

106. Daniel Brower, *Turkestan and the Fate of the Russian Empire* (London: RoutledgeCurzon, 2003), p. 48.

107. For surveys of their activities and writings, see Jack A. Dabbs, *History of the Discovery and Exploration of Chinese Turkestan* (The Hague: Mouton, 1963), and Peter Hopkirk, *Foreign Devils on the Silk Road: The Search for the Lost Cities and Treasures of Chinese Central Asia* (Amherst: University of Massachusetts Press, 1980).

108. Su Rongu, "The Reception of 'Archaeology' and 'Prehistory' and the Founding of Archaeology in Late Imperial China," in Michael Lackner and Natascha Vittinghoff, eds., *Mapping Meanings: The Field of New Learning in Late Qing China* (Leiden: Brill, 2004).

109. Raphael Pumpelly, "Archaeological and Physico-Geographical Reconaissance in Turkestan," in Raphael Pumpelly, ed., *Explorations in Turkestan* (Washington, DC: Carnegie Institution of Washington, 1905); and, more generally, Pumpelly, *Travels and Adventures of Raphael Pumpelly: Mining Engineer, Geologist, Archaeologist and Explorer* (New York: H. Holt & Co., 1920).

110. Langdon Warner, *The Long Old Road in China* (New York: Doubleday & Page, 1926).

111. William T. Rowe, "Owen Lattimore, Asia, and Comparative History," *Journal of Asian Studies* 66, 3 (2007), pp. 759–86.

112. Imre Galambos, "Japanese 'Spies' along the Silk Road: British Suspicions Regarding the Second Ōtani Expedition (1908–09)," *Japanese Religions* 35, 1–2 (2010), pp. 33–61, and Galambos and Kitsudō Kōichi, "Japanese Exploration of Central Asia: The Ōtani Expeditions and Their British Connections," *Bulletin of the School of Oriental and African Studies* 75, 1 (2012), pp. 113–34. See also Kogi Kudara, "Silk Road and Its Culture: The View of a Japanese Scholar," *Berlin-Brandenburgische Akademie der Wissenschaften: Berichte und Abhandlungen* 6 (1999), pp. 331–347, and Werner Sundermann, "Turfan Expeditions," in *Encyclopaedia Iranica*.

113. Galambos (2010), pp. 34–38.

114. Yasushi Inoue, *Tonkō: Sabaku no Dai Garō* (Tokyo: Nihon Hōsō Shuppan Kyōkai, 1980), translated by Jean Oda Moy as *Tun-huang: A Novel* (Tokyo: Kodansha International, 1978).

115. James Boyd, "In Pursuit of an Obsession: Japan in Inner Mongolia in the 1930s," *Japanese Studies* 22, 3 (2002), pp. 289–303, and Boyd, *Japanese-Mongolian Relations, 1873–1945: Faith, Race and Strategy* (Folkestone: Global Oriental, 2011).

116. Huang Wenbi, *Meng Xin kaocha riji*, ed. Huang Lie (Beijing: Wenwu chubanshe, 1990).

117. Rongu (2004).

118. Justin M. Jacobs, "Central Asian Manuscripts 'Are Not Worth Much To Us': The Thousand-Buddha Caves in Early Twentieth-Century China," *Journal of Inner Asian Art and Archaeology* 4 (2009), pp. 161-68; and Jacobs, "Confronting Indiana Jones: Chinese Nationalism, Historical Imperialism, and the Criminalization of Aurel Stein and the Raiders of Dunhuang, 1899–1944," in Sherman Cochran and Paul G. Pickowicz, eds., *China on the Margins* (Ithaca, NY: Cornell University Press, 2010), pp. 65–90.

119. Edgar Boulangier, *Voyage à Merv: Les Russes dans l'Asie Centrale et le chemin de fer trans-caspien* (Paris: Hachette, 1887).

120. Daniel Brower, *Images of the Orient: Vasily Vereschagin and Russian Turkestan* (Berkeley: Center for German and European Studies, University of California, 1993).

121. Max Albrecht, *Russisch Centralasien: Reisebilder aus Transkaspien, Buchara und Turkestan* (Hamburg: Verlagsanstalt und Druckerei A.-G., 1896); for the railroad section, see pp. 7–21.

122. Hans-Hermann von Schweinitz, *Orientalische Wanderungen in Turkestan und im nordöstlichen Persien* (Berlin: Dietrich Reimer, 1910), pp. 9–11.

123. Albrecht (1896), pp. 9–10, and Dr. O. Heyfelder, *Transkaspien und seine Eisenbahn: Nach Acten des Erbauers Generallieutenant M. Annenkow bearbeitet* (Hannover: s.n., 1888).

124. Jes P. Asmussen, *Studies in Judeo-Persian Literature* (Leiden: E. J. Brill, 1973), p. 4; and Emile Marmorstein, *The Scholarly Life of Elkan Adler* (London: Jews College, 1962).

125. Ella R. Christie, *Through Khiva to Golden Samarkand: The Remarkable Story of a Woman's Adventurous Journey Alone through the Deserts of Central Asia to the Heart of Turkestan* (Philadelphia: J. B. Lippincott Company, 1925), pp. 18–24, 110–12.

126. Hornbostel's account is found as an appendix in Richard Karutz, *Unter Kirgisen und Turkmenen: Aus dem Leben der Steppe* (Leipzig: Klinkhardt & Biermann, 1911).

127. Brower (2003), p. 145.

128. Luigi Barzini, *La metá del mundo vista da un'automobile: Da Pechino a Parigi in sessanta giorni* (Milan: Ulrico Hoepli, 1908).

129. Clärenore Stinnes, *Im Auto durch zwei Welten* (Berlin: Reimar Hobbing, 1929), and Clara Stinnes (Clärenore Stinnes), *En Auto a Través de los Continentes* (Barcelona: Editorial Juventud, 1930).

130. Stinnes (1930), pp. 137, 151.

131. Lady Macartney, *An English Lady in Chinese Turkestan* (London: Ernest Benn, 1931), and Ella Sykes and Percy M. Sykes, *Through Deserts and Oases of Central Asia* (London: Macmillan, 1920).

132. Rosita Forbes, *Forbidden Road: Kabul to Samarkand* (New York: E. P. Dutton & Co., 1937).

133. The newspaper articles have been collected in Annemarie Schwarzenbach, *Alle Wege sind offen: Die Reise nach Afghanistan 1939/1940* (Basel: Lenos, 2000). For the full account of the journey, see Ella Maillart, *The Cruel Way* (London: W. Heinemann, 1947).

134. Note that the Belgian first edition of *Tintin in Tibet* was not published until 1960.

135. Muhammad Iqbāl, "*Musāfir,*" in Iqbāl, *Maykada-yi Lāhūr: Kulliyāt-i Fārsī-yi 'Allāma Iqbāl*, ed. Muhammad Baqā'ī (repr., Tehran: Iqbāl, 1382/2003), pp. 489–504, and Sayyid Sulaymān Nadwī, *Sayr-i Afghānistān* (repr., Lahore: Sang-i Mīl, 2008). For analysis of these texts, see Nile Green, "The Trans-Border Traffic of Afghan Modernism: Afghanistan and the Indian 'Urdusphere,'" *Comparative Studies in Society and History* 53, 3 (2011), pp. 479–508.

136. Nile Green, "The Road to Kabul: Automobiles and Afghan Internationalism, 1900–1940," in Magnus Marsden and Benjamin Hopkins, eds., *Beyond Swat: History, Society and Economy along the Afghanistan-Pakistan Frontier* (New York: Columbia University Press, 2012).

137. Leo Matthias, *Griff in den Orient: Eine Reise und etwas mehr* (Leipzig: Bibliographisches Institut, 1931).

138. David Chioni Moore, "Colored Dispatches from the Uzbek Border: Langston Hughes' Relevance, 1933–2002," *Callaloo* 25, 4 (2002), pp. 1114–1135.

139. Langston Hughes, *A Negro Looks at Soviet Central Asia* (Moscow: Co-operative Publishing Society of Foreign Workers in the USSR, 1934).

140. Moore (2002), p. 1118.

141. Margarita D. Marinova, *Transnational Russian-American Travel Writing* (New York: Routledge, 2011).

142. Ferdinand Ossendowski, *Beasts, Men and Gods* (New York: E. P. Dutton, 1922).

143. Colin Ross, *Das neue Asien* (Leipzig: F. A. Brockhaus, 1940).

144. Shaw (2011), pp. 338–339.

146. Ibid., p. 332.

146. Cf. John Pemble, *The Mediterranean Passion: Victorians and Edwardians in the South* (Oxford: Clarendon Press, 1987).

PART I

IDENTITY, INFORMATION, AND TRADE,
C. 1500–1850

1 Early Modern Circulation between Central Asia and India and the Question of "Patriotism"

Sanjay Subrahmanyam

Huran-i bihishti ra dozakh bud a'raf,
Az dozakhyan purs ki a'raf bihisht ast.

To the huris of paradise, purgatory (*a'raf*) seems hell.
Ask the denizens of hell; to them purgatory is paradise.

—Sa'di, *Gulistan*

Variable Geometries

Some years ago, an Uzbek soccer coach who had just been employed by a team in India was asked by a Delhi newspaper to comment on the degree of cultural difficulty he expected to face in his new position. The Central Asian sportsman simply shrugged off the question. People tended to forget, he stated confidently, that North India and Central Asia were all pretty much a part of the same continuum. Circulation between the two spheres had gone on for centuries if not millennia, and the mountain ranges that had allegedly been "Indian-killers" (thus, *hindu-kush*) had in reality barely posed a barrier to the process. Invoking such figures as the Timurid (or Mughal) dynast Zahir al-Din Muhammad Babur in the early sixteenth century, he suggested that there was scarcely any need to speak of difference—except perhaps in minor matters such as language—between his own homeland and Hindustan.[1] While the response was no doubt reassuring to our soccer coach's employers and wards, it was actually not based on a close reading of the *Baburnama*, Babur's autobiographical text in Chaghatai Turkish, which is at times quite insistent precisely on the differences between the hot and dusty plains farther south and the cool climes of the Ferghana Valley or even Kabul, where Babur had spent a certain time in exile. The question then naturally arises of the categories that Babur, as well as other writers from the Central Asian and Indian worlds, deployed in the sixteenth, seventeenth, and eighteenth centuries to speak of spatial difference as well as spatial belonging. And how is one to discern how such changes were experienced in a context of movement?

This chapter focuses on the corpus of Indo-Persian travel narratives and other related texts between about 1500 and 1800 that traverse the worlds of Central Asia and South Asia.[2] It argues that in an era that clearly preceded that of modern nationalism, other forms of local belonging—to town (*shahr*), patria (*watan*), and community (*qaum*), for example—played a crucial role in how movement was experienced. At the center of the chapter's reflections are comparisons made by early modern travelers and wanderers themselves regarding the nature and quality of life in different regions of Central Asia and India.[3] While framing their thoughts in a variety of ways, I shall nevertheless attempt here not to straitjacket them in alien categories of thought but rather to give their own original attempts to grapple with displacement pride of place. The materials used in the discussion will go beyond the narrow confines of the so-called *safarnama* genre to embrace a variety of other first-person accounts. This can be justified in a variety of ways, some pragmatic (and relating notably to the paucity in the period of travel accounts in the strictest sense) and others more broadly reflective of the fluid nature of genre classifications themselves. Further, the authors and texts under consideration here date mainly from after 1500, which Nile Green has persuasively set out in the introduction to this volume as marking the beginning of a distinct period of writings about travel. By so doing, we will be able to gain a sense of the changes that came about with the consolidation of Timurid rule over northern India in the course of the reign, in particular, of Jalal al-Din Muhammad Akbar (r. 1556–1605) and his immediate successors, which also corresponds broadly with the collapse of the Shaibanid Sultanate in Transoxiana.

In an important and wide-ranging survey of the place of Central Asia in world history after about 1200 written some two decades ago, S. A. M. Adshead notes that definitions of the region could be quite variable: at their narrowest, they could embrace merely "the three Turkestans" and, at their broadest, could be "as broad as Inner Asia or even as Central Asia."[4] Much depended, he went on to argue, on the time frame within which the historian chose to pose his questions. Like Adshead and, before him, Joseph Fletcher, the focus in this chapter is indeed on that moment of "the interlocking of histories" that follows "the Mongolian explosion" that is synonymous with the expansion of the polity of Chinggis Khan in the early thirteenth century. The Chinggisid and Timurid legacies will be crucial in more ways than one to the discussion that follows, as will the classic question of the relationship between nomads and sedentarists. Further, since our perspective will take us above all to the Central Asia–India axis, it is the southern part of Central Asia rather than the northerly steppes that will be our principal concern. Like Adshead, we too shall look to how a sort of "republic of letters" emerged in the period and came to encompass the two regions in some measure.

Much historical literature on the early modern world—and no doubt on earlier periods as well—has posed the question of circulation I address here in terms of a familiar triangle: Central Asia–India-Iran or, if one prefers, Turan-Hind-Iran. But the three legs of this triangle have for a variety of reasons not received equal attention.[5] The relationship between India and Iran, though once perhaps neglected, has been the object of a number of consequent studies in the past quarter century, particularly as regards the early modern period of the Safavid and Mughal dynasties. These studies have highlighted a number of features, of which a few may be mentioned. The consolidation of a prosopography of the *mansabdar* class in Mughal India, and above all its upper (or *umara'*) echelons, by authors such as M. Athar Ali demonstrated the extent to which Iranian emigration between the reigns of Humayun in the mid-sixteenth century and Aurangzeb-'Alamgir in the late seventeenth century continued to be a major factor in Mughal elite politics.[6] These migrants may at times have been classified primarily as administrators, but they were equally poets, chroniclers, calligraphers, musicians, and painters, as well as lexicographers. They carried with them the seeds of a distinct tension, for many of them intended to assert that, even if they were seeking employment from a new patron, their culture of origin was of course far superior to that to which they were migrating. Iranian poets were thus often less-than-gracious clients of Mughal patrons, happily biting the hands that fed them and complaining of how they were underappreciated and underpaid. The case of the poet Ashraf Mazandarani, who was born in Isfahan in the early 1620s and died in Bengal in 1704, is a telling example.[7] Ashraf migrated to India in the 1650s and had a number of powerful patrons and supporters there, even among the Mughal royal family. Though he returned for a time to Iran, he therefore eventually was drawn back to the Mughal domains, where he spent the last decades of his life. Despite that, his verses are at times disdainful enough:

> With the lands of Iran?
> Can black soil ever equal a rose garden?[8]

It scarcely needs to be recalled that the process of migration between India and Iran during the reigns of the Safavids and Mughals was both complex and asymmetrical. If the more significant and visible movement was from Iran to India, Indians too migrated to Iran, but they rarely if ever came to occupy positions of significance in the Safavid administrative hierarchy. (The partial exception to this were some Mughal princes who exiled themselves and took refuge in Iran in the seventeenth century.) Rather, they were more often than not traders and could be found in appreciable numbers both in interior cities like Isfahan or Qazwin and in ports such as Bandar 'Abbas, Bandar Kung, Jarun (or Hurmuz), or even Basra. Their numbers seem to have expanded considerably over the course of the seventeenth century, though already in 1618, the English East India Company's factors in Iran noted the formidable presence of "the bannians, the Cheife Marchantes whoe vende Linene of India, of all sorts and prices, which this countrey cannot bee without."[9] It has been claimed that by the 1670s,

Isfahan alone hosted some 10,000 *baniyas*, that is to say traders from a variety of Hindu and Jain merchant castes from western and northern India. Some of these possibly settled there, but others are more likely to have circulated between the Mughal and Safavid domains, using either the classic overland route via Lahore, Kabul, and Qandahar or the maritime routes that joined the Gujarat ports and those of the Indus delta with the Persian Gulf. To all of this movement, we must add another variant, namely the connections between the Deccan and Iran that had flourished since the time of the Bahmani dynasty in the later fourteenth and early fifteenth centuries. Traders and political entrepreneurs, as well as religious specialists from Iranian centers like Kerman, Gilan, Astarabad, and Mazandaran, had regularly set up in the great courtly and regional nodes of the Deccan, and there had been moments such as the late fifteenth century when Iranian dominance over elite Deccani politics was very substantial indeed.

If these Indo-Iranian links of the early modern era have been studied over the past decades, beginning with the works of scholars such as Ghulam Yazdani and H. K. Sherwani, and continuing with the detailed research of the French savant Jean Aubin, the connections with Central Asia, or "Turan," have been somewhat harder to discern or delineate in a systematic fashion.[10] If we go back as far as the eleventh and twelfth centuries, when first the Ghaznavids and then a series of Mamluk rulers established themselves initially in the Punjab and then in the Ganges-Jamuna *do-ab*, the familiar pattern emerges of a Turko-Persian condominium in which the Turks dominated over warrior functions and the Persians over secretarial and related duties.[11] The Turks in question were of course predominantly Central Asian in origin, though some had spent a generation or two in centers farther south such as Ghazna and Ghur. The tension and mutual incomprehension that could at times exist between the two groups are a staple element in the writings of the chroniclers of the Delhi Sultanate, as well as in the reflections of the sultanate's most famous literary figure, Yamin al-Din Amir Khusrau (1253–1325), himself a Turk of Central Asian origin whose family had resided for a time in Balkh. The invasion of Delhi and its environs in 1398–99 by the Central Asian ruler Timur then led, paradoxically, for a time to a diminution in the power of the Turkish clans and a corresponding rise in that of Afghans, both in Delhi and farther east. It is also likely that as a consequence, the fifteenth century saw a shrinking in direct contacts between the plains of northern India and Central Asia. The emergence in the middle decades of the same century of the Kashmir Sultanate as a substantial polity also changed the nature of relations somewhat. Rulers like Sultan Zain al-'Abidin of Kashmir maintained diplomatic and other contacts with several lines of Timurid princes in Central Asia, including Mirza Shahrukh and Mirza Abu Sa'id.[12] Relations between Kashmir and regions to the east and northeast, such as Tibet, but also centers like Yarkand and Kashgar (today in Xinjiang) seem similarly to have been strengthened in the period.

Babur and His Legacy

The irruption of the Timurid dynasty into power in northern India in the 1520s eventually transformed this structure of dealings. This southward move on the part of Babur to take Delhi and Agra from the Afghan Lodi dynasty was itself the consequence of complex circumstances, notably the growing power of a rival Chinggisid clan, led by Shaibani Khan, which emerged into prominence around 1500. These latter rulers, sometimes designated with the epithet "Uzbek," seized first Bukhara and Samarqand and then the great center of Herat after the death of its celebrated Timurid ruler Sultan Husain Baiqara in 1506.[13] The defeat and killing by the Safavids of Shaibani Khan in 1510 gave some temporary respite to Babur, but he was eventually and comprehensively expelled southward by 'Ubaidullah Khan, Shaibani Khan's successor. He then spent the next decade in and around Kabul, and as he later wrote in the 1520s, "From the year 910 H. [1504–5], when Kabul was conquered, until this date I had craved Hindustan. Sometimes because my *begs* [commanders] had poor opinions, and sometimes because my brothers lacked cooperation, the Hindustan campaign had not been possible and the realm had not been conquered."[14] He also noted that he had made four unsuccessful campaigns into northern India in the late 1510s and early 1520s and eventually succeeded in 1525–26. Nevertheless, it seems that in reality Babur was not enthused about Hindustan, which is to say, the northern Indian plains. As he wrote rather bluntly a few pages after the passage quoted above: "The cities and provinces of Hindustan are all unpleasant. All cities, all locales are alike. The gardens have no walls, and most places are flat as boards." India, in short, was "unpleasant and unharmonious," wrote Babur, adding, "there is no beauty in its people, no graceful social intercourse, no poetic talent or understanding, no etiquette, nobility or manners." Its chief attraction then, especially to a prince who was coming to the end of his tether, was that "it is a large country with lots of gold and money." But there is little doubt that he felt that his wanderings had brought him too far south for comfort. Thus, he wrote:

> Hindustan lies in the first, second, and third climes, with none of it in the fourth clime. It is a strange country. Compared to ours, it is another world. Its mountains, rivers, forests, and wildernesses, its villages and provinces, animals and plants, peoples and languages, even its rain and winds are altogether different. Even if the Kabul dependencies that have warm climates bear a resemblance to Hindustan in some aspects, in others they do not. Once you cross the Indus, the land, water, trees, stones, peoples, tribes, manners, and customs are all of the Hindustani fashion.[15]

This view, and an abiding nostalgia for the Central Asia that had been left behind, were not Babur's alone. He notes the case of one of his companions, a certain Khwaja Kalan, who, on the eve of his return from Delhi to Ghazna, is reported to have scribbled a rude verse as graffiti on the wall of his quarters: "If I cross the Indus in safety, may my face turn black if I ever see Hindustan again." We cannot know how humbler foot soldiers or cavalrymen from Central Asia felt, though Babur indicates that as the hot season came upon them in 1526, "many began to sicken and die as though under the influence of a pestilent wind," and murmurings were heard that the chiefs in the army wished to contemplate an early departure. But Babur's argument in council at the time was implacable: "Shall we go back to Kabul and remain poverty stricken?" After all, he notes, many of the men had sent back "gifts for relatives and kinfolk," as well as offerings to the shrines of holy men in areas around Samarqand and Khorasan from which they came. His memoir is equally helpful in providing an understanding of what such men looked back to. Here, for example, is his idealized view of Samarqand, which in his view lay "at the edge of the civilized world." Not only was it termed the "well-protected town" (*balda-i mahfuza*) since it had never been stormed and seized; it was in his opinion one of the most pleasant cities in the entire world. Its virtues were many but could be broadly classified as follows. First, the area had been dominated by Muslims from the time of the early Caliphs and was thus a great center for theologians and the writing of important Islamic texts. Second, despite the harsh winters, the air was generally good and the water sufficient to irrigate orchards so that grapes, apples, melons, and other excellent fruit could be found there. Third, the city itself was a marvel, and its architecture had been greatly improved by the intervention of both Timur and his descendant Mirza Ulugh Beg in the matter of buildings and gardens. These included a famous observatory where great texts on astronomy were produced, far superior to those in India, according to Babur. Finally, there was the question of the artisanal and commercial activity in Samarqand, with "each trade [having] a separate market." In respect of every one of the trades in question, from baking, to velvet production, to papermaking, Babur apparently saw Samarqand as a city with practically no equal in the world.[16]

But his enthusiasm did not extend equally to every part of Central Asia. Ferghana, with which his memoir begins, is described (like Samarqand) as being "on the edge of the civilized world" and marked by the plentiful availability of grain and fruit. Its seven major towns are depicted by him as pleasant, somewhat bucolic places, with fat pheasants and game, beautiful tulips and violets, and excellent agricultural products—in particular, melons, which are actually something of an obsession with Babur. At the same time, he does not hesitate to call the town of Khojand a "miserable place," on account of its lack of resources and capacity to provide for a man of his stature.[17] In this sense, Samarqand does represent an unusual combination: not only is it located in an excellent and sufficiently northerly clime—the fifth one; it is also notably urbane and sophisticated, a worthy residence therefore for a man from a courtly lineage. As we shall see below, it would remain something of a yardstick against which other cities and centers—particularly those of Hindustan—were compared.

It is probable, at any rate, that Khwaja Kalan was not the only one among Babur's companions to return for a time to Kabul or even Central Asia. But by the time of the ruler's death, and the succession of his oldest son Humayun in 1530, the regular flow of Central Asians, or Turanis, into northern India was an established fact. These

Table 1.1 Composition of Upper Mughal Mansabdars, 1555–1707

Period	Turani	Irani	Rajput	Indian Muslim	Other	Total
1555	27	16	—	—	8	51
1565–75	38	37	8	9	4	96
1575–95	64	47	30	34	9	184
1605	30	21	17	5	22	95
1606–11	30	21	19	16	5	91
1637–38	43	60	26	20	45	194
1655–57	53	75	46	27	47	248
1658–78	67	136	71	65	147	486
1679–1707	72	126	73	69	235	575

included warriors, to be sure, but also a number of divines and mystics, given the proximity of the Mughals to a particular branch of Naqshbandi Sufi Khwajas, the Ahraris, from Central Asia. Babur himself had been closely linked while a child in Central Asia to Khwaja 'Ubaidullah Ahrar, a powerful entrepreneurial figure who controlled enormous resources in terms of land and other revenues, and several direct descendants and disciples of the great Naqshbandi Sufi accompanied him into Hindustan.[18] While we do not have clear information concerning the composition of the upper echelons of the *begs* and *amirs* who surrounded Humayun in the first decade or so of his reign, there is little doubt that these included a substantial number of Turanis. One of these to whom we shall turn below was Mirza Muhammad Haidar Dughlat from Kashgar. Even after Humayun's exile to Iran, and his eventual return to Hindustan in the 1550s—when his entourage clearly contained a conspicuous Iranian element—there is little doubt as to the significance of the Turani presence in the Mughal court. Through the second half of the sixteenth century, and despite several rebellions by Turani groupings against the rule of Humayun's older son, Akbar, this remained the case. To be sure, the numerical significance of the Central Asians declined, but still roughly a third, sometimes a little more and sometimes a little less, of the higher echelons of the great *mansabdars*—as the *amirs* came to be called in reference to the numerical ranking system (of *mansabs*) that was consolidated in this period—remained Central Asian, usually bearing the characteristic place-name *nisbat* denominations, such as Bukhari, Samarqandi, or Andijani, that indicated this. These denominations were themselves indicative of a form of patriotism on the part of those who carried them.[19]

What this meant in turn was that one of the chief motors of factional politics in the Mughal court throughout the sixteenth and seventeenth centuries (when the proportion of Turanis eventually declined to under 15 percent under Aurangzeb, even if their absolute numbers increased) was identification with ethnicity and *patria*, a logic that modern historians have sometimes naively called "the racial composition of the nobility." Two other factors further exacerbated it. The migrants from Central Asia were more often than not Sunnis, while those from Iran were usually—though not always—either Shi'i or somewhat heterodox in their religious orientation. From a legal point of view, once again it was the Central Asian migrants who tended—together with other groups in close contact with the Hijaz and the Ottoman domains—to strengthen the Hanafite legal orientation of the Mughal courts. Further, even if some of the migrants from Iran who bore names such as Qazwini or Gilani were ethnically Turks, a linguistic cleavage regarding the relative place of Persian and Turkish in the Mughal court did exist.

Beyond faction, there were thus real questions of ideology regarding the nature of rulership, of succession, and so on. Within a half century of Babur's conquest of Hindustan and over the course of just two generational successions, the Mughals acculturated considerably in the face of Indian realities, sometimes leaving their Turani *amirs* aghast at the compromises they were willing to countenance. It is clear now that two rebellions, in the 1560s and then again in the early 1580s, in which many of the Turanis rose up in support of Akbar's half brother Mirza Muhammad Hakim, who ruled over Kabul, were in fact a reflection of this unease. Mirza Hakim's court was far more closely tied to Central Asia than that of Akbar, and he also maintained very close ties with a number of Naqshbandi Khwajas, one of whom, Khwaja Hasan, was not only his brother-in-law but the real éminence grise in his court.[20] Such figures obviously preferred the relatively orthodox Sunnism of the Kabul court to the eclectic Islam that had emerged around Akbar, who was attempting at this very time to manage a complex court in which Central Asians and Iranians stood side by side with Afghans, Indian Muslims, and prominent Rajput princes. Even those Turanis who remained faithful to the central Mughal lineage of Humayun and Akbar (rather than, say, to Mirza Kamran and Mirza Hakim) seem to have been rendered anxious, as we see from the career of a certain Qilij Muhammad Khan Andijani, who was a prominent administrator in Gujarat and elsewhere. Qilij Khan is described in various Mughal texts, as well as in the great Mughal biographical dictionary the *Ma'asir al-Umara'*, as an orthodox Sunni Muslim whose ancestors had already been in the service of Sultan Husain Baiqara at Herat.[21] Though made uneasy by a number of changes and reforms in the reign of Akbar, he seems broadly to have stood firm in his loyalty and was hence rewarded with a series of significant provincial governorships. But the great *amir* apparently knew rather well who he was and what he and his ilk stood for. The account of Asad Beg Qazwini of the end of Akbar's reign notes, for example, that when the ruler was on his deathbed, two prominent *amirs*, Mirza 'Aziz Koka and Raja Man Singh, attempted to mount a conspiracy to set aside his son Salim and replace him with Prince Khusrau (Salim's son and the nephew of Man Singh). It is claimed, however, that those who vehemently opposed the proposal, and who eventually triumphed, were the Turanis. These included a certain Saʻid Khan, a great Turkish noble from Central Asia and related to the Mughals by clan, who was strongly supported by none other than Qilij Khan Andijani. What is also of significance is that their principal argument lay in how this proceeding of the Timurids, who belonged after all to the Ulus Chaghatay, would be wholly contrary to the normal Chinggisid customs (*shiʻar-o-tura-i chaghatay*).[22] In other words, they wished to keep the Mughals true to their Central Asian roots rather than let them be contaminated by the newfangled ways of the Rajputs and others, with whom they had increasingly begun to intermarry.

Mirza Haidar's Odyssey

Still more complex attitudes can be found among the Central Asians of these first generations. A particularly intriguing example is that of Mirza Haidar Dughlat, an adventurer and the author of a somewhat neglected text in Persian titled the *Tarikh-i Rashidi*, who had been born in Tashkent around 1500 in a clan closely related to that of Babur's lineage but which saw itself as quite distinct in its ambitions in many ways. Mirza Haidar spent the first years of his life in personal proximity to Babur but then chose from his mid-teens to place himself in the service of another important clan, that of Sultan Saʻid Khan to the east. Over the next two decades, he fought more or less ceaselessly for this patron in the area between Kashgar and Khorasan, often extending his operations southward into the Tibetan plateau as well. This altogether brutal high-altitude campaigning with small forces and high casualty rates took Mirza across the Pamirs on more than one occasion. In 1531, he invaded Ladakh, Tibet, and western Kashmir on behalf of his patron in what he termed in his text as a form of *jihad* against prosperous and powerful infidels. Again, in 1533, he mounted an attack on Lhasa, which he had understood possessed considerable riches on account of its density of Buddhist monasteries, but was eventually forced back by a lack of material resources. However, when his chief patron, Sultan Saʻid, died in 1533, in the course of these strenuous mountain campaigns, Mirza Haidar began to fear with some justification that a powerful warlord like himself would not be treated well by the sultan's successors. Rather than test the murky waters of loyalty, he therefore chose exit as an option. After a complex set of dealings and negotiations, he managed in 1536–37 to attain Badakhshan, and then Kabul, from where he sought to revive his far older dealings with the lineage of Babur. His initial contacts were in Lahore, where in 1538 he entered briefly into the service of Mirza Kamran, Babur's younger son and the rival of Humayun. Then in 1539, he entered the service of Humayun himself and fought briefly at the latter's side in his disastrous campaign in the Gangetic valley against the Afghan-led armies of Sher Shah Sur. After Humayun's defeat at Kannauj, Mirza Haidar proposed a retreat to the north in the direction of Kashmir, with which he had some earlier familiarity. When the Mughal ruler chose otherwise, Haidar Dughlat himself marched north and in November 1540 entered Kashmir and took it over with very little initial resistance.

Over the next decade, and until his death in 1551, Mirza Haidar's activities in Kashmir remain quite enigmatic. Initially, he seems to have chosen to act as a mere "regent" to one of the claimants to the throne in Kashmir, Nadir Shah. Thereafter, from the mid-1540s, he issued coins in the name of Humayun and seems largely to have acted in his name, even though the Mughal ruler was absent in these years, in distant Iran and then in the Kabul region. In this same period, as discontent with his rule grew, Mirza Haidar was obliged to defeat various rebellions mounted either by members of the displaced Kashmir dynasty or by other powerful local warlords. A common modern narrative presents him as a ruler whose intolerance grew apace with time and power, and who increasingly revealed himself as an orthodox Sunni Muslim of a Hanafite persuasion and therefore quite unable to stomach the heterodox Sufi-inflected Islam of the region, as incarnated in particular by the Nurbakhshiya order of mystics. As an important recent historian of Kashmir portrays matters, "the Nurbakhshiyas suffered a great setback in the time of Mirza Haidar Dughlat, who persecuted them thinking that if there was uniformity of religion in Kashmir there would be peace in the country."[23]

It is thus convenient, no doubt, to contrast Babur and Mirza Haidar and their texts from a number of viewpoints, starting with the linguistic: Babur's text is written in eastern Turkish and that of his cousin in Persian. Further, if the former author appears flexible, pragmatic, and human (and even "humanistic," as one of his recent apologists has it), to which one can add his metro-sexual self-presentation as a further virtue, the latter can easily be presented as the bigoted Sunni from eastern Mughulistan, the failed country cousin of the cosmopolitan dynast.[24] In this process, we may, however, sell Mirza Haidar somewhat short. In fact, even if the *Tarikh-i Rashidi* borrows extensively from other texts—as its author himself freely admits—the attitudes and perspectives it captures cannot be quite so easily dismissed. These attitudes are, moreover, not simply those of a nostalgia for a Central Asia from which the author found himself exiled. The text of the *Tarikh-i Rashidi*, we may recall, was written while Mirza Haidar was in Kashmir in the 1540s, even though historians of Kashmir have often complained that he says rather too little about that region itself.

On the one hand, Babur's own self-perception is clear enough. He saw himself as a Timurid and also as a Chinggisid; his direct descendants continued until much later to use terms for themselves such as the "Chaghatay princes" (*salatin-i Chaghata*) or the "lineage of Timur" (*khandan-i Timuriyya*), and broadly destested the term "Mughal" or "Mogor," which others—notably the Europeans of the sixteenth century—used for them. On the other hand, Mirza Haidar saw himself precisely as a Mughal and a native of a region he termed "Mughulistan" (with the second *u* being long in his usage), though he also sometimes identified with the Qara-Khitai—an older usage.[25] He noted that when he was born in around 905 AH (or 1499), the towns in his native region were in poor shape and most of his fellow Mughals "had never lived in villages; indeed, they had never so much as seen a settlement, 'A group like beasts of the mountains.'"[26]

This referred then to the easterly groups, in contrast to the more fortunate, prosperous, urbanized, and settled westerly lineages to which Babur belonged. But Mirza Haidar's own reflections on Kashgar and Yarkand can only be termed ambiguous in the extreme. An extended passage from the *Tarikh-i Rashidi* makes this clear enough.

> Just as it [Kashgar] had advantages, it has disadvantages too. At the beginning of spring constant dark, black, adverse winds full of dust and grit blow. Although Hindustan is famous for this, it happens even more in Kashgar and Yarkand. Agriculture is laborious and bears little produce. In Kashgar it is impossible to maintain an army on one harvest. In comparison with the Qipchaq steppe and Qalmaq, Kashgar resembles a city; but relative to real cities, it is as hell compared to purgatory.[27]

This can hardly be termed a ringing endorsement. In Mirza Haidar's imagination, the area around Kashgar and Yarkand was once prosperous; he writes that "in ancient times there were great cities [in these wastes, but] . . . all have sunk beneath the sands." He even adds the claim that "some hunters who go to hunt wild camels relate that occasionally buildings of a city are uncovered, but when they return after a time there is no trace, and they have sunk back beneath the sands. There were such cities, but of them neither name nor trace remains (*nam-o-nishan-i u baqi nist*)." Indeed, only Yarkand seems to retain some vestiges of its former glory in his eyes, and he tells us briefly of its impregnable high citadel, with "lofty and charming buildings" and "gardens in which lofty structures have been built, each of which contains a hundred rooms, more or less." Yet despite its excellent water—"the best in the world"—and superb fruit and roses that were "better than those of Herat," it would seem that even Yarkand is a place that by the early sixteenth century was a pale shadow of what it once was.[28] One can fruitfully compare Mirza Haidar's tone while describing it with his broadly enthusiastic view of the physical environment of Kashmir, which, he notes, "is among well-known countries of the world [and] . . . famous throughout the world for its various delights." Writing in the mid-1540s, he congratulates himself for having conquered it, especially since, "for the delightfulness and verdure of its gardens, meadows, mountains, for the pleasantness of its weather throughout the four seasons, and for perfect temperateness, no place like Kashmir has ever been seen or heard of."[29] Like Babur then, Mirza Haidar was obliged to move south from Central Asia; unlike the grumbling Babur, however, he seems quite contented with his lot in Kashmir, looking back at his land of origin as a place in more or less terminal decline that, in the final analysis, had little to offer a man of large ambitions.

The Question of Patriotism

Writing in the late 1990s, the Cambridge historian C. A. Bayly proposed that it was necessary to "reconsider the origins and periodization of Indian nationalism from the perspective of late pre-colonial history" and that the most appropriate way of doing so would be to consider the question of "old patriotisms," that is, "how successive generations of Indian commentators understood and contested sentiments of attachment to land and local custom in the political realm."[30] In relation to terminology, he proposed a closer look at not only the powerful term *desh* but also other terms such as *watan* and *qaum*, referring broadly to a sense of belonging to a place and to a community respectively. Although he then went on to briefly examine Indo-Islamic treatises on governance, and pointed to the circulation of such ideas in a wider sphere including Iran and Central Asia, Bayly's attempt foundered largely on two issues: the constant specter of a teleological relationship between "patriotism" and "nationalism" and a too-close adherence to the Maratha case, which he defined as "the paradigmatic example of pre-colonial Indian patriotism." To be sure, he argued that a more elaborate typology of patriotisms could be laid out, and he provided several other examples: (1) a patriotism deriving principally from personal ties of loyalty to an overlord, as was often the case with the Rajputs and similar warrior groups; (2) a concrete attachment to land (or *bhumi*) itself as a sentiment; (3) patriotism that was defined primarily through the emergence of a more acute sense of "ethnicity" and language community; and, finally, (4) a patriotism that rested above all on alterity or "a fear of the outside other." But even if one were to take the Marathas as "paradigmatic," how would one deal with those lineages that consolidated their rule not in the heartland of the *svadesh* or *svarajya* but in places such as Gwaliyar, which was ruled over by the migrant Shinde clan?[31] In other words, what would be the relationship between patriotism and circulation, given that so many of the elite groups whose activities were centrally in question with regard to state building, whether Rajputs, Marathas, Iranis, Turanis, or Afghans, were precisely given to ceaseless to-and-fro movement?

At roughly the same moment when Bayly was refining these reflections on "old patriotism" in a South Asian context, the Austrian historian of Iran and Central Asia Bert Fragner independently put forward his own reflections on the question of "Iranian patriotism in the seventeenth century."[32] Here, Fragner argued that under Safavid rule, and particularly after the kingdom had been consolidated and stabilized by Shah 'Abbas I, conditions emerged for a discourse on the part of the literati regarding terms such as *Iran-shahr* and *Iran-zamin*. He proposed moreover that this seventeenth-century conception was distinct both from the classical and medieval vocabulary regarding place and belonging deriving for example from authors such as Firdausi in the *Shahnama* and from nineteenth- and early twentieth-century Iranian nationalism. Fragner's view, like that of Bayly, was not entirely devoid of teleological overtones since he moved easily between "patriotism" and "protonationalism" as terms. But what is of particular interest is the central figure he chose to exemplify the new tendencies of the seventeenth century, namely, Muhammad Mufid Mustaufi Yazdi. This member of the secretarial class from the town of Yazd has left behind at least two important works: the *Jami'-i Mufidi* and the *Mukhtasar-i Mufid*. Yet his reflections on his own identity and loyalties were clearly not those of a stay-at-home; instead, they emerged precisely in the context of his move to first Mughal India and then the Deccan in the 1670s.

Of these works, Fragner draws above all on the *Mukhtasar-i Mufid*, a text that begins with Mufid congratulating himself on his own hard-won knowledge in comparison to the "fools who remained at the surface" (*bikhiradan-i zahir-bin*) and those "illiterates regulated by stupidity" (*nadanan-i himaqat a'in*) whom he frequently encountered in the salons of India.[33] Irritated by the claims of these others, who usually held forth on the greatness of the rulers of Cathay and China, the armies of the Turks, and the vastness of Rum and Magna China (Machin), Mufid wished to insist even in exile on the great achievements of the Safavids, and in particular those of the founder figure, Shah Isma'il Safavi, who had provided stability over a vast area including Iran and its neighborhood. His exasperation seems particularly marked when he meets other exiles from Iran, including his fellow townsmen (*ham-shahr*), who unlike him seem quite well settled in India and do not spend the greater part of their time in a state of discontent. Mufid further notes that his intention was to write a work highlighting the topography, urban centers, and certain political facts, with reference in particular to the Safavids. It would seem to have been completed while in "a state of exile (*diyar-i ghurbat*) in Lahore in Hind" in the late 1670s or early 1680s. Its closing passages are marked with the twin sentiments of exilic bitterness and loyalty to a homeland that are characteristic of much of this author's writing while in India.

> Since the year 1089 AH until the completion of these stories, the sadness of exile and the desire to meet my brothers has become so overwhelming, that I am unable to continue writing and describing. From the first light of dawn to the last light of dusk, I am preoccupied with the idea that this exile, who is wandering in the valley of perdition, may be able to return to his own country.[34]

For the most part, we are unable to capture much of the expression of the sentiments of those Indians who found themselves in Central Asia in the same period. A single important exception comes to us from the 1740s, when the Delhi-based intellectual Khwaja 'Abd al-Karim Shahristani found himself in Transoxiana and left us some of his impressions of the region in his text *Bayan-i Waqi'*.[35] Of course, this does not mean that there were no Indians to be found in Central Asia, quite the contrary. Both the Mughals and other northern Indian courts maintained diplomatic relations with the courts of Central Asia. Despite the occasionally rancorous tone of the correspondence and potential border problems at the time of the Shaibanid ruler 'Abdullah Khan in the last decades of the sixteenth century, a reasonable level of relations was maintained from at least the early 1570s onward.[36] In the mid-1580s, for example, 'Abdullah Khan sent Akbar a gift of special pigeons and a trainer for them along with his envoy to the Mughal court, Nizam-ud-Din Amir Quraish. A few years later, Akbar sent a return embassy, headed by the important courtier Hakim Humam Gilani.[37] While several of the letters to this envoy while he was away on his mission have come down to us, and we know that he was given quite a lavish "expense account" so as to make influential contacts in the Shaibanid court, we do not possess either his letters or the report he must certainly have prepared on his return.[38] It would seem that besides managing the difficult frontier issues that were emerging at this time as a consequence of Shaibanid expansion into Khorasan, one of Hakim Humam's tasks in Turan was the purchase of valuable books on such diverse subjects as bird rearing and mysticism. Some years later, while he was in Kashmir, Akbar also opened correspondence and diplomatic relations with Muhammad Khan, the ruler of Kashgar, and sent an envoy, who was himself of Central Asian origin, by the name of Mirza Ibrahim Andijani. In the letter carried by this envoy, the Mughal ruler declared his eventual intention to send an embassy to the Ming court and asked the Kashgar ruler to mediate in the matter by providing him information on a variety of subjects: the religion followed in China, the nature of Ming administration and justice, the strength of Chinese armies, and the principal arts and crafts.[39] Once again, the responses to these requests have not come down to us, nor do we have details of a great merchant called "Fataha" who was apparently sent out by the Mughals on an exploratory mission to China via Kashgar. But it must have been merchants such as these in whose company the Portuguese Jesuit Bento de Góis set out in 1603 from Lahore, to make his way via Kashgar into western China, where he eventually died in Gansu province in 1607.[40]

The relatively fragmentary evidence we have suggests that the Indians who traveled or settled in Central Asia between the sixteenth and eighteenth centuries were a complex lot. If some of them were Muslims, such as the unfortunate 'Ala-ud-Din Khan, who went to trade in Balkh in the 1640s but was eventually enslaved and sold on the Bukhara market, a substantial number were Hindus from the Punjab and Sind. These included a large number of Aroras and Khattris (sometimes with sub-caste names like Kapur and Chaddha), often generically identified in the records as "Multanis" even though their geographical origins are likely to have been more diverse than that. A listing from Astrakhan at the mouth of the Volga river in 1747 allows us a reasonable sense of many of their names: Brajnath Bhavanidas, Jagatrai Fatehchand, Ramdas Jassu, Kasiram Madhodas, Tekchand Lal, Sukhnath Dharamdas, Amardas Multani, Lajjaram Brindaban, and Kesardas Kriparam are some examples.[41] Many of these names suggest that these travelers were Vaishnava in their orientation, though undoubtedly there would have been some variation as regards this matter. Evidence as to their activities indicates that they maintained close solidarities and tended to live in distinct streets and quarters of their own in the towns where they found themselves, such as Samarqand or Bukhara.

Our real difficulty in penetrating their world, to discern the nature of their sentiments concerning both their *patria* and where they eventually found themselves, is the absence of first-person accounts. Muzaffar Alam, whose analysis of the question remains the most complex to date, suggests an interesting pattern based on his examination of Persian administrative records like those in the *Majmu'a-i Wasa'iq*, a collection of court papers maintained by the chief *qazi* of Samarqand. Alam argues that in the fifteenth century, Indian merchants and craftsmen in towns such as Bukhara and Samarqand often lived in "mixed" quarters; he suggests, moreover, that "many abandoned their ancestral religion, took Muslim names, married Uzbek women, and were identified with their in-laws."[42] However, as their numbers grew, and with the passage of time, one can actually discern a decline in such assimilation. Hindu merchants and craftsmen now cohered under the leadership of a designated head, a *kalantar* or *aqsaqal*. They sometimes had their own places of worship and attempted to settle their disputes internally, including on matters of commercial interest. Their model thus came to approximate that with which the Armenians regulated their commerce across the Central Asian world in the sixteenth, seventeenth, and eighteenth centuries, even if Multan never quite acquired the status held by New Julfa.[43]

Studies of modern nationalism have often proceeded from the premise that "absence makes the heart grow fonder" and that exile is therefore often the cradle for nationalist sentiment. But equally, it may be the case that wandering, rather than being the handmaiden of patriotism, promotes assimilation into a new culture. This is one possible opposition, but another, equally fruitful, would oppose the "patriot" to the "cosmopolitan," those who—according to the celebrated phrase—felt they were in fact strangers nowhere in the world. But this was scarcely more than illusion when applied to most of the inhabitants of the early modern world, who were heavily circumscribed in their sense of belonging by such factors as language, religion, and access to cultural traditions other than those in which they had been brought up. However attractive a "trickster" figure like the Hungarian traveler to Central Asia Ármin Vámbéry (1832–1913) may be, he cannot be seen as characteristic of the period on which this chapter has focused.[44]

Mutribi's Musings

A final and somewhat extended example should help demonstrate the complexities of the problem of belonging and "patriotism" for people traveling between early modern India and Central Asia. This is the intriguing text written by the Central Asian poet Mutribi al-Asamm al-Samarqandi in the latter half of the 1620s regarding his conversations with the Mughal emperor Jahangir.[45] Mutribi's *Khatirat* is certainly not a classic example of travel literature, since it contains no clear itinerary, no sense of movement in space and time together, and the text is in fact essentially a memoir of amusing conversations and discussions. Nevertheless, it touches on a central problem that we are concerned with here, namely the comparison between two adjacent but somewhat separated cultures, Central Asia and Mughal Hindustan. The text is situated in a period in Mughal history for which source materials are by no means in short supply. The monarch Nur al-Din Muhammad Jahangir (r. 1605–27) is after all himself the author of a highly accomplished autobiographical work in Persian, the *Tuzak-i Jahangiri* or *Jahangirnama*.[46] In this work, Jahangir shows off his vast culture and curiosity, concerning both nature and artifacts; nothing, from melons, to elephants, to the themes favored by local poet-composers, seems to escape his probing pen. The court chronicles of the reign, such as that of Mu'tamad Khan, the *Iqbalnama-i Jahangiri*, supplement this "internal" perspective, of kingship seen from the inside out, and we may add a number of other personal memoirs (and travel accounts) that date from this reign and shed light on a variety of political and cultural institutions at work in this epoch of the Mughal meridian. Among these, one finds ʿAbd al-Latif Gujarati's elusive travel text from 1607–10, Mirza Nathan Isfahani's well-known memoir, and Asad Beg's account of his vicissitudes both in the Deccan and in his early years at Jahangir's court.[47] Finally, the important text of ʿAbd al-Sattar Lahori regarding the nightly conversations in Jahangir's court during the early period of his reign has begun to attract increasing attention among scholars.[48] In each of these works, comparisons both implicit and explicit are made between different cultures and lived experiences. A variety of voices speaks to these questions, sometimes even in the form of an explicit debate with contradictory opinions.

Mutribi Samarqandi was a quite well-known figure of the early seventeenth century, and the author of several texts including a *tazkira*, or biographical dictionary, of poets composed in around 1604.[49] He was the grandson of Zain-ud-Din Mahmud Wasifi, a poet from Sultan Husain Baiqara's court at Herat, who then migrated to Transoxiana and moved between Samarqand, Bukhara, and Tashkent. Mutribi himself had studied in Bukhara with a certain Khwaja Hasan Nisari and also traveled extensively in the course of his life, initially in regions such as Khorasan and Badakhshan but eventually to Hindustan as well. Being the writer of a biographical dictionary, he was aware that other poets from Central Asia had sought Mughal patronage before him, albeit with somewhat mixed success. As Maria Szuppe notes: "the attraction of the imperial courts of the Great Mughals made India the preferred destination for Central Asian poets and literati, despite the rather significant distance and the difficulties, even the dangers of crossing the Afghan mountains. Not everyone succeeded in obtaining a position at the Mughal court; one finds some of them later having returned to their own country, or in attendance on less prestigious patrons."[50] This included a certain Mushfiqi Bukhari who had tried his luck in Akbar's court only to return disappointed; fortunately, he was then given a place of great importance in ʿAbdullah Khan's court in Bukhara. More successful acquaintances of Mutribi include a certain Mulla Hisari Samarqandi and Salihi Nadaʾi Shaikhi Bukhari, both of whom had left for India in the late sixteenth and early seventeenth centuries.[51]

Mutribi himself had quite carefully prepared the ground before entering the Mughal court, and he begins his work with a brief introduction reflecting on the twin ideas of thanksgiving and patience. His patience with respect to one of the greatest rulers of the age, namely Jahangir, has proved fruitful, and thus his text is naturally one of thanksgiving to Allah. It recounts a set of meetings with Jahangir that appear to have taken place in Lahore through the mediation of a certain Khwaja Fakhr al-Din Husain, who was the son of Maulana Khwaja Khan Diwan. They began on Wednesday, 19th Rabi I, 1036 AH, in the afternoon, thus rather late in Jahangir's reign; the text itself was written down from Thursday, 9th Jumada II, of the same year, when the recollections were still fresh in Mutribi's mind.[52]

Mutribi describes the meetings using the term *waqi'a* (happenings), but there is a clear sense of orchestration present rather than mere chance. It all begins rather coyly. When the poet appears in court for the first meeting, Jahangir asks Mutribi why, after spending a whole month in Lahore, he has only now come into his presence. The poet answers that he was finishing a text in honor of Jahangir (titled the *Nuskha-yi Ziba-yi Jahangir*) and had only now found a chronogram to close it.[53] On duly being presented the text, Jahangir is pleased and asks Mutribi whether he would rather stay in the Mughal court, go back to his homeland of Turan, or make the hajj to Mecca and Medina. Mutribi, ever the courtier, says that he is at the ruler's disposal. Jahangir then tells Mutribi that he has four gifts for him but would give them one after the other. They are, respectively, money for his expenses, a *khil'at* (ceremonial and honorific robe) to wear, a horse and a saddle, and a slave to serve him. Which of these does he want first? Mutribi replies in poetry on the importance of money (*zar*) and is at once given a platter full of money, amounting to 1,000 rupees and another 500 rupees on the part of the ruler's wife Nur Jahan. Mutribi immodestly compares himself to Hafiz Shirazi before Jahangir's ancestor Timur on the occasion of the conquest of Shiraz by the latter and recounts an elaborate anecdote regarding the meeting between the two. Timur too had given Hafiz money and a *khil'at*, though not a horse and a saddle. Clearly, the poet's opening gambit has succeeded and he now has a foothold in the court.

The stage has been set for subsequent meetings and conversations, which will have a more explicitly comparative and reflective nature for the most part. Present at the second meeting are the ruler's brother-in-law Khwaja Abu'l Hasan Asaf Khan the *diwan*, Khawass Khan, and a certain Bahadur Khan from Mawarannahr (Central Asia), as well as several other *amirs*. Jahangir comes quickly to the point with regard to his own interest in Central Asia: this is the burial site of his illustrious ancestor, Timur, in Samarqand. Mutribi replies that details about the spot are to be found in his text, the *Nuskha-yi Ziba*, but the emperor wishes to have answers to a set of precise questions regarding the color of the gravestone. He requests that a square black stone be brought and asks Mutribi to compare it in his mind's eye with the gravestone. Mutribi replies that there some differences, since the stone before him is duller than the other. He now gives the reader details of the construction of Timur's burial place by way of an aside. He further reports that Jahangir was content with the tenor of his response and once again gave him a *khil'at*, as well as a Kashmiri shawl, a turban, and other gifts. Besides, his son Muhammad 'Ali, who has accompanied him, is given a suit of expensive brocade clothes.

We quickly comprehend that Mutribi represents a window into Central Asia for Jahangir, as a sort of authentic eyewitness (*bayan*) to affairs in Transoxania. Despite the emperor's alleged fascination with Iran and its ruler, it is clear that his curiosity ranges farther afield as well. Mutribi and Jahangir spend the next conversation comparing objects of wonder. The emperor shows the poet a small booklet (*kitabcha*), four fingers long, that has been presented to him by European merchants. He writes on the book with a pencil and then shows Mutribi how to rub off the writing. On receiving it as a gift, Mutribi reports his intention to carry the book back to Turan and give it to the ruler there, Imam Quli Khan, as a valuable gift from Hindustan. He also recounts an anecdote from the time of 'Abdullah Khan Uzbek in Bukhara, when a certain physician (*hakim*) called Maulana Jalali possessed a strange box (*sanduq*) the height of a man in his house, with the heads of animals (a monkey, a lion, and a horse) sculpted on it. These heads, especially that of the monkey, would move about, the apparatus would make a noise, and the passage of time could be measured thereby. Mutribi is obviously referring to a rather complicated clockwork mechanism of some sort. Now, Maulana Jalali had an ingenious use for this contraption. He would ask his guests to make a wish and then to take a seal made of a mix of seven metals that he gave them and place it in the mouth of the horse. The seal would fall into the box with a bang but would then rise up again with a rattling sound, emerge from the lion's mouth, and fall into a jar. At this time, a window concealed on one side of the box would open, and a man would be revealed sitting on a throne with a rolled-up paper in his hands. Taking the paper, Maulana Jalali would read out loud from it and recount details of his visitor's future and impending fortune or misfortune. At the end of this, the window would close up, and the entire structure would once more resemble a box. So if Jahangir had his fancy magic tricks brought to him by the European traders (*tujjar-i firang*), the denizens of Central Asia had their own magic too, it seemed.

In the fourth meeting, matters took a literary turn, as Jahangir had by now read Mutribi's book and commented on a verse in it. A discussion took place on its authorship, as Mutribi had taken it from another writer (a fact that Jahangir apparently recognized). Mention was made of the presence in court of a certain seventy-year-old courtier called Maktub Khan, himself a poet from Shiraz and in charge of the imperial library and picture gallery. Maktub Khan had on an earlier occasion cited the same verse, and the issue arose of who in fact had the earliest claim to the verse. Did Shiraz have precedence over Samarqand and Bukhara? Happily, Mutribi reports, the matter was eventually settled with tact.

In the next meeting, Jahangir brought up the issue of hearsay and eyewitness. He asked Mutribi if he knew a certain Mirza Baqi Anjumani, and the latter replied that he was 'Abdullah Khan's son, who had taken refuge in Akbar's court, and gave details of his stay in the Mughal court. Jahangir was surprised at his knowledge of these details and asked him how he came by them. Mutribi replied that he had received news of him in Samarqand and then in Lahore from a traveler called Brahman, who claimed to have made the hajj with Mirza Baqi and told of his death. Jahangir insisted that this hearsay was incorrect and that Mirza Baqi had never left the Mughal court but had in fact died there. This led Mutribi to reflect on the nature of truth and falsehood, and he noted that Jahangir was rigorous in investigating the veracity of statements. Jahangir then wished to test Mutribi. He hence asked him if he knew a certain Abu'l Bey, and Mutribi replied that he did. Jahangir had two men brought in to stand before him and asked Mutribi which one was Abu'l Bey. Mutribi hesitated and said he did not think either was Abu'l Bey; at this, Jahangir smiled and said that Mutribi was right, for in fact one was Afzal Khan and the other Musawi Khan. The emperor was simply toying with the poet, it seemed. Indeed, on a later occasion, Mutribi espied Abu'l Bey in the court, and Jahangir was satisfied with his powers of observation and devotion to the truth.

A certain level of intimacy is being established over these meetings, and even by their rather ludic nature. In the sixth meeting, Jahangir is being weighed on the occasion of a celebration. Mutribi too receives two platters of coins worth 2,000 rupees and other valuables. Pleased, the poet recites verses in the court in praise of the emperor, and Jahangir, pleased, in turn, by the verses, gives Mutribi still more gifts. He also asks Mutribi which sort of horse and saddle he wants. Mutribi somewhat greedily asks for the most expensive sort of horse and saddle, and a discussion ensues on the relative quality of different sorts. Finally, he receives an Iraqi horse (rather than a less valuable Turkish one) and a saddle of velvet (rather than a more expensive but less durable one in scarlet).

At the next meeting, the question of "patriotism" takes on a somewhat different flavor as we turn to the question of the wonders of Hindustan. A massive sugar candy (weighing half a Bukhara *maund*) has been placed on a silver seat in the court in anticipation of Mutribi's arrival. Jahangir then proudly asks Mutribi whether such a thing could be found in Transoxania. When Mutribi says that he has never seen such an object, Jahangir notes that it is rare in India as well; a certain Muhammad Husain had brought it from the region of Lucknow, and now he offers it to Mutribi as a gift. The latter, for his part, decides to take it back to his home and to give it either to Imam Quli Khan or to the man he terms the "Axis of the Age," Hazrat Ishan. Intrigued, Jahangir asks who this latter person might be, and Mutribi replies that he is a great Sufi master called Khwaja Hashim Muhammad Dehbedi. It turns out that Jahangir knows this Sufi and is even devoted to him, a measure perhaps of the continuing Mughal connection with the Central Asian Naqshbandi order.

In the encounter that follows, Jahangir, who has just returned from a hunt, gives Mutribi a special bird (*surkhab*) that he himself had shot. He then jokingly asks Mutribi for something in return, and Mutribi recites a verse on the occasion. Pleased, the emperor gives him some money as a gift. In the next meeting, he is again given two birds (*murghabi*), from which he has a kind of pilaf dish (*mutanjana*) made. Such birds, it is noted, were simply not to be found in Transoxania and were a peculiarity of Hindustan. What we have then is an implicit reversal of Babur's view that so much of the best flora and fauna of Central Asia cannot be found in India.

At a subsequent meeting, the conversation takes a more explicitly "anthropological" turn. Jahangir asks Mutribi rather bluntly whether he thinks white skin is better than black, obviously wishing to test the Central Asian's color prejudices with regard to Indians. Mutribi replies evasively, saying that it is all a matter of opinion, but Jahangir insists that he wants to know *his* opinion. Mutribi for his part says that he could judge only by seeing (*binam wa guyam*), and so Jahangir advises him to look right and left and decide. On the right, Mutribi finds a dark young Indian princeling (*rajabacha*) who is so handsome that Mutribi claims he loses control of his heart. But on the left is an equally fair and handsome boy who dazzles Mutribi's eyes. How can he now decide? Having looked twice at each, he says to Jahangir that it is not a matter of dark and fair but of the pleasantness of the countenance. Jahangir is pleased and recites a verse in the same sense, to which Mutribi replies with a supporting hadith, in which the Prophet boastfully states that his brother Yusuf is fair, but he is the one whose countenance has a more agreeable (literally, "salty") quality (or *malahat*).

The remaining meetings also contain anecdotes intended to pursue this comparison between Mutribi's native land and the country to which he has come. During one of them, the emperor has organized a tournament with camels and fighting bucks. Mutribi marvels, for he has never seen such a fight in Transoxania, and Jahangir rubs it in by asking whether Mutribi had ever witnessed such in his homeland. Mutribi has to confess that he had not and admits that Hindustan holds wonders unheard of in his own country. In another episode, the eighteenth meeting, the nature of empirical verification is again at issue. A freshly made set of portraits from the Mughal ateliers is brought before Mutribi, who sees that they depict the former ruler of Turan, 'Abdullah Khan Uzbek, and his son 'Abd al-Momin Khan. He tells Jahangir that there are defects in the representation of 'Abdullah Khan's chin and of his son's headgear. At this, the painter is at once summoned and asked to correct the paintings, which he does by the next day. Another Turani courtier expresses a contrary opinion on the matter of 'Abd al-Momin Khan's headgear, but finally Mutribi's view is upheld. He is once more impressed by the empiricist spirit on display in Jahangir's court: seeing is believing, and Jahangir does appear to be seriously invested in Central Asian matters.

There can be little doubt, then, that a persistent thread running through the conversations concerns Jahangir's effort to demonstrate the hierarchical superiority of Hindustan over Central Asia. Thus, in the twenty-second conversation, he asks Mutribi for the names of worthy persons from Central Asia whom he can invite to his court, never for a moment thinking that such an invitation would be refused. Mutribi suggests that a certain Maulana Sabri Tashkandi be invited, and Jahangir accepts the suggestion. In the same conversation, Jahangir asks how much money should be sent to repair the Gur-i Amir, Timur's tomb. When Mutribi suggests 10,000 rupees, Jahangir says that he will send this sum back with Mutribi to Central Asia, with the implication being that those in Central Asia are incapable of raising the funds themselves.

By the time of the last meeting, Mutribi has begun to feel homesick and also mentions his advanced years. However, he approaches the question obliquely and, on an occasion when Asaf Khan and others are present, offers a *ghazal* and says he wishes to leave for Samarqand, promising however to spread the word of Jahangir's greatness there. Jahangir asks him instead to come to Kashmir with him and promises that he will send money to bring some more of Mutribi's relatives over. After some discussion, he allows Mutribi at last to go but insists that he return in a year. The poet then departs, leaving Jahangir—who has transformed himself through Mutribi into a sort of arm-chair traveler—behind in Hindustan. Yet, in effect, in this text, Mutribi has become the vehicle for the expression of Jahangir's opinions and prejudices and, willy-nilly, a propagandist for "Hindustani patriotism." To be sure, Jahangir still spoke Turkish as a mark of his Central Asian heritage, but we cannot forget that he combined this with Persian (his language of preference) and with some form of Hindawi (or northern Indian vernacular), speaking each of them as the occasion demanded. A century had elapsed since Babur had entered Delhi, and much had changed. Conceptually, this would not have been entirely strange to the Indo-Islamic theorists of the time, who recognized that miscegenation, as well as the simple fact of taking in the air and water (*ab-o-hawa'*) of a place over time, could work substantial changes in human beings.

Visiting the Central Asian steppe a century after Mutribi was in the Mughal court, in the 1740s, the Delhi intellectual Khwaja 'Abd al-Karim Shahristani was to mention this very fact in regard to some prisoners from Khorasan who had been held for a long period by the people of Khwarizm and then released. He noted:

> The Turkomans, at the advice and with the connivance of their own ruler, had invaded Khorasan and had captured many women and children there. In each house, there were ten or twelve Khorasanis. The cultivation, irrigation, and the dig-ging of deep ditches from the Jaihun river which went all through Khwarizm, had been entrusted to these prisoners from Iran. They were busy in these works day and night and because of the climate of that land, their faces had become like those of the Turanian Turkomans. Some of them were as old as fifty and sixty, and said that they had been brought there as children.[54]

Further, when they were released at last and some tried to persuade them to return to their "homeland," they showed considerable reluctance, on account (it is claimed) of their affection for the people of Khwarizm and because they had heard of the ruination of Iran with the fall of the Safavids. Many of them hence turned back to Khwarizm while halfway along the road to Khorasan; others, from the intensity of the winter and the lack of proper provisions, died on the way; and those who reached Khorasan regretted that they had left Khwarizm. Human adaptation is thus stressed by Khwaja 'Abd al-Karim as much as innate qualities attributed to different ethnic groups. Not only is it not the same river twice over; it is not the same body that bathes in it.

I began this chapter by noting that the early modern relationship between Central Asia and India, like that between India and Iran, was undoubtedly an asymmetric one. But the asymmetries were by no means as simple as those that emerge from comparing the "vastly greater natural and human resources" of Mughal India to those of Iran and Turan and concluding thereby that "its economy . . . overshadowed its neighbors in terms of its overall size, diversity and sophistication." The invocation of the Wallerst-inian and Braudelian world-systems perspective has thus often led to an understanding in which a South Asian "core" dominated Iranian and Central Asian "peripheries," with the presence of "thousands of merchants from the Mughul empire [who] resided semi-permanently in Iran and Turan . . . [and who] were, in essence, personifications of India's stature as a regional world economy."[55] Rather, the difficulty lies in coming to terms with a Mughal India that was itself a jigsaw puzzle of different ecological zones, from mountains and scrubland, to marsh and mangroves. It will simply not do to equate the Gangetic valley with the Mughal domains. Further, it is of crucial importance to note that movements of humans between Iran, India, and Central Asia in the early modern period were never a form of one-way traffic. To be sure, Indian merchants and entrepreneurs found themselves in the towns of Central Asia (even if they wrote little about them), but so did Central Asians—whether poets, warriors, or horse traders—find themselves in the Mughal domains. Rather than the language of "core" and "periphery," the appropriate paradigm within which to comprehend these movements is thus one of circulation.[56]

Equally important is the recognition that processes of circulation are for the most part also processes of transformation. This is perhaps inadequately taken into account in a part of the literature, which attributes an immutable "Central Asian" character to, for example, the Mughals and suggests that throughout the sixteenth and seventeenth centuries, the conquest of Central Asia remained one of their significant preoccupations. The concrete evidence for this centers largely on Shahjahan's campaign—which has incidentally long divided and puzzled historians—against Balkh, which began in 1645 but ended in a rather ignominious retreat in 1647. Yet scholars have concluded largely on this basis that "in the end it was their Central Asian roots that defined much of the pysche of the Mughal emperors" and often led their policies to be driven by their "obsession with Central Asia."[57] If anything, the Balkh campaign shows the extent to which the Mughal princes who led it, such as Murad Bakhsh and Aurangzeb—now in the fifth generation after Babur, it should be recalled—were simply unable "to withstand the snow and cold of the country" as well as the "rigor of the winter" (as contemporaries noted). They had come a long way indeed from hardened winter campaigners such as Babur and Mirza Haidar Dughlat. What had once been a snowy paradise had become instead a frozen hell, while the dusty roads of the Deccan were now precisely the places where the erstwhile Central Asians made their camps with the greatest alacrity.

Notes

Epigraph: Interestingly enough, this verse from Shaikh Sa'di's *Gulistan* (*bab* 1, *hikayat* 7) is cited in Mirza Haidar Dughlat's *Tarikh-i Rashidi*. For the Persian text, see the recent reprint, *Mirza Haydar Dughlat's Tarikh-i Rashidi: Tarikh-i Khawanin-i Mughulistan (A History of the Khans of Moghulistan)*, ed. and trans. Wheeler Thackston (Cambridge, MA: Harvard University Department of Near Eastern Languages and Civilizations, 1996), text, p. 247; translation, p. 193. I have preferred this recent edition and translation to the older one, *A History of the Moghuls of Central Asia*, ed. and trans. Ney Elias and E. Denison Ross, 2 vols. (London: Curzon Press, 1898).

1. This was ironic in view of persistent (and perhaps malicious) Indian press reports that the Uzbek coach Rustam Akramov was frequently in difficulty in India in the 1990s on account of his "lack of English knowledge."

2. Some of the themes dealt with here have also been treated at some length in Muzaffar Alam and Sanjay Subrahmanyam, *Indo-Persian Travels in the Age of Discoveries, 1400–1800* (Cambridge: Cambridge University Press, 2007).

3. See the useful general reflections in Simon Digby, "Some Asian Wanderers in Seventeenth-Century India: An Examination of Sources in Persian," *Studies in History*, n.s., 9, 2 (1993), pp. 247–64.

4. S. A. M. Adshead, *Central Asia in World History* (New York: St. Martin's Press, 1993). Adshead draws for his conceptual apparatus on the dispersed work of Joseph Fletcher, much of which has since been gathered together in Joseph Fletcher, *Studies on Chinese and Islamic Inner Asia*, ed. Beatrice Forbes Manz (Aldershot: Variorum-Ashgate, 1995).

5. On relations between Central Asia and Iran, see Thomas Welsford, "The Re-opening of Iran to Central Asian Pilgrimage Traffic, 1600–1650," in Alexandre Papas, Thomas Welford, and Thierry Zarcone, eds., *Central Asian Pilgrims: Hajj Routes and Pious Visits between Central Asia and the Hijaz* (Berlin: Klaus Schwarz Verlag, 2012), pp. 149–68, and Robert D. McChesney, "Barrier of Heterodoxy? Rethinking the Ties between Iran and Central Asia in the 17th Century," in Charles Melville, ed., *Safavid Persia* (London: I. B. Tauris, 1996), pp. 231–67.

6. M. Athar Ali, *The Mughal Nobility under Aurangzeb* (Bombay: Asia Publishing House, 1966). Also the more recent overview in Masashi Haneda, "Emigration of Iranian Elites to India during the 16–18th Centuries," in Maria Szuppe, ed., *L'Héritage Timouride: Iran-Asie centrale-Inde, XVe–XVIIIe siècles*, special issue of *Cahiers d'Asie Centrale* 3–4 (1997), pp. 129–43.

7. Stephen Frederic Dale, "A Safavid Poet in the Heart of Darkness: The Indian Poems of Ashraf Mazandarani," in Michel Mazzaoui, ed., *Safavid Iran and Her Neighbors* (Salt Lake City: University of Utah Press, 2003), pp. 63–80, also published in *Iranian Studies* 36, 2 (2003), pp. 197–212. For Ashraf's poetry, see also Ahmad Golchin-i Ma'ani, *Karwan-i Hind: Dar Ahwal wa Asar-i Sha'iran-i 'Asr-i Safawi ki bi Hindustan Rafta-and* (Mashhad: Astan-i Quds-i Rizawi, 1990), vol. 1, pp. 70–74.

8. Alam and Subrahmanyam (2007), pp. 219–21.

9. Ronald W. Ferrier, "An English View of Persian Trade in 1618: Reports from the Merchants Edward Pettus and Thomas Barker," *Journal of the Economic and Social History of the Orient* 19, 2 (1976), pp. 182–214 (citation on p. 192).

10. Jean Aubin, "De Kûhbanân à Bidar: La famille Ni'matullâhi," *Studia Iranica* 20 (1991), pp. 233–61, and Aubin, "L'Inde dans le contexte du monde islamique," *Purusârtha* 9 (1986), pp. 23–27. For another attempt at a synthesis and overarching interpretation, see Sanjay Subrahmanyam, "Iranians Abroad: Intra-Asian Elite Migration and Early Modern State Formation," *Journal of Asian Studies* 51, 2 (1992), pp. 340–62.

11. Sunil Kumar, "The Ignored Elites: Turks, Mongols and a Persian Secretarial Class in the Early Delhi Sultanate," *Modern Asian Studies* 43, 1 (2009), pp. 45–77.

12. Mohibbul Hasan, *Kashmir under the Sultans* (1st ed., 1959; Delhi: Aakar Books, 2005), pp. 78–80.

13. Maria Szuppe, *Entre Timourides, Uzbeks et Safavides: Questions d'histoire politique et sociale de Hérat dans la première moitié du XVIe siècle* (Paris: Association pour l'avancement des études iraniennes, 1992).

14. Zahir al-Din Babur, *The Baburnama: Memoirs of Babur, Prince and Emperor*, trans. Wheeler M. Thackston (New York: The Modern Library, 2002), p. 329.

15. Ibid., pp. 332–33.

16. For the long history of the town, see Frantz Grenet, "Maracanda/ Samarkand, une métropole pré-mongole: Sources écrites et archéologie," *Annales HSS* 59, 5–6 (2004), pp. 1043–67.

17. Babur (2002), p. 72.

18. On this important figure, see Jürgen Paul, "Forming a Faction: The *Himayat* of Khwaja Ahrar," *International Journal of Middle Eastern Studies* 23, 4 (1991), pp. 533–48, and the valuable materials in Jo-Ann Gross and Asom Urunbaev, *The Letters of Khwajah 'Ubayd Allah Ahrar and His Associates* (Leiden: E. J. Brill, 2002). For the Naqshbandis in Mughal India, also see Muzaffar Alam, "The Mughals, the Sufi Shaikhs and the Formation of the Akbari Dispensation," *Modern Asian Studies* 43, 1 (2009), pp. 135–74.

19. This data is taken from Iqtidar Alam Khan, "The Nobility under Akbar and the Development of His Religious Policy," *Journal of the Royal Asiatic Society of Great Britain and Ireland* 100, 1 (1968), pp. 29–36; Afzal Husain, *The Nobility under Akbar and Jahangir: A Study of Family Groups* (New Delhi: Manohar, 1999), p. 191; and Athar Ali, *Mughal Nobility under Aurangzeb*. The data for 1565–75, 1575–95, and 1605 pertain to *mansabdars* with a rank of 500 and above, and that for the period after 1605 to those with a rank of 1,000 and above. The information for 1555 pertains to all *amirs*.

20. Sanjay Subrahmanyam, "A Note on the Kabul Kingdom under Muhammad Hakim Mirza (1554–1585)," *La Transmission du savoir dans le monde musulman périphérique, Lettre d'information* 14 (1994), pp. 89–101. The main conclusions of and sources for this study were reprised with a few additional materials in Munis D. Faruqui, "The Forgotten Prince: Mirza Hakim and the Formation of the Mughal Empire in India," *Journal of the Economic and Social History of the Orient* 48, 4 (2005), pp. 487–523.

21. Nawwab Samsam al-Daula Shahnawaz Khan, *Ma'asir-ul-Umara, Being Biographies of the Muhammadan and Hindu Officers of the Timurid Sovereigns of India from 1500 to about 1780 A.D.*, trans. H. Beveridge and Baini Prashad (Calcutta: Asiatic Society of Bengal, 1952), vol. 2, pp. 534–37; for the Persian text, see Shahnawaz Khan, *Ma'asir al-Umara'*, ed. Maulavi 'Abdur Rahim and Maulavi Mirza Ashraf 'Ali (Calcutta: Asiatic Society of Bengal, 1890), vol. 3, pp. 69–74.

22. Muzaffar Alam and Sanjay Subrahmanyam, *Writing the Mughal World: Studies in Political Culture* (Ranikhet: Permanent Black, 2011), pp. 156–58. For an earlier discussion of the question, also see Ahsan Jan Qaisar, "Jahangir's Accession: An Outcome of Orthodox Revivalism?" *Proceedings of the Indian History Congress, 23rd Session* (Aligarh, 1960), pp. 251–52.

23. Hasan (2005), p. 312. On the Nurbakhshiya, see Shahzad Bashir, *Messianic Hopes and Mystical Visions: The Nūrbakhshiya between Medieval and Modern Islam* (Columbia: University of South Carolina Press, 2003).

24. For the presentation of Babur as a "humanist," see Stephen F. Dale, "Steppe Humanism: The Autobiographical Writings of Zahir al-Din Muhammad Babur, 1483–1530," *International Journal of Middle Eastern Studies* 22, 1 (1990), pp. 37–58; however, compare the rather more convincing analysis in Ali Anooshahr, *The Ghazi Sultans and the Frontiers of Islam: A Comparative Study of the Late Medieval and Early Modern Periods* (London: Routledge, 2009), pp. 15–37.

25. Cf. Michal Biran, *The Empire of the Qara Khitai in Eurasian History: Between China and the Islamic World* (Cambridge: Cambridge University Press, 2005).

26. *Tarikh-i-Rashidi*, trans. p. 90; text, p. 111 (the last phrase is a proverb).

27. Ibid., trans. pp. 192–93; text, p. 247.

28. On Mirza Haidar's description of the region, also see Robert B. Shaw, "A Prince of Kashgar on the Geography of Eastern Turkestan," *Journal of the Royal Geographical Society* 46 (1876), pp. 277–98.

29. *Tarikh-i-Rashidi*, trans. pp. 258–60; text, pp. 363–65.

30. C. A. Bayly, *Origins of Nationality in South Asia: Patriotism and Ethical Government in the Making of Modern India* (Delhi: Oxford University Press, 1998), pp. 1–30.

31. For the ambivalence of some of these "expatriated" lineages to their own Marathi-speaking origins, see Prachi Deshpande, "The Making of an Indian Nationalist Archive: Lakshmibai, Jhansi, and 1857," *Journal of Asian Studies* 67, 3 (2008), pp. 855–79.

32. Bert G. Fragner, "Iranian Patriotism in the 17th Century: The Case of Mohammad-e Mofid," paper delivered as part of the Yarshater Lectures, Harvard University, 30 April–5 May 2001.

33. Muhammad Mufid Mustaufi Yazdi, *Mohtasar-e Mofid des Mohammad Mofid Mostoufi*, ed. Seyfeddin Najmabadi (Wiesbaden: Ludwig Reichert, 1989), vol. 1, p. 2. Also see the earlier examination of this work in Jean Aubin, "Quelques notices du Mukhtasar-i Mufid," *Farhang-i Iran Zamin* 6 (1958), pp. 164–77.

34. Yazdi (1989), vol. 1, pp. 386–87.

35. Khwaja 'Abdul Karim ibn Khwaja 'Aqibat Mahmud Kashmiri, *Bayan-i Waqi': A Biography of Nadir Shah Afshar and the Travels of the Author*, ed. K. B. Nasim (Lahore: University of Punjab, 1970).

36. Mansura Haider, "Relations of Abdullah Khan Uzbeg with Akbar," *Cahiers du monde russe et soviétique* 23, 3–4 (1982), pp. 313–31.

37. Riazul Islam, *A Calendar of Documents on Indo-Persian Relations (1500–1750)* (Karachi: Institute of Central and West Asian Studies, 1982), vol. 2, pp. 209–13.

38. See the letters sent to Hakim Humam by his older brother Hakim Abu'l Fath Gilani, in *Ruq'at-i Hakim Abu'l Fath Gilani*, ed. Muhammad Bashir Husain (Lahore: Research Society of Pakistan, 1968), pp. 90–92, 117–20, 123–26.

39. This letter, dated 28 Zi-Hijja 1005 AH (August 2, 1597), was drafted by Shaikh Abu'l Fazl and appears in his *insha'* collection. For a summary, see Islam (1979–82), vol. 2, Letter Tx. 336, pp. 225–26.

40. Hugues Didier, *Fantômes d'Islam et de Chine: Le voyage de Bento de Góis S.J. (1603–1607)* (Paris: Chandeigne, 2003).

41. Stephen Frederic Dale, *Indian Merchants and Eurasian Trade, 1600–1750* (Cambridge: Cambridge University Press, 1994), pp. 113–16.

42. Muzaffar Alam, "Trade, State Policy and Regional Change: Aspects of Mughal-Uzbek Commercial Relations, c. 1550–1750," *Journal of the Economic and Social History of the Orient* 37, 3 (1994), pp. 202–27 (citation on p. 219).

43. On Armenian trading practices, see Sebouh D. Aslanian, "Social Capital, 'Trust' and the Role of Networks in Julfan Trade: Informal and Semi-Formal Institutions at Work," *Journal of Global History* 1, 3 (2006), pp. 383–402.

44. For example, Jacob M. Landau, "Arminius Vámbéry: Identities in Conflict," in Martin Kramer, ed., *The Jewish Discovery of Islam: Studies in Honor of Bernard Lewis* (Tel Aviv: Tel Aviv University, 1999), pp. 95–102.

45. *Khatirat-i-Mutribi Samarqandi (Being the Memoirs of Mutribi's Sessions with Emperor Jahangir)*, ed. Abdul Ghani Mirzoyef (Karachi: Institute of Central and West Asian Studies, 1977). For a somewhat approximate translation, see Richard C. Foltz, *Conversations with Emperor Jahangir by 'Mutribi' al-Asamm of Samarqand* (Costa Mesa: Mazda Publishers, 1998). For discussions of this text, see Surinder Singh, "The Indian Memoirs of Mutribi Samarqandi," *Proceedings of the Indian History Congress, 55th Session*, Aligarh, 1994 (Delhi: IHC, 1995), pp. 345–54. Also Richard Foltz, "Two Seventeenth-Century Central Asian Travellers to Mughal India," *Journal of the Royal Asiatic Society of Great Britain and Ireland*, series 3, 6, 3 (1996), pp. 367–77.

46. Wheeler M. Thackston, trans., *The Jahangirnama: Memoirs of Jahangir, Emperor of India* (Oxford: Oxford University Press, 1999), which largely replaces the older version by Alexander Rogers and Henry Beveridge, trans. and eds., *The Tuzuk-i-Jahangiri or Memoirs of Jahangir*, 2 vols. (London: Royal Asiatic Society, 1909–14). For a full discussion of this text, see Corinne Lefèvre, "Recovering a Missing Voice from Mughal India: The Imperial Discourse of Jahangir (r. 1605–1627) in His Memoirs," *Journal of the Economic and Social History of the Orient* 50, 4 (2007), pp. 452–89.

47. For a conspectus of sources from this period, see Corinne Lefèvre, "Pouvoir et noblesse dans l'Empire moghol: Perspectives du règne de Jahangir (1605–1627)," *Annales HSS* 62, 6 (2007), pp. 1287–1312.

48. Alam and Subrahmanyam (2011), pp. 249–310, and Corinne Lefèvre, "The *Majalis-i Jahangiri* (1608–11): Dialogue and Asiatic Otherness at the Mughal Court," *Journal of the Economic and Social History of the Orient* 55, 2–3 (2012), pp. 255–86.

49. Mutribi Samarqandi, *Tazkirat al-Shu'ra'*, ed. Asghar Janfida and 'Ali Rafi'i 'Ala Marwdashti (Tehran: Markaz-i Mutala'at-i Irani, Ayina-i Miras, 1377 sh./1998).

50. Maria Szuppe, "Circulation des lettrés et cercles littéraires: Entre Asie centrale, Iran et Inde du Nord (XVe–XVIIIe siècle)," *Annales HSS* 59, 5–6 (2004), pp. 997–1018 (citation on pp. 1015–16).

51. On Central Asian poets in Mughal India, see Syed Muhammad Fazlullah, "Some Persian Poets of Transoxiana (beyond the Oxus) Who Migrated to India during the Early Mughal Period (10th century H./16th c. AD)," in R. N. Dandekar et al., *Sanskrit and Indological Studies: Dr. V. Raghavan Felicitation Volume* (Delhi: Motilal Banarasidass, 1975), pp. 113–26.

52. The meetings thus took place in December 1626 and January 1627, and Jahangir himself died in Rajauri (near Lahore) in late October 1627.

53. For this text, see Mutribi Samarqandi, *Nuskha-yi Ziba-yi Jahangir*, ed. Isma'il Bikjanuf and Sayyid 'Ali Mawjani (Qom: Kitabkhana-yi Mar'ashi Najafi, 1377 sh./ 1998).

54. Khwaja 'Abdul Karim, *Bayan-i Waqi'*, pp. 88–89. On humoral theory and "patriotism," also see the remarks in Bayly (1998), pp. 13–16, and Alan Mikhail, *Nature and Empire in Ottoman Egypt: An Environmental History* (Cambridge: Cambridge University Press, 2011), pp. 204–13.

55. See the somewhat unsatisfactory discussion in Dale (1994), pp. 20–21, 45.

56. This is amply demonstrated in Claude Markovits, Jacques Pouchepadass, and Sanjay Subrahmanyam, eds., *Society and Circulation: Mobile People and Itinerant Cultures in South Asia, 1750–1950* (New Delhi: Permanent Black, 2003).

57. Richard C. Foltz, *Mughal India and Central Asia* (Karachi: Oxford University Press, 1998), pp. 153–54.

2 Prescribing the Boundaries of Knowledge

Seventeenth-Century Russian Diplomatic Missions to Central Asia

Ron Sela

IN THE BEGINNING of the seventeenth century, Central Asia was still a mysterious and relatively faint blip on the Russian radar.[1] Although diplomatic and commercial missions to the region had, with intervals, been ongoing for some time, they were yet to properly begin in earnest. Partly because Russia was ensnared in its own "Time of Troubles," partly because Muscovy still seemed "isolated, self-obsessed, and hyper-xenophobic," and partly because relations with its near-west and near-south would command Russia's attention for most of the nascent empire's history, Central Asia was not of primary concern.[2] The region's image in Russia (assuming there was one) probably relied on visions imprinted on the Russian historical imagination that associated the world to the east with migrants, Muslims, and Turks.[3] Age-old relations with Turkic nomads (be they *torki, pecheneg, polovtsy,* or others), Kievan connections with Abbasids, Khazars, and Byzantines, legendary accounts of Muslim competition for Prince Vladimir's conversion, early trade with the steppe regions, and, most notably perhaps, the two centuries of Mongol rule that became known as the "Tatar Yoke" may all have served to forge negative impressions of what lay beyond Russia's eastern borders. More recent accounts of the commercial voyages of Afanasiï Nikitin (in the 1460s) and Anthony Jenkinson (in the 1550s), although both published and accessible in certain quarters, did little to revise such notions.

Since the middle of the sixteenth century, the Russian czardom under Muscovy's hegemony had begun to expand eastward, crushing the remnants of the Turco-Mongol khanates in Kazan and Astrakhan and bringing newly conquered populations closer to its core. Even with the changing nature of interactions between Russia and its neighbors—shifting from general acquiescence to conquest and annexation, and transforming Russians' self-portrayal from Christianity's medieval defenders and the (more or less) heroic victims of the Mongols to the first subjugators of Siberia—the focus of the new state was still the west, and early expansion beyond the Urals began as a private enterprise. In the seventeenth century, Russia was only beginning to view itself as an "empire."[4] Russians were yet to engage in drawn-out internal debates over their own conflicted, part-Asiatic part-European character; Russian Oriental Studies, responsible more than any other field of inquiry for advancing our scholarly knowledge of Central Asia, was yet to be founded; and Central Asia was yet to become, in Dostoyevsky's memorable words of 1881, Russia's "destiny."[5] All this would emerge much later, in the course of the fast-paced developments of the nineteenth century.

In the seventeenth century, Russian embassies to Central Asia were crossing a threshold into a world that had recently experienced wide-ranging changes. In the late fifteenth and early sixteenth centuries, massive migrations swept through the region, bringing Turkic steppe nomads known as Uzbeks, with Qazaq offshoots, and governed by Chinggis Khan's male descendants. The newcomers overran the region's sedentary states and drove off the remnants of their princely houses, descendants of the renowned Timur (Tamerlane). They intermingled with and largely overwhelmed the Iranian population and pushed East Turkestan's nomads farther east. In the process, they reinvigorated Chinggisid imperial charisma, stimulated the development of an extensive and multifaceted indigenous historiography in Turkic and Persian, and were instrumental in supporting the rise of Sufi orders and cultivating new alliances between ruling houses and religious and mercantile networks. Several powerful seats of government were established in Khiva, Balkh, and Tashkent, with Bukhara rapidly becoming the region's most powerful and centralized sedentary center. New cultural and political boundaries—both real and perceived—came into being between the Central Asian khanates and other surrounding, expanding, foreign polities led by emerging dynasties: the Romanovs to the north, the Safavids to the southwest, the Mughals to the south, and later the Qing to the east. Remarkably, most of these key developments remained unnoticed in the travel writings of seventeenth-century Russian envoys to Central Asia.

Russia and Central Asia: Travelers' Early Impressions

The passing of Ivan IV ("the Terrible") in 1584 threw Muscovy into anarchy. Succession struggles, false monarchs, resilient Cossack outlaws, Polish and Swedish invasions, severe famines, and other woes wreaked havoc on both the population and the land. Only with the rise of the House of Romanov and the implementation of copious reforms did Russia endure. Muscovy was still receiving ambassadors from Central Asia during its "Time of Troubles," but these diplomatic and mercantile gestures were not being reciprocated.[6] Ongoing internal strife and uncertainty in Russia guaranteed that Central Asia had little role in Muscovy's more pressing priorities.

Reports by earlier travelers to Central Asia were also not very reassuring.[7] Afanasiï Nikitin, sailing south on the Caspian Sea on his arduous and unpredictable voyage to Hindustan in the 1460s, had pointed to a hazardous route involving more risk than the journey was worth.[8] Nikitin's troubles had begun shortly after leaving Astrakhan, when Tatars shot and killed one of his men, boarded one of his two vessels, plundered his possessions, and took four other men as slaves. As the voyage continued on the Caspian en route to Derbent, a storm crushed the smaller boat, and its crew and passengers washed ashore only to be captured by Caucasian Kaitaks.[9] Although intermediaries finally secured their release (all travel through these regions required constant negotiation and substantial assistance from mediators), the journey's future was in jeopardy. After some deliberation and much doubt (and significantly fewer resources), Nikitin resumed his voyage, presumably because he was heavily in debt back home and could not risk a premature return. And so he reached Persia and, after a yearlong stopover, headed to Hindustan. Nikitin's sojourn among the Muslims of Hindustan occupies the greater part of his narrative, but beyond reports of select curiosities, what was his message to his potential audiences?[10] Clearly, the journey was perilous and yielded no financial or spiritual reward. The Tver merchant repeatedly cautioned prospective voyagers that dealing in trade in such parts of the world would require leaving the Christian faith in favor of that of Muhammad. On several occasions, Nikitin warned Christians that such a journey would "lead to sin" and force them to "abandon their faith." The religious divide also carried with it a financial burden, as all toll-free goods were reserved exclusively for Muslims.[11] Nikitin concluded that life in the imposing city of Bidar, then the capital of the powerful Bahmani Sultanate, was too expensive for the merchant. He also found nothing worthwhile for Russians to trade in. It is not clear whether such statements deterred his compatriots from engaging in commercial activities in Hindustan, but they undoubtedly invoked strenuous expectations.

A century later, the Englishman Anthony Jenkinson, aspiring to minimize Portuguese maritime commercial success by envisioning water- and land-based trade routes through Asia, composed a more elaborate but equally cautionary report. A member of the Muscovy Company, a joint-stock English company that was chartered in 1555 to expand England's trade with Russia and Asia, Jenkinson was a very different traveler than Nikitin. He came from a wealthy family, boasted more experience in foreign settings, was better funded, and seems to have had a larger and more efficient support network.[12] His company was to have a monopoly over trade between England and Russia all through the seventeenth century.

Although the new company's activities started rather dismally—the first four ships launched from England were either lost or wrecked—the prospect of potential wealth was too tempting to relinquish. Jenkinson arrived in Moscow on Christmas

Day 1557, soon after Russia's triumph over the khanates of Astrakhan and Kazan.[13] Four months later, he began his journey southward and was soon greeted by dreadful sights, which were the dire consequences of the recent Russian conquests. Internal wars among the scattered Tatars ensued, and persistent famine and plague spread uncontrollably. Sown fields were being ravaged, Noghay children were being sold into slavery, and in the port city of Astrakhan, the streets were overflowing with unburied corpses, which were "very pittifull to beholde."[14]

Like most other travelers of his era, Jenkinson chose the Caspian Sea as his preferred route.[15] The Englishman and company sailed from Astrakhan in a southeastwardly direction, trying (and mostly succeeding) to keep within sight of land. As they anchored near the Yayik River estuary, a band of thirty men boarded their boat seeking infidels, presumably to sell them into slavery. One of the travelers, a respected Muslim, assured the raiders that there were no infidels on board, and Jenkinson was spared an unpleasant fate. Another brush with ruin came on the twenty-seventh day of the sea voyage, as the company barely survived a vicious storm before making landfall in the vicinity of the Manghishlaq Peninsula. The local population—"very badde and brutish"—from whom they procured camels for the desert leg of the journey, harassed them incessantly, fighting, stealing, begging, and inflating prices. Traveling overland in harsh desert conditions for nearly three weeks and finding no water and no adequate sources of food, the weary wayfarers were forced on several occasions to slay and eat their own beasts of burden.

Finally, they arrived in the city of Urgench, the capital of Khorezm, where they stayed for a month. Trade opportunities were virtually nonexistent. Continuing southward, on the river, they came upon a castle near Kat whose ruler was brother to the king of Urgench and "who ment to haue robbed all the Christians in the *Caravan*."[16] Incidents with other robbers and thieves also take up much of the report on the journey to their next destination, Bukhara, where they arrived on December 23, 1558. But even if Jenkinson's description of the "very great" city—the first real city since they had departed from Russian territory—was much more approving than that of Moscow, and even if he seemed to enjoy the convivial hospitality offered to him by Bukhara's ruler, 'Abdallah, business prospects—the merchant's highest priority—were still pitiable. The king's revenues were minute—he even owed the Englishman some money—and the polity was in a state of continual war with the Persians, which harmed commerce further. Jenkinson's disappointment with the merchant fair was unmistakable.[17] He had heard of other cities in the region and was also eager to explore the road to Cathay, but he quickly realized that "barbarous nations" made the routes impenetrable.[18] Tashkent was in a state of war with the Qazaqs, and Kashghar was impossible to reach. Seeing that succession struggles among Chinggisid factions in Bukhara (of which he was only partially aware) would not come to an end in the foreseeable future, the English merchant decided to leave. "[A]nd if we had not departed when we did," he wrote, "I and my companie had bene in danger to haue lost life and goods." During his journey back along the same route, Jenkinson continued to observe destroyed roads, plundered caravans, and slain merchants.

Yet the Englishman's account is more than just a cautionary tale, and though he seems to have been interested chiefly in commodities and prices, his voyage should be measured for other reasons as well. His report includes notes on the geographical features of the routes to Central Asia. It is also imbued with "ethnographic" tidbits, in which Jenkinson would comment, albeit very concisely, on such things as the makeup of tents and dwellings, on methods of drawing water from wells and irrigation, on types of fruit and grain, on the origins and customs of local royalty, and on hunting and riding. Interestingly, such descriptions were to remain absent from the official reports of Russian envoys in the following century.

On his return journey to Moscow, Jenkinson was accompanied by six Central Asian ambassadors to Russia—one from Bukhara, another from Balkh, another from Urgench, and three other "Soltans," who were brethren of the "king of Vrgence." Together, they became responsible for the establishment of official relations between Central Asia and Muscovy, albeit at least for the time being from the Central Asian side. Jenkinson claimed that the ambassadors were apprehensive about the journey, and although he had promised to protect them, "they somewhat doubted, because there had none gone out of *Tartaria* into *Russia*, of long time before." Throughout the seventeenth century and after, perhaps because of this singular mission, these three locales—Bukhara, Urgench, and Balkh—became synonymous in Russia with the Central Asian sedentary world.[19]

Lastly, even if incidentally, Jenkinson was also responsible for raising the question of Russian slaves in Central Asia, a particularly contentious point of disagreement between Russia and Central Asia for the remainder of their complex history. While in Urgench and Bukhara, Jenkinson made several offhand remarks about the existence of Christian slaves in the khanates, as well as other slaves of "divers countries," and even mentioned that without the czar's letters of introduction he himself would have been taken into slavery. Having managed to obtain some of these slaves, Jenkinson brought with him on his return journey "25 *Russes*, which had been slaues a long time in *Tartaria*, nor euer had before my comming, libertie, or means to gette home."[20] He did not elaborate on the slaves' condition or identities, and he eventually delivered them into the czar's hands.

Clearly, Jenkinson's testimony was not much of an endorsement of Central Asia. This was so much so that subsequent British expeditions to the region opted to journey through Astrakhan and the Volga westward to Shabran and Shemakha (in modern-day Azerbaijan) and then over land to Persia, thus forsaking Central Asia for the next 180 years.[21]

Bukhara Initiates Relations in the 1610s

Shortly after ascending the throne of the khanate of Bukhara, Imam-Quli Khan (r. 1611–41) began to strive for the revitalization of relations with Russia.[22] Such relations, he thought, could boost economic growth in his country, inform him of events in the western and southern parts of the steppes (particularly in light of recent violent incursions by Cossacks and Kalmyks), and perhaps also help alleviate pressure from Bukhara's chief contemporary troublemakers, namely, Imam-Quli's competitors in Balkh and Qazaq agitators in Tashkent and the Ferghana Valley.[23] In September 1613, the khan Imam-Quli sent an envoy, Khoja Nauruz, to Moscow to establish relations, seek opportunities for trade, and discover what authority rested in the hands of the newly elected ruler, the seventeen-year-old first czar of the Romanovs, Mikhail. However, the ambassador did not reach Moscow. Instead, together with a large group of Bukharan and Khorezmian merchants, Khoja Nauruz was detained for fourteen months in the town of Samara on the bank of the Volga river, because the Russians had more urgent affairs to deal with. Still at the closing stages of the "Time of Troubles," the czar was concerned that Astrakhan's port (then held by both Russian and Cossack rebels) was about to fall into the hands of the Persian Shah 'Abbas I.[24] In order to secure safe passage through Khivan—and possibly Bukharan—territory for the czar's ambassador to Persia, Mikhail Tikhonov, the Central Asians were therefore held hostage in Samara until Tikhonov successfully completed his mission. Central Asia was not the objective of the Russian embassy and was merely an ad hoc conduit for accomplishing a more urgent objective.[25] In 1619, another ambassador, Adam Bek, was sent to Moscow from Bukhara. As an incentive, Imam-Qulī Khan even offered to send back all the Russian slaves that Bukhara had purchased from Noghay and Crimean traders in return for a permanent Russian ambassadorial presence.[26] This time, the Bukharan ambassador was well received. When he was permitted to leave, he was joined for the first time in many years by the czar's official envoy, Ivan Danilovich Khokhlov.[27]

Russia Responds: Ivan Khokhlov's Mission, 1620–1622

Following decades of diplomatic inactivity, Khokhlov's mission may be regarded both as a template for other Russian missions and as an exception to them. Born in response to a Bukharan promise to release Russian slaves, the embassy had clear goals. In addition to freeing the captives—primarily Russian imperial servicemen and noblemen— Khokhlov was to conduct himself in a manner in keeping with new Russian diplomatic etiquette and deliver the czar's gifts to the khan.[28] He was instructed to explain to Imam-Quli the new political circumstances in Russia, namely, that the "Time of Troubles" was over and that Russia had renewed its sovereignty over the "mountain people" in the north Caucasus and the steppe nomads. Furthermore, he was also to try to negotiate better trading conditions with mutual access to border cities. Although directed not to volunteer information, if asked, the envoy was to clarify that Russia enjoyed good relations with Turkey, Persia, and Europe but was hostile to Poland and Lithuania.

Like most other envoys of the era, Ivan Khokhlov was provided with a set of instructions (*nakaz*), the likes of which became common practice for Russian ambassadorial missions to Central Asia and elsewhere. The *nakaz* was composed of specific directives that were to be followed to the letter. They concerned all manner of behavior and protocol, from the style of the envoy's self-introduction to the proper recitation of the czar's titles. They also prescribed the travel routes that the embassy was to follow and the mission's more specific goals and how they were to be accomplished. The envoy had to abide by the instructions and not deviate from them: there was little or no room for improvisation. As a serviceman of the lowly nobility, Khokhlov emerges from his account, perhaps appropriately, as a seasoned soldier, stubborn and persistent, and with a knack for following orders. Although he had had experience in dealing with foreigners from distant lands,[29] he was no professional diplomat, as his "official report" clearly shows.[30]

When Ivan Khokhlov returned to Russia after the conclusion of his mission, he was interrogated by the authorities in December 1622. The results of this interrogation—the report refers to it as "questioning" (*rospros'*)—form the main specimen of "travel writing" that we have at our disposal.[31] At this time, Russian ambassadors were not yet in the habit of keeping detailed logs of their journeys or personal—sometimes confidential—diaries.[32] However, they did take notes throughout their expedition in order to facilitate their responses at the formal debriefing that would be held upon their return. Thus, we read the following insert in Khokhlov's interrogators' report:

> It seems that there are roughly thirty cities in the Bukharan land, but he [that is, Khokhlov] does not recall their names. He had a note (*zapiska*), [but] when he was in the territory of Iurgench he lost his note. Fearing for himself because of the blood-thirstiness of Prince (*czarevich*) Abesh of Iurgench [that is, Sultan Habash, son of 'Arab Muhammad Khan], he buried his instructions and all kinds of letters in the ground. Later, when he was released from Iurgench, he searched but could not locate [them].[33]

It is unclear how the apparent loss of his notes affected his questioning, though Khokhlov's awkward explanation indicates some degree of negligence or thoughtlessness. His interrogators, however, were most methodical in following the envoy's original instructions (after all, copies of the *nakaz* were preserved at the court) and adhering to the mission's chronological sequence of events. Consequently, they were upholding the embassy's original objectives. Just as the envoy could not and did not deviate from his charge, the interrogators were likewise bound by the same commitment. In trying to complete the mission's goals, the envoy and his interrogators were bound to expand Russia's knowledge of Central Asia, but at the same time, such expansion was pursued only in very specific—and quite limited—directions.

Records of official interrogations are not what we might typically associate with "travel writing" in other parts of the world during this era. As opposed to the textual legacy of some other late Renaissance travelers, the Russian mission reports required neither the "interdependence between fact and fiction" nor the establishment of the "authority of the traveler as narrator" that necessitated an erudite interpretation of the traveler's personal experiences. Since much of the official report consisted of the repetition and implementation of prior instructions, there was also less need to develop sophisticated literary skills.[34] Furthermore, if they were not asked directly—and ordinarily they were not—the czar's envoys took no notice of "ethnographic" information. They disregarded stories of the supernatural and legendary and offered little to no commentary on the religious divide that had so preoccupied former visitors to the region. This stands in sharp contrast to the presumed undertaking of European travelers of the period to "explore human diversity through geography."[35] The results of the Russian ambassadorial missions of the seventeenth century also leave little room for the scholar to probe the "transformation" of the text "from a literal journey to a psychological or symbolic one."[36]

However, certain features of Khokhlov's narrative—particularly the climatic and cultural challenges of the journey—are reminiscent of earlier travels in the region. But moving from private travel impressions (with Nikitin) to state-sanctioned testimony (with Khokhlov) created conditions that fostered a more monotonous and restricted narrative. For a merchant like Nikitin, boundaries of description were constrained mostly by his own disposition and background and by the era's conventions. But for Khokhlov and the other envoys that followed him, the reports contained almost entirely those specific materials that directly concerned Russian state authorities. Khokhlov's report makes us realize that the knowledge collected while operating within such confined limitations was perhaps not as vast, stimulating, or varied as it could otherwise have been.

Returning to Khokhlov's account itself, we may well ask what the Russians had learned of Central Asia. To begin with, obstacles on the path to Khiva and Bukhara were many and were becoming increasingly foreseeable. Much like earlier travelers, Khokhlov and his party had found themselves in similar predicaments: the envoy was accompanied by the returning Central Asian ambassadors (and they, in turn, by "non-Christian" slaves they had purchased in Kazan), as well as translators, interpreters, bodyguards, merchants, and various retainers.[37] Their boat crashed on the Caspian shore in the middle of the night, and they were forced to disembark in an unfamiliar land. Their Tatar escorts collided with Turkmen nomads who were after their wares, and they found themselves wandering in "a land with no sovereign." Attacked by more nomads, they resorted to building provisional fortifications to defend themselves. According to Khokhlov's testimony, the attacking nomads had no idea who the Russians were and at first thought they were envoys of the mortal enemy of the Sunni Turkmens, the Shi'ite Safavid ruler.[38] Through trade and numerous negotiations undertaken by interpreters, the returning ambassador from Urgench, and chance acquaintances, the envoy was able to ally himself with some of the nomads. But he still had to fight with others. After a twenty-day siege, Khokhlov's party was able to proceed, only to encounter another ambush in which Khokhlov himself managed to kill one of the attackers. Surrounded by Turkmens who were demanding lives or slaves in return for their dead and realizing that they were about to perish from hunger and thirst in the inhospitable desert, Khokhlov had to buy his and the other men's freedom by giving up some of his goods, including cloth, leathers, knives, and dishes. If Russian officials had been aware of Nikitin's and Jenkinson's accounts while listening to or reading Khokhlov's testimony, they would have surely had a distinct feeling of déjà vu.

In Urgench, the residence of the khan's son Habash Sultan, much of Khokhlov's report details his determined and even violent (if successful) resistance to the blatant extortion attempts of the sultan and his officials, who wanted to seize his possessions. They were especially excited by the gyrfalcons that he was carrying as presents for the Bukharan ruler. In response, the envoy's interrogators in Moscow were interested chiefly in the goods that Khivan officials wanted to confiscate (sable and mink furs, woolens and cloths, leathers, flagons of wine) and in their formal behavior toward the embassy. They wanted to know about the food that was served at an audience with the sultan (flat cakes, half a melon, dried fish), about matters of protocol at official meetings, about provisions given (a sheep, firewood, bread, and melons) or denied. If this type of information dominates Khokhlov's depiction of the mission's stay in Khiva, then it is still pithily described. Since Khokhlov's primary mission was to reach Imam-Quli Khan in Bukhara, and perhaps also because of the Russians' already sour opinion of Khiva, he carried no message from the czar for 'Arab Muhammad Khan of Khiva and so had no reason to remain there. Nevertheless, the khan ordered him to appear at court.[39] Khokhlov brought some gifts with him (wool, squirrel furs, leathers, wine, plates), but the khan found the lack of greeting from the czar more difficult to accept. He manifested his displeasure in miserliness, offering scanty food to the envoy (bread, half a melon, and the very wine that Khokhlov had brought himself). Although the embassy did later receive some provisions—by way of bread, melons, and berries—the hospitality in Khiva was stingy, and the khan even refused to allow them to leave. Khokhlov's interpreters and translators did their best to negotiate, but various dignitaries in Khiva had their eyes on the embassy's goods, and it was unclear who had the authority to sanction their release. One of the royal princes even threatened to assassinate the envoy.[40] Having bribed one of the officials, Khokhlov and company managed to leave Khiva, only to learn that they were being pursued. They hastened their efforts to reach Bukhara by crossing a harsh sandy desert (the distance to Bukhara from the Amu Darya, or Oxus, river was twelve days).[41]

When they arrived, the khan was not in Bukhara but in Samarqand, where he was launching a campaign against the Qazaqs. Bukhara was under the control of a governor, who housed Khokhlov's party in guest quarters and supplied them for ten days with daily provisions of sheep, bread, millet, and firewood. The governor also tried several times to get his hands on the falcons, and each time, Khokhlov had to deny him, even shooting at his hosts and chasing them away. Finally, Khokhlov and his party were allowed to leave for Samarqand and meet the khan there. The long-awaited audience with Imam-Quli Khan went well. Even if His Highness complained that "for many years there had been no high-level envoy" from Russia, the embassy was treated much better in Bukhara than in Khiva.[42] Matters of protocol (such as reading the czar's letter, presenting the falcons, and exchanging other gifts) were carefully observed. These were followed by negotiations for the slaves' release, during which the khan allowed Khokhlov to ransom eight men with the envoy's own money.

Khokhlov was then sent to speak to the khan's uncle, Nadir Divan-begi, the official in charge of the treasury. Their conversation—indeed, the longest conversation that Khokhlov seems to have had with anyone in the region—is one of the more intriguing parts in the interrogation document. Since the majority of the discussion consists of Nadir's questions to Khokhlov, it points to the concerns of Bukhara rather than Russia. The khan's uncle displayed notable interest in the steppe regions, particularly the Noghays, and much less in Russia itself. In answer to a question concerning the extent of the new czar's sovereignty over the steppe nomads, Khokhlov confessed that "during the time of trouble and anarchy" (*v smutnoe i bezgosudarnoe vremya*), the Noghays had become independent, but now sovereignty had been restored. Perhaps paradoxically, Nadir indicated that most of the information that Bukhara had on conditions in the steppes came from the slaves brought to Bukhara by Noghay slave traders. Nadir also suggested that some of the Russian captives were soldiers who had been fighting in Bukharan service against the Qazaqs.[43]

Before leaving Bukhara, Khokhlov was informed that conditions in Khiva had worsened. The khan's sons had abducted their father and put out his eyes, and people were fleeing the country. Realizing that he should circumvent Khiva through Persian territory, Khokhlov sent the interpreters to negotiate safe passage, but the new Khivan rulers tricked him into passing through their territory. Much of the remainder of the report describes Khokhlov's attempts to leave Khiva by sending his men in different directions and negotiating an escape with Afghan Sultan, who would became the new Khivan ambassador to Russia.

Toward the end of his testimony, Khokhlov was asked about other conditions in Central Asia. He painted a picture that must have sounded chaotic to his interrogators. Politically and militarily, Balkh and Persia were hostile to each other; the Safavids had been at war with the Mughals; Bukhara was at odds with the Mughals over Balkh (yet Balkh and Bukhara were portrayed as one kingdom that had been divided between two brothers and the people seemed to love the younger brother in Balkh more); Bukhara was at war with the Qazaqs in Tashkent; Khiva and Bukhara were in conflict; and the Kalmyks were raiding Khiva.[44] Khokhlov also observed that there were no cannons and guns in the cities, save for one old iron cannon in Bukhara, and that most soldiers were riders, archers, and lancers.

Khokhlov's deplorable experiences in Bukhara and Khiva and his subsequent report seem to have irritated the Russian authorities, and the czar decided to send no more missions to Central Asia. It took nineteen years for the Russians to dispatch another official embassy, during which time there were at least five official Central Asian embassies to Russia.

The Long Hiatus: Gribov's Two Missions in the 1640s

In the spring of 1641, Anisim Gribov was sent to Bukhara and Khiva with clear instructions to gain the release Russian slaves, obtain information on the khanates' relations with the Ottomans and Georgia, and seek trading opportunities.[45] Unlike Khokhlov, Gribov was a merchant, not a military man. He had been to Central Asia before and could speak Turkic. Accompanied by Savin Gorokhov, Gribov took a long time to reach the khanates, traveling under harsh and hazardous conditions. Gorokhov fell ill and passed away in Qabaqlï, and because of entanglements with the Turkmens, it took Gribov six additional months to travel from Qabaqlï to Urgench (though it was usually a three-week journey), where he arrived in mid-January 1643. In Khorezm, the ambassador encountered more difficulties and was denied food provisions and other supplies. When he finally reached Bukhara, he was surprised to receive the same treatment. The new khan, Nadir-Muhammad, did not inquire after the czar's health and remained seated when the czar's letter was read to him. He also refused to release any Russian captives who had yet to work off their bondage.

Not unlike other envoys, Gribov tried to secure the trust of other Bukharan officials in order to skirt the khan's apparent stubbornness. He tried bribing, through one of his interpreters (who, as usual, were accomplishing much of the work but always remain voiceless in the reports). One of the Russian captives with whom he came into contact explained to him that the khan had thought he was a spy. In such ways, the captives acted as conduits of knowledge, not only about the circumstances of their servitude, but also on matters of intelligence.

In trying to negotiate with the khan's officials and not with the khan directly, Gribov was again deceived, and the khan had already left Bukhara and went to Qarshi. Gribov chased him and managed to secure an audience with His Majesty, but the khan refused to release any slaves and even denied knowledge of their existence. Gribov's attempt was doomed to fail: not only did the khan believe him to be a spy, but Gribov had given eight falcons to the khan of Khiva and only four to the Bukharan. While Gribov was still in Bukharan territory, significant events were taking place in the region. Bukhara annexed Khorezm, and a large-scale battle was launched against the Zunghars, which led to Bukharans and Qazaqs forming alliances. Gribov wanted to inform the czar about these developments and returned to Moscow in August 1643, accompanied by a Bukharan ambassador. Save for two women and one man whom he was able to ransom, Gribov could not secure the release of any other Russian captives. He even had to turn down the request of forty who had come to meet him and plead for their freedom in person.[46]

Toward the end of 1646, Gribov undertook a second mission, which was aimed at announcing the passing of the old czar, Mikhail, in 1645 and the accession of his son, Aleksei.[47] In addition, Gribov was to explore trade opportunities, try to negotiate the release of slaves, and explore opportunities for trade with the Mughals in India.[48] Because the Caspian-to-Khiva route was deemed unsafe, this time the envoy was sent to Bukhara through Persian territory. Because of various circumstances, primarily an ongoing civil war in Bukhara, he opted to remain in Persia rather than proceed to the khanate.

The Pazukhin Mission (1669–1673) and the Beginning of Change

After another long pause, Moscow was ready to renew relations and, on behalf of Czar Aleksei Mikhailovich (r. 1645–76), dispatched an embassy in July 1669, as before, to Bukhara, Balkh, and Urgench. It was headed by two half brothers, the elder and higher-ranking Boris Pazukhin and the younger Semen Pazukhin.[49] The orders given to the Pazukhin brothers harked back in part to earlier Russian goals in the region, but this time the mission seemed to be operating with a wider and more "international" mandate. Central Asia was now considered to be a player in a much larger arena.[50] The envoys were instructed to ransom Russian captives, gather information about roads leading to India, learn about the bones of the holy martyr Simeon, and persuade Bukharan merchants to sell more silk to Astrakhan and Muscovy.[51] Furthermore, while in the region, the embassy was ordered to learn more about relations between the khanates and Turkey, Persia, and India and also find out whether Indian travelers from Hindustan to Astrakhan paid taxes in Urgench, Bukhara, or Persia. In addition, the envoys were instructed on how to behave in case there were other foreign ambassadors at the Khivan or Bukharan courts. Closer to home, the envoys were directed to gather information on the whereabouts and condition of the rebel Stenka Razin and his Cossack followers.[52]

Instructions and preparations for the journey indicate a far better understanding of the region by 1669 and of the ways and methods of getting there. This was by no means a complete picture, but it seems that previous embassies, as well as private contacts and ambassadorial representatives from the region, had served to better inform the Russian authorities. By now, the Russians realized that there were three clear options for reaching sedentary Central Asia. The shortest and quickest route—if, given the ferocious sea storms and hostile desert nomads, frequently the most dangerous— was to cross the Caspian from Astrakhan to Karagan in the Manghishlaq Peninsula and from there make the swift, four-week journey to Khiva. The longest route—fourteen weeks by Boris Pazukhin's estimate—was to reach the Caspian via Astrabad, sail to Mekhshet, and arrive in Bukhara from the southwest via Merv. Finally, there was the overland route to Khiva through Kalmyk-controlled territory, the least dangerous according to Astrakhan's governor at the time. Luckily, relations with the Kalmyks were good, and the Pazukhin embassy could rely on the assistance of the Kalmyk *tayi-shi* Daichin, who would supply Kalmyk guides.

Perhaps because Boris Pazukhin was an experienced and poised individual, and perhaps because the Russian government had learned to expect difficulties on the road to Central Asia, the envoys were allowed to decide for themselves which road to take based on conditions along the way. Indeed, on several occasions, it seems that Boris was allowed—or at least not punished for—exercising more judgment than his predecessors. The *nakaz* instructions stipulated that letters of safe passage should be displayed to indicate the embassy's purpose and that, to alleviate unnecessary distress, a hefty quantity of walrus tusks should be used for barter. Furthermore, the envoys were instructed to hire a good many guards to protect them from rogues and brigands. Given past experiences, the Russian authorities also anticipated snags in the region's courts. Although, as we have seen earlier, the envoys were directed to gain the confidence of other dignitaries in the realm in addition to the khan, they were now cautioned against trusting people in 'Abd al-'Aziz Khan's retinue who might demand excessive payoffs. In all matters, the envoys were to parley only with the khan himself. They were to be courteous, show respect for local customs, and throw a banquet in the khan's honor in order to encourage him to free the Russian captives. In the elaborate explanation on the circumstances of ceremonial and official presentations, the envoys were to emphasize the good relations that had existed "for many years" with the previous czars ("our ancestors"), while still acknowledging that they regretted that "for many years there has not been ambassadorial contact between the rulers."[53]

Boris and company followed the advice of Astrakhan's governor and skipped the Caspian in favor of traveling through the Kalmyk lands all the way to Khiva. Relying on the assistance and guidance of Daichin and his grandson, Nazar-Mamut, the journey passed uneventfully. As in previous embassies, upon their arrival, the Pazukhin brothers were ordered to pay close attention to matters of court protocol. According to their report's detailed descriptions, both in Khiva, where Boris and the khan displayed tact, politeness, and patience, and even more so in Bukhara, the gatherings, greetings, eating arrangements, and other ceremonial matters were much more elaborate than previous ones.[54] The hospitality awarded to the embassy in Bukhara surpassed anything they had expected, and even if Boris complained from time to time about lack of provisions, the embassy seems to have been generously treated. Their quarters included benches for sleeping, various rooms adorned with carpets and furs to keep them warm in the winter, and adequate food supplies of rice, bread, oil, grapes, apples, melons, and onions. But by far the most remarkable were the courtly gestures and spectacles offered by the Bukharan authorities, probably an effect of the embassy's more composed and well-mannered approach and the khan's desire to show off. This was all a far cry from Ivan Khokhlov's portrayal of the meager and harsh treatment that he had received.

The display of ceremonial and courtly life culminated in an official dinner in Bukhara. Boris and his companions were sitting at the table with the dignitaries of the realm, who had been summoned from different cities, all wearing their finest garb. There were no other foreign ambassadors present. 'Abd al-'Aziz Khan, flanked by his attendants, was sitting at the head of the table; his sword, bow, and shield lay before him. In front of him sat the *khojas*, old and revered holy men, with books that had been brought from the mosques; "for many hours" they were discussing and explaining legal matters to the audience.[55] The table was covered with gilded brocade, and on it were placed fine cuts of meat and an assortment of berries and sweets, all served in fine vessels. While the feast was going on, nine men were singing and playing "Muslim games" (*busurmanskie igrie*). At one point, the khan commanded a wild animal to be brought in; a black horn towered above its lip, and Boris was asked if they had such a creature in Russia (he had never seen one before). At another dinner several days later, the khan ordered other animals to be paraded before the guests, including a lion, tiger, elephant, deer, and various birds. Then additional "Muslim games" were played.[56]

Such vivid descriptions had not been part of any previous ambassadorial account. Yet the fanciful images created by Pazukhin's report remained restricted to the realm of court ceremonial. The report provides no information on what the khan looked like, where his dignitaries came from, who the *khojas* were, or what was meant by "Muslim games." Beyond the court, Pazukhin was silent on all matters of "ordinary" life, whether on urban and rural space, the economy, or religion. Even the report on the pressing matter of the Russian slaves—which the Pazukhin embassy was unable to resolve and which would be concluded only with the Russian conquest of the region two hundred years later—was limited to the numbers and positions of slaves. Even so, the report was revealing in its own way.

Like the previous embassies and almost every Russian embassy that would follow, Pazukhin requested release of the slaves and permission to take them back to Russia. Unsurprisingly, the discussion that followed was less convivial and more contentious and hinged on the question of the slaves' religion. Boris had asked all the Christians to be freed, and the khan knowingly (and much like other khans before him) replied that they had all converted to Islam and thus were no longer Christian. Boris contended that they had been forced to convert, and the khan claimed to have no knowledge of it. After some deliberation, the khan agreed to release nine slaves and to allow the envoys to purchase twenty-two others. This was not enough, and Boris decided to try to speak with the Russian captives "in secret" (*tainym obychaiem*) and find out about their conditions. This resulted in his securing from them several handwritten petitions that he later submitted to the czar. In them, the captives offered prayers for the czar's health, pleaded for their liberation, restated their loyalty to Orthodox Christianity, and told of the numerous times they had tried to escape, only to find themselves alone in the desert, parched and hopeless.[57] These discussions with the captives helped the Russians obtain knowledge of the slave trade in the region. Apparently, Bukharans purchased Russian captives from Khiva for 40 rubles or more. Kalmyks and Bashkirs often supplied the slaves, while Kalmyks and Persians sometimes sold captives as far away as India. The number of Russian slaves amounted to 150 men and women in the inner city of Bukhara (their numbers were much higher outside the city); 100 in Balkh (with similar ignorance as to their numbers outside the city); and 50 in the Khivan palace (with no clear idea of how many there were outside it).[58]

Boris and company also learned that Bukhara, Balkh, and Khiva had erratic relations. They had no connections with the Ottomans, but when Boris was there, Bukhara and Balkh were on good terms with India and Persia, while Khiva and Persia were at war. Khiva also had good contacts with India—in fact, the Khivan ambassador to India passed Boris on his way there. Boris estimated that the route from Astrakhan through Persia to India was long, difficult, and very dangerous, partly because India and Persia were hostile to each other. He added that Russians were not allowed to pass through their lands, with special permits given only to merchants.[59] Pazukhin estimated that it took four and a half months by camel to travel from Astrakhan to the Indian city of Zhanabat (that is, Shahjahanabad, the Mughal capital since 1639), where the "Indian czar Uranzep [the Mughal emperor Aurangzeb (r. 1658–1707)] lives." Unusually, Boris commented on the lineage of the Indian "czar": "Temir-Aksak [Timur the Lame, or Tamerlane] was the great-grandfather (*praded*) of Uranzep czar; their ancestry is Chagatai."[60] The historic connection of the Mughals to Central Asia seems to have been well known, but whether Boris's statement was meant to point to a familiar story or to imply any clearer relations between the khanates and Hindustan remains unknown. Returning through Persian territory, the Pazukhin embassy's journey back to Russia was much longer than its journey to Central Asia. The embassy had to wait for months for permission to cross Persian country, and once it was granted, the brothers ran into problems with some of the local population southwest of the Caspian. Taking a boat to Baku and finding no adequate transport to the north, the Pazukhins fell too deeply into debt to finance the rest of their journey home.

Throughout the seventeenth century, official contacts between Russia and Central Asia grew steadily but were still in their very early stages. In Russia, Central Asia had been associated with a remote and mysterious world that was challenging to get to, unyielding, and difficult. The routes to Khiva, Bukhara, and Balkh were long and treacherous, and navigating them required perseverance, extensive planning, and the effective cooperation of locals. The early seventeenth-century missions had some knowledge of the journey's complexity but did not have the required networks in place to sustain them. As more and more embassies were sent to the region, however, and as Russian expansion continued, the slow learning process continued. In 1670, when the well-prepared Pazukhins set out, their journey proceeded as smoothly as was possible.

While increasing acquaintance with Turkic-speaking Muslims along the Volga river basin (who were also employed as interpreters and intermediaries in embassies to Bukhara and Khiva) facilitated communication, it did not necessarily translate into a better understanding of the Central Asian world. Since the Russian envoys were given strict stipulations and compelled to report only on matters of interest to their state sponsors—such as official meeting protocols, court ceremonials, military capabilities, and whether specific goals were attained or missed—the knowledge they accumulated remained useful but incomplete and restricted. Indeed, Central Asia was still of limited (but growing) significance for the Russians. Before responding to the diplomatic challenge, before developing an awareness of the delicate slave situation (an issue that remained a thorn in Russia's side for the next two centuries), and before realizing the significance of Bukhara, Khiva, and Balkh both as channels to other parts of Asia and as crucial players in the affairs of the steppes, Russia had to overcome its own period of disorder and uncertainty. The Russian embassies that began rather disappointingly around 1620 with Khokhlov, a determined but rather unpolished envoy, progressed over the decades to become subtler and more observant. As a result, they also produced more elaborate narratives. This type of travel record evidently increased Russian knowledge on Bukhara and its neighbors. Yet even though we can appreciate the cultural awareness displayed by the Pazukhin brothers in the early 1670s, the avenues for exploration were still wide open. The emergence of more perceptive travelers—or at least ones who had more freedom to display their insights—would have to wait several more decades.

Notes

1. In this chapter, the term "Central Asia" corresponds to the territory governed by the khanates of Bukhara, Khiva, and Khoqand in the early nineteenth century. It stretches to the Caspian Sea in the west, framed by the Qazaq steppe to the north and by East Turkestan to the east. Most of our discussion concerns Russian embassies to Bukhara, Khiva, and Balkh and their pathways there.

2. Quoted from Mark Bassin, "Russia between Europe and Asia: The Ideological Construction of Geographical Space," *Slavic Review* 50, 3 (1991), p. 4. The "Time of Troubles" (Smutnoe Vremya) refers to the three-decade-long period preceding the establishment of the Romanov dynasty in 1613. The era was characterized by political and social chaos, dreadful natural disasters, constant challenges to the throne and encroachment on Russia's borders by neighboring states.

3. Scholarship on Russian perceptions of Asia and the Orient tends to begin with Peter the Great in the early eighteenth century.

4. For a brief summary of the applicability of the term "empire" for contemporaneous Russia, see the recent discussion by Ricarda Vulpius, "The Russian Empire's Civilizing Mission in the Eighteenth Century: A Comparative Perspective," in Uyama Tomohiko, ed., *Asiatic Russia: Imperial Power in Regional and International Contexts* (Abingdon, UK: Routledge, 2012), pp.13–31, particularly pp. 14–18.

5. See also the introduction and chapter 1 in David Schimmelpenninck van der Oye, *Russian Orientalism: Asia in the Russian Mind from Peter the Great to the Emigration* (New Haven: Yale University Press, 2010).

6. Between 1589 and 1619, only one official embassy was sent from Russia to Bukhara, during Tzar Fedor Ivanovich's reign; *Materialy po istorii Uzbekskoĭ, Tadzhikskoĭ i Turkmenskoĭ SSR*, ed. A. N. Samoilovich (Leningrad, 1932), pp. 400–401.

7. By and large, in analyzing travelers' reports from the fifteenth to seventeenth centuries, scholars' attention has been drawn more to economic and commercial data and less to the images of Central Asia that this type of writing generated in Russia.

8. Afanasii Nikitich Nikitin, *Khozhenie za tri moria Afanasiia Nikitina 1466–1472 gg.*, ed. I. G. Verite et al. (Moscow, 1960).

9. The treacherous Caspian was best sailed during the spring and autumn, thus avoiding freezing winter conditions and fierce summer storms. The shallow water rendered the boats more likely to capsize and more susceptible to raids. On the dangers of the sea voyage, see Audrey Burton, *Bukharan Trade, 1558–1718*, Papers on Inner Asia 23 (1993), p. 5.

10. Nikitin's text survived in different renditions from the sixteenth and seventeenth centuries, with fragments from the late fifteenth century, and seems to have been known in official circles. See Iakov Solomonovich Lur'e, "O mirovozzrenii Afanasiia Nikitina," *Polata Knigopisnaia* 16 (1987), pp. 94–111.

11. Perhaps in order to overcome this hurdle, Nikitin assumed a Muslim name, Khoja Yusuf Khorasani. On Nikitin's religious identity, see Gail D. Lenhoff and Janet L. B. Martin, "The Commercial and Cultural Context of Afanasij Nikitin's Journey beyond Three Seas," *Jahrbücher für Geschichte Osteuropas* 37, 3 (1989), pp. 321–44.

12. Although several Soviet authors (Sreznevskiĭ, Bogdanov, and others) suggested that Nikitin was receiving state backing, there seems to be no definitive evidence to support this assessment (Lur'e [1987], p. 100).

13. For Jenkinson's account, see E. Delmar Morgan and C. H. Coote, eds., *Early Voyages and Travels to Russia and Persia by Anthony Jenkinson and other Englishmen* (London: Hakluyt Society, 1886), vol. 1.

14. Ibid., p. 57.

15. The most common overland alternative was the route from Saraychiq to Urgench or, since 1640, from Gur'ev to Urgench, crossing the river Emba and the Ust Yurt plateau. A north-south route through the Qizil Qum desert, circumventing the Aral Sea from the east, seems to have been less popular.

16. All italics appear in the Hakluyt Society edition of the text.

17. ". . . [B]ut these Marchants are so beggerly and poore, and bring so little quantitie of wares, lying two or 3 yeeres to sell the same, that there is no hope of any good trade there to be had worthy the following." See Morgan and Coote (1886), p. 87. The Englishman's opinion of Urgench was equally damning (ibid., p. 72).

18. Ibid., p. 91.

19. Urgench remained the capital of Khorezm until the reign of 'Arab Muhammad Khan (r. 1603–21), when the capital was moved to Khiva. The city of Urgench was then abandoned, for lack of water, during Isfandiyar Khan's rule (r. 1623–42).

20. Morgan and Coote (1886), p. 95.

21. Iuldashev's suggestion that Jenkinson's negative evaluation may have been fashioned deliberately in order to throw off potential competition is not substantiated by the sources. See M. Iu. Iuldashev, *K istorii torgovykh i posol'skikh sviazeĭ Sredneĭ Azii s Rossieĭ v XVI–XVII vv.* (Tashkent: Nauka, 1964), pp. 17–18.

22. Bukhara's role as the initiator of relations was accepted by early Russian scholars (such as Bartol'd, Veselovskiĭ, and Zhukovskiĭ) but was later rejected by other scholars in Soviet times. It seems that the sources support the former conclusion. See the summary in Iuldashev (1964), p. 21.

23. The 1603 raid on Urgench by Yayiq Cossacks (whom the Central Asian sources identified simply as "*rus*") under ataman Nechai seems to have been well known in the region. The raid left about one thousand dead in Urgench, but the Khivan khan was eventually able to fend off and kill the attackers. From the early seventeenth century, sedentary Central Asia was also susceptible to occasional raids by Kalmyks. Both Bukhara and Khiva kept ambassadorial and commercial contacts with the steppe peoples.

24. Despite its growing cosmopolitan nature, especially since the 1640s, Astrakhan would remain "on the distant periphery of the Muscovite state" for most of the seventeenth century. See J. T. Kotilaine, *Russia's Foreign Trade and Economic Expansion in the Seventeenth Century* (Leiden: Brill, 2005), pp. 57–58.

25. Tikhonov did become aware, inadvertently, of a growing hostility between Balkh and Bukhara and a temporary reconciliation between Bukhara and Khorezm. He conveyed these impressions to the czar. See Audrey Burton, *The Bukharans: A Dynastic, Diplomatic and Commercial History, 1550-1702* (Richmond: Curzon Press, 1997), pp. 140–42.

26. Of no less importance was Imam-Quli Khan's request of four gyrfalcons to be sent to him from the czar. These hunting birds were one of the most prized gifts a seventeenth-century ruler could solicit (ibid., p. 147).

27. Khokhlov was accompanied by the Bukharan and Khivan ambassadors, as well as merchants who were hoping for duty-free opportunities. The coveted gyrfalcons also formed a part of the convoy.

28. Burton (1997) suggested that the czar needed troops to fight the Polish and therefore expected the freed Russian captives to join the military effort. Given the relatively small number of captives, their roles, and the time it would take them to reach Russia (assuming they were in good condition to fight), it seems less likely to be a concern.

29. Khokhlov had been attached to the Persian ambassador to Muscovy in 1600 and later had spent two years in Persia as an envoy on behalf of the Cossack rebel Ivan Zarutskii (Zarutskii, an enemy of the czars, based himself for a while in Astrakhan until his final capture and execution in Moscow in 1614). For Khokhlov's short biography, see N. I. Veselovskiĭ, *Ivan Danilovich Khokhlov: Russki poslannik v Persiiu i v Bukharu v XVII viekie* (Saint Petersburg, 1898).

30. Reforms in diplomacy would come about nearly a century later under Peter the Great and would include the introduction of permanent diplomatic missions and the recruitment of higher-ranking nobility and better-trained (often Western-educated) diplomats, even to the point of incorporating foreigners into the service. See Avis Bohlen, "Changes in Russian Diplomacy under Peter the Great," *Cahiers du monde russe et soviétique* 7, 3 (1966), pp. 341–58.

31. Khokhlov's report and accompanying materials are found in Grigoriĭ Dmitrievich Khilkov, *Sbornik kniazia Khilkova* (Saint Petersburg, 1879), pp. 388–491. The documentary record of such missions includes the original set of instructions or copies thereof; the czar's official messages; correspondence with dignitaries along the route who provided essential resources (provisions, lodgings, personnel, letters of introduction, and safe passage); lists of goods and gifts taken, delivered, and received; and the final report of the embassy, typically the record's longest portion.

32. Only a century after Ivan Khokhlov's journey would official Russian diplomats such as Florio Beneveni begin to keep personal diaries in addition to their official reports. See Florio Beneveni, *Poslannik Petra I na Vostoke: posol'stvo Florio Beneveni v Persiiu i Bukharu v 1718-1725 godakh*, ed. V. G. Volovnikov (Moscow, 1986), and Nicola Di Cosmo, "A Russian Envoy to Khiva: The Italian Diary of Florio Beneveni," *Proceedings of the XXVIII Permanent International Altaistic Conference* (Wiesbaden: Harrassowitz, 1989), pp. 73–114.

33. Khilkov (1879), p. 423.

34. See in this regard Jenny Mezciems, "'Tis Not to Divert the Reader': Moral and Literary Determinants in Some Early Travel Narratives," in Philip Dodd, ed., *The Art of Travel: Essays in Travel Writing* (London: Frank Cass, 1982), p. 2.

35. Jaś Elsner and Joan-Pau Rubiés, "Introduction," in *Voyages and Visions: Towards a Cultural History of Travel* (London: Reaktion Books, 1999), p. 39.

36. Casey Blanton, *Travel Writing: The Self and the World* (New York: Twayne Publishers, 1997), p. 3.

37. Khokhlov's mission is the subject for a recent study by David Aaron Knighting, "Ivan Khokhlov: Russian Envoy to the Court of Imam Quli Khan" (MA thesis, Indiana University, 2008).

38. Khilkov (1879), p. 390.

39. "They [namely, Khokhlov and his interpreter] were there against their will," recorded the interrogator (ibid., p. 394).

40. 'Arab Muhammad Khan even threatened that Khokhlov would suffer the same fate as the Russian merchant Iudin, who had been killed in Khiva several years earlier. See Khilokov (1879), p. 396.

41. Ibid., p. 397.

42. Ibid., p. 400.

43. Khokhlov told his interrogators that the Qazaq leader, Tursun Sultan, ruled his nomadic people, the Qazaq Horde (Kazach'ia Orda), from a city (Tashkent) and that leadership of the horde was his, "according to their Muslim law." See Khilkov (1879), p. 421. Cf. Jenkinson's identification of the Qazaqs as followers of Muhammad's laws in Morgan and Coote (1886), p. 90.

44. Khokhlov also noted that in a war between the Bukharans and the Tashkent Qazaqs, an army of 40,000 Bukharans killed 10,000 Tashkentians. He also remarked that Bukhara could recruit 100,000 soldiers. Decades later, Boris Pazukhin estimated that the Bukharans could recruit the largest army in the region, about 150,000 soldiers, but their horses were in very poor shape.

45. A. A. Preobrazhenskii, "Iz istorii snoshenii russkogo gosudarstva so Srednei Aziei v XVII v. Dva posol'stva kuptsa Anisima Gribova," *Istoricheskie zapiski* 36 (1951), pp. 269–86.

46. Burton (1997), p. 221.

47. Ibid., pp. 242–56.

48. The first Russian official envoy to India was dispatched in 1646. Before then, economic connections between Muscovy and northwest India were exclusively private, with the initiative left to the Indian merchant class. See N. B. Baïkova, *Rol' srednei Azii v russko-indiiskikh torgovykh sviaziakh, pervaia polovina XVI-vtoraia polovina XVIII v.* (Tashkent, 1964), p. 52. India's value for Russia grew during the Russo-Polish War of 1654–67, as the czar hoped that the Indian "shah" would send large sums of silver to Muscovy to help fund the war effort (ibid., p. 60). Following Boris Pazukhin's mission, in the early 1670s, when it became clear to the Russians that the Persian and Indian rulers were in a state of war, it was decided to send more Russian missions to Bukhara and Balkh as a means of reaching India.

49. Two other, very short expeditions from Tobol'sk to Bukhara in 1669 left little documentary record. See Burton (1997), p. 291. The Pazukhin embassy attracted the attention of geographical societies in the late nineteenth century. A short summary of the mission in English was published in the *Proceedings of the Royal Geographical Society of London* 21, 3 (1877), pp. 218–21. A longer outline in French was included in N. Charykow, *Un voyage dans l'Ouzbekistan en 1671 (D'après des documents conservés aux Archives Principales du Ministère des Affaires Etrangères à Moscou)* (Saint Petersburg, 1880).

50. Pazukhin's orders, the missions' official report, and all related materials are found in A. N. Truvorov, ed., *Nakaz Borisu i Semenu Pazukhinym, poslannym v Bukharu, Balkh, i Iurgench, 1669, Russkaia istoricheskaia biblioteka* 15 (Saint Petersburg, 1894), pp. 1–91. See also Jennifer Johnson, "The Pazukhin Embassy: A Look at the Political Portrayal of Power between Seventeenth-Century Russia and the Uzbek Khanates" (MA thesis, Indiana University, 2010).

51. According to a rumor in Muscovy, the bones of the holy martyr were located in a church by a Persian village, and any Muslim who chanced to look upon them promptly became blind. The embassy was unable to find the bones.

52. Stenka Razin was leading an open rebellion against the Russian government. At the time of the writing of the *nakaz* (June 1669), Razin had already been driven out of his old encampment on the Yayik River, had sailed to Baku, and then proceeded to Persia.

53. Truvorov (1894), pp. 5, 11.

54. Ibid., pp. 38–42.

55. Earlier, the khan had commanded Boris to meet with the families of *khojas*—alleged descendants of the Prophet Muhammad—in Bukhara. Boris was made to understand that the ruler's legitimation stemmed from his connections (marital and historic) to these respected families, though he did not seem to understand either who they were or their religious significance.

56. Truvorov (1894), pp. 52–53.

57. These petitions are included in the documentary materials of the embassy.

58. Truvorov (1894), pp. 59–60.

59. Ibid., p. 63.

60. Ibid., p. 62. Boris added that Aurangzeb was a Muslim and did not convert to the Indian religion.

3 Central Asians in the Eighteenth-Century *Qing Imperial Illustrations of Tributary Peoples*

Laura Hostetler

ETHNICITY IS SALIENT to the ways in which we think about identity today. Our global obsession with ethnicity, our confidence in naming and defining a people by a marker as mutable as ethnicity, stems largely from the modern nation-state's proclivity to build its legitimacy on the ethnic identity of its citizens. The centrality of ethnicity to political legitimacy at once invites contestation over who wields power or has voice, and who remains silent within any given political power structure. Thus questions of belonging and difference within the nation often serve not only as ideological glue but also as a source of potential volatility or weakness. Thus ethnicity is, at least in part, both politically constructed and wielded politically. Central Asia is, of course, no exception to this global phenomenon. In this chapter, I look closely at eighteenth-century imperial Chinese understandings and representations of the peoples of Central Asia. The *Qing Imperial Illustrations of Tributary Peoples* (Huang Qing zhigong tu), commissioned by the Manchu emperor of China in 1751, offers us the opportunity to view Central Asia and its inhabitants from the perspective of the Qing court. Based both on accounts of Qing officials who traveled to Central Asia and on records of court visits by Central Asians who traveled to China's imperial center bearing tribute, this illustrated ethnographic compendium allows us to explore questions of ethnicity during the Qing by looking outward from the court toward Central Asia and gives us a glimpse of Central Asian ethnicities in the making.

Questions of ethnic identity in the context of Qing imperial expansion have received a significant amount of scholarly attention in recent years. With regard to Manchu identity, Pamela Crossley has argued that in eighteenth-century China we see ethnic formation in a process of becoming. She supports her claim by demonstrating that Manchu ethnicity was created by a court eager to bring unity to formerly disparate Jurchen tribespeople as as a way to both foster loyalty and bring legitimacy to the Asian Gioro clan. This creation of a Manchu identity was bolstered by the invention of founding mythologies and the recording of supporting histories. Mark Elliott in turn has explored the perpetuation of Manchu identity through the institution of the banners.[1] While arriving at somewhat different conclusions, Crossley and Elliott are both interested in the way that the court used Manchu identity to create and to maintain difference between the rulers and the ruled. How would the court attempt to understand and to categorize the many peoples that would come under Qing influence or direct rule as a result of military intervention and conquest, from Tibet in the southwest to Chinese Turkestan in the northwest? Was ethnicity a category the court used—or would create—to understand and to categorize these new subjects in relation to the growing Qing polity?

Scholars have already given considerable attention to questions of ethnic representation of "others" in the context of late imperial China's southern frontiers, where a variety of culturally non-Chinese peoples were seen and constructed as "other" during the eighteenth century. Following its conquest of China in 1644, the Qing empire continued to consolidate its control and expand its influence to the south and southwest. Taiwan, which had served as a base for Ming loyalism and piracy, was incorporated into the empire by 1683. To the southwest, Yunnan, Guizhou, and Guanxi provinces were gradually incorporated more firmly into the empire during the first century of Qing rule with a shift from the old *tusi*, or native chieftain, system of indigenous rule through native officials to the system of regular administration used elsewhere in the interior.[2] These territorial acquisitions would be mapped successively in local gazetteers and also in imperial surveys carried out with Jesuit assistance under three emperors.[3] At the same time that lands were acquired and mapped, the people inhabiting these frontier areas were also separately mapped out or surveyed. This process has been documented in Taiwan and in southwest China, where "Miao albums" made by local elites categorized and described the native inhabitants according to their tribal or ethnic affiliations, costumes, and customs.[4] While culturally non-Chinese peoples are represented as "other" in these contexts, Chinese documents sometimes use such phrases as "they are becoming more like Han" to convey a civilizing process at work.

In time, parts of Central Asia would also come under Qing influence and control. Starting during the reign of the Kangxi emperor (1661–1722), Tibet also increasingly came under Qing influence as the court became involved in matters of succession and governance in the face of Mongol counterpressures in the region.[5] Finally, Qing power and westward expansion would reach its height with the conquest of the Zunghars in 1759.[6] Yet because of their different forms of governance and different relationships to Qing power, Central Asian peoples were not seen as targets for sinicization in the same way that those in south and southwest China sometimes were. How would the peoples of Central Asia be understood? Would they be ethnicized in the same way as the various peoples (*zu*), and later "nationalities" (*minzu*), of south and southwest China? Or would a type of relationship to the Manchu rulers of the Qing that was different from what southwestern peoples had long experienced vis-à-vis Chinese imperial power make a difference in how the court viewed and understood them?

In 1751, the Qianlong emperor commissioned an ambitious project through which we can explore these questions. Related in nature to the Miao albums of southwest China, this document was much more comprehensive. The *Imperial Illustrations* would picture and describe more than three hundred different groups of people with whom the court had trade or tribute relationships. Its geographical scope ranged from Southeast to Central Asia and included everyone from Europeans to indigenous peoples from southwest China. Some of the relationships described in the compendium had been established with imperial China centuries before. Other groups, such as those in recently conquered parts of Central Asia, were only coming into direct contact with the Qing, or under direct Qing jurisdiction, as the document was being compiled. Thus, especially with regard to Central Asia, the *Imperial Illustrations* gives us a glimpse into a moment in which the Qing court first recorded newly established administrative relationships with a wide variety of inhabitants of Central Asia. Not to be confused with travel writing, which has tropes and generic characteristics of its own, the compendium is primarily an administrative document designed both for reference and for posterity. While not necessarily accurate—as ethnographic accounts made by outsiders in an uneven power relationship never fully can be—its contents do give us a window onto the Qing view of these groups at the time and onto nascent systems of categorization for them.[7]

A close reading of the text demonstrates that the production of ethnographic knowledge of Central Asia and the extension of Qing administrative control are inextricably linked throughout the narrative. Significantly, although not surprisingly, regions farther from the center of Qing power are generally treated both more cursorily and in more derogatory ways that tend to rely on hackneyed tropes for describing savagery in the Chinese imperial context. Exceptions to this general pattern occur in cases in which pilgrimage or tributary visits made by individual leaders or groups of leaders allowed for closer observation and direct questioning.[8] The same is true of the visual representations in which groups farthest from the imperial reach are portrayed as least civilized, dressed, for example, in leaves or fur and barefoot.

The layout of the *Imperial Illustrations* pairs individual textual descriptions with illustrations to identify and enumerate those peoples with whom the court had tributary or trade relations of some sort.[9] I refer to each of these pairings as an "entry." This catalog-type presentation coupled with our own familiarity with the official iteration of fifty-six (albeit contested) ethnic nationalities in the People's Republic of China might lead a casual reader to presume that the identities of those portrayed were fixed or determined according to a logic in which ethnicity is a major factor in identifying a people: Miao, Gelao, Luoluo (now Yi), and so on, for southwest China, and Dutch, English, Swedes, Poles, and the like, for Europe. Yet this would be an erroneous and anachronistic assumption. Far from a fully formed systematic accounting, we find instead a complex hodgepodge of conceptual categories that relies on a combination of region, tribal affiliation, religion, administrative relationship to the Qing, and internal structures of leadership as referents. In short, the very complexity of the compendium's organization at once reveals a lack of uniformity in administrative practices and also documents the wide variety of factors that the Qing would need to take into account in its efforts to govern the region. Although tribal affiliations are occasionally mentioned, ethnicity itself seems not to be a category of analysis. For instance, while different peoples resident in Tibet are described, there is no mention of "Tibetans" per se. While we may see here the nascent beginnings of what would become ethnic categories in later times, and we certainly see textual passages that can be described as ethnographic (or ethnological) in nature—pertaining as they do to habits of dress, diet, livelihood, and religion—we do not see fully formed ethnic categories. In other words, it is accurate to say that at the time of compilation, ethnicity itself, as we would later come to understand it, was not the primary factor identifying the various Central Asian peoples represented in the *Imperial Illustrations*. Yet we can see the nascent stages of what would later become ethnic categorization, with people of various places being identified according to costume and customs. Ethnicity would become an increasingly important referent for identity in the region over time, particularly as ethnic identity became associated with national identity—whether realized or longed for—in the twentieth century.

Organizational Categories of Central Asian Peoples in the *Imperial Illustrations*

Although there are no formal structural divisions within the document itself, the overall organization of the Central Asian portion of the *Imperial Illustrations* can be described as falling into half a dozen categories based on the order and sequence of their contents. These are peoples in and around Tibet; residents of pacified Ili; tribal headmen and commoners beyond Zungharia and in the Western Regions (Xiyu); Hui peoples grouped according to region; Torghuts; and areas beyond Yunnan province. These primary divisions are composed of different kinds of categories, sometimes overlapping. For example, three sections take location or region as their primary referent (Tibet, Ili, beyond Yunnan). At least two are organized around levels of leadership within groups, that is, tribal headmen (*toumu*) and commoners, as among the Qazaqs and Bulute beyond Zungharia or a more stepped division of administration as in Ili. Religion serves as another fundamental, but not exclusive, organizational rubric (Hui). The Torghuts stand on their own, distinguished by their unique history as a people (described below). Within these major geographical, religious, and historical divisions, the groups are further sub-divided into additional categories.

The first seven entries of the Central Asian portion of the *Imperial Illustrations* use Tibet as their geographical referent. The first three refer to peoples living in places under the jurisdiction of Tibet (*Xizang suo shu*), the fourth and fifth to peoples within Tibet but not said to be under its jurisdiction (*suo shu*), and the last two to peoples beyond Tibet. Those living under the jurisdiction of Tibet include both subjects (*min*) and strangers, or frontier people (*fanren*). The "subjects" are described as living in garrisons that were established under Qing projection, namely Wei, Zang, Ali, and Khamu (Khams). The "strangers" are identified as belonging to the Bulukeba and Mu'anba tribes (*buluo*) within Tibet. The second category of Tibetans comprises peoples who live within Tibet but are not described as being under its jurisdiction—the Baliekamu tribe and Miniyake frontier people. The third category described with reference to Tibet are those living *beyond* Tibet, the Lukabuzha tribe several thousand *li* to the southwest and a Balebu or Gurkha headman and his servant. A careful reading shows no term equivalent to our present-day "Tibetan."

After Tibet, the next series of illustrations turns to Ili. Individual pages are organized according to administrative hierarchies. The divisions are *taiji*, *zaisang*, common subjects (*minren*), and Hui, or Muslim, people. *Taiji* and *zaisang* are titles for leaders within the area, and these leaders and their wives appear in the illustrations in finery that corresponds to their positions. Commoners are depicted in clothing of similar style made from plainer materials. The Hui people are given their own page in the section on Ili but are also described in fuller detail later in the *Imperial Illustrations* along with other Muslim peoples in the pages devoted to the Hui.

From this point onward, the organization of the document continues to reflect administrative structures within the different regions of Central Asia. The next entries are devoted to the leaders of tribes in and beyond Zungharia, namely, the Kazakhs and Bulute respectively. Here too there is overlap with contents found in other parts of the scroll that also describe leaders of tribes in Western Qazaq. The move into Muslim areas is very smooth, retaining as it does the continuity of organization in which the organizing principle is the leaders of tribal groups juxtaposed to commoners under their leadership. The initial entries on the Hui are for leaders of Hui tribes in the Western Regions, namely, the walled cities of Ush, Kuche, and Aksu; Badakhshan (in present-day Afghanistan), described as 2,000 *li* west of Kashgar; and Anjiyan, described as being located more than 1,000 *li* to the northwest of Kashgar, bordering on Bulute.

From discussing tribal leaders of the Hui and commoners under their leadership, the attention of the scroll then turns to Hui subjects (*Huimin*) and Hui peoples (*Huiren*) from different places, some of whom had come under Qing administration and some who had not. Populations covered include Hami *Huimin* in Anxiting, *Huimin* of Luguqing, which had pledged allegiance to the Qing under the Yongzheng emperor, and *Huiren* in areas as distant as Aiwuhan and Huohan. Aiwuhan was is described as being an additional three-month journey from Badakhshan, and Huohan as another 3,000 *li* north of Badakhshan. These Hui, while resident in different places, are identified primarily by their religion and secondarily by their place of residence. They are not described by tribal affiliation or ethnicity. The final section that mentions *Huiren* is, by contrast, divided according to individual leaders of specific tribes of the Western Qazaqs, namely Nulali of the Qiqiyusu tribe, Batu'er of the Qiqiyusu tribe, and Hayabu of the Wu'ergen tribe.

At this point, the *Imperial Illustrations* turns its attention to a unique story in the history of Central Asia. Two pages are devoted to the return of the Torghuts from Russia to the Qing empire after a five-generation sojourn, a historical episode discussed more fully below. Not being attached to any specific regions, they are identified as an ethnic group, distinguished by their historical experience of migration and return. The last portion of the Central Asian section of the scroll takes up a description of individual leaders from beyond the Yunnan border, namely Xianmaiyandi, headman of Zhengqian, and Xian'ganhong, headman of Jinghai. The naming and picturing of individuals in this section demonstrate how a system of personal loyalties continued to coexist with a more institutional approach to diplomacy, in which administrative positions such as *taiji* and *zaisang* identified those in leadership positions, in the imposition of Qing influence on frontier areas.

Overall, this overview of the organization of the *Imperial Illustrations* conveys a sense of the complexity of relationships that existed between the court and the peoples on the Qing frontiers. In its efforts to understand and—where possible—to govern these frontier peoples, the court used a variety of tools at its disposal. Region, religion, and history were all taken into account in the conceptualization of groups. Furthermore, a wide variety of forms of leadership—from indigenous headmen, to Qing administrators, to religious leaders—all played a role in the administration of empire and establishment of foreign relations. But to appreciate the relationship between Qing colonial administration and the level of knowledge that the court obtained regarding frontiers people, we must take a close look at the actual contents of the *Imperial Illustrations*.

Ethnographic Descriptions of Central Asian Peoples in the Tibet and Beyond

As mentioned above, the first seven sets of illustrations and textual annotations in the Central Asian portion of the *Imperial Illustrations* are all in some way or another presented in reference to Tibet. I will refer to these paired groupings of text and illustrations as "entries."[10] Significantly, if not surprisingly, the farther from the center of power, the more barbaric and exotic the groups appear, even as the actual amount of ethnographic information presented diminishes. The first entry is the only one that refers to the people in question as subjects, or frontier subjects, *fanmin*, as opposed to simply frontier people, or strangers (*fanren*). Titled "*Fanmin* under the jurisdiction of

Wei, Zang, Ali,[11] and Kamu in Tibet," it begins by locating Tibet in relation to dynastic China both geographically and historically. In ancient times, the term "Tibet," the reader learns, referred to lands of tribes located in the southwestern regions beyond the borders. During the Tang and Song, it was under the Tufan tribes but "now" follows the Dalai Lama. The entry records that the Qing sent imperial troops to garrison Tibet, which was divided administratively into four regions: Wei, Zang, Ali, and Kamu (Khams). Altogether, more than sixty towns are said to have been controlled by the garrisons.

Having established the relationship of the Qing empire to the area, the text moves on to an ethnographic description of the people:

> The men in these regions wear tall, red, tasseled terai hats, brown long-collared upper garments, and plain bead necklaces. Women let down their hair to their shoulders. There are also women who braid their hair. Sometimes they wear red terai hats. Those who are from wealthy families often wear gems and pearls to show off their wealth to each other. Their upper garments are made of multi-toned brown cloth. The inner layers are longer than the outer one. They are good at making brocade felt. They all cover their feet with leather. Their taxes are paid entirely to the Dalai Lama.

This first entry on Tibet demonstrates Qing familiarity with the habits of the residents of the areas where garrisons were prevalent. The fact that the people were tax-paying subjects, even while those taxes went to the Dalai Lama, qualified them as *min*. In the illustration, they appear well off. They are dressed in brocade and wear boots and ornamentation. The woman holds what appear to be several bolts of cloth, presumably felted brocade that she has woven. The man has a sword at his waist—not a hostile gesture among subjects. Relative proximity to these tax-paying subjects would have been required to get a sense of the physical appearance of the women and to know something about their economic contributions to the group, as well as how they displayed their wealth.

The second and third entries in the Central Asian portion of the scroll are on the Bulukeba and Mu'anba *fanren*—as opposed to *fanmin*—of Tibet. The difference in suffix indicates that while they are still under the jurisdiction of Tibet (*Xizang suo shu*), they are not settled in towns as the *fanmin* are, and do not pay tax. Both the Bulukeba and Mu'anba are referred to specifically as tribes (*buluo*). As such, their social organization was different from that of the *fanmin*, and they may have been nomadic, although this is not specifically noted.

We learn that the Bulukeba were formerly under the jurisdiction of lands farther west but that Lord Poluonai of Tibet, known in the English-language literature as Polhanas, first received their submission. At the time of writing, they sent envoys to Tibet annually to reverently pay their respects, express gratitude, and inquire after his majesty's well-being. They are described as adherents of the Red sect of Tibetan Buddhism (*hong jiao*). Both according to the textual description, and according to the illustration, their dress is quite different from that of Tibet's *fanmin* as described above:

Men let down their hair and wrap a piece of white cloth around it. They wear brown, long-collared clothes and wrap a white scarf around their shoulders. They carry plain beads in their hands. Women coil their hair and let it hang down in back and wear a plain hat. Their upper garments are red, and they pair them with a long brown outer skirt with a floral pattern. They wear a dark shawls around their shoulders and long pearl and gem necklaces that go all the way around their backs.

The illustration depicts the man in plain clothes rather than in brocade. He holds a set of Tibetan prayer beads, which evinces a certain amount of piety, but the image does not project political authority. He is depicted without knives or other weapons. The woman is finely dressed in a brocade skirt and sports a long strand of pearls. Both wear brightly colored boots. Unlike for the *fanmin* living in the garrisoned areas, the text gives no information on the general means of livelihood for men or women.

The Mu'anba, like the Bulukeba, are described as having been under the jurisdiction of West Fanguo (Xifanguo),[12] but the scroll makes no mention of tribute or formal visitation to Tibet of any sort. Rather, we learn simply that they frequently go to Tibet because their lands adjoin those of the Bulukeba. Presumably, they were located quite a bit farther out and were less well known; the ethnographic description of the Mu'anba is shorter than for the Bulukeba and includes no information at all beyond mention of the dress of men and women, which is described as follows:

Men wear their hair down, and on their heads they wear strands of red yak hair, which hang down in every direction. They wear brown clothing, leather boots, and yellow shawls. The women let their hair down and restrain it with golden barrettes. They also wear pearls and accessories inlaid with gold. They dress in brown and go barefoot. Some wear leather boots.

This is the kind of information that could be picked up relatively easily through observation of members of the group when they traveled to regions of Tibet under Qing domination. Additional knowledge would have required a familiarity with the Mu'anba in their own territory. The illustration appears to closely reflect the wording in the text, with the man's yellow cape, red yak hair hanging down "in every direction"—appearing only on the top rather than worn alongside and nearer the length of his own hair as customary—and the woman's bare feet. Farther from the points of Qing power and presence, those portrayed appear gradually wilder, with men's heads and women's feet becoming uncovered.

At this point, the scroll moves on to discuss two more groups both described as frontier people of Tibet (*Xizang fanren*), but not as under the jurisdiction of, or "belonging to" (*suoshu*), Tibet. The Baliekamu are specifically described as a "tribe" in the text, but this language is not used for the Miniyake. Both were located in the eastern part of Tibet (*zang di zhi dong*), the Baliekamu having jurisdiction of Li'ang, Bada'ang, and Chamuda'ao, and the Miniyake residing beyond the Dajianlu enclosure.[13] Both are mentioned as adhering primarily to the Red sect of Tibetan Buddhism. The garb of both the men and women of the Baliekamu tribe is described fairly extensively. The men are known for wearing protective amulets over their hearts and for trading brocade and other goods in Tibet. Women, unlike their traveling men, do not wear shoes. Their work is, again, not mentioned, and the illustration gives no clues about their livelihood.

In contrast to the depiction of the Baliekamu, the men of the Miniyake tribe are portrayed as fierce and warlike. They are described as mainly hunters and as wearing armor and carrying both knives and bows and arrows, an image echoed in the illustration. Women's clothing is also described, but women's work is not mentioned. The entry ends by remarking that the Miniyake may be related to the Miaoman peoples in Sichuan province.[14] The illustration depicts the woman offering a chalice to her mate. These people are so at such a distance that there is no mention of religion.

The last peoples mentioned in relation to Tibet are the Lukabuzha[15] and Balebu or Gurkha, who both actually resided beyond Tibet. The Lukabuzha, denoted as *fanren*, are also specifically described as a tribe living several tens of thousands of *li* to the southwest of Tibet. Truly beyond the pale, the region where they live is not named but is described only as "a wild and desolate place where people are foolish and stubborn." As if to bring home this point, the text adds that "they are not [even] aware of Buddhist teachings." A trope also found in Miao albums of southwest China describes the most wild (*sheng*) of all the miaoman groups: both men and women wear animal skins in the winter and leaves in summer, and they catch different types of poisonous insects for food. They are so remote that they do not even travel to Tibet. No mention at all is made of any kind of relationship with the Qing.

The Balebu or Gurkha are, according to the text, located to the west of posterior Tibet, approximately 20,000 *li* from the capital, in a region that used to be home to four separate tribes—the Yangbu, Guoukamu, Yiling, and Mugong—who have more recently been united by the Gurkha king. In the fifty-fourth year of the reign of the Qianlong emperor, the Balebu/Gurkha sent two envoys on a pilgrimage to enter the imperial presence. This audience may be the reason that despite the great distance separating the Balebu from the center of Qing power, a fair amount of ethnographic detail is included, as well as information on local products. The text relates that they are Buddhist, and that as part of a Buddhist ceremony they rub a dot of incense on their foreheads—undoubtedly a reference to *puja*, a kind of worship prevalent in South Asia but not in China. According to the description, the people have brick walls and houses similar to those in the interior of China as well as paddy agriculture. Local products include coral, turquoise, gold, silver, and otter. The people are described as dexterous, many of them working as tradesmen or craftsmen in Tibet. The most unusual feature of this entry is that the illustration depicts two men rather than a male and a female figure, and female attire is not described at all. The two men are most likely a "big headman" and his servant, as described in the heading; one man is carrying a hookah—a pose mentioned in the text as a characteristic of the servant class. The absence of a woman in the illustration is a significant departure from precedent and would seem to indicate that the image was based on a visit to the capital, an activity in which women presumably did not participate.

The portion of the document devoted to Tibet and realms beyond Tibet mentions a variety of different peoples, with an array of relationships both to Tibet and to the Qing polity. Nowhere, however, is "Tibetan" itself used as an ethnic category. Different tribes exist but are identified by specific names. Ethnicity is always in flux and tends to be defined in relation to the state. Tibetan now is considered very much an ethnic category, both by Chinese and those abroad; however, around 1750, there was no single category of "Tibetan" but rather a variety of relationships between different peoples resident in Tibet both between one another and with the Qing state. The formation of the ethnic category of "Tibetan" would come later. Yet the state took an interest in the various regions and peoples of Tibet and created a framework for understanding their practices, natures, and relationship to administrative power structures.

The Ili Region

At this point, the *Imperial Illustrations* leaves Tibet behind and moves north to Ili, which forms the geographical focus of the next four entries. By way of introduction, the reader is told that "Ili" refers to the ancient Quli land that used to belong to the Eleuth tribes. In the twentieth year of the Qianlong emperor's reign, however, Qing troops pacified and settled (*pingding*)[16] the area, after which time Ili was considered Qing territory (*li bantu*), or more literally, "became attached to the map." The term "Ili" is clearly being used in a broad sense to include much of the area that would later become Xinjiang province. The first three of the four sections of the scroll related to Ili depict different levels of administration, namely, the *taiji, zaisang,* and common subjects. The fourth depicts the Muslim populations, which are referred to as Hui *min-ren,* from various regions. The ethnographic content of the entries on Ili is concerned primarily with livelihood and costume. While Hui or Muslim is used as a category of identification, religious practice itself is not described and is of much less interest than questions of administrative hierarchy and the identification and administrative roles played by peoples of different ranks.

The first textual description of Ili is the longest, as it deals both with the conquest and with general information applicable to the *taiji, zaisang,* and commoners. The people are described as nomadic and moving according to the season. Some irrigation is provided by snowmelt, and some hire Hui to help them cultivate the land. We further learn that they grow millet and wheat, melons, and grapes, as well as peaches, plums, pears, and apricots. Their leaders are called *taiji.* Their costume is not only pictured in the accompanying illustration but also described in detail:

> A *taiji* wears a tall, red-tasseled, flat-edged terai hat and a pearl earring in his left ear. His clothing and belt are made of brocade. He wears a small knife by his waist, which is also hung with a towel. His boots are made of red yak leather. The wife of a *taiji* braids her hair in two plaits that are tied with red silk and pearl accessories. She

wears pearl earrings in both ears. Her clothes are made of brocade and embroidered. Her hat and boots are the same as those of the *taiji.*

Of the three groups, they are clearly the most well dressed.

The *zaisang,* who merit their own entry, are described as being under the leadership of the *taiji* and responsible for administering the commoners, with functions and powers varying according to the size of the area they were assigned to manage. Their dress and that of their wives are described as being quite like that of the *taiji* and their wives but are depicted as somewhat less lavish. Commoners, by contrast, wear sheepskin hats and clothing and bronze rather than pearl earrings. Commoners are described as not engaging in agriculture but depending entirely on the Hui for food.

The Hui were clearly in a different category from other residents of Ili as far as Qing administrators were concerned. Already it has become apparent that they were better with agriculture than their nomadic neighbors, but that does not necessarily mean they were entirely sedentary. At the very beginning of the textual description, we learn that the Hui people of various clans and surnames were engaged in trade in Ili with the Eleuth and that they came from a variety of places. The entry also states that in addition to those dwelling in and around Taleqi and Chahanwusu, there were five other groups of Hui located in locations as far-flung as Aksu, Kuche, Yarkand, Kashgar, and Huteng. Each of these groups had its own walled town where they made a living as farmers and herdsmen.

This entry, like the others in this section, notes that imperial troops pacified and settled Ili in the twentieth year of the Qianlong reign; however, the language of the subsequent description of submission and administration is quite different from that used to describe other groups. According to the text, two leaders surrendered and submitted to Qing rule. They then went on a pilgrimage to Rehe to have an audience with the emperor, who bestowed rewards on them and then sent them back. The language of this description is quite significant in that it uses the term "pilgrimage" (*chaojin*). As Chia Ning has explained, this term refers to a special pilgrimage to the court that distinguished Central Asians who were under the authority of the emperor from those who merely presented tribute.[17] Theirs was in that sense a subject position, but also one that enjoyed the privilege of reciprocity, which is signaled by the use of the term *silai* in the emperor's return gifts.

As is customary in the scroll, the garb of the men and women is described in some detail:

> Men wear red-topped mink hats. Their clothes are made of filigree brocade. The wrap their waists with a brocade band and wear leather boots with appliqué. Hui women wear their hair in two braids tied with red silk and decorated with pearl accessories. Their hats and garments are similar to those of the men.

The costumes depicted in the accompanying illustration seem particularly ornate, perhaps reflecting the emperor's largesse as well as the women's skill in weaving.

According to the notation, women wove brocade so exquisite that each length could be exchanged for more than ten horses or dozens of sheep.

Headmen and Commoners: Qazaqs, Bulute, and Hui

The next ten pairs of illustrations pertain to headmen, namely, *toumu* and *Huimu*, and the common people whom they govern.[18] The *toumu* are, more specifically, the leaders of Qazaq and Bulute[19] found to the northwest and southwest of the Zunghars respectively. The *Huimu* are described as inhabiting the Western Regions. After treating the Qazaq, Bulute, and Hui headmen and the populations under their leadership, the scroll moves on to depict Hui living within other polities. As such, in understanding and categorizing Central Asian frontier people, the scroll's organization seems to privilege location, patterns of governance, and religious affiliation, in that order. In any case, the similarity in the presentation of the entries on the headmen and commoners forms a kind of coherent pattern in which leaders are paired with commoners and the moment in which the leaders pledged allegiance to the Qing is well documented. More perfunctory attention is given to livelihood and dress.

According to the text, Qazaq was called "Dayuan" during the Han, and it had no contact with China even from ancient times. However, in the twenty-second year of the Qianlong reign, two leaders successively came over and sincerely submitted. One sent a son and the other a nephew to the capital to look upon the emperor with reverence. Moreover, they presented horses. Qazaq was thereupon included in Qing territory.

The ethnographic portion of the text relates that while the Qazaq are traditionally nomadic, they also know how to farm. Their leaders wear tall, red and/or white, square, leather-edged hats, brocade outer garments with long sleeves, and striped leather boots. The wives of their leaders braid their hair in two plaits and wear pearl earrings. They wear embroidered brocade outer garments with long sleeves, and their hats and boots are identical to those of the male leaders. The commoners, however, whether male or female, wear terai hats and brown clothes. In this instance, the illustration does not follow the text closely. The boots of the headman are plain, and his robe is made of brocade. That of his wife is plain but has an embroidered border. The commoners' clothing is blue and plum, with a subtle stripe, not brown. The commoners depicted in the scroll are designated *minren*, or "subjects."

The textual entry on the headmen of Bulute recounts a story of submission similar to that of the Qazaq. The reader first learns of their location, which was to the southwest of Zungharia, and that they are also Hui. In the twenty-third year of the Qianlong reign, its two leaders, Mamutekuli from "left Bulute" and Halabotuo from "right Bulute," successively led their tribes to sincerely submit. Like the Qazaq, they each sent envoys to the capital to look upon the emperor with reverence, whereupon their territory was incorporated into the empire. Headmen among the Qazaq and Bulute clearly had a special relationship with the throne, which invested them with their titles and special privileges and entitled them to special attention in the *Imperial Illustrations*. The commoners under the Bulute leadership are also designated as *minren*, or "subjects." The made a living by farming and grazing.

Men are described as wearing tall, rimmed hats tied with four white strips and brocade outer clothing with long collars and a red band around their waists. They also wear red leather boots. Women braid their hair in two plaits and wear pearl earrings. They have brocade outer garments with long sleeves and hats and clothing identical to those of the men. Oddly enough, the illustrations in the scroll seem to have reversed the order of the Qazaqs and Bulute; the illustration of the Bulute resembles the textual description of the Qazaqs and vice versa. Apparently, those at court doing the painting or the layout for the scroll were not entirely familiar with what they were representing.

Several Hui leaders enjoyed a status similar to that of the Qazaqs and Bulute. The first annotation on the Hui leaders is followed by an illustration of Hui commoners, or *Huiren*. The textual description presents some geographical overlap with the earlier entry on *Huiren* in Ili; both textual annotations mention the cities of Kuche and Aksu. Here Ush (Wushi) is also named.[20] Whereas the entry on the *Huiren* in Ili served as a follow-up to include Hui populations not specifically mentioned in the sections on Ili that were organized around non-Muslim leadership positions (*taiji, zaisang*), here, by contrast, we are provided more detailed information on the administration of specifically Muslim populations. In these regions, Hui leaders are called *hezhuomu*, and each town is governed by a *beg*.

Having outlined this basic administrative organization, the narrative turns to what has become a recurring theme—surrender to the Qianlong emperor. In the twenty-third year of the reign of the Qianlong emperor, Houjisi, the *beg* of Ush had his son Mozapa'er come to the capital to look upon the emperor with reverence.[21] The next part of the text reads like a moving tableau of his appearance and clearly records a scene from the audience, and one recorded carefully in the accompanying illustration:

> Mozapa'er wrapped his head with a brocade scarf, inserted gold sticks on the top, which were shaped like flowers and leaves. When he walked, his accessories created a tinkling sound. His clothes and band were made of brocade. He wore leather boots with a decorative design.

The remainder of the text includes a description of the dress of both nobility and commoners, means of livelihood, and local products. Their lives, we are told, are generally similar to those in Turfan. There are towns, villages, houses, and huts. Men plow and women weave. They grow five kinds of grain, melons, and fruit and raise various animals including camels, horses, cows, and sheep. No mention is made of specific gifts to the emperor, return gifts, or the incorporation of this territory into the map. Perhaps this is why the commoners under his control are referred at as *Huiren* rather than *Huimin*.

The other two Muslim headmen described in subsequent entries are from farther afield. The Hui leader of Badakhshan (located in present-day Afghanistan), described in the scroll as more than 2,000 *li* west of Kashgar, is mentioned in relation to the military alliance made with the Qing in the twenty-fourth year of the Qianlong reign. During that year, imperial troops arrived in the area while pursuing two rebel Muslim leaders, or *hezhoumu*. The text records that their chief, Su'ertansha, sealed off the passage of the rebels, killed the rebel leaders, and cut off their left ears, which he subsequently presented to the commanding Qing general. Su'ertansha, the reader is told, then sincerely submitted and entered dependency. He sent envoys to the capital to look upon the emperor with reverence and to offer tribute of horses, dogs, and weapons. Hui people in the neighboring town of Poluo'er also submitted when they heard the news.

After a brief description of clothing and diet—described simply as identical to those of Hui in other towns such as Kashgar—the final lines on Badakhshan mention that their language is called "Pa'erxiyu," or Parsi. The commoners over whom the Hui leader presided are referred to as *Huimin*. They are pictured, but as in the other illustrations of commoners in this section, no additional text accompanies the illustration. In contradistinction to the text, the illustration shows the Hui headman of Badakhshan in ways that distinguish him from other Hui leaders. His head covering has a cloth that drapes behind his head in more Arabic fashion. The fur-lined brocade of his clothing is a distinctive patterned purple. Finally he is more heavyset than most men pictured thus far, his girth adding a certain distinction to his bearing. His wife is also well clad in fur-lined brocade and hat.

The last entry devoted to a Hui headman is for the region of Anjiyan, located more than a thousand *li* to the northwest of Kashgar and bordering on Bulute (in present-day Kyrgystan). It was an area where many different Hui people went for trade. The text is more limited than that for the other headmen but follows a similar pattern. It records that in the twenty-fourth year of the Qianlong emperor's reign, their leader, the *beg* Erdeni, surrendered following the pacification and settlement of the area. Subsequently, he submitted and made payment. The local people are described as engaging primarily in trading and farming. Their speech, dress, and eating habits are said to be identical to those of Hui in Kashgar and other towns.

As compared with the other headmen and commoners, this pairing shows more similarity in the fabric and design of the clothing than the others, although the robes of both the headman and his wife are fur lined, whereas those of the commoners appear not to be. Both men are in striped mustard-colored robes, and the women's robes are blue. The headman's costume is set off with a red hat, boots, and sash, while the commoner wears a white hat and sash and brown boots. The headman's wife has brighter trim on her gown, and, like her husband, she wears a red hat and red boots. The other woman wears brown boots and no hat. A bit of red appears at her collar, however.

The textual focus in this portion of the scroll dealing with newly submitted head-men and the people under their leadership is first and foremost their acceptance of Qing authority, with descriptions of distinctive aspects of dress, livelihood, and customs playing a secondary role. In general, the ethnographic focus is primarily on livelihood and dress, yet we also learn something of local products, diet, and language, depending on the group in question. Parallels between different groups of Hui are explicitly drawn in this section. In this respect, we see an emerging concept of "Hui" as a group with common customs.

Other Muslims

After describing Muslim headmen and the commoners they governed, the scroll moves on to describe other Muslim groups in Central Asia. These include Hui subjects (*Huimin*) designated by their dwelling places, and Hui led by tribal leaders—all of whom are identified as being branches of the Western Qazaq. The tribal leaders described in this section are even more far-flung geographically than the Qazaq, Bulute, and Hui headmen.

The first of the entries, on Hui subjects in various places, describes those in Anxi. This area came under the sway of the Qing empire before the Qianlong reign. The administrative status of its population is indicated by the suffix *min* in a way that parallels the use of *min* in the discussion of Tibet's *fanmin* above. The text gives a fairly extensive synopsis of the region's relationship with imperial China. The reader learns that the Hami *Huimin* are descendants of the Huihe of the Tang dynasty, and that during the Ming, the government established a military station in Hami whose descendants later came under the jurisdiction of the Zunghars. Ever since the founding of the Qing, the reader is told, the *Huimin* have been submitting tribute and inheriting feudal titles. During the Kangxi reign, troops were sent to the west to establish garrisons for the military and officials, thus making Hami strategically important. Every year they sent Hami melons and other items as tribute. The reader further learns that the *Huimin* in Guazhou surrendered and were assigned to banners during the Yongzheng reign.[22]

The textual description of the clothing of *Huimin* in Anxi is fairly cursory. We are told that males wear red hats with black brims and long-collared outer garments with sleeves of equal length. Women let down their hair in four directions and wear skullcaps. Their clothes are made of cloth of different shades of brown. Their dress and diet are said to be identical to those of the Hui in the interior. The illustration, particularly the rendering of the woman, is far more colorful and detailed than the textual portrayal. Her face is markedly paler than that of her mate. Her dark hair hangs down from under her blue skullcap. Around her shoulders she wears a dark brown cape. Her blouse is a deep gold with green trim that extends down the center closure and around the collar. Pale blue trousers peek out from under her skirt. She wears brown shoes.

The man wears a brown, fur-lined robe belted with a blue sash. He has yellow shoes and a red cap.

The second group of *Huimin* to be pictured and described are Luguqing and Jintasi lineages (*zu*) in Suzhou, both of which are characterized as Turpan tribes. This is the first and only time that we see the term *zu* in regard to Central Asians in the *Imperial Illustrations*. Like the *Huimin* from Anxi, the *Huimin* are presented as descendants of the Huihe people of the Tang dynasty. The text says that in the fourth year of the Yongzheng emperor's reign, they sincerely surrendered and were made part of the interior. They were assigned to Suzhou's Jintasi military station, and agricultural lands were given to them for their support. The dress of men and women is described somewhat cursorily. Men wear green-topped leather hats and long-collared brown robes. Married women let down their hair in two tufts. They wear red hats decorated with sand grouse feathers on the side and tie their boots crosswise with cloth laces. These small details of dress would help an administrator to distinguish one group of Hui from another. Their diet and other customs are said to be like those of Hui subjects in the interior. The illustration in general echoes the textual description with the exception that the man's fur-lined robe is a vibrant blue, not brown.

Hui Tribal Leaders

At this point, there is a break in the scroll, and when it continues, a textual annotation unaccompanied by any illustration serves as an overall introduction to the five entries that deal with Hui from Western Qazaq and beyond. The annotation was apparently inserted after the scroll had already been completed; a note explains that at the time of writing, there was no illustration available for inclusion and no room left in the scroll. The emperor therefore issued an edict to append a drawing at the end of the work. The note serves to indicate where the annotated illustrations would have come in proper sequence.[23]

Of these five groups, two are identified primarily by location (Aiwuhan and Huohan) and three as under the leadership of specific tribal leaders, who are denoted by name. Representatives of these groups apparently traveled to the court together, arriving at the end of the twenty-eighth year of the Qianlong emperor's reign to present tribute. The general annotation states that the Huohan of Aiwuhan, along with the leaders of the Qiqiyusu and Wu'ergenqi tribes from Western Qazaq, all brought foals to offer. Aiwuhan is more than three months' journey from Badakhshan.

The illustration devoted to the Aiwuhan *Huiren* is accompanied by a fairly long annotation. The text relates that the Aiwuhan Hui are a tribe from the extreme west and, reiterating what was expressed in the previous passage, that heading southwest from Badakhshan, it takes another three months to reach the area, which boasts three major towns: Habu'er, Mashate, and Kaidaha'er. The entry is long and detailed, probably because it records the first-ever tributary visit from this distant land. Because of its extensive nature, I reproduce most of it here:

The Khan, Aihamotesha, lives in the walled town of Kaidaha'er.²⁴ Aiwuhan is sur-
rounded by mountains on all sides. It is full of rich fields. The people engage in
agriculture. Local residents build their own houses and live spread out from each
other. There is no record of a census having been made. They use shotguns, knives,
and long lances in the battlefield. They do not use bow and arrow. Among the Hui
tribes they have long been declared powerful and prosperous. Recently again they
annexed a neighboring tribe, Hindustan. They are growing bigger and stronger.

In the twelfth month of the twenty-seventh year of the Qianlong emperor's
reign, looking up to [the emperor's] majesty and virtue, Aihamotesha sent the envoy
Hezhuomi'erhan with tribute horses. Their letter to the emperor was respectfully
written on gold paper, and it had to be translated by the siyi guan.

The people are tall and stout. They wrap their heads with silk that has a decorative design. They wear brown, long-collared upper garments with a long, brocade-
rimmed, open-front overcoat. The women also wrap their heads with silk that has a
decorative design and wear pearl hair accessories. They wear long strings of pearls
on their ears, which hang all the way down to their shoulders. Their upper garments
have brocade borders. They are diligent in weaving and spinning. The region produces good horses. The four horses of their tribute are all seven chi tall and eight
chi long.²⁵

The court may have been particularly interested in the Aiwuhan *Huiren* because they
were an expanding tribe, noted here for annexing neighboring territory. Their tributary visit to the court provided an opportunity to learn about these distant peoples,
their livelihood and local products.

The illustration of the Aiwunahn *Huiren* holds unique interest for the costumes it
portrays. The man wears a gold-colored turban with flecks of blue and red and sports
a full beard. Over his long-sleeved mustard robe he wears both a white tunic and a
peach-colored shawl with a floral border, which drapes around his body in many folds.
His brown leather boots have heels. The woman has an elaborate headdress made out
of the same fabric as the man's, but folds of fabric cascade down her back, and she
wears a five-pronged hair ornament. The illustration shows a double strand of pearls
as described in the text. Her long outer garment is of red patterned brocade and is
trimmed with blue. She holds a green sash around her waist. No mention is made in
the text of whether women traveled with the tributary party.

Houhan, the topic of the next entry, was just as far away as Aiwuhan but located
3,000 *li* to the northeast of Badakhshan. Its people were known for bringing sheep and
horses to trade in Ye'erqiang and Kashgar. After imparting this information, the scroll
recounts that in the twenty-fourth year of the Qianlong reign, imperial troops reached
Badakhshan. Their leader, E'erdeni Beg, sent envoys to the military camp to reverently
inquire about his majesty's health. Several years later, in the twenty-seventh year of the
Qianlong emperor, envoys were sent to submit tribute, presumably arriving with the
group from Aiwuhan in the twenty-eighth year of the Qianlong emperor's reign. As
is customary, the scroll describes the clothing of both men and women. Males wear
brown outer garments and leather hats. Women wrap their heads with patterned silk

ornamented with pearl hair accessories and wear long, patterned, brown outer garments adorned with brocade handkerchiefs. The region boasts city walls and houses,
the entry relates, but the people also live as nomads. Customs are said to be identical
to those of Eastern Qazaq.

The illustration of the man's outfit departs significantly from the textual description in this instance. While he wears a brown robe, it is largely covered by a red overcoat sewn from several pieces of joined fabric or sheepskin. He wears a fur-lined red
hat of the same material. The woman wears a headdress similar to that of the Aiwuhan
Huiren but with three rather than five prongs. The fabric of her gown is much less
showy. One message that comes through strongly from the illustrations is that these
two groups of Hui dress differently from each other. Presumably, the Aiwuhan Hui did
not dress like those in Eastern Qazaq.

The next three entries on the *Huiren* are more cursory. Significantly, they all
specifically name the individual leaders of the groups that came to pay tribute, demonstrating a system of foreign relations in which relationships with individuals was
still paramount over agreements made between states or other polities. All three
were from Western Qazaq. In the twenty-seventh year of the Qianlong reign, the
Hui people under the jurisdiction of Nulali and the Hui people under the jurisdiction of Batu'er—both of the Qiqiyusu tribe—sent tribute. Although the text is not
explicit on this point, it seems likely that they may have traveled together with the
envoy from Houhan. The inclusion of the third group of Hui from the far west, who
were under the jurisdiction of Hayabu of the Wu'ergen tribe, is somewhat perplex-
ing because there is no mention of them traveling to the capital or even submitting
to Qing authority. They are simply alluded to as a branch of Western Qazaq, their
nomadic area is said to be close to that of the Qiqiyusu tribe, being more than 2,000 *li*
from Ili, and they sometimes travel with other Hui people from neighboring tribes to
Ili and other places to engage in trade. Apparently, their identification was deemed
important enough that they were included in the *Imperial Illustrations* even though
they had not formally submitted.

Ethnographic detail is somewhat limited for these distant tribes, but we do learn
that the *Huiren* under the leadership of Nulali brought sheep and horses to trade in
Ili. The other groups also engaged in trade, to supplement their nomadic lifestyles,
but the text does not record in what type of goods. Details on clothing are also scanty.
The clothing of the Hui under Nulali is described briefly, with men wearing brown
clothes and leather hats, and women wrapping their heads with patterned silk. Some
also wear small white hats. Customs of this group are described as identical to those
of East Qazaq. The *Huiren* under Batu'er are described simply as having customs and
costumes identical to those of East Qazaq. Details of dress are not even mentioned for
those under the leadership of Hayabu, which is perhaps not surprising as there is not
record that he, or any of his followers, traveled to the capital. Despite the dearth of
textual information on dress, all three groups are visually portrayed in the scroll. Two

of the women wear small white skullcaps as described in the text. With the exception of some variety in head coverings, the style of the clothing of all three groups is similar although the colors and patterns vary in the scroll. The outer garments of the women in tribes under the leadership of Batu'er and Hayabu are similar but not identical.

Torghuts

The story of the Torghuts is one of the most intriguing of the Qing relationship with polities from Central Asia. In January of 1771, Ubashi Khan, their leader, left Russia with more than 30,000 tents and more than 150,000 people and headed for Zungharia. It was a difficult passage complicated by weather, the pursuit of Russian troops, and hostilities from other tribes who did not support their passage. He would lose half of his company before making contact with Qing officials in Ili.[26]

While this history can be interpreted and told from a variety of viewpoints, what most interests us here is the representation of the event in the *Imperial Illustrations*. Two textual annotations describe the Torghut return. One stands alone without an illustration, much like the introductory text to the section on the various *Huiren*. The other is devoted specifically to the *taiji* of the Torghuts but is followed by labeled illustrations of *zaisang* and commoners as well.[27] The first notation serves to give a historical overview of the negotiation for the return of the Torghuts. We read that Wobaxi/Ubashi, the Torghut leader, in a meeting with two others, Cebokeduo'erji and Sheleng, decided to give up their old nomadic place, Ejile, which was part of Russia, and lead their subordinates to return and submit to Qing authority.[28] Their request was granted, and they were ordered to select a group of elders and to appear with them before the emperor. The audience was held in the Yimian valley. Each person present was granted caps and clothing, saddles and horses. They then spread out around the emperor and followed as he led them to Shanzhuang, where they were banqueted and the emperor conferred rank and official positions on them.[29] From this time forward, we read, the four Eleuth tribes have been in the imperial service. The final words of the annotation remark that their old customs, clothing, and fabrics are not like those of the other Zunghar tribes. Thus the emperor issued an edict to make new drawings.

The *taiji* of the Torghuts and his wife merited their own illustration and annotation, in keeping with the organization of the earlier portion of the scroll, with entries devoted to the *taiji* and *zaisang* of Ili. The annotation on the *taiji* of the Torghuts states that the Torghuts had been one of the four Eleuth tribes of Zungharia, but their ancestor and E'erle Khan did not get along well with Chuoluosibatuluhun Taiji. He thus led his people to move to E'jile in Russia. After five generations, the position of khan was passed down to Guolubalashi. In the twenty-first year of the Qianlong emperor's reign, Guolubalashi sent an envoy to the court with tribute. In the thirty-sixth year of the same reign, Guolubalashi's son Wobaxi/Ubashi worked with the *taiji* of each clan and led all the people—more than 10,000—to return to submission.[30] After they had entered to be observed, honors were bestowed on them. Afterward, they were settled in various parts of Ili. Following this account of their return and resettlement, the scroll moves on to more ethnographic description. The reader learns that the Torghuts are adherents of the Delugspa Yellow sect of Tibetan Buddhism and have a nomadic lifestyle. The dress of the *taiji, zaisang*, and commoners is then described. The *taiji* wear red-tasseled, flat-topped rimmed hats, long-sleeved brocade clothes, and striped leather boots. Their wives braid their hair in two queues and wear pearl earrings and tall, red-tasseled hats. Their clothing and boots are identical to those of the men. The illustration departs in minor ways from the textual description. The *taiji* wears red, not striped, boots, and his wife wears brown boots or shoes; only the very tips of her feet peek out from under her fur-lined brocade robe. The *taiji*'s hat is distinctive, unlike any other head-covering shown in this section of the scroll. The *zaisang* are described only as wearing tall, red-tasseled hats and clothes and belts of brocade, the commoners as wearing nothing more than plain hats and brown clothes. The illustration, while definitely depicting the commoners in the poorest clothing, shows the *zaisang* wearing not brocade but rather a plain blue robe belted with a white sash. His wife is in brown and wears a red-topped hat and shoes.

Leaders from beyond Yunnan

The final entries for Central Asia are for areas beyond the province of Yunnan. A purely textual note precedes annotated illustrations of the peoples in question. It relates that during the thirty-fourth year of the Qianlong reign, Zhao Jiao, headman of Zhengqian, and Diao Bie, headman of Jinghai, surrendered and expressed their willingness to become part of China and requested from afar to present their services. Keeping in mind the extreme distance of their lands, it was ordered that they present only once every six years, as a manifestation of the emperor's favor and compassion. In the winter of this same year, their headmen offered ivory and rhinoceros horn.[31] His majesty ordered the envoy to join in at the end of the New Year tributary groups. Therefore drawings were made of their dress and ornamentation and appended to the back of this work.

In keeping with the overall organizational structure of the *Imperial Illustrations* that we have discussed so far, this introductory note to the tributaries from beyond Yunnan province is followed by an annotated illustration of headmen from each of the areas already alluded to. The first is of Xianmaiyandi, headman of Zhengqian. The text is fairly cursory. We learn that Zhengqian is located outside the border formed by the Jiulong River, more than 1,000 *li* from Pu'er prefecture, and that it produces elephant tusk and rhinoceros horn. There are more than ten affiliating villages, with a total of sixteen headmen, including Xianmaiyan. The dress of men and women is briefly described, but only one man, presumably Xianmaiyan himself, is depicted in the illustration. The second illustration is of Xian'ganghong, headman of Jinghai, which is also located outside the border formed by the Jiulong river, another few hundred *li* from Zhangqian. The region includes a total of more than twenty leaders at various levels,

Xian'ganghong presiding over them all. Local products and attire are noted simply as being the same as Zhengqian's.

While altogether there are thirty-two pairs of annotated illustrations of Central Asians in the *Imperial Illustrations*, only some of them actually allude to journeys to the court or the payment of tribute. This close look at the representation of Central Asian peoples in the scroll gives us an idea of the way in which the Qing saw itself in relation to frontier people in the northwest during a time when those relationships were very much in flux. We see reflected everything from areas and peoples that had become part of the map of the Qing and settled into the banners, to those who paid tribute but were considered beyond the actual territorial reach of the empire, to those so far beyond that no meaningful remarks could be made about their environment. We have seen too that the ethnographic context of the scroll is closely melded with the account of political relationships between dynastic China and the peoples of the frontier. In cases in which audiences occurred, the drawings seem to stem from that particular occasion. In other instances, in areas that were fairly settled, we get a glimpse into not only what people looked like (or were believed to look like) but also what constituted their livelihood and the distinctive local products of their region. For more distant areas, the clothing of the peoples living there could only be sketched out in the crudest of terms, and there was no clear information about the livelihood of the people and their customs. Yet whether near or far, subdued or savage, the Qing empire made a comprehensive record of them all.

In these representations of tributary peoples, we can distill the beginnings of a basis for what would become a system of ethnic categorization of peoples in later times. Under the Qing, ethnic difference served the Manchus as a means of maintaining difference from those they ruled but unity among themselves. This was true whether we think of Manchu ethnicity as created through a shared imagined history or perpetuated by the institution of the banners. The *Imperial Illustrations* scroll shows that the Qing also recognized that the various Central Asian peoples who had pledged allegiance to its imperial authority also had their own distinctive customs and ways of dressing. Furthermore, some of them, such as many of the Hui, shared commonalities among themselves. Yet for the Qing, the compilation of the *Imperial Illustrations* was more about creating a record of the relationships of various groups of peoples *to its own imperial power* than anything else. To the imperial center, where peoples lived, how they were locally governed, and what relationship they held to Qing imperial authority (including what they might contribute to the imperial storehouse) were of primary importance. Their local customs and beliefs were secondary and, along with costume, provided a means of identifying who they were. Establishing differences between these groups was important insofar as it helped to distinguish them for reasons of governance. Individual tribes are mentioned, and Qazaqs, Bulute, and Eleuth are identified. The Zunghars, the main target of the western conquests, do not appear as a category represented and are mentioned only once in passing. The Qing had for all purposes annihilated them, and the organization of the scroll would work to annihilate them from the historical record through omission as well. They had no place in it or in the Qing world because they had not submitted.

Many ethnic groups that we take for granted as existing today are not mentioned. The ethnic categories that have become familiar to us in the early twenty-first century are only partly in evidence. While people from Tibet are described, "Tibetan" is not a category as such. The word "Mongol" (Menggu) does not appear at all. "Hui," by contrast, is a common identifier, but not a specific category within the scroll. Hui are discussed separately according to the type of governance structures under which they lived. These categories, and others, would evolve later out of a different political configuration of power and in an age when the imperatives of the nation-state would take priority over those of empire. In this later context, ethnic identities of "others" would continue to be not only constructed by the state but also used by individual groups in order to attempt to preserve a measure of their own autonomy in the face of external pressures to conform.

Notes

I would like to thank Ying Liu and Wu Xuemei for assistance with translation.

1. Pamela Kyle Crossley, "Manzhou Yuanliu Kao and the Formalization of the Manchu Heritage," *Journal of Asian Studies* 46, 4 (1987), pp. 761–90; Crossley, *A Translucent Mirror: History and Identity in Qing Imperial Ideology Translucent Mirror* (Berkeley: University of California Press, 2002); and Mark Elliott, *The Manchu Way: The Eight Banners and Ethnic Identity in Late Imperial China* (Stanford: Stanford University Press, 2001).

2. Pamela Kyle Crossley, Helen F. Siu, and Donald S. Sutton, eds., *Empire at the Margins: Culture, Ethnicity, and Frontier in Early Modern China* (Berkeley: University of California Press, 2005); Charles Patterson Giersch, *Asian Borderlands: The Transformation of Qing China's Yunnan Frontier* (Cambridge, MA: Harvard University Press, 2006); John E. Herman, *Amid the Clouds and Mist: China's Colonization of Guizhou, 1200–1700* (Cambridge, MA: Harvard University Asia Center, 2007); and Herman, "Empire in the Southwest: Early Qing Reforms to the Native Chieftain System," *Journal of Asian Studies* 56, 1 (1997), pp. 47–74. Laura Hostetler, *Qing Colonial Enterprise: Ethnography and Cartography in Early Modern China* (Chicago: University of Chicago Press, 2001); Leo Kwok-yueh Shin, *The Making of the Chinese State* (Cambridge: Cambridge University Press, 2006); and Kent C Smith, "Ch'ing Policy and the Development of Southwest China: Aspects of Ortai's Governor-Generalship, 1726–1731" (PhD diss., Yale University, 1970).

3. Nailene Chou, "Frontier Studies and Changing Frontier Administration in Late Ch'ing China: The Case of Sinkiang, 1759–1911" (PhD diss., University of Washington, 1976); Wang Qianjin and Liu Ruofang, eds., *Qing Ting San Da Shi Ce Quan Tu Ji* (Beijing: Waiwen chubanshe, 2007); Laura Hostetler, "Early Modern Mapping at the Qing Court: Survey Maps from the Kangxi, Yongzheng and Qianlong Reign Periods," keynote address for "Chinese History in Geographical Perspective," Little Rock, Arkansas, February 19, 2011.

4. Hostetler (2001) and David M. Deal and Laura Hostetler, trans., *The Art of Ethnography: A Chinese "Miao Album"* (Seattle: University of Washington Press, 2006); Nicholas Tapp and Don Cohn, *The Tribal Peoples of Southwest China: Chinese Views of the Other Within* (Bangkok: White Lotus Press, 2003); and Emma Teng, *Taiwan's Imagined Geography: Chinese Colonial Travel Writing and Pictures, 1683–1895* (Cambridge, MA: Harvard University Press, 2004).

5. Yingcong Dai, *The Sichuan Frontier and Tibet: Imperial Strategy in the Early Qing* (Seattle: University of Washington Press, 2009).

6. For an extensive account of the Zunghar campaigns, see Peter C. Perdue, *China Marches West: The Qing Conquest of Central Eurasia* (Cambridge, MA: Belknap Press of Harvard University Press, 2005). On the place of war in Qing imperial culture, see Joanna Waley-Cohen, *The Culture of War in China: Empire and the Military under the Qing Dynasty* (London: I. B. Tauris, 2006).

7. On problems of ethnographic representation, see James Clifford, *The Predicament of Culture: Twentieth-Century Ethnography, Literature, and Art* (Cambridge, MA: Harvard University Press, 1988), and James Clifford and George E. Marcus, eds., *Writing Culture: The Poetics and Politics of Ethnography* (Berkeley: University of California Press, 1986).

8. This distinction between pilgrimage and tribute is described in Chia Ning, "The Lifanyuan and the Inner Asian Rituals in the Early Qing (1644–1795)," *Late Imperial China* 14, 1 (1993), pp. 60–92.

9. Distinctions in the different types of tributary and trade relationship with the peoples of Central Asia will be taken up by the author in a separate article. A preliminary paper on this topic, under the title "Central Asians in the *Qing Illustrations of Tributary Peoples*," was presented at the "Administrative and Colonial Practices in Qing Ruled China: Lifanyuan and Libu Revisited" workshop, April 7–8, 2011, Max Planck Institute for Social Anthropology, Halle, Germany.

10. Different editions of the *Imperial Illustrations* appeared in different formats. The one published as part of the *Siku quan shu* is paginated; the more elegant Xie Sui edition now housed in the National Palace Museum, Taipei, is a handscroll and so is not paginated.

11. The *Siku quan shu* edition reads "A'er" rather than "Ali."

12. *Fanguo* is sometimes translated as "India." *Fan* also means "Sanskrit" or "Pali" and "Brahma." It can also be used in combination with other characters to refer to Buddhist institutions and objects.

13. "Dajianlu" is now known as "Kangding" in Chinese and "Dardo" or "Darzedo" for the Tibetans. The area is now under the administration of Kangding city, located in western Sichuan.

14. Part of eastern Tibet would later come under the jurisdiction of Sichuan province.

15. The *Siku quan shu* edition reads "Lukangbuzha."

16. For this interpretation of *pingding*, see Perdue (2010), p. 410.

17. Chia (1993).

18. These illustrations of commoners are not reproduced in Jifa Chuang, *Xie Sui "Zhigong Tu" ManwentTushuo jiaozhu* (Taipei: Guoli gugong bowuyuan, 1989).

19. Bulute are equated with modern-day Kyrgyz.

20. A number of additional walled towns are also mentioned in the text, all in Hutian, which formed part of the ancient Yutian kingdom.

21. He was also known as Muzafar.

22. "Muslims in Hami and Turfan were organized, unusually, as banners" (Perdue [2010], p. 339.

23. They may have been spliced in at a later date, but having worked from reproductions of the scroll, I cannot state this with great certainty.

24. Aihamotesha is also known as Ahmad Shah of Kandahar, the Afghan state-founder.

25. Three *chi* are equal to forty inches (100 centimeters).

26. Perdue (2010), p. 297. For more on their experience in Russia, see Michael Khodarkovsky, *Where Two Worlds Met: The Russian State and the Kalmyk Nomads, 1600–1771* (Ithaca: Cornell University Press, 1992). For an account of a Chinese embassy to the Torghuts during the Kangxi reign period, see Tulišen, *Narrative of the Chinese Embassy to the Khan of the Tourgouth Tartars, in the Years 1712, 13, 14, & 15*, trans. Sir George Thomas Staunton (Arlington, VA: University Publications of America, 1976).

27. The illustrations of the *zaisang* and commoners are not reproduced in Jifa Chuang, *Xie Sui "Zhigong Tu" ManwentTushuo jiaozhu* (Chu ban. Taibei Shi: Guoli gugong bowuyuan, 1989).

28. They had made the move to this area some generations earlier.

29. Peter Perdue confirms that the audience took place at Chengde, where Ubashi was banqueted, had many gifts bestowed on him, and allowed to keep his title of "khan"; however, "he was no longer in charge of his people. They were split up into ten banners in four leagues dispersed across hundreds of kilometers in northern Xinjiang in order to make sure that these Mongols would never unite to challenge the empire." See Perdue (2010), p. 298.

30. The estimate is quite a bit lower than that in ibid.

31. This occurred in year 40 of the Qianlong reign.

4 The Steppe Roads of Central Asia and the Persian Captivity Narrative of Mirza Mahmud Taqi Ashtiyani

Abbas Amanat and Arash Khazeni

In the widely read nineteenth-century Oriental novel *The Adventures of Hajji Baba of Ispahan* (1826), James Morier imagines in descriptive detail the turbulence of a Turkmen raid on Iran's Central Asian frontier:

> At length, what we so much apprehended actually came to pass. We heard some shots fired, and then our ears were struck by wild and barbarous shoutings. The whole of us stopped in dismay, and like a flock of birds when they see a hawk at a distance, huddled ourselves together into one compact. But when we in reality perceived a body of Turcomans coming down upon us, the scene instantly changed. Some ran away; others, losing all their energies, yielded to intense fear, and began to exclaim, "Oh, Allah! Oh, Imams! Oh Mohamed the prophet! we are gone! we are dying! we are dead!" . . . A shower of arrows, which the enemy discharged as they came on, achieved their conquest, and we soon became their prey. The invaders soon fell to work upon the baggage, which was now spread all over the plain. . . . The Turcomans having completed their plunder, made a distribution of the prisoners. We were blindfolded and placed, each of us, behind a horseman, and after having traveled for a whole day in this manner, we found ourselves on roads only known to the Turcomans. Passing though wild and unfrequented tracts of mountainous country, we at length discovered a large plain, which was so extensive that it seemed the limits of the world, and was covered with the black tents and numerous flocks and herds of our enemies.[1]

Morier's fictional account of the Turkmen slave raids (*alaman*) was not so far-fetched. During the nineteenth-century, the Qara Qum (Black Sands) Desert was infamous

as a transit route for the Central Asian slave trade. Raiding the eastern Iranian borderlands during the Qajar period (1785–1925) and taking Shi'i Persians as captives,
Sunni Turkmen pastoral nomads of the steppes held slaves for ransom in their yurts or
sold them in the markets of the Central Asian oases of Khiva and Bukhara. Turkmen
slave raids disrupted caravan trade on the roads, and created a space of danger and
uncertainty on the eastern borderlands of Iran, leading the Qajar dynasty to strive to
assert its imperial authority through often futile military expeditions into Central Asia
throughout the nineteenth century.[2]

These nineteenth-century expeditions produced a number of travel books (*safarnama*) that surveyed the steppes and depicted.[3] Nineteenth-century Persianate travel
and borderland narratives on Central Asia were part of an effort to describe distant
places and peoples on the eastern edges of Qajar Iran. Drawing on the conventions
of the Persian travel book (*safarnama*) and prompted to a certain extent by the growing body of printed Western geographical and ethnographic literature, Qajar frontier
histories and travel narratives mapped Central Asia as a natural environment and left
ethnographic accounts of encounters with Central Asian peoples. As ethnographic
texts of difference , narratives on the Central Asian borderlands were prone to employ
cultural preconceptions in their representations of distant peoples and places encountered on the road. In Qajar travel narratives on Central Asia, the Turkmen are cast as
rapacious raiders and wicked tribes (*tawayif-i ashrar*) from the steppes of the Oxus.[4]
The pastoral nomadic Turkmen were notoriously feared by the settled townsmen and
villagers for their surprise forays (*chapu*) and violent slave-raiding expeditions (*alaman*), which had carried away thousands of Persians from the eastern provinces of
Astarabad and Khurasan as captives (*asir, bandah, bardah*).

Numerous Persianate travel books on Central Asia from the nineteenth century
detail cross-cultural, inter-Asian encounters in the steppe borderlands of Central
Asia.[5] This body of travel writing includes captivity narratives that offer rich material
for the study of the Central Asian slave trade and encounters between the settled agrar-
ian world of Iran and the pastoral steppes of the Oxus. Nineteenth-century narratives
of captives from Iran trace the paths and encounters of journeys across steppe roads,
recounting cross-cultural contacts and exchanges.[6] At the same time, captivity narratives are records of the troubles of central state along distant borderlands. Nineteenth-
century travel accounts and captivity narratives from Iran to Central Asia trace the
paths and encounters of journeys across steppe roads. Among these Persian captivity
narratives is an account written by Mirza Mahmud Taqi Ashtiyani 'Imad Daftar (the
dates of his birth and death are not known), a calligrapher and scribe (*munshi*) who
served as an accounting secretary (*karguzar*) on the Qajar military campaign against
the Turkmen stronghold of Merv in 1860–61.[7] Following the defeat and desertion of
the Persian army, Mirza Mahmud was taken captive by the Sariq Turkmen and kept
in their encampments in the oasis of Panjdih in what is today northern Afghanistan
for three years before being sold in the slave markets of Bukhara, where he remained

in captivity before he managed to buy his freedom and return to Iran six years hence. During his captivity among the Turkmen, he was forced to work in the fields and graze herds of camels in the Qara Qum Desert under the most abject conditions. He endured long marches, was tied in chains, and escaped three times before leaving the steppes and finding his way to Bukhara, where he served while still in captivity as a scribe and record keeper. Along the way, Mirza Mahmud thus offers firsthand observations of the inner workings of Turkmen slave raids, the lives and experiences of captives, and the networks of slave traffic in nineteenth-century Iran, Afghanistan, and Central Asia.

Upon his return to his homeland, Mirza Mahmud wrote down his experiences in the form of a memoir, which he titled *'Ibratnama* (Book of Reflections). His captivity narrative recounts the travails of individuals caught in the networks of the Central Asian slave trade. Through a reading of Mirza Mahmud's *'Ibratnama*, this chapter argues that the Central Asian steppe was a contact zone, a "middle ground" of encounters between pastoral, nomadic, Sunni Turkmen populations and the Shi'i subjects of Qajar Iran, that hardened into a borderland through the violence of the Central Asian slave trade in the nineteenth century.

Oxus slave raiding and traffic in Central Asia had ecological, economic, and religio-political roots. During the late sixteenth century, the Oxus River (Amu Darya) changed course, its waters swerving eastward from the Caspian to the Aral Sea. Writing in the seventeenth century, the Khan of Khiva, Abu'l Ghazi Bahadur (1603–1642) confirms in his *Shajarah-yi Tarakima* (Genealogical History of the Turkmen) that around the year 1576 the Oxus River changed course, diverting toward the Aral Sea, turning the lands between its former bed and the Caspian Sea into a waterless wasteland and creating an ecological crisis for surrounding dynasties.[8] With the resulting expansion of the Qara Qum Desert, the steppes between the Caspian and the Oxus were transformed into an arid frontier ground between the Safavid, Mughal, and Uzbek empires.

As the Oxus River changed course, Turkmen pastoralists found new possibilities in the expanding arid steppes of the Qara Qum, making it the center of their vast equestrian culture distant from the reach of empires. Between the sixteenth and nineteenth centuries, the Turkmen carved out a loose trading and raiding confederacy built on the power and speed of horses capable of making seemingly impossible sorties across the steppes. The Safavid and the Qajar dynasties of Iran saw the contours of their imperial borderlands shaped by encounters with the new ecology of the steppes and the equestrian culture of the Turkmen. The fluctuation in the course of the Oxus River in effect spurred ecological changes on the frontiers between the steppe and the sown.

Extremely harmful though it was to the sedentary populations in the towns and villages of Khurasan, slave traffic was economically viable for the Turkmen. Slave traffic was facilitated by the Turkmen's immersion as raisers in the currents of the Central Asian caravan trade. Networks of trade and economic exchange linked a wide geographical terrain spanning Iran, Afghanistan, and Central Asia, and souther rims of Russian stepps connecting pastoral nomads, merchants, and travelers of all sorts.[9] Turkmen pastoralists and other itinerant societies were integrated within networks that connected the steppes and agricultural settlements in Central Asia, where they found an outlet for Shi'i captives from Iran.[10]

Sunni-Shi'i sectarian divisions between Iran and Central Asia also contributed to and "justified" the slave trade. At the turn of the sixteenth century, as Shah Isma'il I established the Safavid state (1501–1722) and initiated Iran's conversion to Shi'ism, the Shaybanid Uzbeks, and the Turkmen tribes of the Qara Qum, too, bore the banner of a reinvigorated brand of militant Sunnism in Central Asia. The cultural rift between the two empires in turn widened as the Sunni *amirs* and their supporting *'ulama* establishment defined Safavid Shi'ism as heresy and issued decrees sanctioning the enslavement of the Shi'i of Iran. Sunni slave raids on the frontiers of Khurasan and eastern Mazandaran thus signaled the hardening of a seemingly unbridgeable religious and cultural divide.

The Turkmen, who had entered Islamic Central Asia in the Oghuz migrations of the eleventh century, later stood at the center of the networks of the Central Asian slave trade. The militaries and courts of Islamic states were abundant with Turkmen slaves until the sixteenth century, at which point the direction of the slave trade changed, as the Uzbek and Turkmen peoples increasingly began to raid the borderlands of Iran for Shi'i captives to be sold in the slave markets of Central Asia. Turkmen raids and the expeditions sent in response are chronicled in contemporary sources and represented in Safavid paintings of captured Turkmen. Subdued and shackled to blocks of wood, the Turkmen captives and prisoners in Safavid paintings perhaps depict steppe peoples captured as ransom to be traded for Iranians taken as slaves in Central Asia.

Both the Safavids and afterward the Qajars unsuccessfully attempted to reclaim the Central Asian steppes and to reestablish the Oxus region as Iran's northeastern borderlands. Turkmen raids forced the Safavids to mount difficult punitive expeditions to the Central Asian frontiers of the empire. In the 1590s, the Turkmen overran and destroyed the fortress of Mubarakabad (Aq Qal'a), near Astarabad, which was designed to serve as a bulwark against their incursions.[11] In response, Shah 'Abbas I (1588–1629) marched his troops from Isfahan to Khurasan, restoring Mubarakabad, retaking Mashhad and Herat from the Uzbeks, and attempting to drive the Turkmen from the valleys of the Kopet Dagh and ordering a deep trench to be dug from the foot of the mountains to the shores of the Caspian Sea.[12] Shah 'Abbas also relocated numerous "tribes" of Turkish stock from the Zagros Mountains region in western Iran, where they enjoyed great autonomy and local power, to the Central Asian frontier in order to guard against raids. The Safavids could only assume a defensive policy on the Central Asian frontier. Hundreds of miles of the Qara Qum Desert, the homeland of the independent Turkmen tribes, separated Safavid Iran from the Oxus River.[13] With the fall of the Safavid dynasty in 1722 and the century of dynastic instability that followed, these raids increased in frequency, with Turkmen pastoral nomads employed in most of the raiding.[14]

By the nineteenth century, the Turkmen, virtually independent in the steppes of the Qara Qum, intensified their brazen slave-raiding expeditions into Khurasan. The prevalence of Turkmen border raids and slave traffic served as a barrier against Qajar expansion into the tribiutery Marv region and hindered the establishment of cultivation and trade. During the first half of the nineteenth century, the Qajar dynasty undertook repeated military expeditions to reclaim the steppes between the Caspian Sea and the Oxus River. These campaigns were temporarily successful though they were often left incomplete and in due cours rendered ineffective, or ended in defeat. Among the earliest were the expeditions of 'Abbas Mirza and his European-modeled "New Army," known as the Nizam-i Jadid, in 1832–33 to Sarakhs and its envirors. Later, 'Abbas Mirza's son and the successor to the Qajar throne, Muhammad Shah (1834–1848), undertook the Herat campaign of 1837–38 in part to bar Afghan collaboration with the Turkmen. The Merv expedition of 1860–61, which ended in a disastrous defeat for the Qajars, largely because of logistical shortcomings and the formidable terrain, was the last of the dynasty's large-scale campaigns into the Turkmen steppes.

In 1831, 'Abbas Mirza (1789–1833), the crown prince during the reign of Fath 'Ali Shah Qajar (r. 1797–1834), was appointed governor (*bayglarbaygi*) of Khurasan province. It was a time when defeat in a second round of wars with Russia on Iran's northwestern frontiers called for a face-saving victory for the Qajars against the seemingly less formidable pastoral nomadic Tekke and Salur Turkmen tribes on the Central Asian frontier. Turkmen raids on the eastern frontiers of Iran could seriously strain Qajar foreign relations with other regional powers. In 1831, Mahdi 'Ali Khan Jalal al-Dawla, the son of Sa'adat 'Ali Khan, the late Shi'i Nawab of Awadh in India, was taken captive by Turkmen bandits while en route from Iran to India after having made a pilgrimage to Mashhad; the East India Company subsequently appealed to 'Abbas Mirza to secure his release.[15] The following year, in 1832, 'Abbas Mirza resumed campaigning against the Turkmen in Khurasan. Marching on refractory tribes, his troops stormed the frontier post of Sarakhs, razed Turkmen fortresses, pacified several contingents of the Salur Turkmen, and brought about the release of as many as 20,000 Iranian slaves.

'Abbas Mirza died of an illness in 1833 while preparing for another expedition against the Turkmen, who remained in control of the important Central Asian oasis of Merv, leaving Qajar plans for pacifying the steppes unrealized.[16] However, his eastward march was continued by his son, Muhammad Mirza, who in 1836 set out on another expedition against the Turkmen. The following year, he advanced into the contested territory of the Durrani dynasty in Afghanistan, seeking to reintegrate Herat into the Qajar domain.[17] Under intense pressure from the British, however, Muhammad Shah abandoned the siege of Herat in 1838 and ended his campaign for the reclamation of greater Khurasan.

Nasir al-Din Shah's reform-minded premier, Mirza Taqi Khan Amir Kabir (1807–1852), carried on the effort to reclaim Iran's eastern frontier as a measure against Russian and British imperial encroachment. Seeking to reassert Qajar control over the steppes and oases of the Central Asian frontier, in 1851 he ordered a diplomatic mission to the Oxus in order to reach a settlement with the Khanate of Khiva, a major market for Persian slaves, and to seek the liberation of the thousands of Persian Shiʻi captives held for ransom or sold in the slave markets of Central Asia. The measure once again was intended to recover the steppes of the Qara Qum and bring an end to the destructive slave raids of the Turkmen tribes, which had cast serious doubt on the reach of Qajar imperial authority. In 1861, thousands of Persian infantry and cavalry forces that had marched on Merv under the command of Hamza Mirza Hishmat al-Dawla, the governor of Khurasan, resulted in near annahilation of the Persian army and thousands of Persians falling captive of the Turkmen.[18] The disastrous Merv campaign of 1860–61, originally intended to bring an end to Turkmen slave raids, thus became deeply damaging to the Qajar prestige for its demonstrated the state's inability to protect its eastern borderlands. The Merv expedition would be the last serious Qajar attempt to pacify the Turkmen, and the disastrous defeat signaled Iran's diminishing Central Asian frontiers.[19]

The Turkmen Frontier

In the nineteenth century, the Turkmen practiced both pastoral nomadism and agriculture. The tribes who adopted a nomadic life were called *chumur*, and those who were sedentary were called *charva*. The Turkmen tribes included the Tekke, near the oases of Merv and Akhal in the environs of the Murghab and Tejen (Hari Rud) Rivers; the Ersari dwelling on the edge of the Upper Oxus in an area known as Lab-i Ab (River Bank; Edge of the Water); the Salur, with their encampments in the vicinity of Merv; the Sariq, inhabiting the environs of the Panjdih oasis; the Yamut tribes, spread from the Caspian and the eastern Iranian province of Astarabad to the banks of the Oxus River and Khvarazm; and the Chawdur, spread between Manqishlaq on the Caspian to Khiva.[20] Nineteenth-century European and Persian sources offer varying estimates of Turkmen populations according to the number of tents or yurts.[21]

The Turkmen followed, as much as they could, clan and tribal authorities, paying only a nominal tribute, if any at all, to the Qajar dynasty and the Khanate of Khiva. They were effectively beyond the pale of state power, and their territory marked the edges of surrounding empires. Seen from the perspective of Qajar Persia, the Turkmen steppes marked the limits of the guarded domains of Iran (*mamalik-i mahrusa-yi Iran*). The prevalence of Turkmen border raids and slave traffic served as a barrier to cultivation, trade, and state expansion into the Central Asian steppes.

While Turkmen pastoralists were the cause of the disruption of trade on the Khurasan trade and pilgrimage route, they were also inextricably linked to the networks of Central Asian caravan traffic connecting steppes and cities.[22] The Turkmen

Table 4.1

	Fraser (1825)	Burnes (1832)	*Sb* (1844)	Vambery (1863)	Thomson (1876)	Marvin (1881)	Moser (1885)
Tekke	40,000	40,000	80,000	60,000	5,000	80,000	—
Ersari	—	40,000	40,000	50,000	30,000	30,000	—
Salor	—	2,000	8,000	8,000	9,000	—	—
Sariq	—	20,000	12,000	10,000	14,500	13,000	—
Yamut	25,000	20,000	—	40,000	30,000	35,000	20,000
Guklan	10,000	9,000	—	12,000	4,000	6,000	—
Chawdur	—	6,000	—	12,000	8,000	—	17,000

trade in horses, camels, sheep, skins, wool, textiles (and slaves) linked them to the oases of Khurasan and Mavaralnahr (Transoxania).[23] In the urban markets they found such goods as cotton, tobacco, tea, sugar, and rice (which there was insufficient water to grow in the sandy soil of the Qara Qum). The Turkmen dealt and traded with merchants of Khiva, Balkh, Bukhara, Herat, Kabul, Nishapur, and Mashhad. In his *Safarnama-yi Marv*, 'Abdallah Khan Qaragazlu, a Qajar frontier agent (*sarhadd dar*) posted in Sarakhs between 1876 and 1878 (1294 and 1296 AH) noted the Turkmen's involvement in the wider economic networks of Central Asia. Describing Turkmen markets, he wrote that "twice weekly a makeshift bazaar was assembled in Merv near the near the fortress of Qushid Khan Qal'a and that all the tribes gathered there to trade their goods and merchandise from dawn until dusk.[24] The tribes gathered to barter, trade, buy, and sell in the market, where one could find fruits and grains, cloths and textiles, flocks and herds of animals, wool, and dairy products, among other goods. While some locals possessed Persian and Bukharan currency, their wealth consisted of their camels, horses, and sheep, as well as the crops that they farmed.[25]

In the unforgiving environment of the Central Asian steppes, the Turkmen domesticated nature through their skilled horsemanship. Horses were prized animals in Turkmen society and culture. They were part of the ecology of the steppe and the basis of the mobility, independence, and power of the Turkmen tribes. The equestrian culture and horsemanship of the Turkmen allowed them to make seemingly impossible journeys across the steppes. The possession of swift horses, and the mobility it gave, lay behind the violent Turkmen slave raids of the nineteenth century. According to Joseph Ferrier:

> Turcomans would never venture to advance so far over the Persian border to make their forays, if they did not possess so fine a breed of horses. . . . A horse is to the

Turcoman what a ship is to the pirate, it carries himself and his fortunes. In his saddle he is in his fortress.[26]

The steppes of the Oxus provided a suitable environment for the breeding of horses, offering abundant grasses in dry soil for grazing, and according to tradition, the horses of the Turkmen were mixed with Arab breeds introduced to the Central Eurasian steppes during the reign of Timur Lang, who was said to have distributed 4,200 of the best Arabian mares among the tribes, and Nadir Shah, who is said to have revived this crossing of breeds by offering 600 Arabian mares to the Tekke.[27] The most renowned Turkmen horses were from the Tekke of Akhal and Merv, with those from the Yamut being highly prized as well.[28]

During the 1830s, it became custom for the *amir* and *'ulama* of Bukhara "to issue a decree ordering the Turcomauns in the desert to march to Khorassan and Persia, to make '*tchapow*,' i.e. foray; which order those tribes obey, capturing whole caravans, burning down villages, and selling the inhabitants as slaves in the cities of Turkestan."[29] Turkmen slave raids and surprise attacks are described in nineteenth-century Persian and European travel narratives about Central Eurasia as a source of violence on the frontier and the cause of the decline of trade and cultivation. Travelers described ruined villages where the entire population had either taken flight or been carried away or killed. Walls fortified the settlements that survived, and towers were raised where peasants could retreat in case of attack from the Turkmen. The fear of the Turkmen (*khawf-i Turkaman*) was so strong among the peasantry of Khurasan that they carried arms when they worked in the fields and rarely stepped beyond the village walls. The once thriving trade routes of Khurasan had been depopulated and diminished as fewer caravans ventured to cross the eastern Iranian frontier into Central Asia.[30]

Raiding expeditions were led by a commander (*sardar*) and varied in number of horsemen from just a handful up to one thousand, depending on the number of men in an encampment with a good horse, some arms, and the courage to raid.[31] On the roads, raiding parties sought out information about the passing of caravans of travelers, merchants, and pilgrims. Scouts were detached to ascertain the routes of caravans and often joined the caravans in the guise of harmless travelers. Once they had become aware of the value and extent of the caravan's merchandise, they would suddenly disappear and rejoin the band of raiders.[32] In the early morning hours, smaller parties awaited caravans on the high roads, such as the route between Shahrud and Mashhad, which was traveled yearly by fifty thousand to sixty thousand Shi'i pilgrims.[33] In the mid-nineteenth-century Qajar chronicle *Nasikh al-Tawarikh*, Muhammad Taqi Sipihr describes Turkmen raids in the environs of Sharud in 1852 (1268 AH):

A thousand Turkmen horsemen (*savar*) set upon the village of Shahrud until they were driven off and defeated by the troops of the governor of Astarabad, Muhammad Vali Khan. But in this year on the day of Nawruz festival, horsemen from the

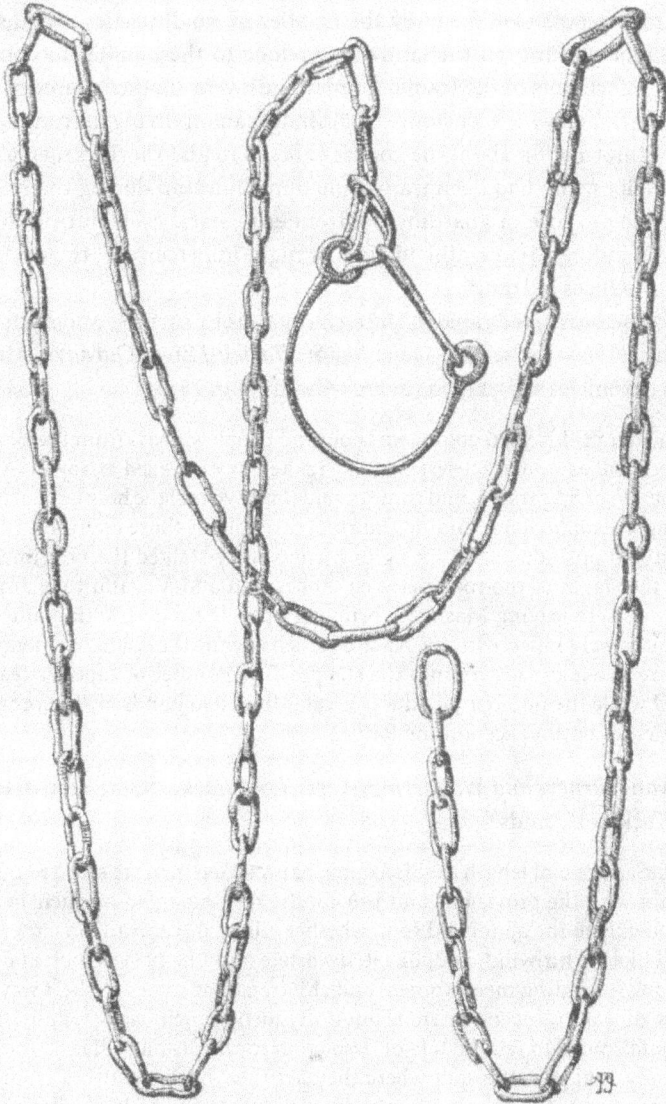

Figure 4.1. A chain (*zanjir*) used by the Turkmen to transport and shackle Shi'i slaves taken captive in Iran and ransomed or sold in Central Asia. From Henri Moser, *A Travers l'Asie Centrale* (Paris, 1885).

Turkmen tribes of Akhal and Tekke from Tejen entered the mosque of light and took thirty women as slaves.[34]

Other Turkmen scouts would survey the frontier in small parties, frequently carrying off peasants working on the land as a prelude to the plunder to come. Persian and Kurdish informants in the Iranian borderlands were another source of reconnaissance.[35] The Turkmen were accustomed to bribing Iranians living in frontier villages in exchange for information about the country and its roads. The Turkmen also paid off the Kurdish tribes who had been transplanted in Khurasan during the reign of Shah ʻAbbas I for the purpose of guarding the frontier to stand aside during their raiding expeditions. "Gliding between the villages at night unperceived," the raiders entered the eastern provinces of Iran.[36]

The raid itself occurred rapidly, taking its victims by surprise and returning to the steppes with captives. In the early Qajar history *Tarikh-i Zu al-Qarnayn*, Mirza Fazlallah Khavari chronicles a Turkmen raid on Khurasan in 1830:

> In the winter of this year, about two thousand people strayed from the heads of the Turkmen, and as is characteristic of the Tekke, they were led astray by Allah Quli Tura, the *vali* of Khvarazm, and came to raid (*takht va taz*) the holy land of Mashhad, galloping (*asbandaz*) and raiding (*turktaz*) throughout those environs. . . . Finding well fortified positions and lurking in corners, they stalked the pilgrimage routes and on the stages of the road between ʻAbbasabad and Mayami they ambush pilgrims who were leaving Mashhad, bringing upon them destruction and ruin. All the old men were killed with the blade of cruelty, while the youth, women, and children were taken as captives into the steppes. The number of captives reached five hundred while the number killed was greater than two hundred. The property that they stole was beyond accounting for.[37]

In his *Caravan Journeys and Wanderings*, Ferrier provides a description of the suddenness of the Turkmen's raids:

> When the attack is at length decided upon, half a dozen men are selected by the chief to remain with the provisions and *yaboos*; the rest, mounted on their best horses, gallop quickly to the appointed spot, whether village or caravan, on either of which they fall like a whirlwind, and, like it, devastate and finally sweep up and carry off everything, including men, women, and children, that comes in their way; in a few minutes all is over. Incendiarism is not unfrequently their last act; and, leaving the flames and smoke to tell the tale of desolation to the distant villages, they fly with their booty, and gain the spot where they left their horses, putting from thirty to forty parasangs behind them without drawing bit; and in an incredibly short space of time reach their encampment.[38]

The sudden nature of Turkmen slave raids and the fear they evoked are reported in both Persian and European sources.

Following the raid, the captives were transported behind the saddles of the Turkmen, tied onto stolen horses, or dragged along on foot by long chains attached to their captors' horses. Upon reaching the Qara Qum territory, some of the captives were put to work cultivating fields and grazing flocks and herds. Most were sold through networks of slave trade and traffic that crisscrossed the borderlands of eastern Iran, Afghanistan, and Central Eurasia, as depicted in Mirza Fazlallah Shirazi's *Tarikh-i Zu al-Qarnayn*:

> Sarakhs is a region among the dependencies of Khurasan and the home of the Salur Turkmen. Its village is great and its fortress thick and there are always five thousand families of Salur Turkmen residing in that region. The chief of this tribe was a descendent of Tuli Khan, son of Chingiz Khan, and his title was Salur Khan and he lived continuously among the tribes of the Atrak. In the time of Bayram ʿAli Khan ʿAzudanlu Qajar's rule in Merv, he invaded that region several times, turning the place upside down and creating havoc. At the beginning of this dynasty's reign, when the Salur tribes were at their fullest, they made a petition to the royal court to make their encampments in Sarakhs and were allowed to stay in peace there. In a word, the Salur tribes were collectively, due to their ties to Tuli Khan, were the leader and foundation for the Turkmen. They considered themselves lords and princes, never setting out to kill and take slaves from Iran. Among the Turkmen tribes, however, the Tekke, Sariq, Yamr ʿAli, and ʿAli Ili, among other tribes, continuously came to Sarakhs as hired mercenaries (*mazdur*), borrowing horses from the Salur and raiding the province of Khurasan. Upon their return, they entrusted half of the slaves and goods in the care of Sarakhs and took the rest with them back to their territories. Associated merchants of slave selling (*tujjar-i asir furush*) from the tribes (*uymaq*) of Hazara, Jamshidi, Taymani, and Taymuri came to Sarakhs to make profit from purchasing Shiʿa slaves from the inhabitants of that province and other strange tribes and then selling them throughout Turkistan. In truth, this province is the harbor of slaves from all lands and the slaves, captives, and slave merchants (*tujjar-i asirdar*) in this land are infinite in number. The Salur tribes themselves regularly conduct trade as merchants of horses and Bukharan skins in Khurasan and Khvarazm. It had been forty years since the province had seen any harm, therefore day-by-day they added to their riches. By means of trade and slave trafficking, they were continuously filling sack after sack with money and storing them in stacks in their yurts.[39]

Ferrier, who traveled through the region in the 1840s, wrote that the slaves were sold through purchase or barter to Uzbek merchants who visited the Turkmen encampments two or three times per year. At the time, the price paid for a ten-year-old boy was forty *tuman*, while a man of thirty was worth twenty-five *tuman*, and so on, with the value decreasing with the age of the slave.[40] Ferrier's estimate overlooks the fact that many of those taken captive were girls and women. Conolly furthermore informs us that "the Toorkmuns capture many beautiful women in Persia . . . , torn from their homes, and taken under every indignity and suffering through the desert, to be sold in the Oosbeg markets."[41] Later in the nineteenth century, Henri Moser reported that Shiʿa slaves were sold in markets of Central Asia for between forty and eighty pieces of gold, with girls between the ages of ten and fifteen years and men between twenty-five and forty years being worth the most.[42] The Turkmen took as captives "the strong and the beautiful," whom they were sure will sell in the slave markets of Bukhara and Khiva. Mid-nineteenth-century European accounts estimate that there were 200,000 Iranian slaves in the Khanate of Bukhara and 700,000 in the Khanate of Khiva.[43]

Mirza Mahmud Taqi and His Captivity Narrative

Mirza Mahmud Taqi Ashtiyani 'Imad Daftar, was a army accountant and a scribe, who served in the Qajar military campaign against the Turkmen in the 1860 Marv campaign.[44] Following the defeat and desertion of the Qajar army, Mirza Mahmud was taken captive and held for nine years, recording his experiences in his *'Ibrat-nama*. Mirza Mahmud begins his narrative by giving the reasons for writing down his experiences:

> The most befitting knowledge for humans to have is an understanding, experience, and awareness of the lessons of the past (*'ibrat*) from the lives of others so that they come to know the pain and suffering of this realm. Therefore, the story of events that happened to me on my travels (*safar*) to Khurasan and Merv, and of my captivity (*asiri*) in the hands of the Turkmen, all of which was written and was my fate and destiny, has been recorded so that others may take some lessons from it.[45]

Mirza Mahmud then details how during the Merv campaign of 1860 he became a captive and was taken by the Sariq Turkmen to the oasis of Panjdih. He unwinds his tale of misery and misfortune by describing the manner by which the Turkmen steppe-dwellers (*sahranishin*) stripped him of all his possessions to the point that even his identity became uncertain:

> In the paws of a bloodthirsty lion, there is no choice but to surrender (*dar kaf-i shir-i nar khun khvarih-i/ ghayr-i taslim va raza ku charih-i*). . . . My clothes and my felt hat are gone. They have given me a sheepskin hat called *shiprima* with long hair that hangs near my eyes and an old green *aqabanu* shawl meant to be worn only by the descendants of the prophet (*sayyids*). As much as I protested, I was made to wear it . . . and with time I came to be known as "Sayyid Taqi" among the other captives and the Sariq.[46]

A reading of the *'Ibratnama* yields glimpses of Turkmen as slave traders and traffickers from the inside perspective of a captive. Mirza Mahmud was bought for fourteen gold pieces (*tala*) by a tight-fisted Turkmen slave trader named Khan Muhammad and put in chains, with his ransom set at one hundred gold pieces at a time when the price of slaves was much lower in Central Asia due to the influx of captives following the Qajar defeat at Merv. Mirza Mahmud consequently spent nearly three years in captivity in Panjdih among the Sariq, whose name as written in the *'Ibratnama* has the same spelling as the Persian word for "robber" (*sariq*), and provided an ethnographic account of the customs, trade, and traffic of the Turkmen tribes.

The slave raid was planned long in advance. Mirza Mahmud recounts how slave-raiding expeditions in the borderlands were organized and carried out by the Turkmen, with the public crier announcing the start of the raid:

> One day, I heard the call of the local crier (*jarchi*) of the Turkmen to the horsemen of the tribes that Mudir Sardar, Qara Bay Sardar, and Aman Sa'd Sardar were going to raid in the direction of Mashhad in fifteen days' time. Any person wishing to come along was ordered to begin preparing their provisions and to give their horses rest—"to keep them raw" (*khami*)—so that they would be ready when the time of the raid came. For two days, the crier kept calling on people in this way and everyone seemed busy preparing their supplies for the raid.[47]

Mirza Mahmud also surveys the geographical span, economy, and networks of the Turkmen slave trade. The slave traffic centered on the Oxus frontier lands, with the circuit of the traffic in slaves extending from the Iranian province of Khurasan in the west to Bukhara and Samarqand to the east. The Turkmen captured Shi'i Iranians during their raids on Khurasan, in the vicinity of Mashhad, Sarakhs, and Herat. Once in their possession , these captives were either held for ransom or sold in the slave markets , in Khiva, Bukhara, Samarqand, and smaller towns like Bashirghan, Urganj, Lab-i Ab, Balkh, and Qarakul. Mirza Mahmud reports seeing two hundred to three hundred slaves a month being trafficked on the caravan routes to and from these Central Asian oases.[48]

Mirza Mahmud also estimated that Iranian slaves sold for thirty to forty *tumans* in the markets of Bukhara, while others such as himself were kept for ransoms of up to four hundred pieces of gold.[49] These ransoms were often paid in the form of orders of exchange (*barat*), which were in effect contractual promises of payment on paper and cash (*tankhvah*) in the form of gold coins sent by the families of the slaves via merchant caravans traveling eastward from Iran to Central Asia.[50] Once eventually everything would have worked out, these middlemen and their caravans of freed slaves would then return to Iran. In other instances, merchants would themselves pay the ransom, carrying slaves in their caravans on the way back to Iran where they were compensated at the destination.[51] Thus, the trade routes that took Iranians into bondage also carried the lucky few back home.[52]

Also involved in the trafficking of freed slaves were Iranian and Central Asian merchants, as described by Mirza Mahmud:

> One day I saw a large caravan from Bukhara traveling to Mashhad and Herat. There were several people in the caravan who had been slaves in Bukhara and having bought their freedom, were returning to their homeland. The head of the caravan were Jura Bay, Badal, Mullah Qul Muhammad and Mullah Hajji Baba Marvi, a Shi'a.[53]

Among the prominent Iranian merchants in Bukhara noted in the *'Ibratnama* were Aqa Muhammad Kazim Tihrani, Aqa Mir Taqi Harati, Hajji Rahim Harati, Aqa Qasim Bay Marvi, Hajji Qurban Mashhadi, and Hajji 'Abd al-Ghaffar Kashani.[54]

The traffic in slaves was thus part of a economy of the region that saw slaves carried on the caravan routes along with horses, textiles, saffron, and opium. The Persian merchants involved in the trade, moreover, did not seem to have had any moral qualms acting as intermediaries in human trafficking of their Shi'i coreligionists. Evidently in their eyes sheer material gains supercdeed any ethical, religious and humaniterain concerns.

Throughout his captivity narrative Mirza Mahmud recalls a host of characters involved in the raiding, selling, and trafficking of Persian slaves in Central Asia. He introduces Turkmen raiders as highwaymen *(qutta' al-tariq)*. One such accomplished plunderer was a certain Bayli:

> Bayli was a Turkmen who was among the most famed robbers *(sariqin-i mashhur)* from the Sariq tribe. Word of his exploits and forays had reached all the Turkmen marauders and he confidently believed himself to be among the most renowned and greatest of highwaymen. He had no talent apart from robbing and never took part in slave selling *(asir furushi)*.[55]

Middlemen and merchants such as a certain Nasim had a different function. He was delivering the ransom for slaves from Iran to the Turkmen captors for a commission.[56] Treading across the pages of the *Ibratnama* also were Turkmen caravan leaders *(qafila bashi)* and slave traffickers such as Qara Bay, whose function it was to transport slaves from the Turkmen camps to Bukhara and Khiva.[57]

Mirza Mahmud's captivity narrative depicts the lives and experiences of Persian slaves in Central Asia, in particular his own captivity and suffering, in stark terms. In order to force Mirza Mahmud to raise his ransom from Iran, Khan Muhammad ensured that his time in the Panjdih was spent in utter discomfort. Mirza Mahmud describes being kept in chains with rings tied to his neck, feet, and hands and being given the minimal amounts of stale barley bread (as opposed to wheat bread). He recalls sleepless nights in the open with nothing more than a dirty, lice-infested felt as a blanket that smelled of smoke and had once been used as a covering for a Turkmen yurt *(alachiq)*. In order to defer the cost of keeping a slave, his owner Khan Muhammad entrusted Mirza Mahmud to one Farajullah Khan of Qazvin, who had supposedly bought several slaves, and kept them unchained, heading for Mashhad.

Yet when Farajullah's deal appeared to have bauched, and he was stalled on the road, he sought to return Mirza Mahmud to the previous Sariq owner. Mirza Mahmud and five others, however, looked for opportunities to escape. They contemplated escape by horse or on foot to Herat, Sarakhs, or Mashhad, devising a plan to escape from Panjdih to Herat along the course of the river flowing between the two cities. In need of horses and a guide with local knowledge of the land, they pinned their hopes on a youth named Rustam, who claimed to know all the roads and swore to deliver them in safety to any place they wished to go.[58] The captives paid Rustam the sum of twenty gold coins and gave him an additional eighty-two gold coins to procure five horses, with saddles and reins. Rustam swore on the Quran that he would keep his word, but he departed with the horses and money, abandoning the captives in the arid steppes.[59]

Back again among the Sariq, Mirza Mahmud was put back in chains and forced to work tending wheat fields from sunrise until late in the afternoon and gathering grass for the Turkmen's camels. As time wore on, Khan Muhammad refused to let his slave go free even for 120 gold coins.[60] In addition to chronicling his own travails, Mirza Mahmud also recalls the burdens of other slaves. He describes "many slaves from Iran cultivating the land and being forced into labor as captives."[61] Meeting a slave named Muhammad from Farahan who belonged to a Turkmen shepherd named Aqqi, he considers the various types of work the captive was forced to undertake, including agricultural labor, sheep herding, and various domestic tasks, such as weaving.[62] He relates the experiences of a child slave, a twelve-year-old named Shahbaz, who fell into the possession of Khan Muhammad.[63] Although allowed to accompany Khan Muhammad in relative freedom, the boy alledgedly suffered frequent abuse and even rape at the hands of his master. According to the *Ibratnama*, Khan Muhammad ultimately had to sell the boy after being confronted by his wife—"beards were pulled off and clothes ripped"—and the entire Sariq encampment became aware of his habits.[64]

Toiling under the sun during the day and sleeping in chains at night, Mirza Mahmud reached the point of utter disparation, crying out in the nights. The Turkmen became convinced that Mirza Mahmud was possessed by spirits and hence performed rituals with fire to drive the evil spirits out but soon came to believe that he was insane. Khan Muhammad began to regret that he had not sold Mirza Mahmud earlier when he had the chance. Seeking simply to survive the ordeal, Mirza Mahmud feigned insanity and as a result was no longer forced to work the fields.[65] When another opportunity for escape presented itself, he was quick to seize it. Over time, Khan Muhammad took to releasing Mirza Mahmud from his chains and sending him to gather grass (*alaf*) from the surrounding steppes for newborn camels. On one such outing, Mirza Mahmud dropped the ropes and the large woolen sack used for gathering fodder and took flight into the desert toward Bala Murghab. Saying a prayer in the name of the Shi'i saint 'Ali ibn Abi Talib and scattering dirt around him to camophlage in the hope that he would not be caught by the Turkmen, he fled with his shoes worn backward so that his tracks appear to be in the reverse direction. When his shoes became worn out, he continued barefooted.[66] He was within one *farsakh* of Qal'a-yi Murghab when he was spotted by men from the Sariq and Salur tribes, who recognized him as a runaway slave. This despite the fact that he attempt to pose as an Afghan. They returned him to his master, Khan Muhammad, in Panjdih for the second time.

For the third time Mirza Mahmud attempted unsuccessfully to flee during the night on one of Khan Muhammad's horses. But he finally abandoned his escape attempts and resigned himself to being sold into bondage in Bukhara, where life appeared to be easier than that among the tribes of the steppes. Recalling the irony of Rumi's verse in the *Masnavi*: "If you're going to Bukhara then you're insane/ Worthy of prison house and the chains (*Gar Bukhara miravi divanih-i / qabil-i zanjir u zindan khaneh-i.*" Mirza Mahmud thus sets his sights on finding an Iranian merchant in Bukhara who would buy his freedom.

After nearly three years of captivity in a Sariq yurt , Mirza Mahmud still holding out hope that he could be sold for 250 gold coins in Bukhara. His master entrusted him accordingly to a Turkmen caravan merchant named Qara Bay who was heading toward Bukhara. Poor Ashtiyani ascribe was thus chained to a camel and marched for twelve days barefoot on a Turkmen caravan. To ensure that he would not take flight yet another time while on the road, he was always kept in chains as the caravan proceeded across the Qara Qum :

> And then the caravan was on its way in the direction of Bukhara. I was bound tightly in chains as prescribed by Khan Muhammad. Because there was a feud between the Sariq and Tekke, the caravan traveled down back roads through the wildlands and did not dare to venture down the main road out of fear of Tekke horsemen. And in this manner they marched me along with them on foot for twelve days. I had no comfort day or night. . . . When the time came for the caravan to move, the chains were tied tightly around my neck and hands and I was taken along on foot.[67]

In the village of Qarakul, a customs agent in the service of Salim Bayg Chur Aqasi spotted Mirza Mahmud and, realizing he was a literate slave (*asir-i sahib savad u nivisandih*), took him from the Turkmen caravan to Bukhara, bringing the most difficult period of his captivity-to an end. In the urban environs of Bukhara, Mirza Mahmud served various masters, and was for a time, the slave of the governor of Bukhara and his minister, serving as a secretary.[68] After six additional years as a captive in Bukhara, Mirza Mahmud bought his freedom and returned home around 1870, bringing to a close his ill-fated travels and adventures. Mirza Mahmud ends the *'Ibratnama* with verses on his alienation and detachment during the course of his arduous experiences. He had "traveled the roads and quit home," had "journeyed to "many cities and countries," but "saw only misfortunes and troubles. (He travelled) in a land (suitable) for the society of outcasts . . . where being a Muslim was full of shame," a place "debauched and far from praise."[69]

Notes

1. James Morier, *The Adventures of Hajji Baba of Ispahan* (London: John Murray, 1824), vol. 1, pp. 19–21. See also Abbas Amanat, "Hajji Baba of Isfahan," *Encyclopaedia Iranica*.

2. Slavery and slave traffic in nineteenth-century Central Eurasia is a little-explored subject. One of the few works in the existing historiography to substantively touch upon the subject is Afsaneh Najmabadi's history of the Iranian Constitutional Revolution of 1906–11. See Afsaneh Najmabadi, *The Story of the Daughters of Quchan: Gender and National Memory in Iranian History* (Syracuse: Syracuse University Press, 1998), pp. 6–7.

3. For some analyses of the Persianate genre of the *safarnama*, see Muzaffar Alam and Sanjay Subrahmanyam, *Indo-Persian Travels in the Age of Discoveries, 1400–1800* (Cambridge: Cambridge

University Press, 2006); Nile Green, *Bombay Islam: The Religious Economy of the West Indian Ocean, 1840-1915* (Cambridge, 2011); Green, "Journeymen, Middlemen: Travel, Trans-Culture and Technology in the Origins of Muslim Printing," *International Journal of Middle East Studies* 41, 2 (2009), pp. 203–24; Green, "Among the Dissenters: Reciprocal Ethnography in Nineteenth-Century Inglistan," *Journal of Global History* 4, 2 (2009), pp. 293–315; Naghmeh Sohrabi, *Signs Taken for Wonder: Nineteenth-Century Travel Accounts from Iran to Europe* (Oxford: Oxford University Press, 2012); Mohamad Tavakoli-Targhi, *Refashioning Iran: Orientalism, Occidentalism, and Nationalist Historiography* (Basingstoke, UK: Palgrave, 2001); Iraj Afshar, "Persian Travelogues: A Description and Bibliography," in Elton Daniel, ed., *Society and Culture in Qajar Iran: Studies in Honor of Hafez Farmayan* (Costa Mesa, CA: Mazda Publishers, 2002), pp. 145–62; Arash Khazeni, "Across the Black Sands and the Red: Travel Writing, Nature, and the Reclamation of the Eurasian Steppe, circa 1850," *International Journal of Middle East Studies* 42, 4 (2010), pp. 591–614.

4. In 1841, Major James Abbott estimated that there were 700,000 slaves in the Khanate of Khiva, roughly one-third of the total population. In the city of Khiva alone there were 30,000 Persian and 12,000 Herati slaves. See James Abbott, *The Journey from Heraut to Khiva, Moscow and St. Petersburgh* (London: Wm. H. Allen and Company, 1843), vol. 2, p. xliv.

5. For some better-known examples of these texts, see Riza Quli Khan Hidayat, *Safaratnama-yi Khwarazm* [*Relation de l'Ambassade au Kharezm. Texte Persan*], ed. Charles Schefer (Paris: Ernest Leroux, 1876); Nasir al-Din Shah Qajar, *Safarnama-yi Khurasan* (1283/1865) (Tehran: Intisharat-i Farhang-i Iran Zamin, 1354/1975); Nasir al-Din Shah Qajar, *Safarnama-yi Duvvum-i Khurasan* (1300/1882) (Tehran: Intisharat-i Kavush, 1363/1984); Muhammad Hasan Khan Sani' al-Dawla I'timad-al-Saltana, *Matla' al-Shams, Tarikh-i Arz-i Aqdas va Mashhad-i Muqaddas, dar Tarikh va Jughrafiya-yi Mashruh-i Balad va Imakan-i Khurasan*, 2 vols. (Tehran: Farhangsara, 1362/1983). For other Persian accounts of nineteenth-century Central Asia, see Anonymous, *Safarnama-yi Bukhara*, ed. Husayn Zamani (Tehran: Vizarati Farhang, 1373/1994); "Safarnama-yi Herat" (1267/1850), in *Sih Safarnama: Herat, Marv, Mashhad*, ed. Qudrat Allah Rushani Zafaranlu (Tehran: Danishgah-i Tehran, 1347/1968), pp. 1–71; Sayyid Muhammad Lashkarnivis Nuri, "Safarnama-yi Marv" (1277/1859), in *Sih Safarnama*, pp. 73–144; Mirza Ibrahim, *Safarnama-yi Astarabad* (1276–1277/1859), ed. Mas'ud Gulzari (Tehran: Bunyad-i Farhang-i Iran, 1355/1976); 'Abdallah Khan Qaragazlu, *Majmu'a-yi Athar*, ed. Inayatallah Majidi (Tehran: Miras-i Maktub, 1382/2003); Qaragazlu, "Kitabchih-yi Marv," *Majmu'a-yi Athar*; Muhammad 'Ali Munshi, *Safarnama-yi Rukn al-Mulk bih Sarakhs*, ed. Muhammad Gulbun (Tehran: Danishgah-i Tehran, 1356/1977); and "Guzarish-i Muhammad Husayn Muhandis" (1893), in *Safarnama-yi Rukn al-Mulk bih Sarakhs*.

6. The literature on this subject is vast. For some examples, see John Demos, *The Unredeemed Captive: A Family Story from Early America* (New York: Vintage, 1994); Linda Colley, *Captives: Britain, Empire, and the World, 1600–1850* (New York: Anchor, 2004); and Colley, *The Ordeal of Elizabeth Marsh: A Woman in World History* (New York: Pantheon, 2007).

7. Mirza Mahmud Taqi Ashtiyani, *'Ibratnama: Khatirati az Dawran-i Pas az Jangha-yi Herat va Marv*, ed. Husayn 'Imadi Ashtiyani (Tehran: Nashr-i Markaz, 1382/2003), pp. 26–28. For another example of a nineteenth-century Persian captivity narrative about Central Asia, see Sarhang Isma'il Mirpanja, *Khatirat-i Asarat: Ruznama-yi Safar-i Khvarazm va Khiva* (1280/1862), ed. Safa' al-Din Tabarrayan (Tehran: Mu'assasa-yi Pajhuhish va Mutala'at-i Farhangi, 1370/1991). Also see Vassili Mikhailov, *Adventures of Michailow, a Russian Captive among the Calmucs, Kirghiz, and Kiwenses* (London, 1822). For some nineteenth-century European-language captivity narratives, see Henri de Coulboeuf de Blocqueville, "Quatorze mois de captivité, chez les Turcomans aux frontières du Turkestan et de la Perse, 1860–1861 (Frontières du Turkestan et de la Perse)," *Le Tour du Monde* (Paris: Hachette, 1866), pp. 225–72; Edmund O'Donovan, *The Merv Oasis: Travels and Adventures East of the Caspian During the Years 1879–1880–1881, Including Five Months' Residence Among the Tekkes of Merv*, 2 vols. (London: Sir R. Phillips and Company, 1882).

8. See Abu'l Ghazi Bahadur Khan, *Shajara-yi Tarakima (Histoire des Mogols et des Tatares)*, trans. Baron Desmaisons (Saint Petersburg: Imprimerie de l'Académie Impériale des sciences, 1871), vol. 1, pp. 221, 312; vol. 2, pp. 207, 291. For further discussion of the Oxus shift, see Arash Khazeni, "The River's Edge: The Steppes of the Oxus and the Boundaries of the Near East and Central Asia," in Abbas Amanat, Michael Bonine, and Michael Gasper, eds., *Is There a Middle East? The Evolution of a Geopolitical Construct* (Stanford: Stanford University Press, 2011).

9. On this "Turko-Persian" space, see Canfield (1991).

10. The buoyancy of early modern trade in Central Asia has recently been discussed in Scott Levi, *The Indian Diaspora in Central Asia and Its Trade, 1550–1900* (Leiden: Brill, 2002). See also Canfield (1991), p. 21.

11. V. V. Barthold, *Four Studies on the History of Central Asia*, vol. 3: *A History of the Turkman People*, trans. V. Minorsky and T. Minorsky (Leiden: Brill, 1962), p. 144.

12. Riza Quli Khan Hidayat, *Safaratnama-yi Khvarazm*, p. 27.

13. In the early seventeenth century, the task of administering and preserving order on this imperial frontier was entrusted to Firaydun Khan (d. 1621), the governor of Astarabad. Firaydun Khan's campaigns against the Turkmen during this time are related in a *fathnama* (book of victory), penned by Muhammad Tahir Bastami, with the title *Futuhat-i Firayduniya*. Interestingly, the author of *Futuhat-i Firayduniya* makes no mention of the Oxus or Ab-i Amuya, instead providing a more modest view of the Atrak and Gurgan rivers as the eastern boundaries of Iran. See Muhammad Tahir Bastami, *Futuhat-i Firayduniya: Sharh-i Jangha-yi Firaydun Khan Charkas-i Amir al-Umara-yi Shah 'Abbas-i Avval*, ed. Mir Muhammad Sadiq and Muhammad Nadir Nasiri-Muqaddam (Tehran: Nashr-i Nuqta, 1380/2001). See also Barthold (1962), vol. 3, p. 146.

14. Charles Marvin, *Merv, the Queen of the World; and the Scourge of the Man-Stealing Turcomans* (London: W. H. Allen and Company, 1881), pp. 178–79.

15. For an account of the episode, see British Library, India Office Records/F/4/1381, January–December 1831.

16. On the campaigns of 'Abbas Mirza against the Turkmen in Khurasan as recorded in Qajar chronicles, see Fazlallah Shirazi, *Tarikh-i Zu al-Qarnayn*, vol. 2, ed. Nasir Afsharfar (Tehran: Kitabkhana-yi Majlis, 1380/2001), pp. 819–36, 872–87; Lisan al-Mulk Sipihr, *Nasikh al-Tavarikh*, ed. Jamshid Kiyanfar (Tehran: Asatir, 1377/1998), vol. 1, pp. 457, 483–88, 500–505; Riza Quli Khan Hidayat, *Rawzat al-Safa-yi Nasiri*, ed. Jamshid Kiyanfar (Tehran: Asatir, 1380/2001), vol. 9, pp. 7948, 8022–29. See also Gavin Hambly, "Iran during the Reigns of Fath 'Ali Shah and Muhammad Shah," in *The Cambridge History of Iran*, vol. 7: *From Nadir Shah to the Islamic Republic* (Cambridge: Cambridge University Press, 1991), p. 166; Homa Nategh, "'Abbas Mirza va Turkamanan-i Khurasan," *Nigin* 10, 112 (1974), pp. 13–17; and Abbas Amanat, "Herat Question," in *Encyclopaedia Iranica*.

17. Hambly (1991), p. 169.

18. For narratives of the disastrous Persian campaign on Merv in 1861, see Hamza Mirza, *Safarnama-yi Hamza Mirza: Sharh-i Lashkarkashi-yi 1276 Hijri Qamari bih Marv*, ed. Muhsin Rahmati (Tehran: Nashr-i Tarikh, 1387/2009), and Blocqueville (1866), pp. 225–72.

19. Abbas Amanat, *Pivot of the Universe: Nasir al-Din Shah and the Iranian Monarchy, 1851–1896* (Berkeley: University of California Press, 1997), pp. 225–32.

20. Anonymous, *Safarnama-yi Bukhara*, pp. 72–73.

21. Population figures based on James Baillie Fraser, *Narrative of a Journey into Khorasan in 1821 and 1822* (London: Longman, Hurst, Rees, Orme, Brown, and Green, 1825); Alexander Burnes, *Travels into Bokhara; Being the Account of a Journey from India to Cabool, Tartary, and Persia*, 3 vols. (London: John Murray, 1834); Anonymous, *Safarnama-yi Bukhara*; Arminius Vambery, *Travels in Central Asia: Being the Account of a Journey from Teheran across the Turkoman Desert on the Eastern Shore of the Caspian to Khiva, Bokhara, and Samarcand Performed in the Year 1863* (London: John Murray, 1864); FO 60/379, "Report by Ronald Thomson on the Toorkoman tribes occupying districts

between the Caspian and the Oxus" (Tehran, February 29, 1876); Marvin (1881); and Henri Moser, *A Travers l'Asie Centrale* (Paris: Librarie Plon, 1885).

22. Writing in the 1920s, the pioneering scholar of Central Asia V. V. Barthold claimed to have come across only one reference to Turkmen merchants and traders, that of the history of Abu'l Ghazi. See Barthold (1962), p. 154. But this is not necessarily the case. For instance, the anonymous author of *Safarnama-yi Bukhara* noted that he encountered the *rish safidan* of the Tekke Turkmen traveling with the caravan of the Malik al-Tujar near Sarakhs. See Anonymous, *Safarnama-yi Bukhara*, pp. 24–25.

23. Qaragazlu, *Majmu'a-yi Athar*, pp. 129, 133–34. For an account of the bazaar of Merv in the late nineteenth century, see O'Donovan (1882), vol. 2, pp. 321–37.

24. 'Abdallah Khan Qaragazlu, *Majmu'a-yi Athar*, pp. 128–29.

25. Qaragazlu, *Majmu'a-yi Athar*, p. 129.

26. Joseph Pierre Ferrier, *Caravan Journeys and Wanderings in Persia, Afghanistan, Turkistan, and Beloochistan* (London: John Murray, 1856), pp. 93–94.

27. Ibid., pp. 94–95.

28. Ibid., p. 95.

29. Joseph Wolff, *Travels and Adventures of the Reverend Joseph Wolff* (London: Saunders, Otley, and Company, 1861), vol. 1, p. 285.

30. The *sarhadd dar* of Sarakhs in the mid-1870s estimated that, at the most, merely two to three caravans per year traveled from Mashhad to Sarakhs. See Qaragazlu, *Majmu'a-yi Athar*, pp. 89, 97, 102. In another late nineteenth-century account, it is reported that due to the raids of the Tekke Turkmen, the eastern Merv Gate had been closed and covered with earth. See Muhammad 'Ali Munshi, *Safarnama-yi Rukn al-Mulk bih Sarakhs*, p. 81.

31. Moser (1885), p. 324.

32. Ferrier (1856), p. 85.

33. Arthur Conolly, *Journey to the North of India, Overland from England, through Russia, Persia, and Affghaunistaun* (London: Richard Bentley, 1834), vol. 1, p. 59.

34. Lisan al-Mulk Sipihr, *Nasikh al-Tavarikh*, vol. 3, pp. 1193–1194.

35. Ferrier (1856), p. 85.

36. Ibid., p. 86.

37. Shirazi, *Tarikh-i Zu al-Qarnayn*, vol. 2, p. 764.

38. Ferrier (1856), p. 85.

39. Shirazi, *Tarikh-i Zu al-Qarnayn*, vol. 2, pp. 826–27.

40. Ferrier (1856), p. 87.

41. Conolly (1834), vol. 1, pp. 181–82.

42. Moser (1885), p. 248.

43. Wolff's statement that "200,000 Persian slaves are sighing in the kingdom of Bokhara" implies a British imperial (and masculine) mission in Central Asia. See Wolff (1861), vol. 1, p. 176. For an estimate of the number of slaves in nineteenth-century Khiva, see Marvin (1881), p. 181.

44. In addition to the account of Mirza Mahmud Taqi Ashtiyani, there are other extant captivity narratives written by those taken as slaves following the 1860 Merv campaign. See Sarhang Isma'il Mirpanja, *Khatirat-i Asarat: Ruznama-yi Safar-i Khvarazm va Khiva*, and Blocqueville (1866), pp. 225–72.

45. Ashtiyani, *'Ibratnama*, pp. 23–24.

46. Ibid., pp. 26–28.

47. Ibid., pp. 60–61.

48. Ibid., pp. 28–29.

49. Ibid., p. 54.

50. Ibid., p. 29.

51. Ibid., pp. 29–30.
52. Ibid., p. 32.
53. Ibid., p. 72.
54. Ibid., p. 74.
55. Ibid., p. 40.
56. Ibid., p. 29.
57. Ibid., pp. 80–83.
58. Ibid., p. 32.
59. Ibid., p. 34.
60. Ibid., p. 29.
61. Ibid., p. 83.
62. Ibid., pp. 39–40.
63. Ibid., pp. 36–39.
64. Ibid., pp. 36–39.
65. Ibid., p. 44.
66. Ibid., p. 52.
67. Ibid., pp. 81–82.
68. Ibid., p. 72.
69. In Persian, the verse begins as follows: "Pas az tayy-i rah u qata' manazil, dar an khakam iqamat gasht hasil / Basi shahr u balad kardam siyahat, chu ahl-i an nadidam bi sa'adat."

PART II
EMPIRE, ARCHAEOLOGY,
AND THE ARTS, C. 1850–1940

5 "The Rubicon between the Empires"

The River Oxus in the Nineteenth-Century British Geographical Imaginary

Kate Teltscher

"THERE ARE MANY places, scattered over the world, that are hallowed ground in the eyes of Englishmen," begins Thomas Kington-Oliphant's *The Sources of Standard English* (1873), "but the most sacred of all would be the spot (could we only know it) where our forefathers dwelt in common with the ancestors of the Hindoos, Persians, Greeks, Latins, Slavonians and Celts—a spot not far from the Oxus."[1] It is a measure of the widespread acceptance of racial thinking in 1870s Britain that a history of the English language should start with an invocation of an Aryan homeland. If the precise location of the holy ground was unknown, it was marked by proximity to the river Oxus. To nineteenth-century British writers, the Oxus was one of the most mysterious and evocative rivers in the world; impossibly remote, yet intimately connected through imagined Aryan ties to Britain. What were the multiple factors that contributed to the nineteenth-century British notion of the river? In this chapter, I will examine the intersecting literary, racial, and imperial discourses that combined to make the Oxus a river of texts.

In adapting the concept of a "road of texts" that Nile Green outlines in the introduction to this volume, I want to suggest a more fluid mode of exchange and influence. The river of texts is one that dissolves fixed distinctions of genre. British writing on the Oxus draws on multiple sources: a poem feeds into accounts of exploration, racial theories mingle with imperial debate. Like Green's road of texts, the tributaries are multilingual. A Persian epic provides the source for an English poem; German philologists furnish the notion of an Aryan homeland; British and Russian geographers engage in furious scholarly debate. The river of texts meanders through different time zones: an imagined Aryan past, the heroic age of Persian epic, and contemporary dip-lomatic negotiation. The writers are diverse yet constantly draw on one another's work: adventurers and geographers, a major Victorian poet, and two British schoolgirls.

The texts that I discuss date from the 1840s to the 1930s, the period that saw a complete transformation in the travel infrastructure of Central Asia. In the 1840s, the journey to the river Oxus was a hazardous horseback affair; by the 1880s, the river could be viewed from the comfort of a Trans-Caspian railway carriage. At the start of the period, British-sponsored travel in the region took the form of clandestine intelligence-gathering missions; by the end of the century, official groups of British and Russian surveyors charted the upper reaches of the Oxus for Boundary Commis-sions. The river Oxus moved from the inaccessible to the known over the course of the century, but it also accrued a dense mythologizing fog as the supposed birthplace of the Aryan race.

The course of the textual Oxus did not run straight, but neither did the actual river. The Oxus was notoriously hard to fix, being one of the world's great wandering rivers, in ancient times discharging into the Caspian Sea, then into the Aral Sea. But for all its fluctuations, the Oxus paradoxically served as a boundary marker. Persian scholars knew of it as the river that divided Iran from Turan (Central Asia). For the classically educated, the Oxus evoked the exploits of Alexander the Great. According to Arrian, the Oxus was the formidable barrier crossed by Alexander in his pursuit of Bessus, the Persian leader. Undeterred by the width or depth of the river, the absence of boats or timber with which to build a bridge, Alexander ordered his men to fashion rafts by stuffing the skins that covered their tents with hay. It took five days to ferry the army across the river, a feat that awed the Persians into surrender, with Bessus's own courtiers betraying him to the Greeks.[2]

For the nineteenth-century British, the Oxus—always known by its Greek name rather than as the Amu Darya—continued to be associated with boundaries and the possibility of military conflict. The Oxus came to prominence in diplomatic negotia-tions between Britain and Russia in the 1870s over the extent of Afghanistan. From the mid-1860s, Russia's steady advance into Central Asia had been greeted with alarm in British India. It was the Russian occupation of Khokand (1866) and Bokhara (1867–68) that focused attention on the ill-defined border of Afghanistan. In 1873, the British and Russians reached an agreement that the as yet uncharted Upper Oxus should mark Afghanistan's northern boundary. But the diplomatic talks ended without for-mal exchange of notes, and the same year saw the Russian occupation of the Khanate of Khiva. It was uncertain how far the Russians would respect the line of the Oxus, a problem compounded by the fact that the river was not clearly mapped.

For the next two decades, the Oxus was a crucial marker in negotiations to delimit Afghan territory. The Anglo-Russian boundary commission of 1885–88 took the Oxus as the end point of its survey of Afghanistan's northwestern border, and in 1895, Rus-sian and British surveyors met at Lake Sarikol, one of the sources of the Oxus, to fix the boundary eastward toward China. The Oxus represented not only the frontier of Afghanistan but, more significantly, the boundary between spheres of Russian and British influence. According to the geographer Henry Creswicke Rawlinson, the Oxus was laden with political and military significance. Invoking the river that in classical times marked the border of Rome (and which, if crossed by troops, amounted to an act of war), Rawlinson dubbed the Oxus "the Rubicon between the Empires."[3]

John Wood's Lake

The first significant British account of the Upper Oxus is John Wood's *Narrative of a Journey to the Source of the River Oxus*, first published by John Murray in 1841 and reissued in 1872 with a long introductory essay by Henry Yule. Wood was a naval lieutenant who accompanied Alexander Burnes as assistant on the 1836 mission to Afghanistan. Wood's brief was to survey the Indus and surrounding land, to ascertain the navigability of the river and the mineral wealth of the region. During the course of his travels, he managed to gain permission from Mir Murad Beg, the Uzbek ruler of Qunduz, to extend his expedition: "The great object of my thought by day and dreams by night," Wood writes, "had for some time past been the discovery of the source of the river Oxus."[4]

Halfway through, the *Narrative* shifts gears and turns into a geographical and personal quest, as Wood adopts the role of the single-minded adventurer. Indeed, it is almost as if the text starts again, at chapter 15, when he embarks on the journey of discovery. Clad in local dress and taking only the minimum of baggage, Wood sets off on horseback with his entourage of servants. Wood and his party are beset by deep snow, the threat of avalanches, and treacherous ice as they travel upstream. He must decide which path to take when the valley of the Oxus divides in two. Which of the two valleys and streams leads to the source of the Oxus: the northern (Pamir) or the southern (Sarhad)? Judging from the water temperature, velocity, and volume, Wood opts for the northern stream (Pamir) and follows it to Lake Sarikol.

Their arrival at the lake is heralded by the discovery of a Kirghiz burial ground, which prompts thoughts of man's transience and the divine. Having thus consecrated the spot, Wood ascends a low hill, where, "at five o'clock in the afternoon of the 19th of February, 1838, we stood, to use a native expression, upon the *Bam-i-Dúniah*, or *"Roof of the World*," while before us lay stretched a noble but frozen sheet of water, from whose western end issued the infant river of the Oxus." The precise date and time accord the moment historic significance, and Wood amplifies the effect by considering dedicating the lake to the monarch: "As I had the good fortune to be the first European who in later times had succeeded in reaching the sources of this river, and, as shortly before setting out on my journey, we had received the news of her gracious Majesty's accession to the throne, I was much tempted to apply the name of Victoria to this, if I may so term, newly re-discovered lake."[5] Wood's claims as an explorer are unusually circumspect; he does not quite accord himself the full status of discoverer, nor does he allow himself to name the lake. Pride of place is awarded to Marco Polo (in whose footsteps he believes he is following), while he takes second place as the "first European . . . *in later times*" to have "*re*-discovered" the lake. Having contemplated the patriotic name, Wood rejects it as likely to cause confusion and opts instead for the local name "Lake Sirikol." But later nineteenth-century cartographers had fewer compunctions and adopted the name.[6] The imprimatur of Victoria laid claim to the source of the Oxus and suggested a parallel with the East African Lake Victoria, the source of that other great river, the Nile.[7]

If Wood could not fully indulge in the gestures of heroic exploration, he did allow himself a moment of reverential awe. As Mary Louise Pratt has noted, one of the conventions of colonial travel writing, much exploited by British explorers in search of the source of the Nile, was the "monarch-of-all-I-survey" trope, often associated with contemplation of an extensive view.[8] Wood's arrival on the Roof of the World may not actually offer a sweeping panorama, but he can imagine one. Walking across the frozen lake, he reflects on the many countries that owe their importance and wealth to the rivers that arise from this chain of mountains: "from it, as from a central point, their several streams diverge, each augmenting as it rolls onwards, until the ocean and the lake of Aral receive the swollen tribute, again to be given up, and in a circuit as endless as it is wonderful to be swept back by the winds of Heaven, and showered down in snowy flakes upon the self-same mountains from which it flowed."[9] From his vantage point on the Roof of the World, Wood sees entire courses of rivers with his far-reaching, geographic eye. The elevated situation seems to demand a heightened rhetoric. Wood's vision of a sublime hydrologic cycle broadens to embrace the many peoples whose lands are watered by the rivers:

> How strange and how interesting a group would be formed if an individual from each nation whose rivers have their first source in Pamir were to meet upon its summit; what varieties would there be in person, language, and manners; what contrasts between the rough, untamed, and fierce mountaineer and the more civilized and effeminate dweller on the plain; how much of virtue and of vice, under a thousand different aspects, would be met with among them all; and how strongly would the conviction press upon the mind that the amelioration of the whole could result only from the diffusion of early education and a purer religion![10]

The Roof of the World provides the meeting place for many races and types, differentiated by language, custom, and morals. Wood's ethnographic fantasy reaches its climax with a pious declaration of the primacy of Christian faith. His *Narrative* received the accolade of a Royal Geographical Society Gold Medal, and his rhapsodic outburst set the model for British writing about the Oxus: a grand vision that associated the river with the sacred and equated it with the stream of mankind.

Matthew Arnold's Majestic River

Just over a decade after Wood's *Narrative* was published, the Oxus made its first full-length appearance in an English poem, Matthew Arnold's *Sohrab and Rustum* (1853). Arnold retells an episode from the legendary exploits of the Persian hero Rustum in Homeric style, using the blank verse associated with English epic form. The Persian and Tartar armies are encamped by the banks of the Oxus, the wide, yellow river of the plains. Sohrab, a young Tartar warrior, is seeking his Persian father, the mighty Rustum, who does not know of his son's existence. To prove his valor, Sohrab dares a Persian champion to meet him in single combat, and the disguised Rustum takes up the challenge. The epic struggle between father and son ends when Sohrab receives his death wound. In his final moments, Sohrab reveals his identity to his anguished father. The poem is introduced by Arnold with a note on his sources. He came to the story, he writes, through two accounts of Firdausi's *Shahnama* published in European works: a footnote in Sir John Malcolm's *History of Persia* (1815) and a version in an essay by Charles Augustin Sainte-Beuve.[11] Neither of these accounts makes much of the setting of the encounter between father and son; it is not mentioned in Sainte-Beuve's version, and there is only a passing reference to the Tartar army crossing the Oxus in Malcolm's summary. But Arnold shifts the focus so that the Oxus is center stage in *Sohrab and Rustum.*

Arnold's conception of the river seems to have been taken from Alexander Burnes's best-selling Great Game account of his first mission to Afghanistan and Persia, *Travels into Bokhara* (1834). Burnes appended a "General and Geographical Memoir" to the second volume of his *Travels*, which included a chapter on the Oxus, tracing the river's course from the "table-lands of Pamere" to the "swampy delta" near the Aral Sea.[12] Burnes described the annual floods caused by melting snow in the upper reaches of the Oxus. He emphasized the military and commercial significance of the river as the most direct conduit between Europe and Central Asia. This larger Central Asian topography provides the frame for Arnold's epic. The poem opens with the early morning fog rising from the river. After a sleepless night, Sohrab leaves his tent and passes through the camp, along

> Of Oxus, where the summer-floods o'erflow
> When the sun melts the snows in high Pamere. (lines 13–15)

The river extends all the way back to its lofty source. The sense of connection between the river of the plains and the snows of the mountains recalls Burnes's account of the annual inundation and Wood's far-reaching geographic eye. At the place of the encampment, however, the Oxus takes on its geopolitical significance as the border between Persian and Tartar territory. The armies are massing for battle, but large-scale slaughter is averted through Sohrab's proposal of individual combat. The two heroic antagonists, leaders of opposed nations, are in fact much more intimately related than they know, so that the river operates as a site of both conflict and affiliation.

Throughout the encounter, the Oxus is closely associated with the central protagonists. The Oxus sands, glittering at the start of the poem, are whipped into a whirlwind by the combat between father and son and stained with blood by the end. The word "sand" recurs with almost incantatory insistence and is identified with Sohrab's tragic end: "Come, sit beside me on this sand," Sohrab urges his father, "Quick, quick! For numbered are my sands of life" (lines 718, 721). The river even responds to the drama unfolding on its banks. When Rustum's marvelous horse Ruksh roars in horror at the combat, the Oxus, we are told, "curdled" (line 508). In the moments before Sohrab's death, Rustum calls for the Oxus to take his life:

> Oh that I saw its grains of yellow silt
> Roll, tumbling in the current, o'er my head! (lines 768–70)

But Rustum is spared death to grieve for his son. The action concludes with Rustum in solitary mourning by Sohrab's corpse; both father and son are shrouded in a fog that "Crept from the Oxus" (line 868). If the action ends at that point, the poem does not. *Sohrab and Rustum* is famous for the final stanza that retreats from the tragic scene by following the course of the "majestic River." The traveler George Littledale observed that the poem's final verse "showed how the imaginative faculty might be linked with physical geography."[13] Arnold's vision once again seems indebted to Burnes, encompassing the entire length of the Oxus from its source, through deserts and marshland, down to the Aral Sea. The flow and extent of the river is conveyed by an ever-extended single sentence that runs inexorably on to the river's mouth:

> Out of the mist and hum of that low land,
> Into the frosty starlight, and there moved,
> Rejoicing, through the hush'd Chorasmian waste,
> Under the solitary moon;—he flow'd
> Right for the polar star, past Orgunjè,
> Brimming, and bright, and large; then sands begin
> To hem his watery march, and dam his streams,
> And split his currents; that for many a league
> The shorn and parcell'd Oxus strains along
> Through beds of sand and matted rushy isles—
> Oxus, forgetting the bright speed he had
> In his high mountain-cradle in Pamere,
> A foil'd circuitous wanderer—till at last
> The long'd-for dash of waves is heard, and wide
> His luminous home of waters opens, bright
> And tranquil, from whose floor the new-bathed stars
> Emerge, and shine upon the Aral Sea. (lines 875–92)

The length of the syntax and meter enact the meanderings of the river; the polysyllabic "foil'd circuitous wanderer" (line 888) disrupts the iambic pentameter and conveys the river's frustration at its serpentine course. Indeed, the verse sentence is so long that the reader shares the river's relief at its eventual arrival at the "long'd-for" destination. The final stanza shifts the river away from its close emotional identification with the poem's two central protagonists. The Oxus grows in stature and assumes a detached grandeur that dwarfs the vicissitudes of human life. Paradoxically, at the same time that the river evinces such disregard for humanity, it is most fully personified, imagined as a male traveler, yearning for home. By the end, the river has eclipsed the humans to become the poem's central character himself.

The Cradle of Our Common Race

Arnold's conceit of the infant Oxus in "his high mountain-cradle in Pamere" intersects with contemporary German racial theories concerning the origins of mankind. The Pamirs were associated with the infancy of the human race. While Arnold's poem dramatizes the ties of blood between father and son, German linguists were exploring notions of consanguinity across nations. Comparative philologists interpreted the idea of an Indo-European language group in ethnological terms. From the early 1820s, German orientalists sought to shift the location of an Indo-European homeland away from India, where Friedrich Schelgel and other enthusiastic Indophiles had placed it. Philologists looked to the areas to the north and west of India in an attempt to avoid close kinship with a dark-skinned people. As Tuska Benes has demonstrated, it was the German linguist Julius Henry von Klaproth who first suggested that Germans originated in Central Asia.[14] In *Asia Polyglotta* (1832), Klaproth argues that humankind had survived the biblical flood by fleeing to the high points of the earth and that the Himalayas were one of these mountain retreats. By 1840, German linguists had situated the Aryan homeland in the region near the sources of the Oxus and the Jaxartes.

In Britain, these ideas were popularized by Friedrich Max Müller, professor of Sanskrit at Oxford and a pioneer in the fields of comparative philology, mythology, religion, and philosophy. In his widely read *Lectures on the Science of Language*, delivered in 1861, Max Müller imagined Central Asia as a kind of linguistic and racial watershed. According to Max Müller, "before the ancestors of the Indians and Persians started for the South, and the leaders of the Greek, Roman, Celtic, Teutonic, and Slavonic colonies marched towards the shores of Europe, there was a small clan of Aryans settled probably on the highest elevation of Central Asia, speaking a language, not yet Sanskrit or Greek or German, but containing the dialectical germs of all."[15] The origins of rivers, languages, and peoples coincided. From a spot near the sources of the Oxus and Jaxartes, the Aryans spread out across continents.

Racial and linguistic theory turned for support to comparative mythology, and the many rivers of the Pamirs were transformed into the well-watered paradises of

Aryan creation myths. In his 1872 introductory essay to Wood's account, the geographer Henry Yule could claim the region as "the centre of primeval tradition as well as modern theory regarding the primitive history of mankind."[16] The search for the source of the Oxus could be framed as a search for racial and religious origins: "Here is the one locality on the earth's surface to which . . . the Mosaic narrative points, in unison with the traditions of Aryan nations, as the cradle of our common race."[17] Arnold's "high-mountain cradle in Pamere" may have influenced Yule's "cradle of our common race," but Yule's resonant phrase gained a currency of its own. In 1884, for instance, the president of the Royal Geographical Society, Lord Aberdale, termed the region of the Upper Oxus "the cradle of the human race" from whence "the great Aryan race from which Englishmen were descended issued forth."[18] The last quarter of the nineteenth century saw the Oxus incorporated into Britain's racial and national mythology.

Gross Geographical Heresy

Celebrated as a primordial point of origin, the Oxus also played a significant role in contemporary politics. In the decades following the First Anglo-Afghan War and the British retreat from Kabul in 1842, the British had little chance of gaining access to Afghanistan. To fill the gaps in their geographical knowledge, the British trained Indians in the art of covert surveying, the so-called pundit surveyors who could travel relatively unobtrusively. But British geographers did not entirely trust the information that they supplied; the rudimentary training of the pundit surveyors, combined with the constraints of secrecy under which they operated, reinforced British prejudice against the reliability of Indian-gathered intelligence.

From the late 1860s, private individuals such as George Hayward and Robert Shaw made their way into Central Asia. Hayward received sponsorship from the Royal Geographical Society to explore the Pamirs but was killed en route to the region. Shaw's trading venture to Yarkand and Kashgar fared better, paving the way for the official missions of Douglas Forsyth to Yaqub Beg, ruler of Kashgar. Forsyth's second mission of 1873–74, sent to counter Russian influence at Kashgar, was a substantial intelligence-gathering expedition that generated a mass of new geographical material.[19] With growing suspicion of Russian intentions in the region came increased skepticism of the reliability of Russian geographical accounts. This distrust exploded in the late 1860s in an outburst of scholarly outrage orchestrated in chief by Henry Rawlinson. The Central Asian explorer and Conservative MP for Frome (1865–68), Rawlinson was considered Britain's foremost Central Asia expert and did not want for prominent platforms to express his views. Obsessed by the threat that Russia posed to India, Rawlinson was one of the most vocal advocates of a "forward" policy in Central Asia. Using his privileged position as vice president (1864–68) and then president of the Royal Geographical Society (1871–73, 1874–76), Rawlinson promoted Central Asian exploration (securing patronage for George Hayward, for example) and frequently broke the rule forbidding political discussion at meetings. In the 1860s, Rawlinson joined forces with

Lord Strangford, president of the Royal Asiatic Society, to uncover what they claimed was a case of geographical fraud that had grievously distorted the cartography of Central Asia. Never one to stint his rhetoric, Rawlinson asserted that the hoax had "caused the spurious delineation of the hydrography of the Upper Oxus to be introduced into almost every Russian and German map of Central Asia that has been recently published, and has thus hitherto vitiated all our geographical knowledge and produced universal confusion."[20]

Rawlinson and Strangford engaged in heated discussion with two Russian geographers, Khanikoff and Veniukoff, over the authenticity of manuscripts recently discovered in the Saint Petersburg archives: one was an account of a Central Asian journey written by an anonymous German, the other, a Chinese itinerary. The British geographers claimed that these manuscripts, and an additional one, lodged in the British Foreign Office, the report of a secret Russian geographical expedition sent by the emperor Paul I to find an overland route to India, were in fact hoaxes.[21] They attributed these forgeries to none other than the German orientalist Julius Klaproth, chief architect of the idea of the Central Asian Aryan homeland. Since the Foreign Office had reputedly paid 1,000 guineas for the purchase of the manuscript, Strangford and Rawlinson concluded that Klaproth had devised the documents for financial gain. Klaproth's authorship was proved by geographical errors shared by all three manuscripts that were untraceable to any other source. Some of these mistakes had found their way into John Arrowsmith's map of Central Asia of 1834, long considered authoritative.[22]

A controversial figure in his lifetime, Klaproth was both a likely suspect and an easy target. He was a phenomenal linguist whose knowledge of Central and East Asian languages far outstripped that of his European contemporaries. Although Klaproth held university professorships in Saint Petersburg and Bonn, his career had been tarnished by a number of scandals. He was suspected of stealing valuable manuscripts from libraries in Russia and alleged to have been a Prussian spy in Paris.[23] It was unclear where such a cosmopolitan and supposedly unscrupulous scholar's allegiances lay, "nor, perhaps," commented Henry Yule, "was there any contemporary capable of accomplishing a fraud of this kind so successfully."[24] In the course of a series of debates and articles, Strangford and Rawlinson repeatedly asserted British geographical rigor over Russian credulity, but their indignation was at least in part generated by the assumption that Klaproth had managed to deceive the British as well as the Russian government. In an effort to assert the integrity of British geographical knowledge against the "gross geographical heresy" of the foreign Klaproth, Wood's *Narrative* was reissued in 1872 as the work of "a genuine living English naval officer, whose work unmistakably expresses the author's truth, candour and good sense."[25]

The 1872 republication of Wood's *Narrative* with Yule's introductory essay "The Geography and History of the Upper Waters of the Oxus" was well timed by the publisher, John Murray. The British were keen to establish the extent of Afghanistan as a buttress against Russian advances in Central Asia. Diplomatic negotiation between

Britain and Russia in 1872 centered on the issue of the northern border of Afghanistan, and the British proposed the Upper Oxus as marking the frontier. For Henry Yule, the region was ominously poised between former and future historical significance: "its past history is interwoven with that of all the great Asiatic conquerors," he wrote, "whilst its coming history looms on the horizon rife with all the possibilities suggested by its position on the rapidly narrowing border-land between two great empires, one of them our own."[26]

In the 1870s, there was a flurry of geographical activity in Britain, collating the material available on the upper waters of the Oxus. This was part of a larger shift in attention toward Central Asia. As Geoff Watson has shown, from 1860 to 1880, the percentage of articles on Central Asia published in the *Journal of the Royal Geographical Society* more than tripled the figure for the previous decade. Between 1860 and 1880, articles on Central Asia accounted for some 15 percent of the *Journal*'s total content (slightly higher than the percentage devoted to Africa).[27] The geographers involved, most notably Rawlinson and Yule, were at the center of intersecting scholarly and political networks: the Royal Geographical Society and the Council of India. For Yule, who had recently published a massively annotated edition of Marco Polo's *Travels*, Polo's understanding of the geography of the Oxus was near visionary: "Information so far in advance of an author's own time is like prophecy, which only becomes clear in the light of its fulfilment."[28] This consecration of geographical knowledge suggests something of the contemporary significance of the region. Henry Trotter, member of Forsyth's 1873–74 mission to Kashgar, declared to the Royal Geographical Society that the unstinting research of Yule and Rawlinson had aroused among geographers "an almost sacred interest" in the Pamirs.[29]

Rawlinson was approached by the Foreign Office for advice on the issue of the Afghan frontier. Reflecting on the process of border negotiation in 1875, Rawlinson had cause to lament the sketchy state of geographical knowledge three years earlier. "Unfortunately our notions of the geography of the Upper Oxus in 1872 were somewhat hazy. We knew little or nothing of the bend of the river to the northward, between the two points explored by Wood . . . and our delineation of the upper feeders descending from Pamir was also far from accurate."[30] The gaps in geographical knowledge were compounded by a clerical error that left it unclear "which, among the several feeders of the Oxus was to be considered the main stream of the river."[31] By 1875, Rawlinson had rejected Wood's Lake Victoria as the source of the Oxus, favoring rather the Little Pamir Lake, discovered by Thomas Gordon, who had accompanied Forsyth on his second mission to Kashgar. The Little Pamir Lake, Rawlinson advised, should form the basis for future maps of Afghanistan.

Rawlinson's conception of Central Asia was as a region divided with almost symmetrical precision between the Russians and the British. Mapping parallels between the Russian frontier capital of Tashkent and the British Lahore, the Russian military post of Samarqand and the British Peshawar, Rawlinson saw "a very remarkable

similarity between the Russians and English positions in Central Asia, both politically and geographically." These parallels extended to Bokhara on the Russian side and
Cabul on the British, with "the Oxus being the ultimate and common boundary."[32] For
Rawlinson, it was a precariously maintained balance, a rivalry that always threatened
to tip into conflict.

Relations between the British and Russians deteriorated in 1878 when Sher 'Ali,
the ruling Afghan *amir*, received a Russian mission at Kabul but refused a British
one. To avenge the perceived insult, the British viceroy, Lord Lytton, declared war on
Afghanistan. The Second Anglo-Afghan War (1878–80) ended with the installation
of Sher 'Ali's nephew, 'Abd al-Rahman, as *amir*. Suspicions of Russia's designs next
peaked with the Russian occupation of Merv, close to the Afghan city of Herat, in 1884,
for Rawlinson and many others considered Herat the gateway to British India. War
between Britain and Russia was only just averted the following year when the Russians
annexed the nearby oasis of Panjdeh, which lay within Afghan territory. By the terms
of their treaty, the British were required to come to Afghanistan's aid in the event of
external aggression, but the situation was defused when 'Abd al-Rahman agreed to
cede Panjdeh to the Russians, on condition that they renounce other claims to Afghan
territory.

The diplomatic solution to the Panjdeh Incident was played out in the geographical sphere with the establishment in 1885 of the Anglo-Russian Boundary Commission to determine Afghanistan's northwestern border. The relationship between British and Russian geographers was inevitably overshadowed by politics. A few months
after the Russian annexation of Merv in 1884, for instance, Robert Michell, a British subject who had spent much of his life in Russia, delivered an account of Russian
expeditions to the Upper Oxus to the Royal Geographical Society. In his introduction,
Michell dubbed the Russian emperor, Alexander III, "the Alexander of our age."[33] Pre-
dicting Russian intervention in Bokhara, Michell modeled Russian military tactics
on the irresistible progress of Alexander the Great's army across Central Asia. "There
are winged soldiers like those of the great Macedonian . . . even now in Asia," Michell
wrote. "[W]ord has only to go forth for the Russian eagles to rest on all the eyries
in Hissar, Kulab, and Darwaz, as on the Pamir at Kara-Kul Lake, which absolutely
command the entire basin of the Oxus river from its very sources."[34] As if the classical parallels were not enough, Michell added an allusion to the terrestrial paradise of
Aryan myth. "It is therefore to be expected," he declared, "that in due time the keys
of the gates of these paradises of Inner Asia will be suspended from the girdle of his
Imperial Majesty the Emperor of all the Russias."[35] A latter-day Alexander the Great
or secular Saint Peter (brandishing the keys to paradise), the Russian emperor loomed
over the region, threatening not only to annex the territory but to absorb its multiple
mythological resonances himself.

The Theodolite and Compass

The romance of the Oxus found its fullest expression in the final decades of the nineteenth century, paradoxically—but perhaps predictably—at the moment that it was more accessible than ever before. The Conservative MP and future viceroy of India George Nathaniel Curzon decided to make his name as an expert on Asian affairs. To this end, he embarked on a tour of Russia and Central Asia in 1888. Curzon traveled through Bokhara on the newly built Trans-Caspian railway, which he saw as dangerous evidence of the extent of Russian influence, its commercial and military capability. Curzon's first sight of the Oxus was through his carriage window. The once impossibly remote river, crossable only by an Alexander, was now spanned by a railway bridge. If the Trans-Caspian railway announced the triumph of modernity and Russian engineering, then the waters of the Oxus spoke to Curzon of antiquity. The train-traveling Curzon could not pose as heroic adventurer, but he could endow the river with epic stature. In his paean to the Oxus, Curzon reaches for many a superlative:

> No river, not even the Nile, can claim a nobler tradition, or a more illustrious history. Descending from the "Roof of the World," its waters tell of forgotten peoples, and whisper secrets of unknown lands. They are believed to have rocked the cradle of our race. Long the legendary watermark, between Iran and Turan, they have worn a channel deep into the fate of humanity. World-wide conquerors, an Alexander and a Tamerlane, slaked their horses' thirst in the Oxus stream; eastern poets drank inspiration from its fountains; Arab geographers boasted of it as "superior in volume, in depth, and in breadth to all the rivers of the earth."[36]

Drawing on the notion of an Aryan watershed and freely borrowing from Yule, Curzon invokes the myriad mythical and historical associations of the Oxus. Yule's "cradle of our common race" is now rocked by the Oxus, so that the river ministers as nursemaid to the Aryans. The nurturer of conquerors and poets, the Oxus is associated with the great achievements of humanity and reveals nothing less than the hidden origins of mankind.

For Curzon, the mystique of the Oxus was most fully conveyed by *Sohrab and Rustum*: "In my ears were continually ringing the beautiful words of Matthew Arnold, who alone of English poets has made the great Central Asian river the theme of his muse, and has realised its extraordinary and mysterious personality."[37] Curzon quotes sections of the poem both as a chapter epigraph and within the body of the text. He would have been of the generation to have read Arnold's *Sohrab and Rustum* at school. With its exotic locale, heroic combat, and poignant depiction of father-son relations, the poem quickly became a childhood favorite. "To some boys at Eton," the poet Algernon Charles Swinburne noted in 1867, Sohrab and Rustum "have been close and common friends," and the Oxus "familiar almost as the well-loved Thames."[38] In fact, Curzon attended Eton some five years after Swinburne's observation. By 1891, the poem had entered the canon of children's literature, included in W. E. Henley's much reprinted anthology *Lyra Heroica: A Book of Verse for Boys*.

The glamour and romance of childhood reading were again exploited by Curzon in his account to the Royal Geographical Society of his second trip to Central Asia. In 1894, Curzon embarked on an expedition to the Pamirs and the source of the Oxus in the company of Francis Younghusband. Curzon recalls his first encounter with the Oxus some six years previously and quotes part of the final stanza of *Sohrab and Rustum* (lines 875–79). But the river of the plains now holds few attractions for Curzon. On this second trip, he is drawn to the "high mountain-cradle in Pamere":

> And with the poet, my imagination had flown eastwards and upwards to that aerial source, and had longed to pierce the secrets that were hidden behind the glaciers of the Pamirs and the snowy sentinels of the Hindu Kush.[39]

By the 1890s, Arnold's epic had become so closely associated with the Oxus that such geographical flights of fancy were acceptable even in an address to a learned society.

Before Curzon formulates the geographical goal of his journey, he repeats and elaborates his earlier paean to the antiquity of the Oxus. The river figures as "that great parent stream of humanity, which has equally impressed the imagination of Greek and Arab, of Chinese and Tartar, and which, from a period over three thousand years ago, has successively figured in the literature of the Sanskrit Puranas, the Alexandrian historians, and the Arab geographers."[40] Curzon's hyperbolic "parent stream of humanity" fuses river with race and places the Oxus at the center of world history. Once the significance of the river has been thus established, Curzon announces his intention to find its source:

> Where did this great river really rise? Which among the several confluents of its upper course was the true parent stream? This was a question that had been obscured by the imperfect information or the erroneous hypotheses of previous travellers, as well as complicated by the diplomatic sophistries of rival statesmen.[41]

Curzon seeks to settle one of the major geopolitical puzzles of the previous fifty years: there were at least four contenders for the title of source of the Oxus. He makes the inflated claim to have located "the true and indisputable source of the Oxus" in a gushing stream issuing from two ice caves within a glacier near the Wakhjir Pass.[42] Peering inside one of the womblike caverns resonating with the "ceaseless noise of grinding, crunching and falling in," Curzon witnesses the birth of the river.[43] This sublime point of origin is, however, also a conclusion. For Curzon, "the era of exploration and discovery in this celebrated region" has come to an end. The geographical questions are now answered, and there can be "no legitimate cause of political quarrel." Having invoked the ancient secrets of the Oxus at the start of his account, Curzon concludes by dispelling them: "the mystery and romance of the Roof of the World," he writes, have "been extinguished by the theodolite and the compass . . . superseded by the accurate delineation of scientific maps."[44]

In declaring the death of the Oxus romance and the end of exploration, Curzon was asserting the final heroic adventure as his own. The Royal Geographical Society ratified his claims with the award of a gold medal. But of course Curzon protested too much. His "true and indisputable" source of the Oxus was simply one among several contenders. The

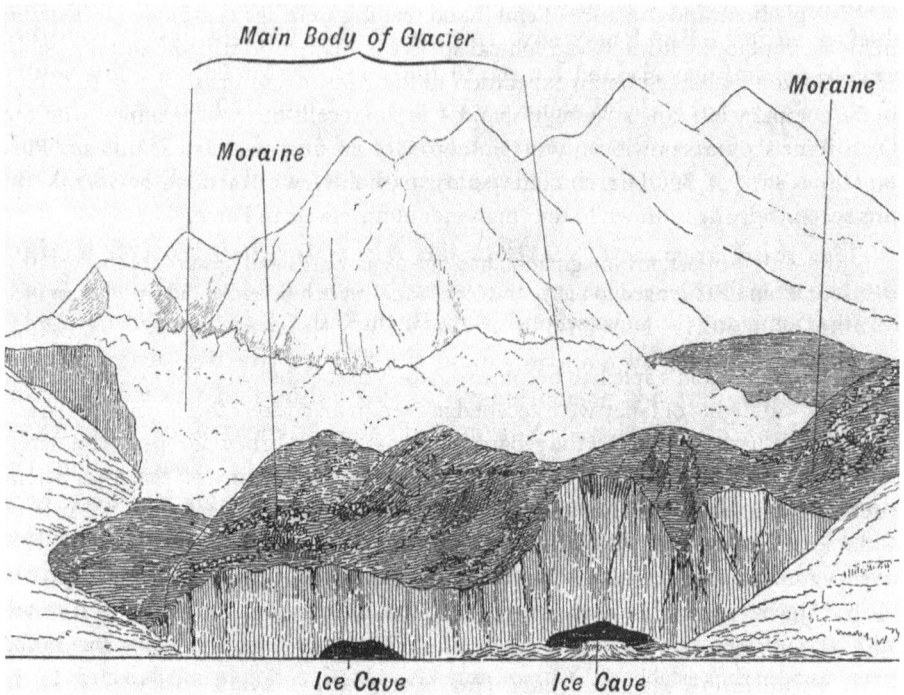

Figure 5.1. Lord Curzon's Ice Cave. Courtesy Royal Geographical Society (with IBG).

theodolites and compasses had indeed been at work throughout Curzon's expedition. The Pamir Boundary Commission of 1895 determined that it was impossible to establish which of four possible sources constituted the fountainhead of the Oxus. For this reason, the Anglo-Russian agreement of 1872–73 that had fixed the border of northern Afghanistan along the course of the upper Oxus proved unworkable on the ground. Moreover, the commission dismissed the very idea that rivers functioned as useful frontiers in the Pamirs. In a telling phrase that effectively rejected decades of geographical and diplomatic endeavor, the report asserted: "Geographically, politically, and ethnographically, watersheds and not rivers are the only true and stable boundaries in these regions."[45]

As the nineteenth century drew to its close, the British preoccupation with the upper reaches of the Oxus dwindled. It had been a fascination fueled by concern over Russian intentions in the region. Henry Rawlinson, probably the most persistent advocate of the need to amass geographical knowledge of the Oxus, acknowledged that "the political element was the most important subject of consideration." Without it, "the Upper Oxus and its tributaries would be comparatively of little interest."[46] The Boundary Commission of 1895 concluded that the Pamirs did not offer a likely path for invasion of India so that there was little to fear from the Russians from that quarter.

In the latter stages of surveying the Pamirs, the Boundary Commission's Russian and British surveyors met by the shores of Lake Victoria (Lake Sarikol). At a cordial

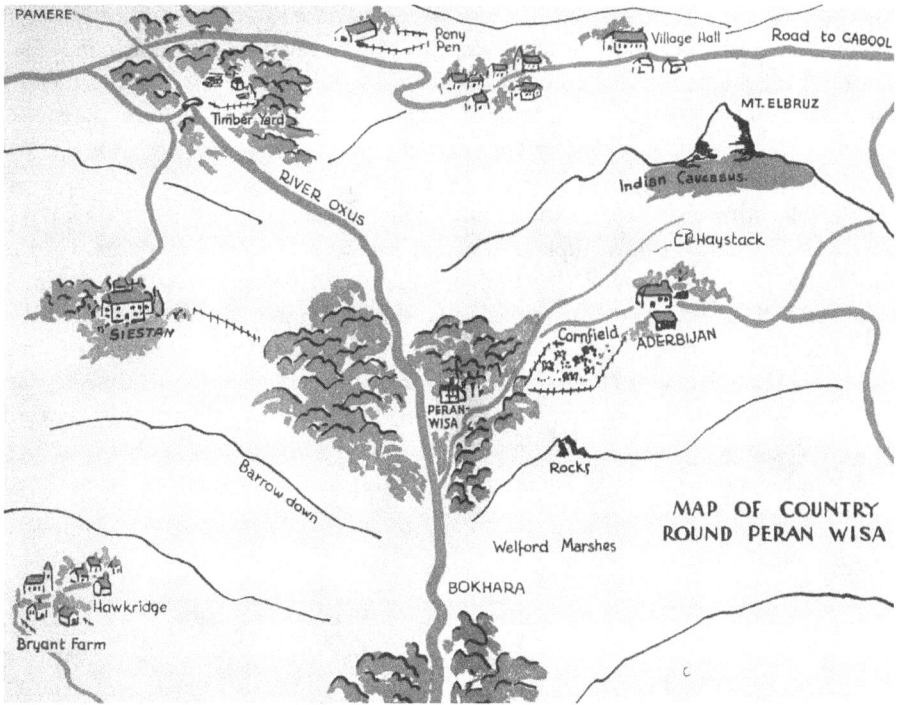

Figure 5.2. "The Far Distant Oxus," from Hull and Whitlock, *The Far Distant Oxus* (1937). Courtesy of Fidra Books.

Anglo-Russian dinner hosted by the British camp, the chief British surveyor proposed the health of the Russian emperor and suggested that some nearby mountains should be named Range Nicolas in his honor. Graciously reciprocating, the Russian commissioner proposed retaining the name "Lake Victoria" for Lake Sarikol on Russian maps. In a final gesture of goodwill, a mountain peak between Lake Victoria and Range Nicolas was named "La Concorde."[47] Carving up the Pamirs between them, the British and Russian surveyors drained the region of its poetic glamour and mythical significance. Familiarized through the rituals of dinner and diplomacy, the sources of the Oxus would never seem so remote and mysterious again.

Some forty years on, the domestication of the Oxus was complete. In 1937, two British schoolgirls, Katharine Hull, age fifteen, and her sixteen-year-old friend Pamela Whitlock, sent a manuscript of an adventure story to their great hero, the children's writer Arthur Ransome. So taken with the manuscript was Ransome that he secured a contract for the novel with Cape and supplied an introduction. *The Far-Distant Oxus* (1937) was modeled closely on Ransome's *Swallows and Amazons* but substituted ponies for boats. The novel borrowed its title from *Sohrab and Rustum*, reworking Arnold's poem as a children's adventure tale set one summer holiday on Exmoor in England. Lines from "Sohrab and Rustum" stood as chapter epigraphs, and the Exmoor countryside was transformed with place-names from the poem. As one of the characters explains: "Well, that's the River Oxus . . . and Peter and Jennifer live at Siestan. Cloud Farm is Aderbaijan and the range behind it the Indian Caucausus."[48] The children call the closest town "Cabool," give the name Bokhara to the nearby moor, and build a raft to ferry their belongings down the Oxus to the Aral Sea. The endpapers of the hardback first edition feature a map of the transfigured Exmoor setting. In the novel, the landscape of the Great Game becomes child's play indeed.

In relocating the Oxus to the English countryside, Hull and Whitlock's novel makes clear what was only implicit in earlier nineteenth-century accounts. For the British, the Oxus was as much a river of texts as an actual river. In retaining its Greek name, rather than the local one, Amu Darya, the British perpetuated the river's classical associations. It was the site of epic and mythmaking. Laden with the allure of the exotic, the Oxus transported the reader to an infinitely remote place and time, be that Alexander's Eastern Empire or the origins of the Aryan race. But the river also marked the borders of contemporary empires and resonated with the possibility of conflict. Nineteenth-century British anxieties about Central Asia converged on the imagined histories, unknowable course, and multiple sources of the river.

Notes

Thanks to Hartmut Walravens and Robert Middleton Bluewin for answering queries about Julius Klaproth.

1. T. L. Kington-Oliphant, *The Sources of Standard English* (London: Macmillan, 1873), p. 1.

2. E. J. Chinook, *Anabasis of Alexander; or the History of the Wars and Conquests of Alexander the Great* (London: Hodder & Stoughton, 1884), pp. 199–200.

3. H. C. Rawlinson, "Book review of H. Yule on *The Book of Ser Marco Polo*," *Edinburgh Review* 275 (1872a), p. 13.

4. J. Wood, *A Journey to the Source of the Oxus* (London: John Murray, 1872), p. 145.

5. Wood (1872), pp. 232–33.

6. A footnote in the 1872 edition suggests that future maps should use the name "Lake Victoria." For claims that the name "Sirikul" designated a caravan stage at the head of the lake and advocates the use of the name "Lake Victoria," see T. E. Gordon, *The Roof of the World* (Edinburgh: Edmonson & Douglas, 1876), pp. 161–62.

7. It was named "Lake Victoria" by John Hanning Speke in 1859.

8. Mary Louise Pratt, *Imperial Eyes: Travel Writing and Transculturation* (London and New York: Routledge, 1992), pp. 201–8.

9. Wood (1872), pp. 234–35.

10. Ibid., p. 235.

11. Sir John Malcolm, *History of Persia* (London: John Murray, 1829), vol. 1, pp. 27–28; C. A. Sainte-Beuve, *Causeries du Lundi* (Paris: Garnier Frères, 1857), vol. 1. pp. 343–50.

12. Alexander Burnes, *Travels into Bokhara: Being an Account of a Journey from India to Cabool, Tartary and Persia* (London: John Murray, 1834), vol. 2, pp. 186–87.

13. George Littledale, "A Journey across the Pamir from North to South," *Proceedings of the Royal Geographical Society* 14, 1 (1892), p. 29.

14. Tuska Benes, "Comparative Linguistics as Ethnology: In Search of Indo-Germans in Central Asia, 1770–1830," *Comparative Studies of South Asia, Africa and the Middle East* 24, 2 (2004), p. 128.

15. Friedrich Max Müller, *Lectures on the Science of Language* (London: Longmans, Green & Co., 1866), p. 238.

16. Wood (1872), p. xxi.

17. Ibid., p. xxi.

18. Lord Aberdale was commenting on Robert Michell, "The Regions of the Upper Oxus," *Proceedings of the Royal Geographical Society*, n.s., 6, 9 (1884), p. 501.

19. Publications generated by the mission include T. D. Forsyth, *Report of a Mission to Yarkund* (Calcutta: Foreign Department Press, 1875); T. E. Gordon, *The Roof of the World* (Edinburgh: Edmonson & Douglas, 1876); and H. Trotter, "On the Geographical Results of the Mission to Kashghar, under Sir T. Douglas Forsyth in 1873–4," *Journal of the Royal Geographical Society* 48 (1878).

20. Rawlinson (1872a), p. 17.

21. The British Foreign Office manuscript is titled "A Journey from the Sibirian frontier through Songaria and Little Bucharia to the western Tibet and the superior branch of the Indus, and from thence back over Badachschan, Kokan, Taschkend, through the Kirghizian step to Orskaia the most oriental fortress in European Russia performed in order to recognize the way over land to India, by a secret expedition, 1801 & 1802." King's College London Library, Foyle Special Collections, FCO Historical Collection, Oversize DS327.7 JOU.

22. Henry C. Rawlinson, "On the Trade Routes between Turkestan and India," *Proceedings of the Royal Geographical Society* 13, 1 (1868–91); Rawlinson (1872a); and Rawlinson, "Monograph on the Oxus," *Journal of the Royal Geographical Society* 42 (1872b), pp. 482–513.

23. Benes (2004), p. 128.

24. Wood (1872), p. liii.

25. Ibid., p. iii, liv.

26. Ibid., p. xxi.

27. Geoff Watson, "Siting the Stage: Representations of Central Asian Environments in British Literature," *New Zealand Journal of Asian Studies* 9, 1 (2007), p. 105.

28. Wood (1872), p. xliii.

29. Trotter (1878), p. 198.

30. Henry C. Rawlinson, *England and Russia in the East: A Series of Papers on the Political and Geographical Condition of Central Asia* (London: John Murray, 1875), p. 310.

31. Ibid.

32. Ibid., p. 303.

33. Michell (1884), p. 489.

34. Ibid., p. 490.

35. Ibid.

36. George Nathaniel Curzon, *Russia in Central Asia in 1889 and the Anglo-Russian Question* (London: Longmans, Green & Co., 1889), p. 144.

37. Ibid.

38. Algernon Charles Swinburne writing in *The Fortnightly Review*, quoted in S. T. Williams, "A Century of Matthew Arnold," *North American Review* 217, 806 (1923), p. 112.

39. Curzon (1896), p. 16.

40. Ibid., pp. 15–16.

41. Ibid., p. 16.

42. Ibid., p. 44.

43. Ibid., p. 45.

44. Ibid., p. 260.

45. M. G. Gerard et al., *Report on the Proceedings of the Pamir Boundary Commission* (Calcutta: Office of the Superintendent of Government Printing, 1897), p. 2.

46. Michell (1884), p. 506.

47. Gerard et al. (1897), p. 18.

48. Katharine Hull and Pamela Whitlock, *The Far-Distant Oxus* (London: Cape Hull and Whitlock, 1937), p. 55.

6 Buddhist Relics from the Western Regions

Japanese Archaeological Exploration of Central Asia

Imre Galambos

I N THE EARLY part of the twentieth century, beside the archaeological exploration of Chinese Turkestan by European explorers, many of whom represented colonial powers, there was also Japanese interest in the region. Most significant in this respect was the series of expeditions organized and financed by Count Ōtani Kōzui (1876–1948). The abbot of the Nishi Honganji branch of the Jōdo Shinshū sect, Ōtani was also a close relative of the imperial family, having married the elder sister of Empress Teimei, wife of the Emperor Taishō, who reigned from 1912. As one of the largest and wealthiest religious organizations in Japan, the Nishi Honganji of which Ōtani was abbot is the head temple for a Buddhist sect comprising ten thousand temples and twelve million followers. The temple is called Nishi (West) to distinguish it from the Higashi (East) Honganji; both temples are located close to each other in Kyoto. The original Honganji was established in the early fourteenth century, and amassed such an immense amount of wealth and power over time that when Tokugawa Ieyasu came to power in the early seventeenth century, he split the temple into an eastern and a western branch in order to reduce its influence. Both temples remained important into the modern period and are among the largest in Japan even today.

With the Meiji Restoration of 1868, Buddhism fell into a state of crisis in Japan as Shinto was established as the state religion and support for Buddhist institutions was withdrawn. The ensuing anti-Buddhist movement caused great damage and led to the destruction of temple property throughout the country. Temples were faced with the need to adapt to the new situation and redefine themselves.[1] The Honganji branch implemented a series of internal reforms, including a complete educational reform.

One of its important efforts in dealing with suppression was to dispatch clerics over-seas to establish contacts with other Buddhist communities and to learn about their practices.[2] The young Ōtani Kōzui, a man of exceptional talent and erudition who was at the time only the heir to the abbacy of the Nishi Honganji, traveled to a number of countries to study the role of religion in modern societies. He was trying to find alternative models for the survival of Buddhism in Japan and in the whole of Asia. It is against this background that the idea of the Central Asian expeditions was conceived, as this was the historical land through which Buddhism came from India to China and ultimately to Japan. The shared Buddhist past of East, Central, and South Asia seemed to provide a conceptual model for a pan-Asian revival under the aegis of Buddhism.[3]

With the Meiji Restoration, Japan instituted an ambitious policy of moderniza-tion, adopting European models for a new economic and legal infrastructure. By 1902, it had signed the Anglo-Japanese Alliance and taken its place among the colonial pow-ers. Along with modern science and technology came a distinct worldview, in which Japan saw itself among Western industrial powers rather than the rest of Asia. Thus, in addition to the traditional Sino-Japanese names of countries and regions, European geographical or geopolitical denominations were also widely used. The term "Shina" was used for "China" instead of the traditional "Shinkoku" (i.e., Qing empire), while Central Asia, which had not existed as a separate entity before, became known as Chūō Ajia. Japan's attitude toward Central Asia was determined by its concern with Russian aspirations in the region. The two powers were in direct conflict over Man-churia, and this eventually led to the Russo-Japanese War of 1904–5, in which Japan achieved a spectacular victory. The Great Game colonial rivalry between Russia and Britain in Central Asia was therefore of interest to Japan primarily because of its ambi-tions in Manchuria.

Having said that, at the turn of the twentieth century, Central Asia did not feature prominently in the public mind in Japan. It was Ōtani Kōzui who, with his expedi-tions, resurrected the region in the popular imagination as the ancient land of the Western Regions so important in Buddhist history. While staying in Europe in 1901–2, he learned about the discoveries of ancient Buddhist ruins in Chinese Turkestan by Sven Hedin (1865–1952) and M. Aurel Stein (1862–1943) and immediately realized their significance for the Buddhist quest in modern Japan. In 1902, he led an expedi-tion himself from London to western China in search of Buddhist ruins, manuscripts, and artifacts, all with the aim of bringing to light the region's long-lost Buddhist past.

A significant part of Chinese Central Asia consists of mountains and deserts. In the center lies the Tarim basin, with the formidable Taklamakan desert, sur-rounded by the mountains of Tianshan, Kunlun, and Pamir. The major cities com-pose a series of oases along the perimeter of the Tarim basin, where the mountains meet the plain and there is enough water from descending rivers. The roads con-necting these oasis cities also run along the edge of the desert. Although at the time the region was the area where British and Russian political interests clashed, it nominally belonged to the Qing empire as the province of Xinjiang.[4] It was part of the imperial administration, with a governor in Urumchi and officials in major cities. While contemporary European narratives commonly depict Xinjiang as one of most desolate and inhospitable places in the world, a sizable population lived there and supported itself by agriculture.[5]

Although no railroads existed, there was a functional network of roads between the cities. Travelers journeyed on horse or mule and could reach Xinjiang via Gansu from the direction of Central China or could cross the border from Russian Central Asia or British India. The common route to Europe was either overland by the Russian railroad or via India and then by sea from there. Thus this "remote" region was part of an increasingly globalizing Central Asia and was connected with other parts of the world. This connection is also demonstrated by the existence of a functional postal service and the continuous efforts made for its improvement. For example, around 1910, the Danish Vilhelm Petersen was posted to Urumchi to reorganize and manage the postal system of Xinjiang. The naturalist Douglas Carruthers, who was Petersen's guest while visiting Urumchi, mentions that at last, thanks to Petersen's efforts, letters could reach Peking in forty-five days and London in thirty days.[6] Even during his expeditions, Aurel Stein maintained extensive correspondence with friends, colleagues, and publishers in India and Europe. He even corrected proofs for his articles and books and sent them by the postal service operated by the British Consulate in Kashgar. The telegraph was also increasingly used from the 1890s.[7] In this way, Chinese Central Asia was connected via an effective postal and telegraphic service to the global community and so was not nearly as remote as it was commonly depicted in the rhetoric of European and Japanese accounts.

Travel Writing in Japan

By the end of the nineteenth century, the genre of travel literature was extremely well developed in Japan. There seems to have been an insatiable appetite for knowledge about the outside world, and hundreds of books were published about journeys to every imaginable corner of the world. The majority of the travelogues, however, except for the extremely popular genre of domestic travel, were about China and European countries, which aptly reflects Japan's orientation in this period. For historical reasons, China occupied a special place in the Japanese mind, as demonstrated by the enormous volume of travel literature about China. In his study of Japanese travelogues from the beginning of the Meiji period until the end of World War II, Joshua A. Fogel utilizes an enormous corpus of nearly five hundred books.[8] The Japanese could claim continuity with the Chinese literary and scholarly tradition and thus assert a direct connection with many of the cultural sites in China, such as the birthplace of Confucius and the old capitals of Chang'an and Luoyang. In addition, there were also travelers who were interested in modern China, in the reforms and intellectual currents of the time. At the same time, this cultural indebtedness to China was juxtaposed with the drive to modernize and catch up with the West. Unsurprisingly, this duality was also represented in the country's political and intellectual factions, some of which tried to preserve traditional models while others opted for emulating European and American examples that would lead the nation to economic prosperity.

Travel literature was also available in translation, especially about regions where few Japanese had the chance to travel. Narratives published until 1912 about sub-Saharan Africa alone numbered in the dozens of books.[9] The translation of Henry M. Stanley's *In Darkest Africa*, for example, was first published in 1893, then again in 1896.[10] This shows that by the turn of the century, there was a rich tradition in Japan of both native and foreign travel literature. Yet there were very few books on Central Asia, and the region was pushed into the foreground only with the archaeological expeditions of Hedin and Stein. Their writings, however, had not been translated yet and came out only beginning in the late 1930s. Hedin's first books translated into Japanese were unrelated to Central Asia (such as *With the German Armies in the West* and *The Flight of Big Horse*), and it was only in 1938 that *Chūō Ajia Tanken Ki* (Record of an Expedition to Central Asia) was published. Similarly, Stein's first book in Japanese is *On Central Asian Tracks*, which came out only in 1939 as *Chūō Ajia Tōsaki*.[11] Apparently, at the beginning of the twentieth century, Central Asia was not a major adventure destination and did not captivate the minds of Japanese readers. The region had few connecting points with Japan, and before the discovery of Buddhist sites there, the memory of medieval pilgrims did not excite the popular imagination. This is of course in sharp contrast to the Japanese preoccupation with the Silk Road, which developed several decades later and continues to this day.

Notable among the available travel accounts written by Japanese authors about Chinese Central Asia is *Chūajia Kiji* (A Chronicle of Central Asia). It was written by the diplomat Nishi Tokujiro (1847–1912), who, after studying in Saint Petersburg, traveled extensively in Russian and Chinese Central Asia between 1870 and 1873.[12] He published his account of the region in 1886. Another well-known travel narrative about this region is *Iri kiko* (Travels in Yili) by Major Hino Tsuyoshi (1866–1920) of the Imperial Japanese Army, who traveled in Chinese Turkestan between 1906 and 1907.[13] Starting from Beijing, he crossed the country westward on horseback, passed through Urumchi, and explored the Yili river region in the northwestern part of Xinjiang before traversing the mountain passes to India and eventually returning to Japan by sea. Both of these narratives combine personal experiences and facts gathered along the way in an effort to make Central Asia more accessible to Japanese audiences, including of course official agencies. They claim no connection with the Buddhist past of the region or the pilgrimage routes of the ancient Silk Road. Instead, they offer down-to-earth descriptions of events and facts.

The First and Second Ōtani Expeditions (1902–1904, 1908–1909)

Although Count Ōtani led the first expedition in person, once he succeeded his father as the leader of his sect, he could only direct the exploration from his headquarters in Kyoto. To be sure, his activities were not confined to western China but also involved other parts of Asia, including China proper, Siberia, Mongolia, Tibet, India, and the islands of South and Southeast Asia. Yet he is remembered today primarily for the exploration of the historical land of the Western Regions in the northwestern part of modern China. While this enterprise is customarily divided into three expeditions, in reality, there were a series of overlapping journeys carried out by his people in different countries. The whole enterprise came to an end in 1914 when Ōtani took responsibility for a financial scandal within his sect and resigned from his position, moving his base to China and the East Indies.

In 1900, Ōtani traveled to Europe with a small group of followers to study European religious institutions. During the two years he spent there, he mostly stayed in England but also found time to visit other parts of Europe and even made a trip to Constantinople. While he was interested mainly in observing European models of the role of religion in contemporary society, it was during this extended stay in Europe that he first encountered reports of the Buddhist treasures of Central Asia. The race for the manuscripts and antiquities of Chinese Turkestan was just beginning. Initially, manuscripts were purchased from local treasure hunters by Russian and British political personnel stationed in Kashgar, but Aurel Stein's exploration of the ancient ruins of the region of Khotan changed all that. He was the first person to introduce systematic excavation into the game, taking the hunt for antiquities from sporadic acquisitions of singular items to a whole new level by clearing out entire sites. At the time of Ōtani's stay in England, Stein had just finished his first expedition (1900–1901), and a preliminary report on his findings was promptly published in London.[14] Sven Hedin's book *Through Asia* (1898), about his daring explorations in Chinese Turkestan, was also extremely popular, and its second English edition was already out.[15] The success of these works in Britain was no doubt due to increasing public interest in Central Asia, which in turn was the result of the growing political rivalry with Russia over dominance in this region. The young Ōtani was equally captivated, but, unlike European audiences, what excited him was not the romanticism of oasis cities and inaccessible deserts but the discovery of Buddhist ruins and texts in a region that had historically been so important for both the introduction of Buddhism to China and medieval pilgrimages to the Western Regions. Accordingly, Ōtani decided to visit Central Asia himself and explore the ancient Buddhist sites in the desert. As he was about to return to Japan, he decided to take the overland route through Russia and China and stop over in Xinjiang.

On August 16, 1902, Ōtani set off from London with four of his followers. The party traveled by rail to Saint Petersburg and Samarqand and thence to Osh, entering Xinjiang through the Terek Pass and reaching Kashgar on September 21. Here they decided to split into two teams and proceed separately. The so-called Indian team, comprising Ōtani, Inoue Kōen, and Honda Eryū, went south to India through the Mintaka Pass. It is here that in January 1903 Ōtani received news of his father's death and promptly returned home by the sea route. In the meantime, the Central Asian team with Watanabe Tesshin and Hori Kenyū carried out excavations in the regions of Khotan and Kucha and visited a number of other sites throughout Xinjiang. But because Stein had already done a thorough survey of Khotan and the Germans had excavated the sites around Turfan, the Japanese team concentrated its archaeological activities on the ruins and cave temples in the vicinity of Kucha. In the end, the explorers left Xinjiang and, heading west, proceeded to the coast via Xi'an. During the expedition, Watanabe kept a detailed diary of the team's activities. After his return to Japan, the *Tōkyō Asahi Shimbun*, one of the major daily newspapers in Japan, serialized a condensed narrative version of this diary (installments of Watanabe's account ran for a week, starting June 27, 1904). Although the Japanese public seemed very interested in the expedition at the time and both local and national newspapers ran stories on the subject, none of the original members published a longer narrative or book about it.

The second expedition began in 1908 when Ōtani was already the abbot of the Nishi Honganji. He organized a new expedition with the eighteen-year-old Buddhist priest Tachibana Zuichō (1890–1968) as the leader and Nomura Eizaburo (1880–1936) as the second team member. It is worth noting that all three Ōtani expeditions were carried out by young men: with the exception of the thirty-one-year-old Inoue, the members of the first expedition had all been in their twenties (including Ōtani himself). This of course meant that they lacked sufficient archaeological training and experience in dealing with the authorities, both of which were to cause problems. The second expedition party traveled from Beijing to Mongolia and entered Xinjiang from the north. First, Tachibana and Nomura did excavations in the region of Turfan at the sites of Yarkhoto, Murtuk, Karakhoja, and Toyuk. Then, at Korla, they split up. Nomura conducted excavations near Kucha, whereas Tachibana traversed the Taklamakan and explored the Lop desert, where he located the ruins of the ancient city of Loulan visited earlier by both Hedin and Stein. Here he discovered an early fourth-century manuscript that would subsequently be declared a national treasure in Japan. The two explorers reunited in Kashgar in June 1909.

The British representative at Kashgar at this time was acting consul Captain A. R. B. Shuttleworth, who was serving in place of George Macartney (1867–1945), then on leave back in England. As a result of a series of miscommunications, aggravated by the general linguistic difficulties of conversing with the Japanese explorers, the young and inexperienced Shuttleworth gradually became convinced that the two men were spies working for the Japanese government.[16] The degree of linguistic difficulties can be gleaned from a comment in the diary of Chester G. Fuson, who was passing through Kashgar and on one occasion dined at the British consulate with the Japanese explorers: "We had great difficulty in conversing with them since our interpreter was not present, and the conversation had to be carried on through five languages—from English through Hindustani, Turki, Chinese, into Japanese, and return!"[17] Meanwhile, Shuttleworth exchanged a series of reports and instructions with his superiors, and in the end, the British authorities concluded that these two men probably were involved in espionage.

After Tachibana and Nomura left Kashgar, they traveled south through the Karakorum Pass into India. There they met with Ōtani, who had just arrived from Japan and was on his way to Europe for a second visit. Suspected of being a spy, Nomura was denied permission to return to China via the Indian frontier. Since he could not go back to Kashgar to retrieve the spoils of the second expedition, which he and Tachibana had left in the care of the British Consulate, Ōtani instructed Nomura to return to Japan by sea. Tachibana, in the meantime, traveled to London with Ōtani and a small group of followers and family members. In London, considerable efforts were made to publicize the results of the second expedition, as a result of which Tachibana was elected a member of the Geographical Society.

Both members of the second expedition kept a diary in which they recorded daily where they went and what they encountered. Once again, neither of these was published at the time, and, moreover, Tachibana's diary was later lost in a fire when his home temple in Nagoya burned down. Part of this diary was discovered only recently, but only for the section of the trip through Mongolia.[18] Thus, the only narratives that appeared in public at the time were shorter reports for the press. In comparison with the previous expedition, however, Tachibana's visit to Europe and Ōtani's publicity campaign there produced a number of responses from the English and French media. The first report about the results of the expedition came out in the *Times* and was written by Sir E. Denison Ross (1871–1940), the renowned scholar of Persian and Central Asian languages who was then principal of the Calcutta Madrasah. He had earlier met Ōtani and Tachibana in Calcutta in December 1909.[19] Acclaim in the foreign popular press and academic circles was in itself a major step forward, as it positioned the Japanese expeditions alongside those conducted by leading powers, officially acknowledging Japan as a major player in the game of colonial archaeology. This was no doubt important to Ōtani, who tried hard to establish his presence in an international field that was concerned with the history of Buddhism.

The Third Ōtani Expedition (1910–1914)

Initially, Ōtani intended to send Tachibana back to Xinjiang with new members and expand the scope of the expedition from archaeology to a number of other disciplines, such as geography and botany. In the meantime, however, Ōtani must have learned about the suspicions of espionage that had surfaced in connection with the previous expedition. His source may have been Sir E. Denison Ross in Calcutta, who was shown some Uighur manuscripts found by the second expedition. Considering Ross's close contacts with the colonial government and his keenness to be given a chance to work

on the newly discovered material, it is not impossible that he had leaked some confidential information to Ōtani and advised him on how to best deal with these compli-
cations. Since Nomura was denied permission to cross the frontier, Ōtani must have
immediately realized that these allegations were going to obstruct his further activities
in Turkestan. He acted immediately to resolve the situation by taking three steps.

First, he sent Nomura back to Japan. British intelligence reports mentioned that
the Russian consul identified Nomura as an officer in the Japanese army. In reality,
this was true only to the extent that he had participated in the Russo-Japanese War
of 1904–5, although this was far from being unusual for a Japanese man of his age, as
more than a million of his fellow countrymen had taken part in that war. Nevertheless,
Ōtani must have realized, or it was explained to him by his source, that in the context
of the Great Game, this military background could be construed by both British and
Russian authorities as extremely problematic. He thus decided not to use Nomura in
further projects in this region but sent him home to Japan. Second, he spared no effort
to publicize the results of the previous expedition and elevate Tachibana's standing in
academic circles. This was to show that the expeditions were purely scientific in nature
and that Tachibana was an acknowledged member of the international scientific community. They submitted reports of their expeditions to the *Geographical Journal* and
also tried hard to push the academic value of these expeditions to the foreground.
Third, Ōtani reorganized the exploration team. Instead of his original plan to send
two Buddhist priests (Hashiramoto Zuishun and Aoki Bunkyō) with Tachibana, he
decided to de-emphasize the Japanese nature of the expedition and convert it into an
international enterprise. Thus he hired the English seventeen-year-old Orlando Hobbs
from Swindon to accompany Tachibana.[20] Once in Saint Petersburg, they also hired a
sixteen-year-old Russian boy as an interpreter. This Russian "team member," however,
had to be let go before reaching the Chinese border because Tachibana and Hobbs soon
realized that although he could converse in Russian, his inability to speak English left
him unable to act as an interpreter. It is hard not to see that these two non-Japanese
members were hired not for their potential contributions to the success of the expedition but because of their nationalities. They were citizens of the two major powers that
faced each other in Chinese Turkestan as part of the Great Game, and the authorities
of these two powers believed that the Japanese explorers had been engaged in espionage a year earlier and thus could obstruct further work in the region.

The third Ōtani expedition ran into no difficulties whatsoever with Russian and
British authorities in Xinjiang. Ironically, to a large extent this was due not to Ōtani's
efforts but to the fact that George Macartney came back from England and Captain
Shuttleworth was recalled. Macartney, who was older and more experienced with
regard to foreign travelers in Xinjiang, saw nothing suspicious about the activities
of the Japanese team. In fact, he became involved with the expedition on account of
an entirely different matter, namely, the death of Orlando Hobbs. After arriving in
Urumchi, Tachibana and Hobbs first visited Turfan and carried out excavations at

the surrounding sites. Then Tachibana went on a desert exploration trip, crossing the Taklamakan and once again visiting the ruins of Loulan. In order to spare Hobbs from the hardship of the desert, he sent him with their luggage to Kucha, instructing him to wait for him there. But by the time Tachibana returned to Kucha, Hobbs had contracted smallpox and died. Before his death, he sent a letter to the British consulate in Kashgar, telling them about his symptoms—evidently unaware of what disease he was suffering from—and asking for help. Macartney immediately dispatched his medical officer, but by the time he arrived in Kucha, Hobbs had already died. Macartney then asked the Chinese authorities to bring the remains of the young man to Kashgar, where he was buried as the first occupant of the English Cemetery.

After learning of the death of his companion, Tachibana rushed to Kashgar and arrived just in time to take part in the funeral. In the following months, grief-stricken and suffering continuous bad luck, he made an unsuccessful attempt to enter Tibet and was lost, deserted by his men, beaten, and robbed. In the meantime, having not heard from him, Ōtani organized a search and sent Yoshikawa Koichirō to relieve and replace Tachibana in Central Asia. The two men eventually met in Dunhuang and together acquired more than 250 scrolls of Dunhuang manuscripts. After conducting excavations together in Turfan, Tachibana returned home with the most precious finds via Siberia on the Trans-Siberian Railway in 1912, while Yoshikawa stayed behind until January 1914.

Publicizing the Expeditions

The archaeological materials obtained during the three expeditions were first deposited at Nirakuso, Ōtani's extravagant villa on Mount Rokkō overlooking the Bay of Kobe. Some of the items were put on display for the general public as part of an exhibition. Both local and national newspapers ran reports about the expeditions and the collection, especially praising the young Tachibana. Shortly after his return to Japan in 1912, the *Ōsaka Mainichi Shimbun* and the *Tōkyō Nichinichi Shimbun*, two major daily newspapers, serialized his account of the last expedition. It drew hundreds of thousands of readers, and due to the overwhelmingly positive reaction, the reports were also issued as a separate volume titled *Chūa Tanken* (Exploration of Central Asia) within a few months.[21] An epigraph at the beginning of the book, in Ōtani's calligraphy, quotes the words of Emperor Taizong (r. 626–49) from his preface to the sutra translations of Xuanzang: "By emphasizing sincerity and disregarding the fatigue of labor, he sought profundity and strived for magnanimity." Evidently, the quote was intended to establish a connection with Xuanzang's pilgrimage to the Western Regions, highlighting the expedition's role in rediscovering lost texts. In other words, it established the expedition as a religious mission, albeit not to convert the local population but to recover a long-lost heritage. The preface was written by Motoyama Hikoichi, general manager of the *Ōsaka Mainichi Shimbun*, and is especially interesting because it places the expedition and its results in a non-Buddhist context, pointing out its significance for the Japanese people in general. It explains that although Japan had made tremendous progress during the Meiji era, by 1912, in the Taishō reign—which had just begun in July of that year—it had to reinterpret its own position within the whole of Asia. In addition, Motoyama raised the issue of the destiny of East Asian nations and highlighted the fact that Japan had to compete with the Western powers both politically and culturally. It is in this context that the exploration of Central Asia by the young Tachibana was significant, as it symbolized Japan's rise to the level of other advanced countries.

A few months before the appearance of this volume, however, a smaller book was published with the title *Shinkyō tanken ki* (Record of the Exploration of Xinjiang).[22] This was the record of a talk on both of his expeditions that Tachibana delivered to a youth association in Tokyo. This book also begins with Emperor Taizong's words from the same preface to Xuanzang's sutra translations, again in Ōtani's calligraphy, and alludes to the hardships of traveling in the Western Regions: "In the morning the fallen snow stirred up and obscured the ground in front of him, in the evening the sandstorm eclipsed the sky above him." The preface to *Shinkyō tanken ki* was written by the newspaper mogul and historian Tokutomi Soho (1863–1957), who put Tachibana's journey alongside the expeditions of Hedin, Stein, and Pelliot, pointing out that the young Tachibana was the first Asian to distinguish himself in a world of exploration and research that was dominated by Europeans.

In the same year, Tachibana also began to edit an academic series titled *Niraku sōsho* (Collectanea from the Niraku Villa), with the aim of publishing the results of research related to the newly acquired material. Two years later, in 1914, he published a short book on the Mongolian language titled *Mōkogo kenkyū* (Studies in the Mongolian Language) and, in the short preface, praised Genghis Khan as his most admired hero. While these were purely scholarly ventures and did not seem to have made an impact beyond Japanese academia, such impact was equally important for Ōtani. In 1915, a beautiful two-volume catalog of the collection appeared, partially illustrated with expensive color plates. This was the *Saiiki kōko zufu* (Illustrated Catalog of Central Asian Archaeology), which provided high-quality images for the study of the Ōtani collection.[23] Due to Ōtani's resignation and departure from the country, the planned series of archaeological reports and popular narratives never materialized, and to this day, these two volumes remain an important source on the collection before its dispersal.[24]

The preface to the catalog was written by Ōtani himself and spelled out his motivation for exploring Central Asia:

> The Western Regions is the land where Buddhism once flourished and through which the Three Treasures spread. The territory of Xinjiang especially, located along the route connecting India and China, at the intersection of these two cultures, occupied a strategic position in the transmission of Buddhism to the East. But Buddhism declined in this area centuries ago, and we did not know what happened here

in the past. For many years I have been aware that a scientific exploration of this area and the whole of Central Asia was necessary but never had the opportunity to carry out these plans. In August of 1902, I happened to be in England, in London, and as I was about to return home, it suddenly occurred to me that I should use the opportunity of my return trip to accomplish this long-standing aspiration. Having made up my mind, I personally visited the holy sites of the Western Regions and also sent others separately to explore the inner areas of Xinjiang. The results of this trip made it increasingly clear to me that the exploration of Central Asia was necessary; thus I sent expeditions over there on two additional occasions.

In this way, Ōtani justified his expeditions to Central Asia by connecting them with the history of Buddhism. He referred to the region's key location in this respect and claimed that he had been meaning to go there for a long time. He also pointed out that the idea of the first expedition came to his mind in London, although he phrased it as if the idea arose merely as a logistical issue of being able to pass through these lands on the way back to Japan. We know, however, that the expeditions had been in large part inspired by the explorations carried out by Sven Hedin and, more importantly, Aurel Stein, which Ōtani had heard about while staying in London.

In 1914, Ōtani abruptly resigned from his position in Japan and left the country for the rest of his life. This was also the end of his involvement in the exploration of Central Asia. He moved his base of operations first to Shanghai and later to Port Arthur (Lüshun), also spending part of the year in the East Indies. He continued to travel extensively and to send his followers to regions and countries that interested him, including Europe, North America, China, Siberia, India, and Turkey. He built or purchased several large villas around the world, where he intended to establish regional headquarters under his leadership. Thus, in addition to such centers in Shanghai, Port Arthur, Dairen (Dalian), and Takao (Gaoxiong, in Taiwan), he also built villas in the East Indian islands of Java and Celebes and even in Lausanne, Switzerland. During these thirty-some years, he rarely visited Japan, retiring to Beppu on the island of Kyushu only shortly before his death in 1948.

Thus, there were only two thin books published on the expeditions while they were in progress. Although a wealth of material was produced in the form of diaries, reports, and letters, these remained hidden from public view, and, with Ōtani's voluntary exile, the collection itself was gradually dispersed.[25] More than two decades after the expeditions, however, a beautiful folio-sized edition in two volumes was compiled with all of the material that was still available. The editors wrote to the original expedition members and asked for their field notes and diaries, which were included in the new compilation. It was published in 1937 with the title *Shin Saiiki Ki* (New Record of the Western Regions).[26] The title referred to Xuanzang's travel narrative *Xiyu Ji* (Record of the Western Region; in Japanese, *Saiiki*), thus directly associating the Ōtani expeditions with Xuanzang's pilgrimage. Echoing the aims of Xuanzang, who traveled to the Western Regions in search of the dharma and scriptures, the modern Japanese explorers were looking for Buddhist manuscripts and artifacts. The new volume contained a significant amount of documentation from the expeditions, although its size and price would have made it largely inaccessible to the general public. In addition, most of the diaries and notes were included in their original format, which was helpful for research but perhaps less interesting for ordinary readers. In contrast, Tachibana's two books (which were also incorporated into the second volume of *Shin Saiiki Ki*) very much targeted popular audiences who were only superficially interested in Central Asia.

The Rhetorics of Exploration

There is an interesting duality in the rhetorics of the Japanese exploration of Central Asia. As we have seen, in their justification of their motives and construction of their travel narratives, the Ōtani expeditions relied on two different traditions. On the one hand, we see an insistent association with the region's Buddhist past, referencing the works of medieval pilgrim-monks who journeyed west from China proper in search of scriptures. On the other hand, Ōtani also referenced European exploration narratives, especially those by Aurel Stein and Sven Hedin. While in Europe, he met both explorers and later sporadically corresponded with them. When Hedin visited Japan for a few days in 1908, he was also Ōtani's guest at the Nishi Honganji temple in Kyoto, which was amply publicized at the time in Japan.

It is interesting how little attention is paid to current conditions in Central Asia in the accounts of some of these archaeological expeditions. The explorers seem to be traveling in an abstract space and make fleeting comments about the people, their customs, and their living conditions only when these matters are pertinent to acquiring medieval manuscripts or visiting ancient ruins. The local population and the Chinese officials are almost a distraction, while the Japanese Buddhist travelers claim this land as their own cultural heritage. Everything is about the past, the author-traveler reads into the land a constructed view of what used to be there, and the only modern reference points are the experiences of other explorers who likewise saw the region through the lens of the past when they had visited these places a few years earlier. Thus we see a process of globalization in the records of foreign explorers, with their fixation on manuscripts and ancient ruins, continually cross-referencing one another. Although the history of any part of the world is a complex narrative involving a variety of different peoples, faiths, and periods, in the context of the archaeological exploration of Central Asia, partly because the ruins in the desert belonged predominantly to Buddhist cultures, this globalization centered around the Buddhist past of the region, disregarding other cultural and religious layers. In this respect, the Japanese experience in Chinese Central Asia was very different from that in "modern" places such as Europe. There Japanese travelers chiefly described the contemporary world around them and made very few references to a history that, albeit just as rich as that of Central Asia, rarely featured in the East Asian tradition of travel writing.

The name compulsively used in connection with the Buddhist heritage of Central Asia is that of Xuanzang, whose seventh-century narrative of his journey to India,

Xiyu Ji, or *Record of the Western Regions*, has been one of the most popular works in the Chinese tradition. Besides being included in the Buddhist canon, the story itself continued to evolve in the popular imagination and was reincarnated in works of popular literature, the most famous of which is the sixteenth-century vernacular novel *Xiyou Ji* (Journey to the West), by Wu Cheng'en.[27] As a result of this long literary tradition, to this day, the very name of Central Asia (i.e., *Xiyu*, or "Western Regions") triggers images of Buddhist pilgrims traveling westward through the desert in search of manuscripts. This Chinese fascination with the region was brought over to Japan in medieval times and since then has also been part of Japanese culture. In a way, exploring the ruins of ancient Buddhist kingdoms was like time travel. The Japanese explorers already knew this land intimately from medieval travel narratives, which had formed part of their cultural memory. Thus when they traveled there in person, they were essentially rediscovering the place.[28] Perhaps this is part of the reason we learn so little about interactions with local populations, as the narratives dwell mostly on the adventures of the explorers or the discovery of ancient manuscripts.

The rhetorics of the Ōtani expeditions consistently utilize the image of Xuanzang and the pilgrimage to the west in general. As mentioned above, Ōtani wrote the opening epigraph in calligraphy at the beginning of both of Tachibana's books, quoting Taizong's laudatory words about Xuanzang. In addition, the preference for using the term "Western Regions" instead of modern toponyms also establishes a link with the heyday of Buddhism in this region during the medieval period and the region's significance for the transmission of Buddhist doctrines and scriptures to China. Nor should we forget that the expeditions were organized, financed, and carried out by members of one of the largest Buddhist organizations in the world. They justified their involvement in this enterprise largely by their spiritual connection with the land of Central Asia and its past. In a rare English-language account of the first expedition written in 1906, Ōtani began his "personal narrative" with the following words:

> After spending two and a half years in study in England, it was my ambition to return to Japan by way of central Asia and India, to visit the ruined cities and remains of Buddhist civilization buried in the desert sands, and to make a pilgrimage through our Buddhist Holy Land in India. I wished to follow the route of Hiuen Tsang [i.e. Xuanzang], the Chinese priest who went to India in the seventh century of the Christian era, spent several years in the Buddhist monasteries of Magadha (modern Berar, Central India) and Kashmir, and brought back many canonical books and previously unknown texts, the expounding of which caused a great revival of Buddhism in China and reinvigorated it in Japan.[29]

This short introduction includes all of the key words that would be used in all later accounts, including "England," "Central Asia," "India," "Xuanzang," "ruined cities," "desert sand," and "pilgrimage." Most importantly, Ōtani connects the manuscripts brought back from India and Central Asia with the revival of Buddhism in China and Japan, which was an important theme in his religious pan-Asianism. Having said that, European explorers were naturally also interested in manuscripts, even if for completely different reasons. As early as the end of the nineteenth century, Russian and British political officers stationed in Kashgar were instructed to acquire available manuscripts and send them back to academic institutions in their home countries. Aurel Stein's excavations in Khotan and Niya only heightened the interest in manuscripts, and Stein's acquisition of part of the Dunhuang cave library in 1907 became a veritable sensation. Ironically, when Stein approached Abbot Wang, the self-appointed caretaker of the Dunhuang cave temples who was also the discoverer of the cave library, he compared himself to Xuanzang. He was like Xuanzang, he claimed, except that he came from the West, and had come looking for Buddhist texts so that he could take the scriptures back to India, the place of their origin.[30] Nevertheless, unlike Ōtani and his men, Stein was not a Buddhist follower but a scholar, and for him the manuscripts had no religious significance.

The role of English-language models for the explorations and subsequent narratives is best demonstrated by the fact that expedition members carried with them many of these earlier books. For example, after Nomura's arrival in Kashgar in the summer of 1909, the British representative Captain Shuttleworth visited him at his residence and made the following observation:

> I noticed he had a large library of English books, including Curzon's *Pamirs*, Stein's *Ancient Khotan*, Putnam Weale's *The Truce in the East and its Aftermath* and books by Deasy, Ellsworth Huntington, Sven Hedin and Cobbold. I also saw several military works, such as *The War in the Far East* by the military correspondent of *The Times*, and one or two naval books by Mahan. Nomura distinctly told me he could neither speak nor read English.[31]

Although Shuttleworth's suspicions were most likely unfounded, as real spies would presumably not carry with them books they could not read, his comment shows the degree of dependence on the results of European exploration of Central Asia. Such a large collection of books, some of which were large and heavy (e.g., the two folio-sized volumes of Stein's *Ancient Khotan*), was not easy to carry around while traveling and its presence was no doubt justified by the books' significance for the Japanese exploration. Ōtani himself was an avid collector of books related to Central Asia and Asia in general.[32] Interestingly, these European narratives seem to have been utilized not only for their geographical, historical, and archaeological content but also as a model for such mundane things as how to travel or even what to wear. For example, since he could not personally participate in the expeditions anymore, Ōtani wrote a detailed how-to handbook for the expedition members, in which he gives instructions on how to handle practical issues, such as the daily distances one should cover on foot or horseback, information that needs to be recorded in a diary entry, or even what to wear when meeting local officials or gentlemen. He points out, for example, that "especially on British territory one should not forget to have a tailcoat at one's disposal."[33]

This indebtedness to the European exploratory tradition was of course no secret. Quite to the contrary, in most writings related to the expeditions, the European explorers are cited at the beginning as worthy predecessors. This shows that Ōtani and his people were trying to establish themselves as part of a lineage of Central Asian explorers. Tachibana, for example, mentions right at the beginning of his narrative of the second expedition that before his departure from England, he had met Stein in London and Hedin in Stockholm and that both of them wished him well, which, in the narrative, functions essentially as a kind of initiation ceremony in an almost religious type of transmission.[34] He then explains how Ōtani took him shopping for expensive scientific equipment for the journey, and his detailed list of the different kinds of chronometers and barometers feels like a device intended to emphasize the scientific (i.e., European) nature of the upcoming enterprise. The reader is reminded that this was no mere pleasure trip but a cutting-edge scientific exploration. In some sense, this also served to demonstrate that, at least with respect to the exploration of Central Asia, Japan was on a par with the European colonial powers. In addition, both of Tachibana's popular accounts were aimed at a Japanese general readership and used the names "Chūa" (Central Asia) and "Shinkyō" (Xinjiang) instead of the earlier term "Saiiki" (Western Regions). This is not to say that the element of Buddhist pilgrimage was absent from these books. As we have seen above, Ōtani chose to underline this with his calligraphy at the very beginning of the books. Yet the narratives in general read not as descriptions of visits to holy sites but as stories of adventure in a dangerous land. The emphasis on Tachibana's young age, stressed throughout the popular accounts, was part of the same narrative framework. The books also follow the European tradition of travel narratives in emphasizing the adventurous and personal aspects of the journey, at times humorous, at other times tragic.

Ōtani also worked hard to publicize the results of his expeditions in Europe. He corresponded with leading European scholars, sent reports and maps to the Royal Geographical Society, and succeeded in having Tachibana acknowledged by the academic community in Europe. He saw the progress of European scholars in the study of the history of Buddhism in Central Asia, India, and Tibet and tried to establish Japan, and more specifically his own sect, among the major players. His grand vision of the pan-Asian revival of Buddhism necessitated that Buddhist scholars were not left out of this field.

As we have seen, the travel narratives of twentieth-century Japanese Buddhist exploration of Central Asia were affiliated with two distinct traditions. On the one hand, they tried to position themselves as part of the tradition of European exploration of Central Asia, which to some extent reflects Japan's contemporary aspirations to align itself with leading colonial powers. This European colonial element shines through in all narratives associated with the expeditions. On the other hand, they also claimed a connection with the medieval Buddhist pilgrimages through the Western Regions. The Chinese monks had brought back scriptures, statues, and relics that all symbolized the dharma, and even their travel accounts functioned as dharma in that they were mementos from the land of the Buddha. The Japanese explorers expressly associated themselves with these medieval movements, effectively sanctifying their archaeological work as a religious pilgrimage in search of relics. When Ōtani learned during his stay in London about the Buddhist ruins and manuscripts found in Central Asia, he immediately realized the significance of these discoveries for his pan-Asian vision of Buddhism. With his expeditions to the region, he meant to reenact the seventh-century journey of Xuanzang, who brought back manuscripts and relics that were to play an important role in the subsequent revival of Buddhism. The ancient land of the Western Regions was the missing link between the East and the West, which provided ideological support for redefining the role of Buddhism both in contemporary Japanese society and throughout Asia.

This might have also been one of the reasons that news of the discovery of ancient Buddhist sites and artifacts in Chinese Turkestan did not trigger much wider interest in China itself. Indeed, Chinese scholars had not paid attention to these finds until the French scholar Paul Pelliot brought some of the manuscripts he purchased in Dunhuang to Beijing in 1909. These were mostly copies of traditional Chinese texts, such as the Confucian canon, classical literature, and geographical and historical treatises. It was mainly these non-Buddhist manuscripts that prompted the interest of the Chinese scholarly community, which eventually was successful in petitioning the Ministry of Culture to rescue the remaining manuscripts. Buddhist scriptures and commentaries, in contrast, excited less attention and were appreciated primarily for their calligraphy and antiquarian value. Even less valued in the first decades of the twentieth century were manuscripts written in foreign languages. Tibetan and Sanskrit texts thus went virtually unnoticed by Chinese scholars, even after scholars had been alerted to the existence of the Dunhuang cave library.[35] In Japan, however, Buddhism was very much a living tradition. The country had a long tradition of collecting and studying manuscripts—many Japanese temples have extraordinary collections of old manuscripts going back to medieval times.[36] Accordingly, Buddhist sutras and artifacts from Central Asia, the Western Regions, were a powerful cultural symbol in Japan that summoned images of religious revival and prosperity.

Notes

This chapter was written while I was a Petra Kappert Fellow at the Centre for the Study of Manuscript Cultures at Hamburg University. I am grateful for Prof. Michael Friedrich and his colleagues at the center for their support.

1. On Buddhism in the Meiji period, see Winston Davis, "Buddhism and the Modernization of Japan," *History of Religions* 28, 4 (1989), pp. 304–39. On the ways in which the Nishi Honganji tries to define its relationship to the state, see Minor L. Rogers and Ann T. Rogers, "The Honganji: Guardian of the State (1868–1945)," *Japanese Journal of Religious Studies* 17, 1 (1990), pp. 3–28.

2. Richard M. Jaffe, "Buddhist Material Culture, 'Indianism,' and the Construction of Pan-Asian Buddhism in Prewar Japan," *Material Religion* 21, 3 (2006), pp. 266–93.

3. Pan-Asianism was one of the consistent themes in Ōtani's life, and he was one of its main proponents in Japan even though he spent the second half of his life away from Japan. On many levels, this nationalistic ideology coincided with Japan's military expansion, and Ōtani has been sharply

criticized for this in the West. See, for example, Ronald S. Anderson, "Nishi Honganji and Japanese Buddhist Nationalism, 1862–1945" (PhD diss., University of California, Berkeley, 1956).

4. At the time, "Xinjiang" was usually spelled "Sinkiang" in European literature. Today it is no longer a province but an autonomous region.

5. In 1907–8, the population of Xinjiang was in the range of 1.65 million to 2 million. See James A. Millward, *Eurasian Crossroads: A History of Xinjiang* (New York: Columbia University Press, 2007), pp. 152–53.

6. Douglas Carruthers, *Unknown Mongolia: A Record of Travel and Exploration in North-West Mongolia and Dzungaria* (London: Hutchinson & Co., 1914), vol. 2, pp. 445–46.

7. Chen Huisheng, *Minguo Xinjiang shi* (History of Xinjiang in the Republican Era) (Urumchi: Xinjiang renmin chubanshe, n.d.), p. 171, n. 2.

8. Joshua A. Fogel, *The Literature of Travel in the Japanese Rediscovery of China, 1862–1945* (Stanford: Stanford University Press, 1996), p. xii.

9. For a list of works, both Western and Japanese, on exploration in sub-Saharan Africa that appeared during the Meiji period, see Aoki Sumio, "Meijiki Nihon ni okeru Sabu-Sahara Afurika he no kanshin (Shoseki mokuroku)" [Japanese Interest in sub-Saharan Africa during the Meiji Period [Bibliography]], *Journal of African Studies* 72 (2008), pp. 61–66.

10. Henry Stanley, *Ankoku Afurika* [Dark Africa], trans. Yabe Shinsaku (Tokyo: Hakubunkan, 1893). The second edition came out as Stanley, *Sutanrētanken jikki* [True Record of Stanley's Expedition], trans. Yabe Shinsaku (Tokyo: Hakubunkan, 1986).

11. Sven Hedin, *Chūō Ajia tanken ki*, trans. Iwamura Shinobu (Tokyo: Fuzanbō, 1938); M. Aurel Stein, *Chūō Ajia tōsaki*, trans. Kazama Tarō (Tokyo: Seikatsusha, 1939).

12. Nishi Tokujirō, *Chūajia kiji* (Tokyo: Rikugun bunko, 1886).

13. Hino Tsuyoshi, *Iri kikō* (Tokyo: Hakubunkan, 1909).

14. M. Aurel Stein, *Preliminary Report of a Journey of Archaeological and Topographical Exploration in Chinese Turkestan* (London: Eyre and Spottiswoode, 1901).

15. Sven Hedin, *Through Asia* (London: Methuen, 1898). The second edition was published by Harper, New York and London, in 1899.

16. On the British suspicions against Tachibana and Nomura during their stay in Kashgar, see Imre Galambos, "Japanese 'Spies' along the Silk Road: British Suspicions Regarding the Second Ōtani Expedition (1908–09)," *Japanese Religions* 35, 1–2 (2010), pp. 33–61.

17. Ibid., p. 49

18. This portion of the diary was published recently under the title *Shimei Ki* (Record of a Mission) by Tachibana's son and grandson with the help of Silk Road scholar Kaneko Tamio. See Tachibana Zuichō, *Shimei ki* (Nagoya: privately published, 2001).

19. "Exploration in Chinese Turkestan," *The Times*, February 3, 1910, p. 5. Although this report appeared anonymously, Ross mentioned having authored the text in his correspondence with Stein. See Imre Galambos and Kōichi Kitsudō, "Japanese Exploration of Central Asia: The Ōtani Expeditions and Their British Connections," *Bulletin of the School of Oriental and African Studies* 75, 1 (2012), pp. 113–34, esp. pp. 116–17.

20. On the tragic fate of Orlando Hobbs and his role in the expedition, see Imre Galambos, "An English Participant in the Japanese Exploration of Central Asia: The Role of A. O. Hobbs in the Third Ōtani Expedition," in Irina Popova, ed., *Russian Expeditions to Central Asia at the Turn of the 20th Century* (Saint Petersburg: Slavia, 2008), pp. 188–202.

21. Tachibana Zuichō, *Chūa tanken* (Tokyo: Hakubunkan, 1912). The volume was actually put together from an oral interview with Tachibana by the journalist Seki Roko, who was closely associated with Ōtani and actively promoted the cause of the exploration.

22. Tachibana Zuichō, *Shinky tanken ki* (Tokyo: Minyusha, 1912).

23. Kagawa Mokushiki, ed., *Saiiki kōko zufu* (Tokyo: Kokkasha, 1915).

24. Since some of the items included in the catalog were subsequently lost, it remains the only record of them. As newer collections become accessible to researchers (e.g., Lüshun Museum), some of these lost items may resurface, and the catalog will provide a much needed reference point.

25. Important parts of the original Ōtani collection are kept today at Ryukoku University Library, the National Museum of Tokyo, the National Museum of Kyoto, the Lüshun Museum, the National Library of China, and the National Museum of Korea, among others. There are also items that have only recently been discovered in private collections in Japan or are still considered lost.

26. Uehara Yoshitaro, ed., *Shin Saiiki ki* (Tokyo: Yukosha, 1937). A reprint, *Shin Saiiki Ki* (Tokyo: Igusa, 1984), includes a small supplement.

27. For an English translation, see Anthony Yu, trans., *The Journey to the West*, 4 vols. (Chicago: University of Chicago Press, 1977–83).

28. Joshua Fogel writes about this aspect of Japanese travel narratives on China, how travelers were confronted with the contrast between the China they knew from their shared cultural tradition and the one they saw upon arriving there in person. See Fogel (1996), pp. 302–3.

29. Count Kosui Otani, "The Japanese Pilgrimage to the Buddhist Holy Land: A Personal Narrative of the Hongwanji Expedition of 1902–03," *Century Magazine* 10 (1906), p. 866.

30. Partly as a result of these rhetorics, today the Stein collection of Dunhuang manuscripts consists mostly of Buddhist texts. Another reason for this was Stein's inability to read Chinese and his lack of sinological training. In contrast, Paul Pelliot, the talented French sinologist who visited the caves a few months after Stein, purchased manuscripts that were more valuable from the point of view of the classical Chinese textual tradition. Ōtani, however, expressly preferred Buddhist texts and in his article on the first expedition writes: "More fortunate than Captain Bower, whose famous manuscripts proved to be chiefly the formula and prescriptions of a medicine-shop, our explorers brought back many pieces of sacred writing—fragments of sutras written in Uigur, Sanscrit, and Chinese characters." See ibid., p. 877.

31. Galambos (2010), p. 54.

32. Part of his collection of books was donated to the Dairen Library (today's Dalian Library), and since the shelf mark of these books begins with an "O," they are still identifiable as a collection. The catalog of the books in European languages shows more than a hundred titles—some quite rare and valuable—that used to belong to Ōtani, mostly on Central and East Asia. See *Classified Catalogue of Books in European Languages in the Dairen Library of the South Manchuria Railway Company* (Dairen: The Dairen Library, 1937). I am grateful to Kitsudō Kōichi of Ryukoku University for pointing out this catalog to me.

33. Ueyama Daishun, "*Tanken shizusho* to *Ryōkō Kyōhan*," *Bunka Issan* 11 (2001), pp. 34–35.

34. Tachibana (1912), p. 2.

35. On the topic of how non-Chinese manuscripts from Dunhuang were initially neglected, see Justin Jacobs, "Central Asian Manuscripts 'Are Not Worth Much To Us': The Thousand-Buddha Caves in Early Twentieth-Century China," *Journal of Inner Asian Art and Archaeology* 4 (2009), pp. 161–68.

36. One of the most sensational finds of recent decades is the medieval library with thousands of manuscript scrolls discovered in 1990 at the Nanatsudera temple. See Ochiai Toshinori et al., *The Manuscripts of Nanatsu-Dera: A Recently Discovered Treasure-House in Downtown Nagoya* (Kyoto: Istituto italiano di cultura, Scuola di studi sull'Asia orientale, 1991).

7 A Russian Futurist in Asia

Velimir Khlebnikov's Travelogue in Verse

Ronald Vroon

Approaches to Asia

Central Asia and the contiguous territories around the Caspian basin have always asserted themselves in Russian cultural consciousness, an inevitable consequence of the role they have played in the social, political, and military life of the land. But Russia's Slavic linguistic roots and its adoption of Greek Orthodox Christianity insulated it to a great degree from the polytheist or Muslim "other" to the east and southeast. They also insulated Russia from the Latin Christian "other" of the West, of course, but the alterity of the East was much more pronounced, so much so that the Russian word *basurman,* etymologically linked to *musul'manin* (Muslim), could be used in peasant speech to designate any non-Orthodox "outsider," including one of the Latin or Protestant confessions. When Russia finally embarked on the path of modernization under Peter the Great, it looked to the West for its literary, musical, and artistic models. The results were in certain respects unnatural: though it was in a position, both literally and figuratively, to understand and exploit the cultural treasures of the East, it initially adopted the oversimplified or otherwise caricatured Orient that was a hallmark of the West. Beginning in the eighteenth century, against the background of a fitfully developing academic orientology initiated by Peter the Great, Russian high culture adopted a similarly colonialist and naive attitude toward its Asian "other."

Three general tendencies seem to dominate cultural production relating to Central Asia and the Caucasus in the period preceding the one in which our hero, Velimir Khlebnikov (1885–1922), emerges as a major literary figure. The first is, for want of a better term, "ornamental." We mean here the tendency to depict the East, in whatever form, as an exotic accessory or ornament adorning an otherwise wholly Western outlook or artistic form. What David Schimmelpenninck van der Oye identifies as Catherine the Great's "Chinoiserie" is a good example.[1] Another is the late eighteenth-century poet Gavriil Derzhavin figuratively donning the costume of a Tatar *murza* and dressing Catherine, the object of his panegyrics, in the costume of a Kirghiz-Kaisatsk princess in his famous ode "Felitsa." The fact that Catherine also engaged the Chinese on matters of trade and spheres of influence and that Derzhavin acknowledged and was proud of his descent from Tatar nobility does not lessen the superficiality of such oriental accoutrements.

For the Romantics and their successors of the nineteenth century, a second tendency begins to emerge and run parallel to the first; a fascination with exoticism still exists, but ideology now comes to the fore, also taking its cue from the West. Depictions of the Caucasus in the works of Alexander Pushkin, Mikhail Lermontov, Aleksandr Bestuzhev-Marlinskii, and other prominent Romantics convey a message of social and spiritual liberation from convention in the spirit of Rousseau. Albeit within a fictional context, these writings—couched in the genres of adventure tales, long narrative poems, and travel notes (Lermontov's *A Hero of Our Times* is the prime example)—also had to integrate Romantic ideology with the reality of Russian colonial interests in the area,[2] and in this respect the Romantic fashioning of exotic mountain landscapes and populations curiously anticipates and parallels the interest in Central Asia's mountain regions by the Great Game's travelers of the 1840s and onward (see Nile Green's introduction in this volume).

The ornamentalization of the East recedes in the Realist period, while ideologization grows in strength. Tolstoy's interest in Confucianism and Daoism are well known, as are Dostoevsky's attempts late in life to claim a unique universalism for the Russian spirit that allowed it to bring both Asia and Europe into its spiritual and cultural embrace. A more ominous ideology emerges in the philosophical works of Vladimir Solov'ev, in which, as Harsha Ram has noted, "the ancient memory of the thirteenth-century Mongol invasions of the Central Asian steppe was recapitulated as an imminent threat to Russia and humanity and a harbinger of the Antichrist."[3] This particular ideological position would subsequently be absorbed and developed in the works of late nineteenth- and early twentieth-century Symbolists, with sometimes ironic twists, including the defiant adoption of a mythologized Asian visage (slanted eyes) and mentality (barbarian) by Alexandr Blok, one of the most urbane and "European" of the Russian Symbolist poets, in his notorious poem "The Scythians."

But a third tendency emerges during this period that finds its parallel in the "archaeological" travels outlined in Nile Green's introduction, one that brings us into range of this chapter's targeted travelogue. A number of writers, among them Vladimir Stasov, Vasilii Grigor'ev, and Esper Ukhtomskii (author of the three-volume travelogue documenting the czarevich Nicholas's eastern journey [1890–91]), took a serious interest in Russia's Central Asian past and its influence on Russian culture and the arts, arguing on the basis of their research and experiences as travelers for a more receptive attitude toward the Asian element manifest in Russia's native arts and its political and spiritual culture. This more studied approach overlapped with the final conquest of Central Asia (1864–84) and gave rise to the considerable fin de siècle ethno-touristic travel literature. Not coincidentally, this period saw the more serious incorporation of Central Asian motifs into mainstream Russian culture in the music of Borodin and Balakirev and the paintings of Vereshchagin.[4] The stage was being set, in short, for a more authentic artistic encounter with Russia's Asian "other" that was not filtered through the prism of Western orientalism.

Futurism

The plays on that stage had their first performances in the 1910s. A new poetic movement, Futurism, arose to challenge the competing orthodoxies of a colonial neo-Realism and a paranoid Symbolism, which had dominated Russian letters at the beginning of the century, and to contend with others vying for attention and readership, among them a resurrected classicism disguised under the odd name "Acmeism" and a less cohesive, but no less competitive, movement associated with an assertive coterie of peasant poets. But there was something different about Futurism, or at least the most avant-garde of its many branches.[5] Not only did it criticize the practices of its immediate predecessors, but, as its name implies, it rejected the literary past in its entirety, favoring either a radical technology-inspired experimentalism focused on the future or an equally radical primitivism focused on the prehistoric—or, at the very least, pre-modern and pre-Western—past.[6]

Such temporal disjunctures were accompanied by an equally dogmatic rejection of spatial centers in favor of peripheries. Unlike their literary rivals, who were for the most part born or raised in Saint Petersburg and Moscow, the Futurists hailed from the provinces and flaunted their provincialism.[7] If one were to draw an arc on a map connecting the birthplaces of the leading Futurists, it would form a gigantic crescent around the star marking Russia's ancient capital, Moscow. Far to the east lies the Kama River, on the virtual border between Europe and Asia, where the poet and aviator Vasilii Kamenskii was born on a barge plying the route between Perm and Sarapul. He would be the first of the Futurists to travel to Asia, long before he had met his literary confreres-to-be. In 1906, fresh out of prison for participating in meetings of the revolutionary underground, he celebrated his freedom by booking passage on a boat from Sevastopol to Istanbul, and from there to Persia, eventually crossing the Caspian Sea to reach Baku, and finally making his way to Saint Petersburg.[8] If we proceed south along the arc whose easternmost tip marks Kamenskii's birthplace, we reach the Kalmyk steppes north of Astrakhan. Here Velimir Khlebnikov was born in a ramshackle encampment, Khanskaya stavka, where his father was temporarily quartered as administrative head of the Russian neo-colonial office overseeing the Kalmyk nomads. Moving farther south and easing our way west along the crescent, we come to Georgia, home of the young Vladimir Maiakovskii. Still farther west and curving north, we reach ancient Hylaea, the fertile area north of the Black Sea first mentioned by Herodotus and currently in southern Ukraine, where the three Burliuk brothers—David, Nikolai, and Vladimir—were born and raised. And finally we arrive at Kharkiv, Ukraine, home of the most incorrigible and long-lived of the Futurists, Aleksei Kruchënykh. If we were to bring the crescent line full circle, significantly, it would exclude all of western Europe. And that, precisely, is how the Russian Futurists conceptualized their own frame of reference.[9]

The nature of this about-face was initially more ideological than cultural. The Futurists were avidly interested in contemporary artistic and poetic developments in the West—the emergence of Cubism in particular—and they were to be heavily influenced by Western trends in the graphic and verbal arts, but Russian fin de siècle culture had achieved a degree of independence and autonomy that gave them the confidence to assert their own path, and if it was not to be Western, then by default it had to be "Eastern," whatever that might imply. And indeed the meaning of such Orientalism was as vague as it was obstreperous. An early poem by Nikolai Burliuk shows the importance of the *juxtaposition* of East and West, as opposed to the elaboration of some genuinely Eastern *Weltanschauung*, philosophy, or aesthetic:

Востока вышивка незримо	The embroidery of the East invisibly
Переживаетъ польскій шелкъ	Outlasts Polish silk.
Во мнѣ арийца голосъ смолкъ	In me the voice of the Aryan is stilled.
Я вижу минареты Крыма.	I see the Crimea's minarets.[10]

A theoretical justification for seeing the East primarily as "not-west" is set forth in Nataliia Goncharova's introduction to a catalog of her works, displayed at a major Moscow exhibition in 1913. Here she focuses on two principles guiding her new orientation: her rejection of Western individualism and her conviction that Russia's native art is essentially Eastern.

> As I set out on my path, I learned above all from contemporary French artists. They opened my eyes, and I grasped the meaning and value of the art of my homeland, and through it the great value of the art of the East. I have assimilated everything that Western art could give me up to the present, and also everything that my homeland created under Western influence. Now I shake the dust off my feet and distance myself from the West, regarding its leveling significance as utterly petty and insignificant; my path leads to the first source of all art, the East. The art of my homeland is incomparably more profound and significant than what I know in the West. . . . I once again open the path to the East, and I am sure many will follow me. Where, if not in the East, is the inspiration of those Western masters at whose feet we have studied so long without grasping the most important thing: not to mindlessly imitate and search out one's own individuality, but above all to create works of art, knowing that the source from which the West draws is the East and we ourselves.

She adds, in a more conciliatory tone, "My pursuit of nationalism and the East is not intended to narrow art's goals, but on the contrary to make it all-encompassing and universal."[11]

Velimir Khlebnikov, Stenka Razin, and the Astrakhan Manifestos

A year after Goncharova published her personal manifesto, Velimir Khlebnikov's first book of poems appeared, with ecstatic prefaces by two fellow Futurists, David Burliuk and Vasilii Kamenskii. The latter's take on Khlebnikov's genius is particularly telling because, like Goncharova's self-characterization, it is rooted in the artist's dual identity: Eastern and native Russian. After praising the authenticity and daring of Khlebnikov's neologisms, Kamenskii presents us with the following portrait of the poet: "Khlebnikov is like an Astrakhan pirate with a constantly bent-over back bearing a sack of semiprecious stones of rare beauty; with the ever concealed quiet smile of a Tatar from beyond the Caspian sniffing the colors of Persian carpets; and with the Russian, o, so profoundly Russian soul of a singer of epics from Novgorod the Great, whose songs from the Lake of Sorrow arc like a rainbow into the Great World of the Present."[12] One detects in this description the clichéd orientalism of European modernism, but localized in a highly original way through the use of a clever cultural double entendre: for "pirate," Kamenskii uses the word *ushkuinik*, an archaic term for bandits plying their trade on the rivers of medieval Novgorod, Russia's westernmost territory; by coupling it with the epithet "Astrakhan," he turns the poet into a modern-day incarnation of Stenka Razin, the leader of a seventeenth-century rebellion against the Muscovite czar who brought together a motley crew of Cossacks, runaway Russian serfs, and representatives of various Central Asian nationalities, sailed up and down the Volga River, besieged and occupied Astrakhan and Baku for a time, raided the Turkmenian and Persian shores of the Caspian, and during one sea battle captured the daughter of the Persian fleet commander. Let us keep her in mind; she has an important role to play later in our narrative.

Kamenskii's idea, significantly, is not entirely his own. He is borrowing from a letter Khlebnikov wrote him four years earlier accompanied by two new poems with Central Asian motifs ("Scythia" and "Crimean") for a new publication Kamenskii was editing. Khlebnikov writes, "How many cities have you destroyed, you red raven? The blood of Novgorodian pirates [*ushkuiniki*], your ancestors, boils in your blood, and the whole publication seems to me the work of a new generation piloting its barks down the Volga to discover a new freedom and new shores."[13] At this early stage in his development, Khlebnikov seems to associate the figure of Razin only with exploration and rebellion, but within a few years, he would also see Razin as a "gatherer" of various faiths and nationalities—in other words, an archetypal embodiment of the Russo-Asian convergence that he championed.[14] Not coincidentally, in another letter, this one to the Russian Symbolist Andrei Belyi, Khlebnikov describes himself as a "son of Asia."[15] He saw his Astrakhan roots as "emblematic of the meeting of Europe and Asia, of civilization and nomadism, the Slavic and the Eastern, in particular the Kalmyk Mongol traditions and, lastly, the meeting place of four landscapes: the desert, the steppes, the sea and the forest."[16]

Khlebnikov, in short, was the "real thing," a true incarnation of that vaguely defined "Turanian" mentality that was artificially cultivated by the Russian avant-garde. But Khlebnikov was also a product of the liberal Russian intelligentsia, and his elaboration of an aesthetic and ideological Eurasianism was a process both gradual and fitful. Much has been written about the Orient in Khlebnikov's works,[17] and here we will briefly outline some landmarks in the development of his Central Asianism. Initially, as we have suggested, his motive for turning to the East was similar to that of his fellow Futurists. It was above all the desire to extend the boundaries of Russian literature and culture beyond the already appropriated territories of Western art and literature. We see this impulse at work, for example, in the 1913 essay "On Expanding the Boundaries of Russian Letters," in which the poet laments that his native literature "is not conversant with Persian and Mongol influences, though Finno-Mongols preceded the Russians in occupying these lands," and that "it has forgotten about the Bulgar state on the Volga, Kazan, the ancient routes to India, relations with the Arabs, Bjarmaland."[18] This cultural parochialism—what Khlebnikov terms "artificial narrowness"—had to be overcome for Russian literature to achieve its full potential.

One of the poet's early works, "The Otter's Children" (Deti vydry), a long dramatic poem written in 1913, is an attempt to do just that.[19] Significantly, in this work he draws from a pathbreaking collection of essays by the Russian orientalist Vasilii Grigor'ev, whose name we have already mentioned. Khlebnikov borrowed from his extensive "archeological" investigations of Russia's ancient contacts with Central Asia.[20] The poem is based on the mythology of the Oroches, an Eastern Siberian people of the Amur River basin, whom Khlebnikov viewed as a repository of the most ancient myths of the Asian continent. The Otter, in their cosmogony, is the mythic progenitor of the people. The speaking persona in the poem and Khlebnikov's alter ego, who identifies himself as "Son of the Otter," travels through time and space in this mythic guise, witnessing the first contacts between the Slavs and the peoples of the Caspian basin. Here Khlebnikov borrows generously from Nizami's *Iskandarnama*[21] (as he had three years earlier in his own reworking of *Layla and Majnun*[22]), gratuitously inserting the figures of the "Herodutus of the Arabs," al-Mas'udi, and the tenth-century Arab traveler Ahmad ibn Fadlan, who quotes anachronistically from the *Iksandarnama*. Later, looking back on this extraordinary pan-Asiatic pastiche, Khlebnikov conceptualized the experiment in the following terms: "Its individual pendentives [i.e., sections] form a complex structure; they speak of the Volga as the river of the Indo-Europeans and utilize Persia as the angle where the line of Russia and Macedonia intersect. The tales of the Oroches, an ancient Amur tribe, astonished me, and I conceived the idea of constructing a pan-Asian consciousness in songs."[23]

At the time he wrote "The Otter's Children," Khlebnikov was primarily intent on enriching, not replacing, the cultural raw material feeding his native literature, but the Asian—and specifically Central Asian—impulse that informed his own consciousness was far too powerful to be limited to the purely aesthetic realm. Around the same time that he wrote "The Otter's Children," Khlebnikov composed a playful but deeply serious open letter, stylized in the language of a seventeenth-century petition to the czar, in which he draws attention to Russia's mixed Asian heritage and calls for the creation of, among other things, a privileged zone in sparsely populated Mongolia, where a certain "society" would be given the right to "call all peoples to itself, and not to burden them, and different peoples will go there and forget what is evil, and therefrom will Mungalia receive its profit."[24] Over the course of the next several years, his interest in the Asian principle would, in this spirit, became increasingly political and utopian. No doubt the outbreak of the First World War and the German invasion of his native land made the look eastward even more attractive ("A united Asia has been born from the ashes of the Great War," he would later write[25]).

As early as 1916, two years after the beginning of hostilities between Germany and Russia but before the February Revolution, he was already proposing publicly the establishment of a coalition of Asian youth—representatives of all the major ethnic groups of the continent—to stand in solidarity against the older generation and its bourgeois traditions, chief among them the maintenance of state borders (see his "Letter to Two Japanese"[26]). Freed from service in the Imperial Russian Army by the Revolution in 1917, he traveled more or less freely about the country, returning for the last time to his native Astrakhan in the late summer of 1918. "Almost every Khlebnikov text composed during the sojourn in Astrakhan," writes Aleksandr Parnis, "is intimately related to the Central Asian problematics and conception of the poet."[27] Chief among these are three manifestos in which he calls for the liberation of the Asian continent from the "oppressors from the islands" (he means first and foremost the British Empire) and the confederation of all Asian nationalities. "Our path," he proclaims, "leads to the unity of the Star [i.e., the globe] via the unity of Asia, and via the freedom of the continent to the freedom of Planet Earth."[28] Khlebnikov took his own impractical steps in trying to realize this dream, publishing an announcement in a new Astrakhan newspaper about his intentions to put out a collection of literary works in Russian, Kalmyk, Kirgiz, Armenian, Georgian, Persian, and Tatar as a kind of emblem of unity and collaboration on the literary front.[29]

Needless to say, these utopian plans were unrealized and unrealizable, but the image of Asia remained a central focus of Khlebnikov's works from this point onward. A hint of the direction his thinking would take is found in an autobiographical tale written during his last Astrakhan sojourn. Titled "October on the Neva" (Oktiabr' na Neve), it recounts his adventures as a soldier on leave in Moscow and Petrograd after the February Revolution of 1917. In a highly poeticized description of Moscow's cityscape, Khlebnikov evokes the image of Qurrat al ʿAyn, the Persian martyr to the

Baha'i faith in mid-nineteenth-century Iran: "And is it not a new black-eyed Qurrat al 'Ayn who yields her wondrous silky hair to the flame which will consume her as she preaches equality and equal rights?"[30] Already in late 1918, this passage suggests, Persia was beginning to move into his field of vision, both ideologically and poetically.

The Road to Asia and the "Grossbuch"

Khlebnikov left Astrakhan in March 1919, made a short trip to Moscow, then headed south to Kharkov (now Kharkiv). There he befriended a young artist, V. D. Ermilov, who had just returned from a three-year stint in Persia as a private in the Caucasian Cavalry Corps of the Russian army. Their conversations served as a kind of telescope, magnifying Khlebnikov's still diffuse thoughts about Asia and bringing the "real" Asia into sharper focus. It is at this point that we can begin to speak of an emerging "travel literature," texts composed by Khlebnikov as he moved toward Persia via the Caucasus: first Rostov-on-Don, then Armavir, Derbent (in Dagestan), Baku, and from there via steamship across the Caspian to Bandar-i Anzali in the Persian province of Gilan. The writings we are referring to include poems that he wrote for local publications (mostly newspapers and miscellanies) but also a large body of works, the majority in poetic form, that remained in rough draft and unpublished in his lifetime. Indeed, many to this day are accessible only in archival repositories.

A major locus of these writings is a sketchbook bound in black cardboard containing more than one hundred leaves (the original number cannot be determined because some may have been ripped out) and roughly eight by thirteen inches (20.5 by 33 centimeters) in size. It has come to be called the "Grossbuch" because it is like a typical ledger in size, though it has no lines or columns for entering data.[31] Much about it is mysterious. We do not know exactly when Khlebnikov acquired the sketchbook: the *terminus a quo* is the spring of 1919, corresponding to the earliest dated text, composed when Khlebnikov was already in Kharkov. The *terminus ante quem* is November 1920, when he was in Baku and, according to one memoirist, was observed carrying a large notebook under his arm.[32] For reasons that remain unclear, he made entries from both the front and the back, inverting the sketchbook so that half the texts are upside down relative to the other half. Among the texts are undated variants of poems known to have been written considerably earlier, so we are dealing here with a mixture of original and reconstructed texts. Why Khlebnikov decided to include the latter is also a matter of conjecture. In some cases, at least, he appears to have assumed that the earlier versions had been lost or destroyed, and so the "Grossbuch" was to serve both as a personal archive repository as well as an ongoing record of current creative activity. Unfortunately, we do not always know whether a given poem is an original composition or the reconstruction of a poem written earlier but lost to posterity, since he himself was robbed during his travels, losing scores of manuscripts he carried about with him, often in a pillowcase.[33] In other cases, he may have simply recopied the text in planning larger composites. All this not only makes the dating of the manuscript itself problematic but introduces an achronicity, or, rather, a synchronicity, of record and recollection that complicates our attempt to reconstruct the direction of Khlebnikov's thought as he made his way from Europe to Asia. Nonetheless, the general contours of vision and its evolution are ultimately discernible through the thickets of the manuscript, and it is this that we will attempt to reconstruct.

During his stay in Astrakhan in 1918, as noted earlier, the poet dictated two manifestos calling for the unification of Asia. This utopian idea was still uppermost in Khlebnikov's mind during his stay in Kharkov, where he produced a poem titled "The One Book," which translates the "one Asia" of the manifestos into a global vision of unity. The opening, however, betrays his orientation on the Asian continent:

Я видел, что черныя Веды	I saw how the black Vedas,
Коран и Евангеліе	The Koran and the Gospel
И в шелковых досках	And the books of the Mongols
Книги монголов	In silky covers
Сами из праха степей	Themselves created a pyre
Из кизяка благовоннаго	Out of the dust of the steppes,
Как это делают	From fragrant kizyak,
Калмычки каждое утро	Like the Kalmyks fashion
Сложили костер	Every morning,
И сами легли на него	And lay down on it,
Белыя вдовы	White widows
В облаке дыма закрыты.	Enclosed in a cloud of smoke,
Чтобы ускорить приход	To hasten the coming
Книги единой	Of the one book.
Эту единую книгу	That one book
Скоро вы, скоро прочтете.	You will very soon be reading:
Белым блещут моря	The seas gleam white
В мертвых ребрах китов	In the whales' dead ribs;
Священн ое пеніе,	Sacred song,
Дикій, но правильный голос	A wild but modulated voice.
А синія реки—закладки	And the blue rivers are the book ribbons
Где читает читатель . . . [34]	Where the reader reads . . .

The poet then enumerates the rivers—the Volga ("where they sing of Razin at night"), Nile, Yangtze, Seine, Danube, Thames, Ob', Mississippi—that are the major page markers in the book of humanity, flowing into its common ocean. The speaker goes on to identify himself as the author of this book, leaving the reader to wonder who this megalomaniac "I" is. The answer emerges in another "Grossbuch" fragment that makes sense only if the lyric subject is identified as planet Earth:

Я, волосатый реками,	It is I, braided with rivers—
Смотрите Дунай течет	Look, the Danube flows
У меня по плечам	Over my shoulders,
И вихорь своевольный	A capricious eddy,
Порогами синеет Днепр.	The Dnepr shines blue in its rapids.
Это Волга блеснула на мне	That is the Volga that glistened on me
Синими водами.	With its blue waters.
А этот волос длинный	And that long strand of hair there—
Беру его пальцами	I take it between my fingers—
Амур где японка	Is the Amur, where a Japanese woman,
Молится небу	Her hands folded,
Руки сложив	Prays to heaven
Во время бури.[35]	In the middle of a storm.

Identifying the speaker (the author of the book) and the reader respectively as the whole planet and all humanity reveals the breathtaking scope of Khlebnikov's vision. But as that vision becomes more concrete on the eve of his journey east, so, too, do the contours and dimensions of the author and reader. Preparing now for the experience of Persia, the poet limits the book's reader to Asia, personified in the following poem as a woman either fomenting rebellion or leading insurrectionary forces:

Азія	Asia
Всегда рабыня, но с родиной царей на смуглой груди	Always a slave, but with the birthmark of kings on her swarthy breast
И с государственной печатью взамен серьги у уха	And with a seal of state in place of a ring in her ear,
То девушка с мечом не знавшая зачатья	Here a girl with a sword who has never known conception,
То повитуха мятежей старуха.	There a crone, midwife of insurrections—
Ты поворачиваешь страницы книги той	You turn the pages of the book
Где почерк был нажим руки морей	Whose script was the pressure of the seas' hand.
Чернилами сверкали ночью люди,	People glistened in the night like ink,
Разстрел царей был гневным знаком восклицанья	The execution of kings was an angry exclamation point
Победа войск служила запятой	The victory of troops served as a comma,
А полем многоточія чье бешенство не робко	The people's wrath was plainly
Народный гнев воочію	A field of ellipses whose madness was not bridled,
И трещины столетій—скобкой.[36]	And the crevices of the centuries serve as a parenthesis

This narrowing of vision is accompanied by an even more striking transformation of the speaking persona. In one of his most daring and beautiful entries in the

"Grossbuch," Khlebnikov describes himself and Asia as lovers, and he calls her to join him in the quest for freedom:

О если б волосами синих рек
Мне Азія покрыла бы колени
И дева прошептала таинственныя
   пени.
И, тихая, счастливая, рыдала,
Концом косы глаза суша.
Она любила! Она страдала!
Вселенной смутная душа.
И вновь прошли бы снова чувства
И зазвенел бы в сердце бой
И Мохавиры и Заратустры
И Саваджи объятаго борьбой.
Умерших их я был бы современник,
Творил ответы и вопросы.
А ты бы грудой светлых денег
Мне на ноги разсыпала бы косы
«Учитель» мне шепча,
«Не правда ли, сегодня
Мы будем сообща
Искать путей свободней?»³⁷

Oh, if only Asia would cover my knees
With the plaits of dark blue rivers
And the maiden would whisper mysterious
   laments
And calmly, joyfully would sob,
Drying her eyes with the tip of her braid.
She loved! She suffered!
The universe's troubled soul.
And feeling once again would course through me
And a battle start to ring out in the heart
Of Mahavira and Zarathustra
And Shivaji, embraced by battle.
I would be a contemporary of their deceased,
Would fashion questions and answers.
And you would scatter your braids over my feet
Like a pile of gleaming coins,
Whispering, "Master,
Isn't it true that today
Together we will search
Out ways of greater freedom?"

Khlebnikov here is already creating the mythic framework for his journey, one based, in all likelihood, on his early reading and poetic reworking of *Layla and Majnun*.³⁸ But this classic tale of star-crossed lovers provides only the barest of paradigms, one that will be filled in with more fully elaborated characters and a journey that has its denouement not only in the uniting of the protagonist and his beloved but in a loftier utopian goal, one implicated by a second project that had enthralled the poet for as many years as his preoccupation with Asia: the discovery of the laws of time, the mathematically definable intervals at which critical events occurred in human history. Central to his investigations, not coincidentally, was the ebb and flow of conquests and migrations east and west, particularly as they involved Russia: the Tatar invasions of the thirteenth century, Russia's "retaliatory" conquest of Siberia in the sixteenth century, the counterthrust of the Japanese victories in the Russo-Japanese War of 1904–5. Indeed, it was Russia's humiliating defeat in that war that had precipitated Khlebnikov's interests in the laws underlying historical flux: upon hearing the news of Russia's horrific losses while he was on an excursion in Russia's Yaroslavl province, he resolved to find the laws of time governing such events and carved his vow to fulfill this mission into the bark of a birch tree.

    With that vow in mind, drawn irresistibly to his beloved Asia, the poet resumed his peregrinations in the autumn of 1920. His destination was Baku, site of a Congress of Peoples of the East, convened by the newly Sovietized Republic of Azerbaijan to propagandize the Revolution being projected now onto Russia's southern neighbors. The concrete dates of his journey from Kharkov to Baku are not known. According to the most recent biography, Khlebnikov left Kharkov in August, spent some time in late August and/or early September in Rostov-on-Don, proceeded to Baku for the congress (September 1–8) and also attended a proletarian writers' conference in Armavir in September, spent two weeks in Dagestan in late September and/or early October, then returned to Baku, where he remained till April 1921.[39]

One of the "Grossbuch" poems that emerged from this period is "Sayan," a strange and beautiful prehistoric idyll set in a mountain range between Mongolia and south-central Siberia.[40] The landscape the poet describes is one in which time has been frozen; the runes and drawings of some unknown artist dress the mountain cliffs and speak of a mysterious covenant between the prehistoric dwellers of the land and their god. A young, nameless visitor makes himself the guardian of an image etched into the bark of a birch tree (reprising Khlebnikov's own vow in Yaroslavl province) while gazing down from the mountaintop at a waterfall that wears its own path in the rocks below—a prescient image to which the poet will return as he moves deeper into Asia.

A second poem, probably reflecting Khlebnikov's wandering in the mountains west of Derbent, had an ominous catalyst: a summons by the Cheka.[41] The narrative, however, focuses not on the interrogation (Khlebnikov often attracted suspicion because of his bohemian appearance and neglect of social proprieties, such as carrying the documents needed to establish his identity) but on the mountainous landscape and how it might be read in the most literal sense:

Вдруг смерклось	Suddenly twilight fell.
Темное ущелье. Река темнела рядом,	A dark ravine. The river alongside grew dark,
По тысяче камней катила голубое кружево	Azure lace rolled down a thousand stones.
И стало вдруг темно, и чехлом холодных капель	And suddenly it grew dark, and we were quickly encased
Покрылись сразу мы. То грозное ущелье	In a covering of cold drops.
Вдруг встало каменною книгой читателя	The terrifying ravine suddenly became the stone book of another reader,
другого	Open to the eyes of other worlds.
Открытое для глаз других мiров	The aul was spread out, the huts
Аул разсыпан был казались сакли	Were like the letters of incomprehensible speech.
Буквами нам непонятной речи.	There a red rock rose to the sky
Там камень красный подымался в небо	Half a mile high, being read by someone to this very day.
На пол версты прямою высотой, кем-то читаемой донынe	But I saw no reader in the sky.
Но я чтеца на небе не заметил.[42]	

The poem continues to elaborate the metaphor of the land as an indecipherable text, like the runes in the Sayan mountains, but author and reader and message all remain a mystery, one corresponding to the poet's own liminal state on the border between Europe and Asia, and on the threshold of a discovery that will alter his perception of himself and his destination.

The discovery took place in December 1920, when Khlebnikov worked out a series of mathematical formulae that he believed underlay the occurrence of major historical events and, because of the patterns they revealed, could be used to predict future events. Metaphorically, this breakthrough was equivalent to the imminent discovery of Asia: "I was the first to ascend this new continent commandeering time," he wrote in a letter to his sister in January 1921. "I was the first to set foot on it, I was drunk with joy."[43] The discovery also altered his perception of himself: in communicating his discoveries to his Baku comrades he presented himself as a new Karl Marx and—to the more conservative Baku populace—as Mohammed's heir. He titled the lecture at which he first presented his discoveries "The Koran of Numbers." Thus Khlebnikov was poised, in the spring of 1921, to pursue two utopian dreams: a unified Asia as a precursor of global unity and the promulgation of the "laws of time."

Three Identities: The Persian Expedition

The opportunity arose in April, when the poet signed on as a propaganda officer for an expeditionary force organized by the Bolsheviks to assist the nascent revolutionary movement in northern Iran.[44] He arrived on April 14 on the steamship *Kursk*, disembarking in Enzeli (now Bandar-i Anzeli). The next three and a half months were spent in Gilan and adjoining Persian provinces on the Caspian, sometimes in the company of the soldiers who made up the Red Army detachment, but often on his own, since his responsibilities were purely nominal and discipline in the ranks was extraordinarily lax. The "Grossbuch" entries document his movements (whether coevally or retrospectively is impossible to determine), beginning with his early impression of the port city through which he entered Iran. "Easter in Enzeli"[45] shows a preoccupation—almost an obsession—with the beauties of the flora, fauna, and exotic sounds of this strange new world: cinchona trees with azure bark, dark green, golden-eyed gardens of *portakal* and *naranj,* the rising moon in a milky sky. But the aural images are, perhaps, more telling: in the background, the poet hears the sound of rowdy soldiers singing a popular song about Stenka Razin, the Cossack rebel with whom, as we have already noted, Khlebnikov's early Futurist confreres linked him at the beginning of his poetic career.

From Enzeli, the detachment of Red Army soldiers moved to the provincial capital of Resht, where they were quartered for a little over a month. Here the street life catches Khlebnikov's eye. In one memorable fragmentary sketch, he talks about the children and the women in their chadors:

Дети пекли улыбки больших глаз	Children baked the smiles of their large eyes
Жаровнями темных ресниц	In the braziers of dark eyelashes
И обжигали случайного прохожего.	And scorched the chance passerby.
Паук-калека с руками-нитками у мечети.	A spider-cripple with hand-webs by the
Темнеет сумрак, быстро падая	mosque.
И запечатанным вином	Twilight grows darker, falling quickly.
Проходят жены. Шелк шуршит.[46]	And women walk by, looking like sealed
	wine bottles.
	The swishing sound of silk.

During these weeks, Khlebnikov was more or less free to wander about at will. From what little documentation we possess, we surmise that he spent some time in a mountainous area northwest of Resht, in the mountains around Khalkhal, probably in mid-June.[47] In several different jottings, he talks about these environs. In one, he introduces himself—in the third person—into the landscape:

Али ала!	Ali ala!
Выбежали с гор	They ran down from the mountains
Встречать	To greet
Чадо Хлебникова.[48]	The child Khlebnikov.

The "they" of this curious fragment is deciphered in drafts outside the "Grossbuch" as dervishes or prophets who welcome the poet as one of their own kind. In another fragment devoted to the same landscape, he introduces two historical figures: Stenka Razin—with whom we are already familiar—and the figure of Fatima Baraghani (1814–1852), better known as Tahirih or Qurrat al-'Ayn, one of the most prominent disciples of the Bab ('Ali Muhammad of Shiraz), executed for her opposition to the Shiite religious establishment.[49] In one particularly graphic description of the Khalkhal landscape, Khlebnikov writes:

Еду—белые горы неподвижныя,	I ride along. White mountains, motionless,
бездыханныя,	lifeless,
Как белое тело Тахирэ	Like the white body of Tahirih
Когда она сама затянула на себе	When she herself drew the shah's rope
веревку шаха	Around her neck. White breasts.
На шее. Белые груди.	The dark nostrils of the mountains greedily
С моря запах Разина жадно	inhale
Втягивают темные ноздри гор.[50]	The smell of Razin from the sea.

Here we see the beginning of a process involving a redefinition of the poet's own core identity and the further personification of Asia as a female figure whom he both honors and rescues from imminent peril.

We can trace the evolution of the poet's self-image as he moves through Persia. From later memoirs by members of the Red Army expeditionary force, we know that they moved out of Resht in an easterly direction along the Caspian coast together with local Persian revolutionaries, with the ultimate intention of veering south toward Tehran and toppling the forces of Reza Khan. They reached Shahsavar (now Tonekabon), remaining there through most of July. Khlebnikov, we read in one these memoirs, his hair and beard grown long, was dressed in "picturesque rags" and walked about barefoot. He and an artist friend, Mecheslav Dobrokovskii, "set up camp in a *chaikhana*, where they were fed for free, given strong tea and *taryak* [opium] to smoke. People always gathered around them."[51]

Three preliminary drafts of poems, in particular, draw attention to the messianic pretensions crystallizing in Khlebnikov's consciousness during his Persian sojourn. One of them, "I saw the youthful prophet . . . ," present in two different variants in the "Grossbuch,"[52] is set deep in the mountains around Khalkhal and describes the thoughts of the "youthful prophet," the author's alter ego, as he contemplates a forest waterfall. The trees, he writes, are like the witnesses to a marriage contract, like elders fingering the prayer beads embedded in the vines that surround them, and the waterfall itself is like an umbilical cord connecting the maternal sources of the stream and their female offspring. Surrounding them are cliffs inscribed with "the alphabet of centuries." Their message seems to be embedded in the metaphor for the boulders lining the cliffs. These giant crags, he says, are like "the shoulders of a forest maiden under a white wave," and they provoke a sudden association:

Что за морем искал священник
  наготы
Он Разиным поклялся быть
  напротив.
Ужели снова бросит в море княжну.
  Противо-Разин грезит.
Нет! Нет! Свидетели высокіе
  деревья!
Студеною волною покрыв себя
И холода живого узнав язык и разум
Другого міра,
Наш юноша поет:
«С русалкою Зоргама обручен
Навеки я,
Волну очеловечив.
Тот сделал волной деву».
Деревья шептали речи столетій[53]

What did this prophet of nakedness seek across
  the sea?
He vowed to be Razin's opposite.
Will he once again toss the princess into the
  sea? Anti-Razin broods.
No! No! The tall trees are witnesses!
Covering himself in the chilled water
And recognizing the language and thought of
  the living cold
Of another world,
Our young man sings:
"I'm betrothed to Zorgam's rusalka
Forever,
Because I made the wave into a person.
That other one turned the maiden into a wave."
The trees whispered the speeches of the ages.

The image of Razin here is evoked with particular reference to the incident we alluded to earlier, in which Stenka Razin captured the daughter of a Persian fleet commander on one of his pirating raids on the Caspian. The popular song about Razin quoted in

"Easter in Enzeli" tells the story of the princess's fate: Razin's fellow marauders, taking his infatuation with the woman as a betrayal of their common cause, start complaining about her presence in their midst. In response, Razin tosses her overboard, sacrificing her to the Volga's waves. The poet, long having perceived himself as a Razin of the poetic world, now asserts that he is "anti-Razin," in that he is prepared to save the Persian princess rather than deliver her to death. But if Khlebnikov is the new "anti-Razin," who is the Persian woman he saves? In the poem, she is called "Zorgam's *rusalka* [water nymph]," identified in some critical sources as the daughter of a well-known khan, Zergam al-Saltana (also Zorgam os-Soltane), whom Khlebnikov tutored for a short time during his stay in or around Khalkhal.[54] But this biographical prototype does not ultimately answer the question any more than does the historical prototype, Razin's captive Persian princess. Within the context of the "Grossbuch" as a whole, we have every reason to identify Zorgam's *rusalka*, the Persian princess, and the forest maiden of the landscape with Asia, to whom the poet-prophet now comes as a bridegroom.

The last line of the poem, "The trees whispered the speeches of the ages," suggests that the landscape, previously indecipherable, is now communicating something intelligible to the young prophet, something about his own identity. In "I saw the youthful prophet . . . ," he is a mirror reflection, a negative doppelganger of the archetypally Russian figure Stenka Razin. But a second poem abandons the Russian antitype for a native one: the messiah of Islam. In the "Grossbuch," curiously, the poem is adjacent to the previous one, almost as though the poet is exploring alternate identities in succession. In this untitled work, which in a later draft bears the title "A Night in Persia," the poet describes himself lying on the sand of the Caspian shore at night. An Iranian passes by and asks him to help balance a stack of firewood on his back. The poet obliges, and the Iranian disappears into the night. The poet lies back on the sand, listening to the waves rolling in, and begins repeating "a name, a single word":

Мехди? Мехди! без смысла, без товарищей соседей	Mahdi? Mahdi! without meaning without comrades, neighbors,
И в то же время таин ст венн ый жук, летевшій прямо с чернаго шумнаго моря,	And at that moment a mysterious beetle, flying directly from the black, sounding sea,
держа путь прямо на меня, сделал два круга над головой	Aiming directly for me, circled my head twice
И сел мне на кудри. Молчал и после	And landed in my curls. I was silent, and then
И внятно заскрипел мне знакомой речью знакомые слова.	It began to clearly chirp familiar words in a familiar speech,
На языке знакомом мне из детства	In a language I knew since childhood.
Он ласково и твердо сообщил мне весть.	Gently and firmly it conveyed a message.

Довольно, жук. Мы поняли друг друга!	That's enough, beetle. We've understood each other!
Таинственный договор. Лети. Прощай в сумраке морском!	A secret compact. Go fly away in the sea's darkness.
Море соленой пеной стирает мой поцелуй	Good-bye! The sea with its salty foam erases my kiss
Вслед уходящему персу.[55]	In the wake of the departing Persian.

This daring association should probably not be viewed as an expropriation of the role the Mahdi is assigned in Shiite Islam, the dominant faith of those in the area where Khlebnikov was wandering. His correspondence at this time indicates, rather, that he was interested in the doctrines, history, and spread of the Baha'i faith. In a letter from Enzeli to his sister, he wrote, "Preparing to leave Baku, I busied myself with the study of Mirza Bab, a Persian prophet, and here I'll be giving a lecture for the Persians and Russians on Mirza Bab and Jesus. I told the Persians that I'm a prophet."[56] In various notebook jottings dating from his stay in Baku, Khlebnikov singles out particular teachings of the Bab's successor, Baha'-u'llah (Mirza Husayn-'Ali Nuri), that corresponded with his own utopian ideals, among them the unity of all humanity and opposition to "states of space" (i.e., political formations that encourage mutual hostility).[57] It seems certain that Khlebnikov, in his encounter with Asia, saw himself in a similar role, coming to Iran and, under the influence of these new surroundings, shedding his Russianness and taking on the mantle of a native prophet.

A third identity, also non-Russian, which is registered in the "Grossbuch" fragments and would later figure prominently in a large, unfinished poem based on them, gives what is perhaps the most frequently occurring self-definition: that of the dervish. In one of these fragments, set in another seaside scene, the poet writes:

Мальчик кричал мне урус	A young boy cried out to me. "Urus!"
Русскій дервиш. Гуль мулла.	"Russian dervish. Gul'-mulla."
Я соглашался, лежал на песке. Мне все равно[58]	I agreed and lay down on the sand. It's all the same to me.

In later expanded versions of this fragment and other poems, these two terms—*dervish* and *gul' mulla*—are frequently repeated. The word "dervish" (identical in Russian) is clear enough and occurs in Khlebnikov's poetic vocabulary well before the "Persian period." "Gul' mulla" is another matter. Khlebnikov himself translated the term as "flower priest" or "priest of the flowers" (*священник цветов*). In using the word "priest," he was probably seeking out a Russian equivalent for "mullah," the word he thought he heard and which (if he had heard correctly) would mean a Shi'i cleric. What he probably heard, according to Russian orientalist K. D. Shidfar, was the phrase "gul-i-moula." "Gol" (or "gul") is "flower"—this Khlebnikov understood correctly—but the second word is not "mullah," but "moula," meaning a spiritual master, mystic, or guru. Shidfar says that the full phrase "gul-i maula"—"flower of the mystics" —is a "folk term for the wandering 'singing dervishes' who were an inevitable part of life in the streets, squares and bazars" of Persian towns. Moreover, it was used by dervishes themselves in announcing their presence and asking for alms.[59] Thus it is clear that Khlebnikov is identifying himself with these mendicants. Moreover, many of his compatriots comment on the literalness of this identification. Not only did Khlebnikov take on the appearance of a dervish—with his long hair, beard, and eccentric clothing and behavior—but he adopted an attitude of utter indifference toward money and all material goods.[60] His use of hashish and other opiates is also well attested. One of his contemporaries reports that during his wanderings around the area of Khalkhal, "a local dervish invited him into a hut. They sat opposite each other the whole night on a carpet spread on the floor. The dervish recited verses from the Koran. Khlebnikov listened in silence and nodded his head, indicating full understanding. Sunrise found them in the same position. When Khlebnikov got ready to leave, the dervish made him a gift of his staff, a tall felt hat (like an Orthodox *kamlaukion*) and *juranki*—colored wool stockings decorated with patterns of the sort you find on a carpet or palas."[61]

Whether or not Khlebnikov intended to settle in northern Persia is difficult to ascertain. On the one hand, he invited his family to join him there; on the other hand, he indicated that Persia was beginning to weigh on him. When a friend, Boris Samorodov, asked him why he had returned to Russia so soon, Khlebnikov said that Persia "oppressed him with the antiquity of its centuries-old culture. He felt like it was the cradle of humanity, and he experienced the weight of its ripeness in everything, even in the red hues of the pomegranates. He needed to recover from the burden of this weight and regain his strength."[62] In fact, his Persian journey was cut short by military and political exigencies: in late July, betrayed by one of the local leaders of the Gilan revolution, the Russian expeditionary force was obliged to retreat from Shahsavar back to Enzeli, and from there, the troops were evacuated to Baku. The Persian Propaganda Council, under whose aegis Khlebnikov still remained, issued him travel papers to Tashkent, a journey that would have taken him from the periphery to the very heart of Soviet Central Asia,[63] but ill health compelled him to retreat to the Caucasus. With the help of friends, he was able to find shelter in Kislovodsk and later subsistence employment in Piatigorsk. Between September and December, he was extremely productive, turning many of the rough drafts, fragments, and sketches composed in Persia into finished poems. Among them are "The Trumpet of the *Gul-Mulla*," a cycle that creates an artificial "diary" out of his Persian impressions, and "Azy iz uzy," literally "A's from a Fetter" or "I's from a Fetter," a montage of poems (including variants of "The One Book" and "Asia" cited above) that focuses on Khlebnikov's pre-Persian reflections on the liberation of the individual and the collective soul of Asia in light of the revolutionary changes taking place in Russia. An analysis of these works, regrettably, lies outside the scope of this study.[64]

The "Grossbuch" manuscript, in conclusion, testifies to two transformations, one involving Khlebnikov's perception of the continent and its multifarious cultures, and the other involving his perception of himself. Initially, the poet saw Asia as an "other" to be culturally appropriated by the avant-garde (both cultural and political) in its rivalry with the West. He could do so with far more confidence than his Futurist colleagues because of his own childhood roots in the Kalmyk steppes and the years he spent in Astrakhan and Kazan, but as a Russian who had been raised with the manners and mores of the Europeanized elite, he was still approaching the East as a target of cultural exploitation. As he matured, however, his attitude changed. The Revolution and its claims to internationalism opened up a literal path to Asia and an encounter that encouraged exactly the reverse process: instead of objectifying Asia as a target of cultural expropriation, he anthropomorphized Asia as a beloved woman or child who was to be protected and who could be a partner in the cause of global unity and liberation.

This transformation, in turn, meant that the poet's own view of himself had to change. His initial self-image was that of a rebel, an insurrectionist intent on upsetting the cultural and political order of his native land by exploiting and deploying the resources of the Orient. But his journey to the East, both figuratively and literally, forced him to reexamine this position. As he approached and then entered Persia, he metamorphosed into a prophet and a dervish. Initially intent on appropriating the East, he was appropriated by her. When he returned to Russia, he did so in the persona of a Persian prophet prepared to share his knowledge of the fundamental laws of time, the discovery of which he believed would put an end to "states of space" and usher in a new world harmony between East and West.

This new identity, inspired, perhaps, by the image of Baha'-u'llah, informs a number of works that Khlebnikov completed following his return to Moscow in December 1921. In the last months of his life, he took many of the fragments we have examined and incorporated them into a cycle of poems called *Zangezi,* dominated by the image of an eponymous prophet. He is now no longer specifically Persian or Asian but retains the same otherworldly cast that he assumed in the "Grossbuch" diary. Significantly, the poem cited above, "It is I, braided with rivers. . . . ," whose lyrical "I" is Earth itself, is now put in the mouth of Zangezi, as though he had earned the right to speak on behalf of all mankind. It is this triumphal globalism, emerging from a lifelong journey that began in the Kalmyk steppes and culminated in the journey to Persia, that defines the poet's ultimate vision.

Notes

1. David Schimmelpenninck van der Oye, *Russian Orientalism* (New Haven: Yale University Press, 2010), pp. 44–59.

2. The admixture of Romanticism and colonial conquest is discussed at length in Susan Layton, *Russian Literature and Empire: Conquest of the Caucasus from Pushkin to Tolstoy* (Cambridge: Cambridge University Press, 1994).

3. Harsha Ram, "The Poetics of Eurasia: Velimir Khlebnikov between Empire and Revolution," in Madhavan K. Palat, ed., *Social Identities in Revolutionary Russia* (New York: Palgrave Publishers, 2001), 211.

4. Schimmelpenninck van der Oye (2010), pp. 74–92, 199–209.

5. We refer, in particular, to the Hylaeans (a group informally constituted in 1912) and the Cubo-Futurists, who succeeded Hylaea in 1913.

6. The history of the movement is most fully explored in Vladimir Markov, *Russian Futurism: A History* (Berkeley: University of California Press, 1968), and A. V. Krusanov, *Russkii avangard, 1907–1932: Istoricheskii obzor* [The Russian Avant-garde, 1903–1932: An Historical Survey], 3 vols. (Moscow: Novoe literaturnoe obozrenie, 2010).

7. "In the characterization of Russian Futurism," writes Vladimir Markov, "social and even geographical factors must be considered. It is important to realize that most Futurists originated in the borderlands and thus that they spent their childhood in a non-Great Russian or a nationally mixed environment, or that they came from the 'plebian intelligentsia.' Osip Mandelshtam fittingly spoke of their *udel'no buistvo*, an expression which defies translation (literally it is 'a tumult in the appanages'), but contains elements of 'militant provincialism.'" See *The Longer Poems of Velimir Khlebnikov*, University of California Publications in Modern Philology 62 (Berkeley and Los Angeles: University of California Press, 1962), p. 8.

8. See his autobiography, "Put' entuziasta" [The Path of an Enthusiast], in Vasilii Kamenskii, *Tango s korovami. Stepan Razin. Zvuchal' vesneianki. Put' entuziasta* [Tango with Cows. Stepan Razin. Soundsong of the Spring-Reed. The Path of an Enthusiast], ed. M. Ia. Poliakov (Moscow: Kniga, 1990), pp.424–26.

9. The majority of the Futurists, write Iu. M. Loshchits and V. N. Trenin, "were in a certain sense a product of the rebellious Russo-Asiatic milieu. Most of them came to literature from the periphery, came as outsiders, like a travelling circus, like a band of nomads." See "Tema vostoka v tvorchestve V. Khlebnikova [The Theme of the Orient in the Works of V. Khlebnikov], *Narody Azii i Afriki* 4 (1966), p. 150.

10. Nikolai Burliuk, "Toboi izmuchennyi ia znaiu" [Tormented by you, I know . . .], in *Trebnik troikh. Sbornik stikhov i risunkov* [A Missal for Three: A Collection of Verse and Drawings] (Moscow: Izd. G. L. Kuz'mina i S. D. Dolinskogo, 1913), p. 53; cf. David Burliuk and Nikolai Burliuk, *Stikhotvoreniia* [Poems] (Saint Petersburg: Akademicheskii proekt, 2002), p. 443.

11. Nataliia Goncharova, preface to *Katalog vystavki* [Exhibition Catalogue] (Moscow: n.p., 1913). Cited in E. N. Petrova, ed., *Nataliia Goncharova: Gody v Rossii* [Nataliia Goncharova: The Russian Years] (Saint Petersburg: Palace Editions, 2002), p. 291.

12. Vasilii Kamenkii, "O Khlebnikove" [About Khlebnikov], in Velimir Khlebnikov, *Tvoreniia. Tom 1: 1906–1908* [Creations. Vol. 1: 1906–1908] (Moscow: "Gileia," 1914), n.p. [= viii].

13. Velimir Khlebnikov, *Sobranie sochinenii v shesti tomakh* [Collected Works in Six Volumes], ed. R. V. Duganov and E. R. Arenzon (Moscow: Institut mirovoi literatury, 2000–2006), vol. 2, p. 118. (Hereafter citations to this edition will be given with the abbreviation SS followed by volume and page number. Volume 6, published in two books, is abbreviated VI-1 and VI-2.)

14. Ronald Vroon, "Velimir Khlebnikov's 'Kuznechik' and the Art of Verbal Duplicity," in Ronald Vroon and John Malmstad, eds., *Readings in Russian Modernsim: To Honor Vladimir Fedorovich Markov* (Moscow: "Nauka": Izdatel'skaia firma "Vostochnaia literatura," 1993), p. 358.

15. Khlebnikov, SS VI-2, p. 311.

16. A. E. Parnis, "'Konetsarstvo, ved' ottuda ia . . . " ["The equine kingdom, whence I hail . . ."], *Teegin gerl (Svet v stepi). Literaturno-khudozhestvennyi al'manakh Soiuza pisatelei Kalmytsskoi* ASSR 1, 67 (1976), p. 150.

17. A highly selective list, in addition to the work of Loshchits and Trenin cited above, must include P. I. Tartakovskii, *Sotsial'no-esteticheskii opyt narodov vostoka i poeziia V. Khlebnikova, 1900–1910-e gody* [The Socio-esthetic Experience of the Peoples of the East and the Poetry of Velimir Khlebnikov, 1900–1910s] (Tashkent: Izd. "FAN" Uzbekskoi SSR, 1987); Tartakovskii, *Poeziia Khlebnikova i vostok, 1917–1922 gody* [The Poetry of V. Khlebnikov and the East, 1917–1922] (Tashkent: Izd.

"FAN" Akademii nauk Respubliki Uzbekistan, 1992); Salomon Mirsky, *Der Orient im Werk Chleb-nikovs*, Slavistische Beiträge 85 (Munich: Sagner, 1975); A. E. Parnis, "V. Khlebnikov v revoliutsion-nom Giliane (Novye materialy)" [V. Khlebnikov in Revolutionary Gilan (New Materials)], *Narody Azii i Afriki* 5 (1967), pp. 156–64, and Parnis, "'Evraziiskie' konteksty Khlebnikova: ot 'kalmytskogo' mifa k mifu o 'edinoi Azii' (1)" [Khlebnikov's "Eurasian" Contexts: From the "Kalmyk" Myth to the Myth of "One Asia"], in V. Ivanov, ed., *Evraziiskoe prostranstvo: Zvuk, slovo obraz* [Eurasian Space: Sound, Word, Image] (Moscow: Iazyki slavianskoi kul'tury, 2003), pp. 299–344.

18. Khlebnikov, SS VI-1, pp. 66–67.

19. Ibid., SS V, pp. 242–79.

20. Among the essays he drew from are "On Ancient Russian Campaigns against the East" and "The Volga Bulgars." See V. V. Grigor'ev, *Rossiia i Aziia: Sbornik issledovanii i statei po istorii, etno-grafii i geografii . . .* [Russia and Asia: A Collection of Studies and Essays on History, Ethnography and Geography . . .] (Saint Petersburg: Tip. brat'ev Panteleevykh, 1876), pp. 1–44, 79–106.

21. Khlebnikov drew, not directly from Nizami, but from retellings of Nizami's *Eskander-nameh* in V. V. Grigoriev, *Rossiia i Aziia* [Russia and Asia] (1876). See Khlebnikov, SS V, p. 437.

22. Khlebnikov, SS III, pp. 55–59.

23. Ibid., SS I, p. 7.

24. Ibid., SS VI-1, p. 212.

25. Ibid., SS VI-1, p. 271.

26. Ibid., SS VI-1, pp. 252–56.

27. Parnis (2003), p. 315.

28. The version published, *Collected Works* (SS VI-1, 272), is not entirely reliable. A corrected text of the manifestos with explanatory notes is published in Parnis (2003), pp. 336–41.

29. Parnis (2003), p. 317.

30. Khlebnikov, SS, V, pp. 185–86.

31. The manuscript is housed in the Russian State Archive of Literature and Art (Rossiiskii gosu-darstvennyi arkhiv literatury i iskusstva), *fond* 527, *edinitsa khraneniia* 64. Hereinafter, references to this manuscript will be identified as "Grossbuch" followed by the leaf number, recto (*r*) or verso (*v*). In citations, the Russian text is given as it stands in the manuscript; the English translation is edited for readability with standard punctuation.

32. Perhaps the origin of the designation "Grossbuch" can be traced to this remark as well. It belongs to Tat'iana Vechorka, who in 1925 published a short essay on her encounters with the poet during his sojourn in Baku from September 1920 to April 1921. See Tat'iana Vechorka, "Vospomina-niia o Khlebnikove" [Reminiscences about Khlebnikov], in *Zapisnaia knizhka Velimira Khlebnikova* [Velimir Khlebnikov's Notebook], comp. and ed. A. Kruchenykh (Moscow: Izd. Vserossiiskogo soi-uza poetov), p. 21.

33. In his moving obituary for Khlebnikov, Vladimir Mayakovskii writes, "The way Khlebnikov worked astonished me. His empty room was always overflowing with notebooks, pieces of paper and scraps filled with his miniscule handwriting. . . . When he travelled the manuscripts would all be stuffed in a pillowcase, which Khlebnikov would sleep on when he travelled, and then he would lose the pillowcase." See V. V. Maiakovskii, "V. V. Khlebnikov," *Polne sobranie sochinenii* [Complete Works], vol. 2: *Stikhi; stat'i, 1917–1925* [Verse and Essays, 1917–1922], ed. V. Trenin (Moscow Gos. izdat. "Khudozhestvennaia literatura," 1939), p. 482.

34. Khlebnikov, "Grossbuch," 9v; cf. Khlebnikov, SS II, pp. 114–115.

35. Khlebnikov, "Grossbuch," 6r; cf. Khlebnikov, SS III, p. 278. See R. V. Duganov, Velimir Khlebnikov: Priroda tvorchestva [Velimir Khlebnikov: The Nature of His Creation] (Moscow: Sovetskii pisatel', 1990), p. 136.

36. Khlebnikov, "Grossbuch," 68v; cf. Khlebnikov, SS II, p.112.

37. Khlebnikov, "Grossbuch," 13v; cf Khlebnikov, SS II, p. 113.

38. Khlebnikov, "Medlum i Leili," SS III, pp. 55–59.

39. Sofiia Starkina, Velimir Khlebnikov (Moscow: Molodaia gvardiia, 2007), pp. 317–18.

40. Khlebnikov, "Grossbuch," 12v; cf. Khlebnikov, SS II, pp. 323–325.

41. There is some dispute about the actual location of the landscape described: the editors of the most recent Collected Works place it in Dagestan during his two-week sojourn there (see Khlebnikov, SS II, p. 536), but this view is disputed by A. E. Parnis, who writes that the actual location remains unknown. See his commentary to the poem in Velimir Khlebnikov, Poeziia. Dramaticheskie proizvedeniia. Proza. Publitsistika [Poetry. Dramatic Works. Prose. Essays], comp. and ed. A. E. Parnis (Moscow: Slovo, 2001), p. 629.

42. Khlebikov, "Grossbuch," 20v; cf. Khlebnikov, SS II, pp. 138–139.

43. Khlebnikov, SS VI-2, p. 200.

44. The history of this incursion is documented in Vladimir Genis, Krasnaia Persiia: bol'sheviki v Giliane 1920–1921: Dokumental'naia khronika [Red Persia: The Bolsheviks in Gilan, 1920–1921: A Documentary Chronicle] (Moscow: MNPI, 2000); and M. A. Persits, comp., Persidskii front mirovoi revoliutsii: Dokumenty o sovetskom vtorzhenii v Gilian (1920–1921) [The Persian Front of the World Revolution: Documents on the Soviet Invasion of Gilan (1920–1921)] (Moscow: Kvadriga, 2009). See also Cosroe Chaquèri, The Soviet Socialist Republic of Iran, 1920–21: Birth of the Trauma (Pittsburgh: University of Pittsburgh Press, 1994).

45. Khlebnikov, "Grossbuch," 7v; cf. Khlebnikov, SS II, pp. 188–89.

46. Khlebnikov, "Grossbuch," 8r; cf. Khlebnikov, SS II, p. 459.

47. See the excerpts from K. B. Tomashevskii's memoirs in A. E. Parnis, "'Prorocheskaia dusha': V. Khlebnikov v vospominaniiakh sovremennikov" ["A Prophetic Soul": V. Khlebnikov in the Memoirs of Contemporaries], Literaturnoe obozrenie 12 (1985), pp. 100–101.

48. Khlebnikov, "Grossbuch," 87r.

49. For a detailed overview of her image in Khlebnkov's works, see Ronald Vroon, "Qurrat al-'Ayn and the Image of Asia in Velimir Chlebnikov's Post-Revolutionary Oeuvre," Russian Literature 50, 3 (2001), pp. 335–62.

50. Khlebnikov, "Grossbuch," 38r.

51. A. Kosterin, "Russkie dervishi" [Russian Dervishes], Moskva 9 (1966), p. 22. Teryak is a form of opium.

52. Khlebnikov, "Grossbuch," 9v and 86r; cf. Khlebnikov, SS II, p. 190.

53. Khlebnikov, "Grossbuch," 86r; cf. Khlebnikov, SS II, p. 190.

54. Khlebnikov (2001) , p. 624.

55. Khlebnikov, "Grossbuch," 85r; cf. Khlebnikov, SS II, pp. 214–15.

56. Khlebnikov, SS VI-2, p. 207.

57. H. Baran and A. E. Parnis, "'Anabasis' Velimira Khlebnikova: Zametki k teme" [Velimir Khlebnikov's "Anabasis": Some Notes], in Ivanov (2003), pp. 290–95.

58. Khlebnikov, "Grossbuch," 40r.

59. Khlebnikov, SS III, p. 479. Dennis Ioffe sheds some light on Shidfar's claim, suggesting that he "had in mind the new western Persian pronunciation of the combination gol-i mowla," admitting, however, that he has been unable to locate authoritative sources that register this "folk name"; Dennis Ioffe, "Budetlianin na obochine islama: 'urus dervish' i 'gul' mulla' v aspekte zhiznetvorchestva i poetiki Khlebnikova (Obzor interpretatsij i dopolneniia k kommentariiu)" [The Futurian on the Margins of Islam: Urus Dervish and Gul'-Mulla from the Vantage Point of Khlebnikov's Biography and Poetics (A Critical Survey and Addenda to the Commentary)], Philologica: A Bilingual Journal of Russian and Theoretical Philology 8, 19–20 (2003–5), p. 242. In our search for such an authoritative source, we contacted Dr. Mehrdad Shokoohy, professor emeritus at the University of Greenwich's School of Architecture, Design and Construction and a native Persian informant, who conveyed in personal correspondence that "in my childhood I often heard dervishes passing in the

street announcing their presence by shouting 'darwish gol-i maula' (the poor flower of the mystics), expecting alms from householders and passers-by." I am also indebted to Professor Shokoohy for his elucidation of the distinction between the terms mulla (or molla) and maula (or mawla).

60. Ioffe (2003–5), pp. 227–31.

61. Ol'ga Samorodova, "Poet na Kavkaze" [A Poet in the Caucasus], Zvezda 6 (1972), p. 189.

62. Ibid., p. 189.

63. See the editorial commentary in Khlebnikov, SS VI-2, p. 268.

64. In addition to the extensive annotations in the standard editions of Khlebnikov's works, see also Markov (1962), pp. 160–67; Mirsky (1975), pp. 53–74; S. Kiktev, "O kompozitsii poemy Khlebnikova 'Truba Gul'-mully'" [On the Composition of Khlebnikov's Poem "Gul'-Mulla's Trumpet"], in Tezisy dokladov III Khlebnikovskikh chtenii (Astrakhan: Astrakhanskii universitet, 1989), pp. 13–14; and P. I. Tartakovskii, "Truba Gul' mully" [Gul'-mulla's Trumpet], in Kiktev (1992), pp. 247–82.

8 Narrating the *Ichkari* Soundscape

European and American Travelers on Central Asian Women's Lives and Music

Tanya Merchant

WOMEN IN UZBEKISTAN tell stories of their musical history that reach deep into the past. The most common versions include living memories of mothers, aunts, and grandmothers who played music and/or sang as a hobby in the privacy of their own homes and their recollections of how this practice was entirely common. "There used to be a *dutar* [fretted, two-stringed lute] hanging in every home," is a phrase that I've heard from many different people from different walks of life. Music is an important part of the oral history of Uzbek home life, and as such, it is part of the history told about and by women. However, women's participation in private musical life is difficult to document, especially since most of the stories of foremothers' participation in private music making focuses on the late nineteenth and early twentieth centuries, when women's lives in the region were little documented. The eldest generation of women I spent time with and interviewed generally had recently retired and spoke of their first memories as occurring in the period during or just after World War II. Acclaimed musicians and dancers such as Viloyat Akilova, Gulshod Ataboeva, and Faizilat Shukurova remember a time when mixed-gender dance troupes toured collective farms, and when young girls with musical talent were selected for places in specialized music schools and the state conservatory, in order to become the very first women musicians in Uzbek Soviet Socialist Republic folk orchestras.

This status as professional musicians, singers, and dancers in official state ensembles was new for men and women of the region at that time. There is a well-documented history of professional male musicians performing *maqom* in the courts of Central Asian cities like Bukhara, Samarqand, and Khiva reaching back to the nineteenth century and earlier.[1] In Middle Eastern and Central Asian contexts, *maqom* denotes a melodic mode and also a musical genre that employs such modes. In Uzbekistan, when used in relation to a genre, the term usually refers to one or all of the three *maqom* repertoires existent in the region: *Shashmaqom* from the courts of Bukhara, Tashkent-Fergana *maqom* from courts in cities of the Fergana Valley, and Khorezmian *maqom* from the courts of Khiva. The repertoires are distinguished by both the pitch collections in the specific *maqomlar* and by other features of the pieces.[2] In more recent times, most music schools, music *kollej* (specialized music high schools), and the Uzbek State Conservatory display rows of pictures of important men, the musicians who shaped the music of the region for the past generations. *Maqom* was transmitted primarily via oral-imitative methods, so relatively little is known about the actual performance practice of this music before the earliest recordings in the first decade of the twentieth century, such as those made for the Gramophone Company in 1909 by Franz Hampe.[3] Indeed, as technologies that allowed great access to and within the region, like the motorcar and railroad, entered Central Asia, sound-recording technology also appeared and allowed for the capture and commodification of musical performance and other sonic material. This combination of access and recording ability in the late nineteenth and early twentieth centuries allowed for the preservation of certain perspectives on Central Asian life. Most often that which was preserved, recorded, and described came from the public realm and the middle and upper classes. Thus, what little we know about the music of Central Asia from Hampe's recordings tells us most about what men's music sounded like, at least within the limitations of gramophone technology.

As little as we know about *maqom* and men's performance practice in the nineteenth and early twentieth centuries, even less is known of women's musical traditions before the *hujum* (assault): forced anti-veiling/emancipation campaigns sponsored by the Soviet government to push women into the public sphere and into the workplace. Historically, respectable women did not have a role in public life. Their domain was the home and hearth, usually called the *ichkari* (inside) and contrasted with the *tashkari* (outside/public) realm, which was the purview of men (or less respectable women) until the forced unveiling campaigns of the 1920s. There is much anecdotal evidence that women of "respectable" classes played instruments and sang in the privacy of their own homes before the *hujum* encouraged such practices on public stages. Although not evident in public, and not notated or remarked upon by many, this musical tradition survives in the stories that women musicians continue to tell about their histories and traditions before Soviet ideological projects brought women's music into the public sphere. Indeed, many stories told by women musicians that culminate in their participation in public performances in Soviet and independent Uzbekistan begin with stories of grandmothers, great-grandmothers, and other foremothers who made music in the *ichkari*, where women of that era were able to pursue entertainments during a time when it was considered inappropriate to appear in public, much less perform music there. As this private realm was little documented, little is known of the music of the *ichkari*. Indeed, although Hampe's recordings include one Tajik woman musician playing the *dutar*, Tajikhan Khajimetova, little is said in the notes about her, and the recording is taken out of the context of the *ichkari*, where one might assume that the music would normally sound. As such, although it is possible to read accounts of the sound and bustle of the streets and bazaars of Tashkent, Bukhara, and Samarqand in the nineteenth and early twentieth centuries, it is much more challenging to create a sense of the soundscape that women most often found themselves in, that of the *ichkari*.[4] Indeed, as little is known about the lives of women who occupied the *ichkari*, even less is known about how those contexts sounded.

One vantage point that we have into women's lives during the early twentieth century in Central Asia comes via the travelers' tales told by European women who spent time in the region and gained access to the private world of those women who were kept largely out of public life. These include accounts by British anthropologist, geographer, and writer Annette B. Meakin (1867–1959) from the early 1900s, American journalist and activist Anna Louise Strong's (1885–1970) writing on the region from the late 1920s, and the work of Swiss travel writer and athlete Ella Maillart (1903–1997) from the 1930s. Beginning with Meakin's colonial-era account and continuing on to Strong's and Maillart's accounts from the early Soviet period, this chapter seeks to place European women's discussion of the sound and music of the *ichkari* in conversation with those provided by (often more well-known) European male travelers, as well as to contextualize these accounts within the stories and remembrances of that era told by Uzbek women musicians in the post-independence era. By doing so, it is possible to sort through the more familiar rhetoric of the independence and Soviet eras to elucidate how they react to and sometimes seem to grow out of colonial-era attitudes and biases toward both women and Central Asian music.

Annette Meakin in Central Asia

Technologies like the railroad and the motorcar allowed greater access to Central Asia for outsiders. A great many of those who took advantage of such developments were men, but a few women did as well. Those who did were often quite active in advocating for increased women's rights and recognition of women's contributions to the world. One such activist voice for women's rights that aimed beyond suffrage in the United States and Europe is that of British anthropologist and geographer Annette Meakin. Although she does not seem to have been directly involved in the suffrage movement (often referred to as the first wave of feminism), Meakin was keenly aware of the issues around women's rights, and her book *Women in Transition* is listed in Elizabeth Crawford's discussion of books and library collections supporting the suffrage movement.[5] She also gained renown as the first woman to ride the Trans-Siberian railroad from end to end, which she did in 1900 along with her mother.[6] Clearly Meakin saw herself as in the vanguard of women's rights and her writings as contributing to the cause.

Emancipation involved changes that she considered imminent and necessary in a global context, not just for the women of Europe and the United States. She addresses the need for women to improve their stations in both her 1903 book, *In Russian Turkestan: A Garden of Asia and its People*, describing her travels in Central Asia, and in her 1907 work, *Women in Transition*. Her most evident call for this, as well as her clearest text describing what she sees as progress on this issue, is in the latter book:

> If Russia's women have made such remarkable progress since they threw aside their veils at the command of Peter the Great, what should hinder the women of Islam from following their example? The Sart women of Central Asia, the most secluded of all women under the sun, are actually beginning to travel, and the year 1903 saw special compartments reserved for them in the Russian carriages on the Trans-Caspian railway.[7]

Meakin obviously views Central Asian women as victimized and forced into seclusion via circumstance as well as powerful men. She takes care to describe women's lives and seclusion via veiling and isolation at home at many places in her 1903 account. She even recounts a conversation that she had with a male Russian acquaintance on the subject of Central Asian women and the veil:

> "Do you consider the Sarts to be a people with a future?" was a question I put to one of the most thoughtful of my Russian acquaintances.
> "They can have no future as long as their women are veiled," was the reply. "Russia should have commanded them to unveil their women from the first; now it would be a more difficult matter."
> "You seem to forget," he continued, "that Russia's own women were veiled till Peter the Great put a stop to it; they had their separate reception-rooms, just as the Sarts have to-day."[8]

Curiously, Meakin chose to open the chapter "Sart Women" with the words of a Russian man. Indeed, Central Asian voices, women's voices especially, are notably rare in the volume, considering how frequently she discusses their fate, their attire, and their standing in society (the chapter displays a rather typical obsession with the veil and modest attire that has not ceased even in current journalistic writings). Indeed, Meakin is so focused on veiling practices and what she perceives as their oppressive and exotic nature that the front cover of her 1903 book features a photograph of the author herself garbed in the *chachvon* and *paranja* head-covering.

Even as Central Asian women's voices are largely unheard in Meakin's book, the work does represent a different view of women's lives than that provided by her male counterparts. She was much aware of this and in fact titillates her readers by describing her book as providing a glimpse into the forbidden world of respectable Sart women: "Gentle male reader! You shall now come with me in spirit where, in the flesh, you will never be permitted to enter. We will go together to the only place where a respectable Sart woman may be seen without a veil—her home."[9] Indeed, men took great notice of Meakin's work, especially as regards the women that she notified them were so securely hidden from their gaze. One reviewer for the *National Geographical Journal* discussed her work soon after its publication and made a general statement about how women might make valuable contributions to the discipline, saying: "This would seem to be the best mission a woman traveler can take upon herself—to bring herself into touch with her native sisters in whatever land she may be, and, by becoming thoroughly intimate with them, to produce work of which a man must always be in a greater or less degree incapable."[10] The issue of women travelers and their contribution was under much consideration in academic circles during the early decades of the twentieth century. During this time period, the Royal Geographical Society was engaged in much debate as to whether and how to admit women into the society. This was largely resolved by 1914, and in fact Meakin was inducted as a fellow in March of 1913.[11] Meakin was also made a fellow of the Royal Anthropological Society in 1903 and later made an honorary member of the Goethe Society of Weimar.[12] She was active and respected in a great many circles at a time when few women were included. In many ways, her gender made her travels and other pursuits more challenging; however, as she herself noted, it did provide her greater access to women's lives.

This advantage of having easier access to the *ichkari* was not just a ploy for attracting attention for her book. She uses her perspective to refute some of the common wisdom expressed about Central Asian women in other travelers' tales. In her *In Russian Turkestan*, Meakin specifically refutes fellow British traveler Francis Henry Skrine's assertion that women make no music (discussed in detail later in this chapter), saying, "I cannot . . . endorse Skrine's remark that 'music is unknown in the cheerless interior.'"[13] She doesn't mention Skrine's coauthor, Sir Edward Dennison Ross (1871–1940), in this challenge to their harsh account of urban home life in Central Asia in their book *The Heart of Asia: A History of Russian Turkestan and Central Asian Khanates from the Earliest Times* (1899):

> Custom, in fact, moulds the Bokharan's inmost being, and the degraded position assigned to women by its teaching places him beyond the pale of civilization. Home-life in the Central Asian Khanates exists no more than it did in ancient Rome. The citizens' houses are ranges of dark and cheerless cells surrounding a central courtyard, and presenting blind walls to the street. The intense cold of the winter months is mocked rather than mitigated by charcoal braziers. Music is unknown in the cheerless interior, and tobacco was till lately tabooed by the arrogant priests.[14]

Even as Meakin refutes the claims that the *ichkari* is a dark and cheerless place, she does emphasize the extent to which women's seclusion was the norm in her experience in Uzbek cities. She is clearly as critical of and fascinated by women's veiling practices as her male contemporaries. Her description provides a bleak assessment of women's lives, even as she challenges such dreary descriptions of women's courtyards:

Not only the absence of windows, but also that of women, has to do with the monotony of the streets. I have roamed Bokhara for days together without encountering one solitary female figure. In the towns that are completely under Russian sway one certainly sees more women about, but even there their presence does little to enliven the scene, for, rich and poor alike, all are enveloped in shapeless outer garments of somber grey with veils of black horsehair.[15]

This rather depressing description extends to her account of bridal customs. She claims to have visited a number of brides, who were all nervous, shy about being interviewed, and completely isolated from wedding festivities going on right outside their chambers.[16] This description of bridal seclusion is especially peculiar, since Meakin goes on to describe wedding festivities at which women musicians performed for family members and other women, which would not challenge the honor of respectable brides:

> Outside in the courtyard, there would be a row of female musicians seated on mattresses, and dancing-girls performed to the tambourine music. . . . Round and round they twirled, the centre of an admiring crowd, singing as they danced, and presently the little boys, without waiting for a pause, threw them coins, which they dexterously caught in their mouths. All this time the bride sat alone in her inner chamber, never attempting to join in the fun. Sart women of good character never dance in public; they consider it undignified.[17]

Meakin's description of wedding music is interesting and is similar to many of the wedding ceremonies that I observed between 2002 and 2009, with women musicians coming to perform for family and other women as a bride is preparing to be escorted to the groom's house or as she is being greeting by her in-laws on the morning after the wedding ceremony (a ritual known as *kelin salom* [greeting the bride]). It is especially curious that Meakin frames such festivities as public space, when they occurred in a courtyard with small children and other women present. During my wedding music research, I did note that the bridal couple very rarely joined in dancing and active festivities and instead acted as observers. This seemed to be less out of modesty than out of a different frame of reference. Guests at weddings were often encouraged by musicians and other guests to dance and provide entertainment for the bridal couple. This, rather than extreme modesty (or lack of agency), may contribute to the reserved behavior that Meakin observed in brides.

The description of wedding music and dance doesn't provide much detail on musical sound or the range of instruments. Meakin does go into greater detail in the later passage, in which she refutes Skrine's claim about music in the *ichkari*. She does this at the same time that, like Strong and many of her male counterparts, she denigrates the quality and musicality of performances in Central Asia. She likens the music to the "squalling of cats" and discusses it in terms of a "monotonous hum."[18] Even while doing this, though, she provides further confirmation of the importance of the *dutar* in women's lives before the Bolshevik revolution, a legacy that many of my consultants in independence-era Uzbekistan take great pride in. Meakin's description provides a rare account of women's role in providing music and entertainment in the home:

> Sart music is peculiar. I should never have recognized it as music but for the instruments by means of which it was produced. . . . The *dutar* comes [second] in importance [to the *karnai*, or long trumpet]. It is a kind of guitar, used chiefly to accompany the human voice, and resembles those found in other Eastern countries. Many of the Sart ladies play, and sing to, the *dutar* in their own houses, or dance while their husband, or brother, accompanies them upon it. I was glad to find that the women had at least this one *tamasha* [spectacle/entertainment] available, for they are shut out from nearly every other kind of amusement. If, when we were visiting at a native house, our hostess considered herself anything of a musician, she was always ready to play or dance at our request.[19]

This description is especially evocative of the important legacy that present-day women *dutar* players describe when explaining the importance of music to their national identity, one that depends on women's performance of it and that was important to women long before they began performing in public in significant numbers. The photograph below is of a woman with a *dutar* outside a "house of entertainment," taken during this era by Samuel M. Dudin (probably during his excursion to Central Asia between 1900 and 1902), a Russian photographer who specialized in Asian and ethnographic photos. This image represents the public and less respectable side of the musical lives available to women in the colonial era.

Anna Louise Strong in Central Asia

In contrast to the other accounts discussed in this chapter, Anna Louise Strong's writings were produced for explicitly political purposes. An American journalist who spent a great deal of time in Moscow and was known for supporting Communist causes, Strong wrote *Red Star in Samarkand*, a travelogue that comments a great deal on the political situation in early Soviet Uzbekistan. While doing so, she describes the role of music in both traditional and modernized contexts, as well as the changing role of women in aspects of Uzbek society in the late 1920s. Unlike the authors of the other accounts discussed in this chapter, Strong has a clear political agenda, and much to say about the revolutionary process under way in the Soviet Union. As such, her account differs significantly from Maillart's and Meakin's, which read more like traditional travelogues, without nearly as much detail (or enthusiasm) about workers' clubs and collective farms. A much greater portion of Strong's writing deals with music; this might stem from the Communist Party's focus on music and the arts as important vehicles for promoting revolutionary values. Indeed, much of her discussion of music contrasts European and what she often calls "native" music. As opposed to Maillart (discussed in detail in the following section), who was so taken with the "pleasurable" drumming of the frame drum, Strong repeatedly calls the rhythms of the music in general, and the sounds of frame drums and other percussion specifically,

Figure 8.1. Woman with a *Dutar*. Photograph by Samuel M. Dudin, 1900–1902. Courtesy of Anahita Gallery, Santa Fe, NM.

"monotonous," which brings her assessment much more in line with those of her predecessor, Meakin.[20] Clearly, Strong saw aesthetic appreciation for local musical practices as outside of the political and cultural process of industrializing and modernizing Central Asia. She saved her praise for musical practices focused more on themes of future prosperity and emancipation, which were most often brought in by Soviet innovators.

The process of modernization in the region fascinated her, and Strong spends a great deal of time discussing various campaigns for workers' rights, the emancipation of women via the public unveiling ceremonies of the *hujum*, and the modernization of musical institutions. These issues combine in her discussion of popular songs performed for a national holiday: "The unveiling of women was the theme of many songs, some pure propaganda, some tragic, some humorous. . . . One of the most delightful songs on women, which cause hearty laughter, told how the wife of a poor workman unveiled, and then demanded that her husband buy her a fine silk shawl and kerchief 'since I am now completely European.' The husband replied that he had no money, whereupon the woman threatened to report him to the police for counter-revolution, since he interfered with the fight for women's unveiling."[21]

Throughout this section, Strong spends many pages translating different song lyrics, many of which mock bureaucrats, singing about peasant life, and glorifying the unveiling movements. She also mentions the Musical High School in Samarqand repeatedly in her book, and traveled with both the students and their instructors on a train trip to perform for villages along with other officials.

In this musical high school and in other contexts, she notes the attempt to add new, modernized lyrics to existing, often well-known, local tunes, a technique used in a variety of areas to propagandize the modernization process. Strong observes that "native" music was one of the things that one could study in workers' clubs, but that "if [someone] prefers ancient music, he will find his classmates composing new topical songs to the old tunes."[22] She lists this along with the Latinization of the alphabet and the modernization of silk production as ways that education was changing to serve the new society. The blending of old tunes with new lyrics served the ideological and aesthetic project of Soviet modernization, which sought to reach out to indigenous populations at the same time that it "elevated" indigenous artistic production by adding elements from Western art music. This brought the musical performance style much more in line with what Europeans were accustomed to hearing, thus addressing many of the aesthetic criticisms launched at Central Asian music by outsiders.

Strong repeatedly criticizes the "wailing" of strings and "monotonous thrumming" of frame drums, but she does note that the indigenous population was quite attached to their musical traditions and didn't care for European songs: "The wailing tones of the strings [in Uzbek music are] monotonous enough to Europeans but dearly loved by the native population. Letters often come to the [radio] station protesting against European music. When it is given the Uzbeks declare 'it hurts the ears.' Their own delights them."[23] This comment came as she was visiting the state-run radio station in Tashkent and interviewing the manager about his programming choices. Just as Strong benefitted from advances in technology that allowed her access to the region, she saw the technological innovations ushered in by the Soviet period as a great boon for local citizens (especially women). Illustrating this idea is the picture accompanying her description of the radio station, which shows a woman in a traditional hat (*duppi*) with headphones on, smiling and holding headphones up to the ears of a smiling baby. The caption underneath reads "Radio comes to the New Generation."[24]

This representation of women interacting with the technologies of modernity is an important trope in Strong's book. As part of her lengthy discussion of the processes and political value of the *hujum*, she calls the *paranja* veil "hideous" numerous times, most clearly in an insert showing two contrasting black-and-white photos, the first captioned "The Hideous *Paranja* Worn by Veiled Women" and the second "The Modern Unveiled Women."[25] She also describes the backlash to these campaigns, citing another song:

> Campaigns on behalf of the veil are waged by the Mohammedan clergy. . . . There is a satirical verse sung by young Uzbeks:
> "On the seventh of March I tore off my veil,

> But before I reached home
> I bought three new *paranjas*
> To veil myself more darkly."[26]

In this sense, although clearly advocating for the emancipation movement, Strong does present the reaction against it, using song to illustrate the arguments on both sides.

Interestingly, Strong's fascination with the musical landscape of a modernizing Uzbekistan did not combine with her fascination with the *hujum* to result in much description of women making music. Indeed, the only mention of women's music making specifically (as opposed to the all-male contexts of the teahouses or the mixed-gender performances sponsored by the Communist Party) comes as she is describing the activities inside the women's quarters of a house in rather derisive terms. In addition to criticizing the upkeep and mood of the area, she once again derides the sound of the women's music:

> On a tiny ledge in the court the baby daughter danced in the sunlight, while her mother and grandmother shook tambourines in monotonous thrumming, and the father gazed in placid content at his assembled family. The child's feet tapped the stones, without leaving their place; there was no room for her to move in any direction. Nor was such movement required for the dance, which consisted in the slow swaying of the body and movements of the arms.[27]

Despite the negative tone of this description, it does bring up the fact that women's music persisted in the *ichkari* even during times of strong emancipation movements. It is certainly possible to read through Strong's bias toward perceiving women actively making music for their children in a contented setting (especially since women's dance styles from the region often feature florid arm movements with lower bodies that are significantly more still, regardless of any notion of oppression). After this description, Strong takes great pains to emphasize that the women performing here are unveiled women who are now accustomed to appearing in public without a veil but who retreat into privacy when men from outside their families appear in their own homes.[28] This provides evidence of the complex layering of what is seen as tradition with the modernity brought in by the Soviet system, one that includes a persistence of music in the *ichkari* that other writers fail to describe.

Ella Maillart in Central Asia

The Swiss travel writer Ella Maillart (1903–1997) was an author, photographer, and Olympic sportswoman who wrote many accounts of her travels through Central and East Asia. Her book *Turkestan Solo: One Woman's Expedition from the Tien Shan to the Kizil Kum* (1934) provides a clear account of Central Asian life during the beginning of the era in which my contacts locate their mothers, when empancipated women were working to educate others in the service of the Soviet state. Maillart visited Central Asia in 1932. This was five years after the *hujum* of 1927, but still a time when the implementation of female unveiling and emancipation policies was not uniform, especially when contrasting urban and rural experiences. Women's transition into public life did not happen instantaneously and, as mentioned above, was complex and multilayered, whether in terms of the women's relation to the *ich-kari* or in other contexts.

Maillart observed women's lives at a time of intense transition, one that provoked significant comment from those she spoke with. Her representation of women's lives, even after the *hujum* of 1927, is typical of Western writers of the time, with the backwardness and the suffering of women in barbaric seclusion strongly suggesting an ancient past to her. At one point, she even comments, "I am living in the heart of the Middle Ages. That fact must not be ignored. We are still in the year 1311, forty years behind the Arabian calendar of the hegira. At every step the fourteenth century rises to face the twentieth."[29]

That said, Maillart does acknowledge the challenge of the stark cultural change that Uzbek culture was facing. She asked one of her contacts in Samarqand, Moroussia, about her identity and her choice to appear uncovered in public:

> "But you yourself are you Uzbek?" "My father was a Persian." "And did you wear a veil?" Marrousia does not smile. "Yes, till 1927, in spite of definite orders to the contrary from my husband, who was a school master. But I had to obey him when I saw he was beginning to get really cross with me." "And the family dramas that they say take place in connection with unveiling: do they still happen?" "Yes: we must go carefully. The liberation of women has created discontent in the home."[30]

This is an interesting account, since it focuses on the imperative to unveil coming from the men of the household, rather than from Party operatives, who were usually European women charged with the task of bringing about this cultural change. In this case, Moroussia presents herself as wielding a great deal of agency in the decision of whether or not to wear a head-covering, and she places herself against the push to unveil coming from both the Soviet state and her husband. As such, unveiling and emancipation are not always as directly related as they are often described in other accounts. Indeed, in this case, the act of unveiling reinforces the patriarchal dynamic that the *hujum* claimed to seek to subvert.

As part of this discussion of women's lives that began with Moroussia's comments, Maillart goes on to describe what she saw as traditional (and "backward") activities in the *ichkari*, noting a buzz of activity for the women "until the man of the house arrives":

> In the daytime there is sunlight round the *karagatch* (the Asiatic elm); in the women's quarter there are flowers, fruits, grapes; round the fountain there is music, tea-drinking, and idle gossip. The stepfather comes in. All fall silent. You can hear the flies buzz. He looks angrily at his daughter and she goes out. The woman takes off his *khalat* [robe], washes his hands, gives him food, and brings in his *chilim* [pipe].[31]

As is somewhat typical of accounts from Western travelers, music does not receive much detailed mention; nonetheless, it is possible to get a sense of the *ichkari* sound-scape here, one that is far from dreary, despite Maillart's insistence on the point. Both the emphasis on dreary "backward" lifestyles and the lack of musical description are common in Western travel accounts from the late nineteenth and early twentieth centuries. Such tales are occasionally accompanied by detailed visual descriptions of instruments and costumes, with little commentary on the sound, unless the authors pointedly complain of "monotony" or "noise." The lack of detail in this particular story may also stem from the fact that this is not Maillart's own account; it is her retelling of a description of the *ichkari* given by one of her contacts, Yann, to whom she was introduced in order to gain access to his Uzbek friends who might provide her with access to the women's quarters. Her short description of the visit to the quarters of Yann's friend Riza's daughters is full of the scorn of backwardness typical of writing of this era. Maillart describes their lack of interest in "the modernity which expires outside [their] very door[s]" as something that she cannot fathom.[32] She depends a great deal on the words of others to bolster her descriptions of women's lives, not giving voice to the women about whose lives she expresses such confusion. Compared to Annette Meakin's earlier account, Maillart neither markets her work as providing special insight into the lives of women nor seems to spend much time in the company of women who were not involved in public life.

Before connecting Maillart with Riza's daughters, Yann took Maillart to a tavern, an outing that produces the most detailed description of a musical performance in *Turkestan Solo*.[33] Her account is of an Armenian tavern in Samarqand where there are women present, whom she identifies as non-Uzbeks (presumably they are Russians or Armenians). She describes the tavern as noisy and smoky, with an orchestra of stringed instruments playing in a manner that is "sharp, grating, and very monotonous, with a constantly changing rhythm which alone reveals the feeling proceeding to a climax. In comparison our own use of richly melodious phrases seems quite orgiastic. The songs are Persian, the dances Uzbek."[34] She goes on to contrast the "monotony" of the strings with "the pleasure of listening to the 'barraban,'" a Russian term for "drum" in general but in this case referring to the *doyra* frame drum with skin membrane and iron rings.[35] Maillart is fascinated by both the instrument and the performer, whom she describes in detail, down to his "stringy wrist" and the rapidity of the rhythmic patterns that he executes on the *doyra*. The level of praise she offers is also remarkable, offering a contrast to Strong's description of "monotonous" *doyra* playing in the *ich-kari* and Maillart's own staunch criticism of other aspects of the performance.

At the end of this description of the *doyra* player and performance, Maillart shifts gears suddenly and discusses dance in more general terms rather than the performance at the tavern. She mentions a renowned dancer (of Armenian heritage), Tamara Khanoum, saying: "it is when she dances that Tamara Khanoum stands rigid, with transfixed shoulders, and rhythmical movements of the seemingly disarticulated head from which a hundred tresses float, while beating time with a metronomic chin. I had already seen her in Moscow with her company."[36]

In this, we have Maillart's only detailed account of music in her book, and this plus the mention of music in Yann's description of the women's quarters represent the only reference to Central Asian music. Maillart does remark on the plaintive songs of Armenian weaving women in Khiva and her own singing of Swiss songs to pass the time on her journey to the Karakul desert.[37] In light of the amount of detail it provides, this account is quite engaging, first in contrasting Maillart's critical impression of the string ensemble with her detailed observations of the *doyra*. Along with timbre of the string instruments, Maillart criticizes the rapid changes in rhythm in the strings that she finds so pleasurable and fascinating in the *doyra* playing. The mention of Tamara Khanoum is interesting here, and represents something of an abrupt transition in Maillart's description of the event. It is unclear whether there was dancing accompanying the instrumentalists, and it seems unlikely that the famous Tamara Khanoum was dancing in a Samarqand tavern.[38] As such, the mention of her dancing style as observed by Maillart in an earlier show in Moscow seems to be an addition of the further knowledge that Maillart had of Central Asian music and dance.

The impact *Turkestan Solo* had on audiences is somewhat unclear, although the book was reviewed and commented on by scholarly journals, implying that Maillart's work did provide important insight for readers (though perhaps not significantly in terms of representations of music and gender). Reviewers of Maillart's book on Central Asia were much impressed with her accomplishments, though they didn't specifically mark her achievement in providing insight into women's lives; this is most certainly a sign of Maillart's work in post-*hujum* Central Asia, as well as the changing approaches to female writers and academics in European and American culture. One reviewer, however, noted that Maillart "seemed able both to grasp the mentality of each of [the groups she encountered] and to record her reactions to them. The whole volume is stocked with interesting anecdotes, contains much valuable information, and includes some of the most pathetic stories that we have ever read."[39] These "interesting anecdotes" are rendered more remarkable because they are told by the woman who experienced them, even if they do not comment significantly on the lives and music-making habits of women at the time.

Pre-Soviet European Accounts: Men Discussing Sart Women and Music

Maillart's book gives more insight into her unique position as a European female traveler than into women's lives at the time; Strong's book clearly represents and propagandizes the emancipatory goals of the Soviet system; and Meakin's book provides glimpses into pre-Soviet and pre-*hujum ichkari*. Regardless of the authors' agendas, their accounts provide important details of women's roles in Central Asia and differ significantly from works by men who traveled through Central Asia in the late nineteenth and early twentieth centuries. Many male travel writers remark on the lack of women in public, on their veiling practices, and on the fact that respectable women would not perform music in public. For those writing before the Soviet period, this discussion of women's absence inevitably leads to lengthy descriptions of the dancing boys known as *bachchalar*, who were common in teahouses, taverns, and other places where music and entertainment could be found until the practice was outlawed by the Soviet government, after which it became much less common. The presence of these dancing boys as a proxy for female dancers often brought about strong emotional responses and descriptions from male travel writers and were at least noted by Annette Meakin, if not discussed with such fascination.

One fairly early account of women's seclusion and modesty practices comes from Scottish Great Game traveler Alexander Burnes (1805–1841), who wrote of his experiences in Central Asia during the 1820s and early 1830s: "Our approach to the Mohammedan countries became evident daily, and showed itself in nothing more than the costume of the women, many of whom we now met veiled. One girl whom we saw on the road had a canopy of red cloth erected over her on horseback, which had a ludicrous appearance."[40] This derisive opinion about the "ludicrous" nature of such practices did not lighten as other men traveled through the area later in the century. Indeed, British travelers Francis Henry Skrine and Sir Edward Denison Ross went as far as to describe the veil as hideous and muffling: "The feminine element, which gives the greatest charm to the crowds of Western cities, is entirely absent in Bokhara. Such women as venture into the streets are muffled in a hideous smock and a thick horsehair veil. . . . The emancipation of women has not begun in Bokhara."[41] These sentiments about modesty practices in the Middle East and Central Asia persist to this day in travel and journalistic writing.

The *bachcha* garnered a great deal of attention from travel writers at the time and clearly intrigued quite a few. They were also used as further evidence of immorality in Central Asian culture that was often linked to the lack of emancipation of women (though such commentary by men was not connected to a similar lack of emancipation at home). The U.S. diplomat Eugene Schuyler (working with coauthor Vasiliy Grigor'ev) traveled to Tashkent in 1873 and provides a typical account of the seclusion of women and the shocking presence of dancing boys:

> In Central Asia Mohammedan prudery prohibits the public dancing of women; but as the desire of being amused and of witnessing a graceful spectacle is the same all the world over, here boys and youths specially trained take the place of the dancing-girls of other countries. The moral tone of the society of Central Asia is scarcely improved by the change.[42]

As mentioned earlier, in terms of Meakin's refutation, Skrine goes even further by claiming not only that women do not dance in public but also that "music is unknown in the cheerless interior," implying that women's lack of music and entertainments extended into the *ichkari* as well. He goes on to explain that "the craving for amusement so deeply implanted in human nature finds an outlet in the performances of the

bachas—lads of between eight and fifteen with long flowing locks, who dance, pos-
ture, and sing with a *brio* which excites frenzy in Bokharan spectators. They supply
the place of our opera-singers, ballet-girls, and actresses."[43] Although many European
and American observers, like Skrine and Schuyler, imply that no women perform (or
appear) in public, other authors make a clear distinction between respectable women
and those of ill repute. Swedish geographer and explorer Sven Hedin, whose 1893–1934
expeditions to Central Asia span both the nineteenth and twentieth centuries, provides one of the rare descriptions of such women in his book, *My Life as an Explorer.*[44]
In it, he takes special care to describe a scene in a "not-too-savoury quarter of the
women dancers" in Samarqand:

> Beautiful women played the *sitara* (zither) and *chetara* (guitar), manipulating the
> strings with dainty little fingers. Others, with like skill and grace, played the tam-
> bourine. In order to keep the drumhead tight, they would now and again hold the
> instrument over a *mangal*, or glowing brazier. As the music rose in the night, the
> dancers appeared, in light, floating garments, with movements full of grace. Some
> of them were Persians or Afghans, others had Tatar blood in their veins. And to the
> rhythmic sounds of music from the stringed instruments, they danced in undu-
> lating measure, like fairies in a dream—messengers from Bihasht and the joys of
> Paradise.[45]

Like Maillart's contact Yann, Hedin and others note the lack of Uzbek (and Tajik)
women in these taverns and other areas where respectable women from those groups
wouldn't deign to be seen. This observation is consistent with observations from both
the czarist era and during and immediately after the Soviet *hujum*. The increased presence of unveiled women on the street does seem to have resulted in a less dramatic tone
in descriptions of situations in which Uzbek women are markedly absent. The seclusion practices before the *hujum* seemed to stir up more alarm from Western observers
and thus possibly resulted in more discussion of activism. Notably, the scandalous
activities of less respectable women in which Hedin and others were so interested do
not feature in present-day discussions of women's musical heritage. My contacts tell
more personal tales of their beloved and deeply respected foremothers' music making
when they lay out the historical context for their own musical successes.

Latter-Day Accounts of the Soundscape in the Late Nineteenth and Early Twentieth Centuries

The women musicians I spoke with and learned from in Tashkent have a sense of
heritage that traces back to women of moneyed classes who played music for themselves and their families as part of a broad and vibrant home life. Although the
women I worked with have very public lives and receive much attention for their
public performances, they link the legitimacy of their musical practice as much to
those women performing in the *ichkari* as to the history of male performers and cre-
ators of their musical traditions in the nineteenth century and earlier. My primary

teacher on the *dutar*, Malika Ziyeeva, was the first female instrumentalist in the *maqom* ensemble of the Uzbek State Radio Station and remained with the ensemble for almost twenty years. She often spoke of her very traditional upbringing in the Fergana Valley and how, in her grandmother's day, if a woman's pinky finger was visible in public, it brought dishonor on her. At the same time, she often narrated a story of women's circumscription in the pre-Soviet era that contrasted with her experience of opportunities to seek education, employment, and renown within the Soviet state-run system in the 1970s and 1980s.

Remembering women's histories in this fashion was common, using the early Soviet period as a fulcrum that enabled the shift from a time of tradition and enclosure, a time that is often remembered fondly because of the rich experience of a home that is described as warm and full of music. This pre-Soviet time is one that many, including Ziyeeva, still mention as one in which there was music in every house, insisting that traditional music was not necessarily performed only by professionals and that every woman could manage to play a little bit on the *doyra* or *dutar* for herself and for her family. Ziyeeva framed this time musically in terms of the instruments that are considered most traditional for Uzbek music: "The *dutar*, *tanbur* [metal-stringed, plucked lute], and *doyra* are our longest-held traditions. These were in every household."[46] The ubiquity of traditional instruments in households is a common way that people remember pre-Soviet times, even though it is currently much rarer to see them in the homes of nonprofessional musicians.

Another of my *dutar* teachers, Rozibi Hodjieva (who performed with the folk orchestra at the Uzbek State Radio Station), spoke of women's roles as musicians in the *ichkari* specifically. Referring to the days before the Revolution, she stated that "women played in the *ichkari*, but there was not a specific school of playing. No one would teach it; rather, women would play for themselves. Maybe one woman would be able to read some notation, or provide a rhythm, and then they would play for themselves."[47] Hodjieva's grandmother played the *dutar* and is considered one of her foremothers and contributors to her musical talent, even though she died before Hodjieva's birth. As such, Hodjieva was able to trace a very important musical lineage for herself, establishing private musical practices from the *ichkari* as an important precursor to her current very public career.

Folk orchestra conductor Feruza Abdurahimova also traces her musical lineage in terms of female family members who were musicians and credits the *hujum* with creating a culture in which she could pursue her career. In an interview, she began by discussing her grandmother, who worked in a factory during the 1920s, beginning her work there veiled, since the vanguard of women who threw off the veil were murdered.[48] She went on to note that she came from a long line of strong women and that her mother worked at the local House of Culture and gave lectures on women's rights at collective farms. Abdurahimova's mother was part of the generation of women of respectable classes who transitioned away from seclusion and

embraced the Soviet rhetoric of emancipation of women as part of the emancipation of the proletariat, which was at its most public and remarked upon during the
hujum of the 1920s.

As historian Douglas Northrop has noted, this focus on the veil created a salient
symbol for women and their connection to notions of tradition and nation: "When
the [Communist] party's vision for modernizing Uzbekistan began with a *hujum*
[assault] against the veil, Uzbek women and their *paranjis* [veils] served all too read-
ily as a focus of cultural, religious, gender, and now national resistance to Soviet
incursions into Uzbek society."[49] He suggests that these campaigns were rather successful in some senses, since by 1930, "an Uzbek national consciousness, however
fitful and uneven, had started to take root, a remarkable development with momentous and lasting consequences."[50] Historian Marianne Kamp has also commented
that women became very important symbols for Uzbek Soviet national identity in
the first few decades of the Soviet period. She observes further that the *hujum* was
successful in bringing women into public view and into the labor force, but because
women's adherence to Communist Party values was so strongly associated with the
act of wearing attire common in the rest of the Soviet Union, that is, without head-
covering, the era of the *hujum* became remembered as the time that women threw
off the veil rather than as a moment of great emancipation.[51] The distillation of the
emancipatory goals of the *hujum* into the symbolic act of unveiling (and of public
veil burnings) has been noted by a number of scholars, and the act of publicly covering or uncovering continues to be a highly symbolic act that women discuss in terms
of its historical context.[52]

Indeed, in post-Soviet Tashkent, the choice of whether or not to express religious
observance by wearing *hijab* is a common topic, and many women expressed concern about their career prospects if they chose to adopt the practice. Others felt that
it would be hypocritical to begin the practice after decades of appearing in public in
Western attire. Regardless, most women, like Ziyeeva, Hodjieva, and Abdurahimova,
remember positively both the emancipatory moves of the early Soviet Union and the
opportunities that they provided women in the public sphere while also expressing
great reverence for traditional life that includes seclusion. These two sentiments create
a sense of tension; they are not necessarily seen as contrasting by those women who
are negotiating complex identities that reach for a sense of modernity grounded in a
notion of traditional and historical roles. As such, much of women's lives in Tashkent,
especially those of women who are successful in their careers of performing music in
public, embodies both the values of post-*hujum* emancipation and traditional priorities placed on modesty.

Women musicians have a legacy in Uzbekistan that stretches back before the Soviet
emancipation movements, and this history is often challenging to document. The
seclusion of the *ichkari*, as well as the relative disinterest in the daily lives of women

demonstrated by male writers (who seem much more focused on exoticizing women's absence from public spheres), contribute to the dearth of written accounts about their lives and habits. Indeed, most accounts feature great amounts of speculation about the doldrums experienced by secluded women, which are not borne out in women's recountings of their foremothers' lives. In the early twentieth century, European and American women experienced a complex of privilege and marginalization that put them in a unique (and understandably problematic) position in representing the lives of Central Asian women. Their status as exceptional women in the West produced the authority to garner attention from both publishers and scholarly societies for their representations of Central Asian women. While their status in European and American society gave them access to publishers and funding for travel, their marginalized status as women allowed them to access women in Central Asia in more private contexts.

Female travel writers benefitted greatly from technological innovations that gave outsiders greater access to the region, but these women also established themselves as truly exceptional in their willingness to traverse boundaries that, arguably, ordinary respectable women in their cultures would not dare to cross. Ironically, it is just this boundary crossing and willingness to engage in historically male pursuits that allowed such women as Meakin, Strong, and Maillart access to the home lives of respectable Central Asian women who would not welcome male travel writers into their midst. Their accounts are rife with the arrogance and misunderstanding that is typical of most Western accounts of the time. But beyond the disdain, the reader may gain a broader sense of the bustling soundscape of the *ichkari*, where music and dance thrived, along with the sounds of cooking, tea drinking, children's antics, and handiwork in progress. Although they display a great deal of bias and disdain when discussing the women's lives and music-making habits, Meakin, Strong, and Maillart confirm the oral histories that women in the region continue to tell about themselves. These are important histories that involve seclusion that is not entirely enforced from outside, that feature a lively home life, and that depend on women for music making and entertainment.

Notes

My fieldwork in Uzbekistan spans over a year and a half total during five trips in 2002, 2003, the 2004–5 academic year, 2008, and 2009. This research has been supported by grants from a number of organizations, including the American Councils of International Education, the Graduate Division at the University of California, Los Angeles, the Social Science Research Council, the Fulbright Program, and the Arts Research Institute and the Committee on Research at the University of California, Santa Cruz.

1. Theodore Craig Levin, *The Hundred Thousand Fools of God: Musical Travels in Central Asia* (and Queens, New York) (Bloomington: Indiana University Press, 1996); Otanazar Matyoqubov, "19th Century Khorezmian Tanbur Notation: Fixing Music in an Oral Tradition," *Yearbook for Traditional Music* 22 (1990), pp. 29–35.

2. Note that as a general practice, Central Asian *maqom* is related to *maqam* in the Middle East, *mugham* in Azerbaijan, and the Persian *dastgah* system.

3. *Before the Revolution: A 1909 Recording Expedition in the Caucasus and Central Asia by the Gramophone Company* (London: Topic Records, 2002).

4. The term "soundscape" has come into common usage in ethnomusicology in the twenty-first century, as scholars focus on not simply examining musical objects but taking into account the entire landscape of sound that contextualizes musical and other activities. For early employment of this now quite popular term, see Buckminster Fuller, "The Music of the New Life: Thoughts on Creativity, Sensorial Reality, and Comprehensiveness," *Music Educators Journal* 52, 6 (1966), p. 52, and Steven Feld, "Sound Structure as Social Structure," *Ethnomusicology* 28, 3 (1984), p. 395, in passages describing his work with the Kaluli of Papua New Guinea. Feld's work especially popularized the use of the term along with the examination of sound in context within the field of ethnomusicology.

5. Annette M. B. Meakin, *Woman in Transition* (London: Methuen, 1907). See also Elizabeth Crawford, *The Women's Suffrage Movement: A Reference Guide 1866-1928* (London: Routledge, 2001), p. 347.

6. Times of London (1959), p. 10.

7. Meakin (1907), p. 22. The term "sart" is common in English-language accounts of Central Asia before the twentieth century. It generally describes the settled (as opposed to nomadic) peoples of Central Asia, usually referring to those who currently identify as ethnically Tajik or Uzbek.

8. Annette Meakin, In *Russian Turkestan: A Garden of Asia and Its People* (London: Ballantyne, Hanson & Co., 1903), p. 106.

9. Meakin (1903), p. 107.

10. O.J.R.H. [sic], "Review: A Woman's Work among the Sarts," *Geographical Journal* 23, 3 (1904), p. 372.

11. Morag Bell and Cheryl McEwan, "The Admission of Women Fellows into the Royal Geographical Society, 1892-1914: The Controversy and the Outcome," Geographical Journal 162, 3 (1996), p. 310.

12. *Times of London* (1959), p. 10.

13. Meakin (1903), p. 218.

14. Francis Henry Skrine and Edward Denison Ross, *The Heart of Asia: A History of Russian Turkestan and Central Asian Khanates from the Earliest Times* (London: Methuen & Co., 1899), pp. 368-69.

15. Meakin (1903), p. 55.

16. Ibid., pp. 141-42.

17. Ibid.

18. Ibid., p. 218

19. Ibid., pp. 217-18.

20. Anna Louise Strong, *Red Star in Samarkand* (New York: Coward-McCann, 1929), pp. 31, 132, 238, 310.

21. Ibid., p. 220.

22. Ibid., p. 221.

23. Ibid., pp. 308-9.

24. Ibid., p. 310.

25. Ibid., p. 234.

26. Ibid., p. 274.

27. Ibid., pp. 238-39.

28. Ibid., pp. 239-40.

29. Ella Maillart, *Turkestan Solo: One Woman's Expedition from the Tien Shan to the Kizil Kum* (London: Century Publishing, 1934), p. 242.

30. Ibid., pp. 223–24.

31. Ibid., p. 229.

32. Ibid., p. 238.

33. Ibid., pp. 235–36.

34. Ibid., p. 235.

35. Ibid.

36. Ibid., p. 236.

37. Ibid., pp. 292–93, 142–43.

38. Tamara Khanum (1906–1991) was a much beloved Uzbek dancer of Armenian origin who was the first woman to dance in public without a head-covering. See Kate A. Baldwin, *Beyond the Color Line and the Iron Curtain: Reading Encounters between Black and Red, 1922–1963* (Durham, NC: Duke University Press, 2002), p. 93. She is known for her association with impresario Muhayiddin Kari-Yakubov, who created Uzbekistan's first touring dance troupe in 1928, as described in Mary Masayo Doi, *Gesture, Gender, Nation: Dance and Social Change in Uzbekistan* (Westport: Bergin & Garvey, 2002), p. 44.

39. D.C. [sic], "Review Work(s): *Turkestan Solo: One Woman's Expedition from the Tien Shan to the Kizil Kum* by Ella K. Maillart; John Rodker," *Geographical Journal* 85, 4 (1935), p. 380.

40. Alexander Burnes, *Travels into Bokhara, Being an Account of a Journey from India to Cabool, Tartary and Persia* (London: John Murray, 1834), vol. 1, p. 61.

41. Skrine and Denison Ross (1899), p. 368.

42. Eugene Schuyler, *Turkistan: Notes of a Journey in Russian Turkistan, Khokand, Bukhara, and Kuldja* (New York: Scribner, Armstrong & Co., 1877), vol. 1, pp. 132–33.

43. Skrine and Denison Ross (1899), pp. 368–69.

44. Sven Anders Hedin, *My Life as an Explorer* (New York: Boni & Liveright, 1925).

45. Hedin (1925), p. 95.

46. Malika Ziyeeva, interview by author, July 29, 2009.

47. Rozibi Hodjieva, interview by author, August 5, 2009.

48. Feruza Abdurahimova, interview by author, July 24, 2009.

49. Douglas Northrop, *Veiled Empire: Gender and Power in Stalinist Central Asia* (Ithaca, NY: Cornell University Press, 2004), p. 68.

50. Ibid., p. 56.

51. Marianne Kamp, *The New Woman in Uzbekistan: Islam, Modernity, and Unveiling under Communism* (Seattle: University of Washington Press, 2006), p. 226.

52. Kamp (2006); Gregory J. Massell, *The Surrogate Proletariat: Moslem Women and Revolutionary Strategies in Soviet Central Asia, 1919–1929* (Princeton: Princeton University Press, 1974), p. 211; and Northrop (2004).

Index

Pax Mongolica, 5, 8
Pazukhin, Boris and Semen, their mission (1669–1673) and the beginning of change, 15, 80–84
Pelliot, Paul (1878–1945), 24, 161, 167
Persia, 16, 80
Persian slaves, 118, 126
Polo, Marco, 5, 8, 14, 15, 138, 144; *Divisament dou monde*, 1, 11

Qajar dynasty (1785–1925), 16, 20; defeat at Merv, 117, 124; military campaigns to reclaim the steppes, 114, 116–18, 124; taking Shiʻi Persians as captives, 114–15; travel narratives on Central Asia, 119–20, 122
Qara Qum (Black Sands) Desert, 113, 115–19, 123, 128
Qazaqs, 77–79, 93; headmen and commoners, 100–103; in Imperial Illustrations, 92, 94, 104, 106.
Qianlong, emperor of China (r. 1735–1796), 91, 97, 98, 99, 100, 101, 103, 104, 106, 108.
Qing Chinese empire, 1, 153–54; Imperial Illustrations of Tributary Peoples, 89–110

Rawlinson, Henry Creswick, 137, 142–45
Razin, Stenka, 174–77
Red Star in Samarkand, by Anna Louise Strong, 199–202
religion: and identity, 92, 94; role in contemporary society, 156, 160
religious and cultural divide, 71, 116
religious *Weltpolitik*, 9, 14, 17
Ross, Colin (1885–1945), 29–30
Ross, E. Denison (1871–1940), 158–59, 197
Rousseau, Jean-Jacques, 21, 171
Royal Geographical Society, 144–45, 147, 197
Rubiés, Joan-Pau, 6, 12
Russia, Russians and Central Asia: travelers' early impressions, 70–73; Central Asia, cultural consciousness, 170, 16–18, 172; Chinese border, 22, 30; cultural consciousness, 170; empire, 4, 20, 23; from great games to railroad savants (1850–1940), 18–31; imperial ethnography, 18; Japanese War (1904–1905), 22, 27, 153, 159, 180; occupation of the khanate of Khiva, 136; occupation of Merv, 145; slaves in Central Asia, 73, 74, 79, 83
Russian Imperial Asian Boundary Commission, 17

Safarnama (travelogue) genre, 44, 114
Safavid dynasty, 5, 45–47, 54–55, 63, 76, 115; fall (1722), 116; and Mughals, war, 78
Samarqand, 8, 21, 28, 56, 58–60, 62, 77–78, 144, 156, 193, 195, 201, 203–5, 207; captured by Rus-

sians, 19, 24; Russian travelogue on, 17; seized by Uzbeks, 47–48, 49; slave trade, 125
al-Samarqandi, Mutribi al-Asamm, *Khatirat-i-Mutribi Samarqandi*, 57–58; musings, 57–64
Sarakhs, 117, 119, 123, 125
Sariq Turkmen, 114, 118, 123, 124
Sart women and music, 205–7
Sayan, 181–82
Schuyler, Eugene, 206–7
Shahnama, by Firdausi, 54, 139
Shahristani, Khwaja Abd al-Karim, 14, 63;
Shaibanid sultanate, 5, 44, 56
Shaw, Robert Barkley (1839–1879), 21, 142
Shiʻi captives/slaves, 114–16, 118, 123, 125, 126
Shin Saiiki Ki (New Record of Western Regions) ed. Ōtani Kōzui, 25, 162–63
Shinkyō. *See* Xinjiang
Shuttleworth, R. B., 157, 165
Silk Road (Paper Road), 3, 4, 12, 22, 155
Skrine, Francis Henry, 197, 206, 207
slave trade, slavery, 6, 10, 15, 16, 72, 78, 82, 83, 114–16, 123–25; living and working conditions of slaves, 127–28; *Sohrab and Rustum*, by Matthew Arnold, 20, 139–41, 146–47, 150
Song dynasty, 8, 95
Spilman, James, 15–16
Stein, Marc Aurel, 24–25, 153–57, 161–62, 163, 165–66; *Ancient Khotan*, 165; *Chūō Ajia Tōsaki* (On Central Asian Tracks), 155
steppes, steppe roads of Central Asia, 6, 10–11, 16–18, 20, 44, 53, 63, 69, 70, 74; and the Persian captivity narrative of Mirza Mahmud Taqi Ashtiyani, 113–23
Strong, Anna Louise (1885–1970), 195, 210; *Red Star in Samarkand*, 199–202
Struys, Jan (c. 1629–c. 1694), 16–17
Sunnis: orthodox, 50, 52, 76, 116

Taiji, 94, 98–99, 101, 107–8
Taishō, Emperor, 152, 161
Taizong, Emperor (r. 626–649), 160–61, 164
Taklamakan desert, 153, 157
Tang dynasty (618–907), 8, 95, 103, 104
Tarikh-i Rashidi: Tarikh-i Khawanin-i Mughulistan (A History of the Khans of Moghulistan), by Mirza Muhammad Haidar Dughlat, 51–53
Tashkent, 19, 22, 51, 58, 70, 72, 74, 78, 144, 187, 194, 195, 201, 206, 207, 209
Tatars, 6, 69, 71
Tekke Turkmen tribes, 117, 118, 122, 123
Through Asia, by Sven Hedin, 156, 157

Contributors

Abbas Amanat is professor of history and international studies and director of the Iranian Studies Initiative at Yale University. His books include *Resurrection and Renewal: Making of the Babi Movement in Iran*; *Pivot of the Universe: Nasir al-Din Shah Qajar and the Iranian Monarchy*; and *Apocalyptic Islam and Iranian Shi'ism*. He is coeditor of *Is There a Middle East? The Evolution of a Geopolitical Concept* and *Iran Facing Others: Identity Boundaries in a Historical Perspective*.

Imre Galambos is university lecturer in Pre-Modern Chinese studies at Cambridge University. He is coauthor (with Sam van Schaik) of *Manuscripts and Travellers: The Sino-Tibetan Documents of a Tenth-Century Buddhist Pilgrim*.

Nile Green is professor of history at the University of California, Los Angeles, and founding director of the UCLA Program on Central Asia. His books include *Islam and the Army in Colonial India: Sepoy Religion in the Service of Empire*; *Bombay Islam: The Religious Economy of the West Indian Ocean*, winner of the Albert Hourani Award from the Middle East Studies Association and the A.K. Coomaraswamy Award from the Association for Asian Studies; *Sufism: A Global History*; and *Afghanistan in Ink: Literature between Diaspora and Nation* (coedited with Nushin Arbabzadah).

Laura Hostetler is professor of history at University of Illinois at Chicago. She is the author of *Qing Colonial Enterprise: Ethnography and Cartography in Early Modern China* and *The Art of Ethnography: A Miao Album of Guizhou Province* (coauthored with David M. Deal).

Arash Khazeni teaches Middle Eastern and North African history at Pomona College, California. His publications include *Tribes and Empire on the Margins of Nineteenth-Century Iran*, recipient of the Middle East Studies Association's Houshang Pourshariati Book Award.

Tanya Merchant is an assistant professor of ethnomusicology at the University of California, Santa Cruz, whose research interests include music's intersection with issues of nationalism, gender, identity, and the postcolonial situation. With a geographical focus on Central Asia and the Balkans, she has conducted fieldwork in Uzbekistan, Tajikistan, Russia, and Bosnia and Herzegovina. She is an avid performer on both the Uzbek dutar and the baroque bassoon, and has given concerts with ensembles in the U.S., England, and Uzbekistan. Her recent publications include articles on Uzbek popular, folk, and traditional musics, which appear in journals such as *Cahiers de Musiques Traditionnelles*, *Image and Narrative*, and *Popular Music and Society*.

Ron Sela is associate professor of Central Asian history in the Department of Central Eurasian Studies at Indiana University, Bloomington. He is the author of *The Legendary Biographies of Tamerlane: Islam and Heroic Apocrypha in Central Asia* and *Ritual and Authority in Central Asia: The Khan's Inauguration Ceremony* and coeditor (with Scott C. Levi) of *Islamic Central Asia: An Anthology of Historical Sources* (Indiana University Press, 2010).

Sanjay Subrahmanyam is professor and Doshi Chair of Indian History at the University of California, Los Angeles. He is the author, coauthor, or editor of nearly twenty-five books, including *Writing the Mughal World*; *Three Ways to Be Alien: Travails and Encounters in the Early Modern World*; and *Courtly Encounters: Translating Courtliness and Violence in Early Modern Eurasia*.

Kate Teltscher is reader in English literature at the University of Roehampton, London. She is the author of *India Inscribed: European and British Writing on India 1600–1800* and *The High Road to China: George Bogle, The Panchen Lama and the First British Expedition to Tibet*. She edited the first scholarly edition of Yule and Burnell's *Hobson-Jobson*, the encyclopaedic glossary of British India.

Ronald Vroon is professor of Slavic Languages and Literatures at UCLA. He is the author of two monographs on the poetry of Velimir Khlebnikov and editor of a variorum edition of Aleksandr Sumarokov's odes and elegies.

www.ingramcontent.com/pod-product-compliance
Lightning Source LLC
Chambersburg PA
CBHW070408270326
41926CB00014B/2758